SCIENCE
AND
ETHICS

D0066974

SCIENCE AND ETHICS

Can Science Help Us Make Wise Moral Judgments?

EDITED BY PAUL KURTZ

with the assistance of **David Koepsell**

 Prometheus Books

59 John Glenn Drive
Amherst, New York 14228–2197

Published 2007 by Prometheus Books

Inquiries should be addressed to
Prometheus Books
59 John Glenn Drive
Amherst, New York 14228–2197
VOICE: 716–691–0133, ext. 207
FAX: 716–564–2711
WWW.PROMETHEUSBOOKS.COM

11 10 09 08 07   5 4 3 2 1

A CIP catalog record for this book is available from the Library of Congress Cataloging
in Publication Division.

Printed in the United States of America on acid-free paper

CONTENTS

8   CONTENTS

INTRODUCTION

1

WHAT IS THE RELATIONSHIP AMONG SCIENCE, REASON, AND ETHICS?

PAUL KURTZ

I

C an science help us to frame ethical judgments? In a world in conflict about moral values and beliefs, this question is especially important today. Dramatic breakthroughs on the frontiers of scientific research provide new powers to human beings for achieving their ends, but they also pose perplexing moral dilemmas.

There are today two contending approaches to morality that ignore the role of science. First is the widely held belief that morality must be derived from religious foundations. It is said that we cannot be moral without guidance from theology, and that God alone provides us with absolute commandments. These are transcendental, conveyed to us from beyond the natural world by human emissaries, though they are actually based on "news from nowhere." This position is virtually the "official doctrine" in the United States and many areas of the world. It presents us with a paradox, however, for belief in God is no guarantee of moral probity (priests have been prone to pederasty), and it often masks immoral hypocrisy (deacons are overcome by greed) and untold evils (the justification of barbaric wars by appealing to the Faith of our Father). Those who destroyed the World Trade Center towers did so in the name of Allah, and many of those who would defend us today from terrorists likewise invoke divine blessing.

11

Even more upsetting to the above thesis is the fact that devout disciples of the doctrine dispute the legitimacy or illegitimacy of other religious-moral creeds. For example, they assert contradictory stances about capital punishment, assisted suicide, or cloning. They all too often line up on opposite sides of the barricades, and many will fight to the end to defend God's commandments as interpreted by their own religious traditions. The extreme religious absolutist, of course, insists that there is a way out—by proclaiming that everyone should accept his or her view of God—to wit, you believe in *your* religion, but I will believe in *God's*: the divine rapture by Jesus, entrance into heaven for males by Muhammad, or the chosen land by Moses, or a latter-day version of heaven by Joseph Smith and the Latter Day Saints. But this has led to bloody wars, holy crusades, and jihads. In the light of this, who can say with any certainty that religion *ipso facto* is a sufficient guide for moral conduct? Others, of course, attempt to find some common ground in all religions—if they are Unitarians or Hindus—but it is often difficult to get a consensus about hot-button issues such as celibacy, assisted suicide, abortion, the role of women, homosexuality, war or peace, or who possesses the right key to unlock the gates to heaven. I submit that religious institutions are created by humans, and they have all the flaws and limitations of other human contrivances.

There is a second approach that has attracted considerable numbers of adherents—sophisticated intellectuals, authors, artists, and students, as well as ordinary men and women, particularly in secular societies. This is the view that ethical choices are merely subjective, expressing tastes; and of tastes you cannot dispute (*de gustibus non disputandum est*). Since they are emotive at root, no set of values is better than any other. If there is a conflict, then the best option is to persuade others to accept our moral attitudes, to convert them to our moral feelings, or, in the last analysis, if this fails, to resort to force, following the old adage that "might makes right." This view has had many kinds of devotees historically.

Classical skeptics denied the validity of all knowledge, including ethical knowledge. The logical positivists of the twentieth century made a distinction between fact, the appropriate realm of science, and value, the realm of emotions and imperatives, claiming that though we can resolve descriptive and theoretical questions by using the methods of science, we cannot use science to adjudicate moral disputes. Most recently, postmodernists in the academy, following the much-maligned French savants and the German philosopher Heidegger, have gone further in their skepticism, denying that there is any special validity to humanistic ethics, or indeed to science itself; for they say that science is merely one mythological construct among others. They insist that there are no objective epistemological standards; that gender, race, class, or cultural bias likewise infect our ethical programs and any narratives of social emancipation that we may propose. "Who is to say that one normative viewpoint is any better than any other?" they demand. Thus many disciples of multicultural relativism and subjectivism have given up in despair, becoming cynics or nihilists. Interestingly, most of these well-intentioned folk hold passionate moral and political convictions, but when pushed to the wall, will they concede that their own epistemological and moral recommendations likewise express their personal preferences?

The problem with this emotive position is apparent; for it is riveted by one horn of a dilemma, and the consequence of this option is difficult to accept. If it is the case that there are no ethical standards, then who can say that the Nazi Holocaust and the Rwandan, Cambodian, or Armenian genocides are evil? Is it only a question of taste that divides sadists and masochists on one side from all the rest on the other? Are slavery, the repression of women, the degradation of the environment by profit-hungry corporations, or the killing of handicapped people morally impermissible, if there are no reliable normative standards? If we accept cultural relativity as our guide, then we have no grounds to object to Islamic law (sharia), which condones the stoning to death of adulteresses. At a humanist convention held in Amsterdam some years ago, I heard some postmodern multiculturalists condone sharia. "Who are we to object?" they asked—this masks our own Western cultural bias. If so, what happens to women's rights?

Both of the above extreme positions—the transcendentalist and the subjectivist—are profoundly mistaken, and they have in some sense, I submit, gotten us into the present moral morass we are in.

II

Is there a third position that can bridge the gap; that would recognize that values are relative to human interests yet allow that they are open to some objective criticisms? This is the position taken by most of the contributors to this volume. I submit that there are, and that upon reflection, most educated people would accept them. I choose to call this third position "objective relativism"; namely, values are related to human interests, needs, desires, and passions—whether individual or socio-cultural—but they are nonetheless open to scientific evaluation. By this I mean a form of reflective moral intelligence that applies to questions of principles and values, and that is open to modification of them in the light of criticism. In other words, there is a Tree of Knowledge of Good and Evil that bears fruit, which, if eaten and digested, can impart to us moral knowledge and wisdom.

In what sense can scientific inquiry help us to make ethical choices? This is the central question of this book. Most of the articles presuppose a naturalistic ethical theory; the thesis is that an increase in *knowledge* can help us to make wiser decisions. By knowledge the authors refer not simply to rational or philosophical analysis, but *scientific evidence*. It would answer both the religionist, who insists that you cannot be moral unless you believe in God, and the subjectivist, who denies there is any such thing as ethical knowledge or wisdom. The main thrust of the contributions to this volume is that rational and scientific inquiry *is* relevant to moral decisions. There is thus a third approach to ethical questions. This has deep roots in the history of philosophical thought, but it is especially important today as the frontiers of science expand, and our knowledge of who and what we are and the means and opportunities to make wiser choices grow.

Before I outline this position, permit me to acknowledge that there have been many skeptical objections to deriving ethics from science, and they have come from some of our leading philosophers. Basically, what are they? First, critics say we cannot *deduce* ethics from science, what *ought* to be the case from what *is* the case. A whole series of philosophers from David Hume to the emotivists have pointed out this fallacy. G. E. Moore at the beginning of the twentieth century characterized this as "the naturalistic fallacy"[1]—mistakenly, I think.

The naturalistic fallacy has been referred to by a great number of philosophers and scientists ever since to claim that science has no role to play in ethics and that a sharp distinction can be made between the two domains. But we should be clear about what the so-called naturalistic fallacy is. Surely there are pitfalls in attempting to derive the ethical principles and norms from the science at any one point in history, but this does not preclude us from drawing upon the sciences and reason in framing our ethical standards. How and what sense remains to be worked out—it is an ongoing process.

I would suggest that, whatever the time slot in history or the social and cultural setting, scientific knowledge is relevant to decisions, and that it is reasonable to refer to the facts of the case, the means at our disposal in evaluating our ends, and the consequences of our decisions. We also need to take account of our preexisting moral principles and valuations that we bring into the context of choice, though these may be justified or modified by reference to empirical evidence—so there are objective facts that are relevant. Our choices are not value-neutral, but values and principles are not encased in concrete and beyond modification in the light of inquiry and deliberation.

First, it is clear that the fact that science discovers that something is the case factually does not make it *ipso facto* good or right. To illustrate: (a) Charles Darwin noted the role of natural selection and the struggle for survival as key ingredients in the evolution of species. Should we conclude, therefore, as Herbert Spencer did, that laissez-faire doctrines ought to apply, that we ought to allow nature to take its course and not help the handicapped or the poorer classes? (b) Eugenicists concluded earlier in the century that some people are brighter and more talented than others. Does this justify an elitist hierarchical society in which only the best rule and/or eugenic methods of reproduction are to be followed? This was widely held by many liberals until the fascists began applying it in Germany with dire consequences. (c) Konrad Lorenz, the Austrian scientist, observed the role of aggression among males in many or most species. He called it the "instinct for aggression," males battling with each other for females and the right to procreate.[2] Should we encourage this literally, or try to find moral equivalents, as he did? Thus you cannot simply deduce moral imperatives from what allegedly is true empirically.

Second, there have been abundant illustrations of pseudoscientific theories—monocausal theories of human behavior that had been hailed as "scientific"—which have been applied with disastrous results. (a) The racial theories of Chamberlain and Gobineau alleging Aryan superiority led to genocide by the Nazis. (b) Many racists today point to IQ to justify a menial role for blacks in society, and/or on that basis they oppose affirmative action. (c) The dialectical interpretation of history was taken as "scientific" by Marxists and used to justify class warfare. (d) Environmentalists decried genetics as racist and thought that changes in species should be induced only by modifications of the environment. Thus one has to be cautious about applying the latest scientific fad to social policy.

Third, we ought not to consider scientific specialists to be especially endowed with special ethical wisdom, nor empower them to apply this knowledge to society—as B. F. Skinner in *Walden II* and other utopianists attempted to do. Neither should scientific- or philosopher-kings be entrusted to design a better world. We have learned the risks and dangers of abandoning democracy to those wishing to create a Brave New World. Alas, all humans—including scientists—are fallible, and excessive power may corrupt human judgment. Given these caveats, most of the contributors to this volume nevertheless hold that scientific knowledge has an important role to play in shaping our moral values and helping us to frame wiser judgments of practice—surely more than our current reliance on theologians, politicians, TV celebrities, columnists, military pundits, or corporate managers!

III

How and in what sense can scientific inquiry help us to make reasonable choices?

I wish to suggest a *modified form of naturalistic ethics*. Perhaps not all of the contributors would agree with me. The term "naturalism" is often used in contrast with supernaturalism. By this is meant that ethical values are *natural*; they grow out of and fulfill human purposes, interests, desires, and needs. They are forms of preferential behavior evinced in human life. "Good," "bad," "right," and "wrong" relate to sentient beings, whether human or other. These values do not reside in a far-off heaven, nor are they deeply embedded in the hidden recesses of reality; they are empirical phenomena.

The principle of naturalism is based on a key methodological criterion: We ought to consider our moral principles and values like other beliefs, *open to examination in the light of evidence and reason and hence amenable to modification.*

We are all born into a sociocultural context, and we imbibe the values passed on to us, inculcated by our peers, parents, teachers, leaders, and colleagues in the community.

Accordingly, ethical values and principles are amenable to inquiry. We need to ask, Are they reliable? How do they stack up comparatively? Have they been tested in practice? Are they consistent? Many people seek to protect them as inviolable truths, immune to inquiry. This is particularly true of transcendental values based on faith and supported by custom and tradition. In this sense, ethical inquiry is similar to other forms of scientific inquiry. We should not presuppose that what we have inherited is true and beyond question. But where do we begin our inquiry? My response is: in the *midst* of life itself, focused on the practical problems, the concrete dilemmas that we confront.

Let me illustrate by reference to three moral problems under dispute today. I do so not in order to solve them, but to point out *a method of inquiry in ethics*.

I will begin by reference to an issue that has been hotly debated: the prohibition of federal funding of therapeutic stem cell research by the United States government during the Bush administration. One argument against reproductive cloning is as follows: (a) It may be unsafe (at the present stage of medical technology) and that infants born may be defective. This factual objection has some merit. (b) There is also a moral objection that we should not seek to design children. Yet we do so all the time, as in artificial insemination, *in vitro* fertilization, and surrogate motherhood. We already are involved in "designer-baby" technology, with amniocentesis, preimplantation, genetic testing, and chorionic villus sampling (the avoiding of unwanted genes by aborting fetuses and implanting desirable embryos).

If it were to become safe, would reproductive cloning become permissible? I can think of situations where we might find it acceptable. For example, if couples are unable to conceive by normal methods. It is a second aspect of this debate that is especially telling. There are those who oppose *any* forms of embryonic stem cell research on moral grounds versus proponents who maintain that this line of research may lead to enormous benefits by curing a wide range of diseases, such as Parkinson's disease, Alzheimer's, or juvenile diabetes. Adult stem cells are now being used, but embryonic stem cells may provide important new materials. The criterion here is consequential: the positive outcomes that may result. Opponents insist that this type of research is immoral because it is tampering with human persons possessed of souls. Under this interpretation, "ensoulment" occurs at the moment of conception. This is said to apply to embryos, many of which, however, are products of miscarriages or abortions. Does it also apply once the division of stem cells occurs in a petri dish? Surely a small collection of cells, which is called a "blastocyst," is not a person, a sentient being, or a moral agent prior to implantation. Leon Kass, former chair of President Bush's Council on Bioethics, maintained that human life cannot be treated as a commodity and that it is evil to manufacture life. He claimed that all human life, including a cloned embryo, has the same moral dignity as a person from the moment of conception. Other researchers deny this claim.

I do not have the time to develop the case pro and con in great detail, but it pits two opposing moral claims against each other: (a) the view that stem cell research may be beneficial because of its possible contributions to human health versus (b) an ethic of revulsion against tampering with natural reproductive processes. At issue here is the question of whether ensoulment makes any sense in biology, and whether personhood can be said to have begun at such an early stage. This is basically a transcendental claim that naturalists object to on empirical grounds. These arguments are familiar in the abortion debate; it would be unfortunate if they are being used to censor scientific stem cell research. Several chapters in this volume will deal with stem cell research, abortion, and the moral status of the embryo.

A second example of the use of science to resolve moral disputes is the argument for euthanasia and assisted suicide in terminal cases, where people are suffering intolerable pain. This has become a central issue in the field of medical ethics, where medical science is able to keep people alive who might normally die. I first saw the emergence of this field thirty-five years ago when I sponsored a conference in biomedical ethics at my university, but could find very few, if any, scholars or scientists who had thought about the questions or were qualified experts. Today it is an essential area in medicine. The doctor is no longer taken as a patriarchal figure. His or her judgments need to be critically examined, and others within the community, especially patients, need to be consulted. There are here, of course, many factual questions at issue: Is the illness genuinely terminal? Is there great suffering? Is the patient competent in expressing his or her long-standing convictions regarding the right to die with dignity? Are there medical and legal safeguards to guard against abuse?

Those who favor active and passive euthanasia draw on several ethical principles: (a) the informed consent of patients in deciding whether they wish treatment to continue; (b) the right of privacy, including the right of individuals to have control of their own bodies and health; and (c) the criterion of the quality of life.

One problem that we encounter in this area is the role of transcendental principles. Some people insist that "God alone should decide life-and-death questions, not humans." This principle, when invoked, is beyond examination, and for many people it is final. Passive euthanasia means that we will not use extraordinary methods to keep a person alive where there is a long-standing interpretation expressed in a living will not to do so. Active euthanasia will, under certain conditions, allow the patient, in consultation with his physician, to hasten the dying process (as practiced in Oregon and the Netherlands). The point is, there is an interweaving of factual considerations with ethical principles, and these may be modified in the light of inquiry by comparing alternatives and examining consequences in each concrete case. These issues are discussed in this volume.

A third illustration of the process of ethical decision making concerns capital punishment. Should we exact the death penalty for people convicted of murder? The United States is the only major democracy that still demands capital punishment. What is the argument for the death penalty? It rests on two basic premises: (a) a factual question is at issue; namely, is capital punishment an effective deterrent against crime, especially murder? and (b) the principle of justice that applies is often called retributive: "An eye for an eye, a tooth for a tooth, a life for a life," so the Old Testament adage reads.[3] Thus people ought to be held accountable for their actions.

The first factual premise can be resolved by sociological studies, by comparing the incidence of murder in those states and nations which have the death penalty in force and those that do not, and/or by states and nations before and after the enactment or abrogation of the death penalty. We ask, "Has there been an increase or a decrease in murder?" If as a matter of fact the death penalty does *not* restrain or inhibit murder, then would a person still hold his view that the death penalty ought to be exacted? The evidence suggests that the death penalty does not to any significant extent restrain the murder rate, especially since most acts of murder are not deliberate but due to passion, or are an unexpected result of another crime, such as robbery. Thus, *if* one bases his or her belief in capital punishment primarily on the deterrence factor, and it does not deter, would one change one's beliefs? The same consideration should apply to those who are opposed to the death penalty: would they change their beliefs if they thought it would deter excessive murder rates? These are empirical questions at issue. And the test of a policy is its consequences in the real world. Does it achieve what it sets out to do? This is discussed in the chapters that follow.

There are, of course, other factual considerations, such as: Are many innocent people convicted of crimes they did not commit (as recently concluded in the state of Illinois)? Is capital punishment unfairly applied primarily to minorities, and so on? This points to the fact that belief in capital punishment is to some extent a function of scientific knowledge concerning the facts of the case. This often means that such measures should not be left to politicians or jurors alone to decide, but that the scientific facts of the case are directly relevant.

The second moral principle of retributive justice is far more difficult to deal with, for this may be rooted in religious conviction—in the Old Testament or the Qur'an, or in a deep-seated tribal sense of retaliation. If you injure my kin, it is said, I can injure yours; and this is not purely a factual issue. There are other principles of justice that are immediately thrown into consideration. Those opposed to the death penalty say that society "should set a humane tone and not itself resort to killing." Or again, the purpose of justice should be to protect the community from future crimes, and alternative forms of punishment, perhaps lifetime imprisonment without the right of parole, might suffice. Still another principle of justice is relevant: should we attempt, where possible, to rehabilitate the offender? At least, all of the above principles are open to debate. The point is, we should not block inquiry; we should not say that some moral principles are beyond any kind of reevaluation or modification. Here a process of deliberation enters in, and hopeful normative recommendations emerge about what are comparatively the best policies to adopt.

I surely do not intend to resolve any of the moral disagreements about capital punishment, active euthanasia, or therapeutic cloning research. I merely wish to point out that scientific factual knowledge is relevant to helping to resolve these issues by being used to modify or justify the ethical values and principles appealed to.

IV

This leads to an important distinction about the basis of values within human experience. Let me suggest two possible sources: (a) values rooted in feelings, faith, custom, or authority, held as deep-seated convictions beyond question, and (b) values that are influenced by cognition and informed by rational inquiry and scientific evidence.

Naturalists say that scientific inquiry enables us to revise our values and principles, if need be, and/or to develop, where appropriate, new ones. We already possess a body of prescriptive judgments that have been tested in practice in the applied sciences of medicine, psychiatry, engineering, educational counseling, and other fields. Similarly, I submit that there is a body of prescriptive ethical judgments that has been tested in practice, and this constitutes normative knowledge.

The question is often raised, what are the sources of naturalistic morality? First, there are what I have called the common moral decencies or virtues. These refer to prescriptions that have been developed over time and are widely accepted in civilization—from truth telling and promise keeping to being reliable, sympathetic, beneficent, and tolerant. I submit that there is a fund of ethical knowledge that is the heritage of humankind. Facing similar problems and needs, humans have developed many similar rules to govern relationships within communities. These are empirically discoverable and they are tested by their consequences in practice. They do, of course, vary from culture to culture, but there are also certain invariant conditions implicit in the human condition—the raising of children, relationships between members of the same kinship group, norms of marriage and cohabitation, making a living, defense, and so on.

Second, there are ultimately some biological roots for moral behavior. Ethical considerations are not simply imposed from without, but are a natural outgrowth of living together. Other species, bees and ants, wolves and lions, display analogous quasi-moral behavior.

The question is thus raised, what criteria should we use to make ethical choices? This issue is especially pertinent today for those living in pluralistic societies such as ours, where there is diversity of values and principles.

In formulating ethical judgments, we need to refer to what I have called a valuational evidential base.[4] Packed into this referent are the preexisting *de facto* values and principles that we are committed to; but we also need to consider empirical data, means-ends relationships, causal knowledge, and the consequences of various courses of action. It is *inquiry* that is the instrument by which we decide what we ought to do, and that we should develop in the young. We need to focus on moral education for children; we wish to structure positive traits of character, but also the capacity for making reflective decisions. There are no easy recipes or simple formulae that we can appeal to, telling us what we ought to do in every case. There are, however, *prima facie* general principles of right conduct, the common moral decencies, a list of virtues, precepts, and prescriptions, ethical excellences, obligations, and responsibilities, which are intrinsic to our social roles. But how they work out in practice depends on the context at hand, and the most reliable guide for mature persons is cognitive inquiry and deliberation.

Theists have often objected to this approach to morality as dangerous, given to debauchery and immorality. Here there is a contrast between two different senses of morality: (a) the obedience/authoritarian model, in which humans are expected to follow moral absolutes derived from ancient creeds, and (b) the encouragement of moral growth, implying that there are within the human species potential moral tendencies and cognitive capacities that can help us to frame judgments.

For a naturalistic approach, in the last analysis, ethics is a product of a long evolutionary process. Evolutionary psychology has pointed out that moral rules have enabled human communities to adapt to threats to their survival. This Darwinian interpretation implies a biological basis for reciprocal behavior—epigenetic rules—according to E. O. Wilson.[5] The social groups that possessed these rules transmitted them to their offspring. Such moral behavior provides a selective advantage. There is accordingly an inward propensity for moral behavior, moral sentiments, empathy, and altruism within the species.

This does not deny that there are at the same time impulses for selfish and aggressive tendencies. It is a mistake, however, to read in a doctrine of original sin and to say that human beings are by nature sinful and corrupt. I grant that there are individuals who lack moral empathy; they are morally handicapped; some may even be sociopaths. The salient point is that there are genetic potentialities for good or evil; but how they work out and whether beneficent behavior prevails is dependent on cultural conditions. Both our genes (genetic) and our memes (social patterns of enculturation) are factors that determine how and why we behave the way we do. We cannot simply deduce from the evolutionary process what we ought to do. What we do depends in part upon the choices we make. Thus we still have some capacity for free choice. Though we are conditioned by environmental and biogenetic determinants, we are still capable of cognitive processes of selection, and rationality and intentionality play a causative role.[6]

Ethical precepts need not be based upon transcendental grounds, dependent upon religious faith, though undoubtedly the belief that they are sacred may strengthen moral duties for many persons; but it is not necessary for everyone.

I submit that it is time for scientists to recognize that they have an opportunity to develop the implications of naturalistic ethics. The naturalistic outlook is relevant to the present: (1) methodological naturalism uses the methods of the sciences to understand nature and human behavior, (2) scientific naturalism offers a physical-chemical and biological-evolutionary perspective of the universe, and (3) ethical naturalism attempts to solve ethical questions, not by faith or feeling but by empirical methods and cognitive inquiry.

We stand at an interesting time in human history. We have great power to ameliorate the human condition. All of this opens wide new opportunities for humankind to create a better world. The "new singularity," according to Ray Kurzweil, are the future prospects of science and technology for extending life and enhancing it enormously. This includes expanding information technology, nanotechnology, biogenetic engineering, and space research.[7]

Yet there are those today who wish to abandon human reason and freedom, and return to mythological legends of our premodern existence, including the impulses of aggression and self-righteous vengeance. I submit that the Enlightenment is a beacon whose promise has not been fulfilled, and that humankind needs to accept the responsibility for its own future.

A Cautionary Note

Some degree of skepticism is a necessary antidote to all forms of ethical certainty. We are continually surrounded by self-righteous moralists who claim that they have the Absolute Truth or Moral Virtue or Piety or know the secret path to salvation, and wish to impose their convictions on all others. They are puffed up with an inflated sense of their own rectitude as they rail against unbenighted immoral sinners who lack their moral faith. These moral zealots are willing to repress or even sacrifice anyone who stands in their way. They have in the past unleashed conquering armies in the name of God, or the Dialectic, or Racial Superiority, or Posterity, or Imperial Design. Skepticism needs to be applied not only to religious and paranormal fantasies, but to other forms of moral and political illusions. These ethical systems become especially dangerous when they are appealed to in order to legislate morality and are used by powerful social institutions, such as the state or church or corporation, to enforce a particular brand of moral virtue. Hell hath no fury like the self-righteous moralist scorned!

The best antidote for this is some skepticism and a willingness to engage in ethical inquiry, not only about *others'* moral zeal, but about *our own*, especially if we are tempted to translate the results of our own ethical inquiries into commandments. The methodological principles of skeptical scientific inquiry have important moral implications. For in recognizing our own fallibility we can learn to *tolerate* other human beings and to appreciate their diversity and the plurality of lifestyles. If we are prepared to engage in cooperative ethical inquiry, then perhaps we are better prepared to allow other individuals and groups some measure of liberty to pursue their own preferred lifestyles. If we are able to live and let live, then this can best be achieved in a free and open democratic society. Where we differ, we should try to negotiate our divergent views and perhaps reach common ground; and if this is impractical, we should at least attempt to compromise for the sake of our common interests. The method of ethical inquiry requires some intelligent and informed examination of our own values, as well as the values of others. Here we can attempt to modify attitudes by an appeal to cognitive beliefs and to reconstruct them by an examination of the relevant evidence. Such a give-and-take of constructive criticism is essential for a harmonious society. In learning to appreciate different conceptions of the good life, we are able to expand our own dimensions of moral awareness; and this is more apt to lead to a peaceful world.

By this I surely do not mean to imply that anything and everything can or should be tolerated, or that one thing is as good as the next. We should be prepared to criticize moral nonsense parading as virtue. We should not simply tolerate the intolerable. We have a right to strongly object, if need be, to those values or practices that we think are based on miscalculation, misconception, or are patently false or harmful. Nonetheless, we might live in a better world if *inquiry* were to replace faith; *deliberation*, passionate commitment; and *education and persuasion*, violence. We should be aware of the powers of intelligent behavior, but also of the limitations of human beings and of the need to mitigate the cold, indifferent intellect with the compassionate and empathic heart. Within the ethical life we are capable of developing a body of melioristic principles and values and a method of coping with problems intelligently. When our ethical judgments are based on rational and scientific inquiry, they are more apt to express the highest reaches of civilized human conduct, perhaps even some excellence and nobility. We are in sore need of these today. What a contrast with current attitudes and approaches!

V

The chapters in this volume deal with a wide range of topics. There are two main themes, however, that appear throughout. First, is the theoretical question: "Can science help us to make judicious ethical choices?" This is a general metaethical question about how we might go about justifying ethical judgments. The second theme is actually concerned with practical questions encountered in concrete scientific inquiries. Actually both questions have a practical normative import since they are concerned with genuine ethical questions that arise in scientific research and practice; so this is not an exercise in purely formal philosophical analyses of hypothetical moral quandaries.

The first theoretical question—can science help us?—is discussed primarily by philosophers: Mario Bunge, Bill Rottschaefer, John Teehan and Christopher diCarlo, Fred Wilson, David Koepsell, Susan Haack, and Paul Kurtz. We generally agree that science is indeed relevant to the resolution of ethical problems, though we cannot deduce in any simplistic way what is good or right or ought to be done from factual considerations alone. These issues are discussed primarily in the introductory section by Paul Kurtz and Mario Bunge as well as in part VIII, "Naturalistic Ethics," by Bill Rottschaefer, John Teehan and Christopher diCarlo, Donald D. Calne, David Koepsell, and Susan Haack. I reiterate, what is herein presented is a kind of modified naturalistic ethics: scientific knowledge adds to our capacity to resolve moral questions. But this conception of science is broadly conceived to involve the use of reason in appraising ethical principles and values and it is continuous with common sense.

The second question concerns the applications of science to practical questions as they are encountered in biogenetic and medical fields and the social sciences. The practical ethical issues are organized around several sections.

In Part I, "Bioethics and Stem Cell Research," Ronald Lindsay and Arthur Caplan—both philosophers and bioethicists—attempt to respond to the objections to stem cell research and find reasons to defend it. Paul Kurtz proposes a general *prima facie* methodological rule that allows scientific research to go on unhampered, unless there are overriding reasons to the contrary. Don Marquis provides a dissenting viewpoint. David Triggle defends biogenetic research.

Part II, "The Embryo in Stem Cell Research and Abortion," evaluates similar arguments about the nature of the human embryo and the beginning of human life used to block research and practice in these areas. Berit Brogaard, Richard and Elaine Hull, and Marin Gillis point out the egregious errors in the case against abortion and stem cell research.

Part III, "Euthanasia and Assisted Suicide," relates the case for voluntary euthanasia on the ethical principle of the "right to privacy" and the difficulty in distinguishing active and passive euthanasia.

Part IV, "Organ Transplants, Sexuality, and Human Enhancement," deals with other moral issues encountered in the biomedical field. John Stacey Taylor examines the ethics governing organ transplants. Vern Bullough deals with moral questions confronting sexologists, such as gender identity, transsexual surgery, circumcision, sterilization, and the morning-after pill. James Hughes raises the question of whether it is meaningful to use the argument that transhumanism and biogenetic techniques used to enhance and alter human life are inadmissible because they are contrary to "human nature."

Part V, "Deterrence and Capital Punishment," deals with the question of whether the death penalty is effective in deterring crime, especially murder. What is the evidence for it? asks Ted Goertzel. What is the empirical justification for retribution rather than rehabilitation in the treatment of offenders? asks Richard Taylor.

Part VI, "Psychiatry and Psychotherapy," presents the opposition of psychiatrist Thomas Szasz to involuntary commitment and the premises of "scientific psychiatry," and Derek Bolton responds. Scott Lilienfeld and Barry Beyerstein, two psychologists, evaluate the scientific credential of mental health practice and what they consider fringe psychotherapies.

Theoretical philosophical questions are raised in the concluding two sections.

In Part VII, "Science, Religion, and Ethics," Fred Wilson evaluates the work of Stephen Jay Gould, who had defended two nonoverlapping magisteria (NOMA), science on the one hand, the domain of scientists, and ethics on the other, the domain of religion. Wilson asserts that science and religion are incompatible and that ethics is capable of naturalistic treatment independent of religion. Paul Kurtz criticizes Gould and sharply distinguishes religion, ethics, and science, though he says that they are only compatible if religion does not seek to compete with science, ethics, or politics and allows them to develop independent of religion. Laura Purdy rejects religious ethics and defends scientific ethics.

Part VIII, "Naturalistic Ethics," presents contemporary defenses of naturalistic ethics by Bill Rottschaefer, John and Christopher diCarlo, Donald B. Calne, and David R. Koepsell. In the concluding chapter, Susan Haack defends science—within reason—and points out its continuity with critical common sense.

This volume grew out of a special Conference on Science and Ethics sponsored by the Center for Inquiry/Transnational, which convened in Toronto, Canada, on May 13–16, 2004. The first conference was on Science and Religion, which also resulted in a volume (*Science and Religion: Are They Compatible?* edited by Paul Kurtz with the assistance of Barry Karr and Ranjit Sandhu [Amherst, NY: Prometheus Books, 2003]). Added to this volume are also papers from another international congress of the Center for Inquiry/Transnational convened at the State University of New York at Buffalo in October 2005 on the theme "Toward a New Enlightenment." Added to it are articles first published in *Free Inquiry* and the *Skeptical Inquirer*, publications of the Center for Inquiry/Transnational.

NOTES

1. G. E. Moore, *Principia Ethica* (Cambridge, 1905).
2. Konrad Lorenz, *On Aggression* (Munich: Deutscher Taschenbuch, Verlag GmbH, 1963).
3. See Leviticus 24:20–21.
4. Paul Kurtz, *The New Skepticism: Inquiry and Reliable Knowledge* (Amherst, NY: Prometheus Books 1992), chap. 9.
5. E. O. Wilson, *Consilience* (New York: Alfred Knopf, 1998).
6. There is a considerable scientific literature that supports this evolutionary view. See Daniel Dennett, *Freedom Evolves* (New York: Viking, 2003) and *Darwin's Dangerous Idea* (New York: Simon and Schuster, 1995); Brian Skyrm, *Evolution of the Social Contract* (1996), Robert Wright, *The Moral Animal* (1994) and *Nonzero* (2000), Matt Ridley, *The Origins of Virtue* (1996), and Elliott Sober and David Sloan Wilson, *Unto Others* (1998).
7. Ray Kurzweil, *The Singularity Is Near: When Humans Transcend Biology* (New York: Viking Adult, 2005).

2

THE ETHICS OF SCIENCE
AND THE SCIENCE
OF ETHICS

MARIO BUNGE

PREFACE

We are currently facing a long list of formidable worldwide challenges—global warming, the exhaustion of nonrenewable resources, resource wars, increasing income inequality, crushing national debts, rising violence on all scales, militarism, the new American imperialism, advertising-driven consumerism, the crisis of the welfare state, the decline of labor unions, the resurgence of religious fanaticism, increasing intolerance, the commercialization of politics, the defamation of classical liberalism and socialism, the decline of student enrollment in science and engineering programs, the popularity of postmodernism, and the displacement of educated art by commercial pop culture.

I suggest that all of the above are symptoms of a crisis of modern civilization. In the face of this crisis, one may take either of two stands: obscurantist or enlightened. Obscurantists will welcome backward trends and will attempt to substitute minor or artificial issues such as abortion, euthanasia, and same-sex marriage for the real ones such as war, hunger, and intolerance. Or they will pretend that the serious problems can be solved with the help of

Originally published as "Enlightened Solutions for Global Challenges," *Free Inquiry* 26, no. 2 (February/March 2006): 29–34.

ready-made recipes, whether religious in character—like the belief that God will provide—or secular, like neoliberalism and globalization.

Obscurantists look backward because, beholden as they are to special interests and frozen belief systems, they fear progress. By contrast, the enlightened are realists: they face facts and look forward to the results of new rigorous research in science, technology, and the humanities. In particular, they realize that every social issue poses moral problems. They also know that ethics did not freeze three millennia ago—or even more recently. Every new stage in history poses problems of its own, which call for original ethical thinking and decision making on subjects such as whether to bomb civilian populations, impose democracy by force, continue to manufacture gas-guzzlers, use torture, reinforce security at the expense of civil liberties, subsidize corporations and confessional schools, and cut taxes at the cost of social services.

For example, obscurantists deny that the environment is being rapidly degraded by gas emissions from factories and cars; or they will admit that this may be the case, but they don't care, either because of civic irresponsibility and moral callousness or because they believe that the end of the world is near. The enlightened, by contrast, will favor regulating gas emissions through taxation together with increased energy efficiency through the redesign of vehicles and other gas-powered machinery. Again, obscurantists will counter grassroots terrorism with state terrorism, whereas the enlightened will attempt to eliminate the roots of group-sponsored terrorism, such as foreign occupation.

All of the global problems we face are social in character. The classical moral philosophies won't help us solve these problems because they ignore society. These problems won't be tackled successfully *unless they are handled in the light of science and technology*, together with well-grounded moral norms capable of inspiring moral passion and prosocial political action.

*   *   *

Traditional philosophy teaches that science and ethics are disjoint. The reason would be that science deals with facts whereas ethics is about values. However, this only holds for mathematics, physics, and chemistry: biology and the social and biosocial sciences tell us a lot about what is valuable for survival and coexistence. Hence, these sciences should not be ignored by the moral philosopher. Besides, all scientists care for certain values and therefore abide by some moral norms, such as respect for truth. Thus, both the ethics of science and scientific ethics must be possible. Let us explore briefly these possibilities. But before doing so we must warn against the popular confusion between science and technology.

1. Do Not Blame Scientists: Frisk Technologists

Half a century ago science enjoyed enormous prestige worldwide. It was seen as the key to solving all problems, not only those concerning the nature of things but also practical problems, particularly those of health and poverty.

Why this optimism? There were two reasons for it. One was that science, or at least natural science, had made sensational strides, particularly in understanding atoms, stars, and the fabric of the human body. The second reason was that, under the influence of journalists and philosophers of all stripes, science was being mistaken for technology. Thus basic science, which is the attempt to understand the world, was mistakenly attributed the power to change it.

Now, obviously, the world can be changed either for the better or for the worse. In particular, technology can be used by industry or government for either good or evil, and thus become vicariously powerful. For instance, nuclear engineering, which is based on nuclear physics, can be used either to design nuclear plants or nuclear bombs.

Note that I have just distinguished nuclear engineering from nuclear physics. The reason is that nuclear physicists study individual atomic nuclei, which are microphysical things, whereas nuclear engineers specialize in nuclear reactors, which contain zillions of atoms. Besides, the vast majority of atomic nuclei are found, whereas all reactors are designed and manufactured.

Nearly six decades ago, the nuclear bombing of Hiroshima and Nagasaki took most physicists by surprise. Everyone knew that the uranium nuclei could be split releasing a large amount of energy, but most physicists had no idea about the way nuclear bombs worked. Even Lord Rutherford, the father of nuclear physics, had declared that nuclear energy would never be tapped. He was a scientist, not an engineer.

Allow me to reminisce for a minute, and go back to Buenos Aires in August of 1945. Guido Beck, my teacher, had invented the layer model of the nucleus, which was to be confirmed experimentally three decades later. But he knew nothing about bombs. At that time he and I were working on a very different problem, and without any practical applications in mind. This problem was: what kind of strange forces hold an atomic nucleus together, overcoming the electric repulsion of the protons in it?

At that time one juggled with three kinds of hypothetical forces, neither of which turned out to be real. The problem was solved several decades later. At that time we were so ignorant about nuclear reactors that we wondered whether engineers would soon invent nuclear cigarette lighters, lasting far longer than the ones we used at the time. We had not heard of critical masses, and had no idea that nuclear power was about to become a large new and ambivalent industry.

The point of this story is that basic science is always innocent, whereas technology can be guilty. The reason for this difference is that basic science is the search for truths about reality, whereas technology is the search for efficiency through the design of artifacts. Thus, whereas for science truth is both means and goal, it is only a means for technology. This is why some scientific findings are rewarded with the Nobel Prize, whereas technological designs can be patented, sold, and implemented. While some experiments and theories are valuable, none are marketable.

2. The Ethics of Basic Science

A piece of scientific knowledge is intrinsically valuable, whereas a technological design is instrumentally valuable: it can be used to produce good artifacts, such as prescription drugs, or evil ones, such as weapons of mass deception.

This difference suggests that scientists and technologists work under different moral rules. The technologist's main moral norm is to work according to the highest technical standards: he is not expected to design shoddy or inefficient products. Of course, if he has a moral conscience, the technologist will try not to harm people or the environment. He may even blow the whistle on socially pernicious projects. But he will do this at a risk, for his employer or client may not have any moral scruples.

The basic scientists need have no such scruples, because his work is unlikely to have practical uses. If it does have any, it belongs in an applied science, such as pharmacology, or in a technology, such as management science, not in basic science.

The first to exhibit the ethics of science was the great American sociologist Robert K. Merton (1973), who founded the scientific sociology of science. In a landmark paper on science and the social order, published in 1938, Merton stated that science has an ethos that consists of intellectual honesty, integrity, epistemic communism, organized skepticism, disinterestedness, impersonality, and universality. (See also Bronowski 1959.)

The postmoderns have attacked this picture of the basic scientist, claiming that it is an idealization. Yet Merton himself warned in the same paper that "the scientist, in company with all other professional workers, has a large emotional investment in his way of life." That is, he is passionate about the search for truth. Merton also denounced the way science was being misused and corrupted in Nazi Germany. A few years later he showed that psychology and sociology were used to manipulate the American public opinion to bolster the war effort.

3. The Betrayal of the Ethos of Science

Like all moral codes, that of the scientist is prescriptive rather than descriptive. Consequently, one should expect some scientists to occasionally fail to comply with it, lending their expertise to unworthy causes. Let us review quickly a few outstanding cases.

Physics. Only one well-known physicist opposed the First World War: Albert Einstein, who signed a pacifist manifesto along with two rather obscure scientists. Nearly three decades later he allowed his friend Leo Szilard to twist his arm, and cosigned their famous letter to President Roosevelt—something both of them came to regret. Shortly thereafter J. Robert Oppenheimer in the United States, and Werner Heisenberg in Germany, were put in charge of the scientific component of their countries' nuclear warfare programs. The German program failed miserably because Heisenberg, a theorist, did not understand that science is not enough to generate technology, much less large-scale industry. By contrast, the Manhattan Project succeeded because it combined science with engineering, management, money, and enthusiasm for a cause.

The scientists in this project had been promised to be consulted before dropping the bomb if it was ever manufactured. But the Truman administration did not consult them. The bomb had ceased to be a weapon to finish the war in the Pacific: it had become a major political weapon to shape the future. The British physicists P. M. S. Blackett and Joseph Rotblat, both Nobel laureates, have told us why. The bomb was not necessary to win the war in the Pacific because Japan lay in ruins, and the Japanese government had asked for terms of surrender. In the winter of 1943, right after the Russians won the battle of Stalingrad, General Leslie Groves, the manager of the Manhattan Project, summoned the leaders of the physics group and told them that the Allied victory was now in sight, but that a new enemy would soon have to be confronted, namely the Soviet Union. The project had to be continued to completion in order to win the next war. Rotblat quietly withdrew and returned to England. The others remained.

At the end of the war a few of those scientists, notably Edward Teller, Johann von Neumann, and Eugene P. Wigner, became ardent cold warriors. In particular, Teller campaigned for the hydrogen bomb. (Ironically, his Soviet counterpart was Andrei Sakharov, who would later become an outspoken critic of the Stalinist regime.) But many other scientists rallied around the outspoken antiwar *Bulletin of Atomic Scientists*. And some of them, in particular Norbert Wiener, the father of cybernetics, swore never to work for the military again. In sum, the moral report card of the physicists in the 1940s is mixed.

Chemistry. Fritz Haber was the eminent chemist who earned the Nobel Prize for synthesizing ammonia, used to manufacture explosives as well as fertilizers. (Note the dual use of this molecule.) In 1915 this scientist donned his patriot's uniform and conducted the first massive essay in gas warfare in history, at the horrendous carnage of Ypres. Back from the front, Haber threw a victory party in the company of other scientists and brass. When the party was over his wife, a fellow chemist, killed herself with his service revolver, out of shame for her husband's crime. Yet hours later, the scientist-warrior, undaunted, traveled to the eastern front to repeat his "experiment." After the war he continued his "patriotic" work on chemical warfare. Yet when the Nazis stormed to power, they did not spare him despite his jingoism: after all, the great scientist belonged to a so-called inferior race (see Cornwell 2003).

Biology and anthropology. Eugenics, or "scientific racism," was hatched by some geneticists and anthropologists one century ago. Its pseudoscientific dogmas were trumpeted by protofascists like Friedrich Nietzsche, as well as by progressives like Margaret Sanger. Eugenics was first put into practice on a small scale in the United States, where some states enshrined it in segregation and sterilization laws. This pseudoscience was applied on a far larger scale in Nazi Germany. We all remember the cruel and utterly useless experiments that Joseph Mengele conducted at Auschwitz. What is far less known is that Mengele did not act on his own: he was an assistant to Professor Otmar von Verschuer, director of one the institutes at the prestigious Kaiser Wilhelm Gesellschaft in Berlin. Earlier, the institute had been supported by the Rockefeller Foundation (see Black 2003). And the Kaiser Wilhelm was presided over by no less than Max Planck, the grandfather of quantum physics, who compromised with the regime although he did not join the party (see Heilbron 1986).

Social science. Nearly five hundred years ago Niccolò Machiavelli, the historian founder of modern political science, wrote *The Prince*. This brilliant tract combined new truths with immoral political advice. Thus modern political science began as a smart whore. Outstanding pupils of the great Machiavelli have been Max Weber, who in 1916 opposed a manifesto of some Berlin professors to seek peace; Woodrow Wilson, the so-called moral idealist and champion of world democracy, who did not object to colonialism and who thought up the vindictive Treaty of Versailles, a root of World War II; Henry Kissinger, who devised some of the strategies and lies used in the Vietnam War; Samuel Huntington, who declared South Africa under the apartheid regime to be a "satisfied society,"and assisted the Pentagon in designing the "relocation" of Vietnamese peasants; and of course the ideologists of the present US administration. All of these politologists have been Machiavellian in the moral sense, but of course, unlike the great Florentine, none of them discovered any new truths about politics.

Besides the just-named delinquents, we must remember the hundreds of German and Soviet scientists who signed declarations of loyalty to their respective dictatorships. Nor should we forget the economists who claim that the natural resources are infinite; that a certain rate of unemployment is healthy for the economy; that free trade is the solution to all economic ills; or that authoritarian governments are good because they protect foreign investments.

In short, basic science is pure, but individual scientists may get corrupted when given the opportunity to double as either technologists or policy consultants.

4. Partial Blindness to Social Reality

Basic research is the search for truth, not for wealth, justice, salvation, or beauty. However, searching for truth is not enough: the genuine scientist knows that reality is enormously complex, so that he is bound to miss much of it. But at least he will not declare that what he leaves aside is not worth investigating. And yet some distinguished social scientists have deliberately underrated or willfully ignored the aspects of reality that did not fit their aprioristic philosophical prejudices. Marx and Weber are two such scientists. Let us peek at them.

Karl Marx is generally recognized as a great economist and a generous champion of equality. But his economic determinism led him to underrate politics and culture, both of which he placed in what he and Engels called "the spiritual superstructure of society," which they regarded as a product and mirror of the economic infrastructure. This one-sided view of society led Marx and most of his followers to miss or underrate some of the most important political and cultural movements of their time, such as nationalism, political liberalism, secularism, bureaucratization, and the sensational growth of basic science and science-based engineering.

When the reaction to economism came within the Marxist camp, it was too radical. Thus Antonio Gramsci emphasized the role of politics and ideology to the point of neglecting the economy and the ways ordinary people manage to make a living. And nowadays innumerable innumerate self-styled Marxist scholars, allergic to economic and social statistics, tend to exaggerate the role of ideology. Some of them have gone to the point of seeing sinister designs behind the most innocent mathematical formulas: they have fallen for the constructivist-relativist sociology and philosophy of science. In the meantime, important social novelties, such as increasing economic inequalities, the decline of the labor unions, the success of cooperative enterprises in the developing world, and the ambivalent results of globalization, are being investigated by non-Marxist scientists.

Max Weber passes for being the anti-Marx although he made no contributions to economics while he was a professor of this discipline. This is because Weber emphasized ideas at the expense of the so-called material factors. Consequently, despite being one of the fathers of modern sociology, he missed all the major social movements of his time. Indeed, he missed colonialism, militarism, the labor movement, and even democracy. Weber fathered the sociology of religion, but he missed the rise of science and technology, for he did not understand that these are the intellectual engines of modernity.

Weber's one-eyed vision of society was not accidental, but stemmed from his combination of historical idealism with methodological individualism, which he learned from the neo-Hegelian Dilthey and the neo-Kantians. For example, when studying the condition of the agricultural workers in East Prussia, Weber focused on the way they felt toward their job and their employers, and deliberately overlooked their material conditions of existence. And because of this preference for inner life over work, Weber chose Protestant ministers as his informants in preference to doctors–a doubly unfortunate choice since most of those laborers were Catholic Poles who spoke hardly any German (Lazarsfeld and Oberschall 1965). Ironically, Weber was also the main critic of the ideological contamination of social science—as long as such contamination came from the Marxist quarter.

Something similar holds also for other followers of the idealist tradition, which focuses on ideas, norms, myths, rites, and the like, to the detriment of environmental and economic factors. For example, the famous contemporary anthropologist Clifford Geertz informs us in detail about cockfighting in Balinese villages, but does not inform us how those villagers make a living, nor how they cope with hurricanes, landlords, and usurers. Nobody can deny the importance of the so-called symbolic factors, particularly nowadays, when millions of people are being mobilized for crusades and jihads. But one should not forget that someone has got to work for fanatics and saints to earn eternal bliss.

5. The Centrality of Truth

It is well known that the main casualties of postmodernity are rationality, objectivism (realism), and reality checks. These values have been displaced by subjectivity, metaphor, rhetoric, and dogma. In recent times the anti-modernist movement, so decadent and so popular among half-baked intellectuals, has forged a tacit alliance with religious fundamentalists—Christian, Jewish, Islamic, and Hindu. All of them know that science is their cultural enemy precisely because science aims at truth through reason and empirical evidence.

Truth is central not only to science but also to technology and, indeed, to everyday life in modern society. Imagine for a moment what life would be like without truth. Imagine a land whose people did not believe in the possibility, much less the desirability, of truth. Call them *analethics*, since the Greek for truth is *aletheia*.

In Analetheia nobody searches for truths, because its inhabitants believe that none are to be found. Consequently, in that land everyone is ignorant of everything, except of course for the maxim "There is no truth." Nobody places any value upon rational discussion, because people do not share any premises regarded as true. Nor is there a common set of rules for arguing in such a way that truth will be preserved. Nobody trusts anyone else, because there is no reason to believe that anyone could or would provide true information. And nobody makes well-grounded decisions, because there are no practical rules based on true generalities.

In Analetheia there is no business other than bartering, because it is deemed pointless to check whether a product is valuable, a deal profitable, a partner loyal, or a supplier trustworthy. There are no physicians, because nobody knows any biology capable of inspiring and justifying therapies. Nor are there any lawyers, because no evidence can be adduced for or against any claim, and no arguments can be conclusive. And in Analetheia there is no binding moral code either, because nobody knows any moral truths—a subject to be considered below.

Analetheia would be an unruly society because it would be bereft of science and technology, as well as of morals and law. Still, such society might produce some art, provided it were purely ornamental and were not intended to help communication. However, it would be impossible to teach art without eliciting such embarrassing questions as "Is it true that mixing blue and yellow yields green?" let alone "Is it true that all beauty is in the eye of the beholder?"

Analetheia might also abide by a formalistic ideology, in particular a pharisaic religion that commanded the performance of certain rituals for purely practical motives: "If you wish to survive, do this, but don't do that—and don't ask why." However, such a society would lack any mechanisms, other than early dressage and coercion, for enforcing such commandments, because no true evidence for either their fulfillment or their violation would be produced.

Consequently the analetheic society, like the early colonial settlements, might have barracks, jails, gallows, brothels, and temples, but neither schools, nor hospitals, nor courts of law, much less laboratories. Therefore life in Analetheia would be, in Hobbes's words, "short, nasty, and brutish."

Of course, Analethia is a dystopia: nobody can live without a modicum of truths. Moreover, I submit that truth is central not only to cognitive and practical pursuits, but also to moral life.

6. The Science of Ethics

According to the traditional moral philosophies, there can be no moral truths because there would be no moral facts: all moral principles and judgments would be emotive, intuitive, or utilitarian. They would be dogmas rather than testable hypotheses.

I submit that there are moral truths because there are moral facts. A moral fact may be defined as a social fact that affects the well-being of others. For instance, starvation, physical violence, political oppression, involuntary unemployment, military aggression, and forcible cultural deprivation are moral facts. So are their duals: relief from starvation, job creation, conflict resolution, political participation, peacemaking, and cultural diffusion.

Since there are moral facts, there must be moral truths. Here are a few: "Life should be enjoyable," "Fairness is right," "Lying is wrong," "The end does not always justify the means," "Exploitation is unjust," "Cruelty is abominable," "Altruism is commendable," "Loyalty is a virtue," and "Just peace is preferable to victory."

Morals need be neither dogmatic nor empirical: it can and should be scientific, in the sense that its rules can and should be compatible with what is known through scientific research about human nature and social life (see Bunge 1989). Three examples will have to suffice to make this point.

First, contrary to the preaching of Utilitarians and neoliberals, reciprocal altruism has a firm basis in social science. Indeed, it is conducive to social justice and social cohesion, and thus to both social harmony and progress.

Second, unlike traditional pedagogy, its contemporary successor emphasizes the joy of learning. Consequently, instead of using punishment as an incentive, it uses reward and the withholding of reward. This reorientation has two roots. One is the thesis that, Martin Luther notwithstanding, we are not condemned to suffer: we may enjoy life and we should have the right to do so. The other root is the finding of modern psychology and pedagogy, that children respond better to reward or the withholding of it than to punishment. Both ideas are alien to the myth of salvation through suffering.

A third example is the case for responsible procreation. Secular humanists hold that it is cruel to procreate children who, being unwanted, will not be properly raised and educated, as a consequence of which they are likely to become unhappy as well as a burden to society. And, since cruelty is abominable, opposition to contraception is starkly immoral. The immorality of condemning the use of condoms is compounded by the current AIDS epidemic, since this deadly sickness is transmitted by the HIV virus through unprotected sex.

Another example of cruelty, and therefore immorality, is the ban on the federal funding of research and therapeutic use of embryonic stem cells to replace diseased or dead tissue, because it condemns to death the victims of such neurodegenerative diseases as Parkinson's, Alzheimer's, and Huntington's, who might greatly benefit from stem cell transplants.

The case of reproductive human cloning is different, for there are scientific reasons against it in addition to religious objections. First, our overpopulated world does not need artificial reproduction: far from being an endangered species, ours is the most endangering of all. Second, too many of the known artificial mammalian clones have exhibited severe defects. A cause of these is the shortening of the telomeres, or tails of the chromosomes. Apparently, artificial clones are born old, hence prone to suffering old-age ailments from birth. Either of the two reasons should suffice to ban human cloning for the moment. And in both cases the moral norm is based on scientific considerations: truth may show the way to the good and the right.

Let us now jump from a handful of cases to a few generalities. A moral code can be either traditional or updated with the help of science and technology. If traditional, a code will ignore or even reject important truths found in recent centuries. Consequently, such a code will condone serious mismatches between morals and modern life, thus contributing to the unhappiness of many people. By contrast, a scientific morality would start by identifying basic needs and the ways of meeting them without harming others. It would adopt the maxim "Enjoy life and help live."

In sum, whereas traditional morals are bound to be obsolete, oppressive, and divisive, a scientific moral code would match modern life and would be liberating and inclusive, in being based on objective truth. Indeed, the scientific truth (or rather its recognition) shalt make thou free!

The view of morals that I have just sketched is called "moral realism," and it is compatible with philosophical materialism, because it is worldly rather than otherworldly or supernaturalistc. However, I do not believe in moral naturalism, or the view that morality is only a survival device. If it were, we should prefer lying to telling the truth, and conformity to independence. In other words, the moral realism and materialism I advocate (Bunge 1989, 2006) is not a form of reductionism. Rather, it is consistent with emergentist materialism, which emphasizes qualitative novelty and the existence of levels of organization, from the physical to the biological to the social (Bunge 2003).

In short, I submit that the moral norms, far from being determined by our genes, are made, repaired, and rejected in the course of history, along with other social norms.

What holds for ethics also holds for its next-door neighbor, namely political ideology. The traditional view is of course that ideology is unscientific. This is indeed the case with all the extant ideologies. But in my view, it is possible to craft a scientific political ideology, that is, one based on social science.

Take, for instance, the problem of social equality. Why should social justice be objectively desirable? First, because social psychology has shown that people are dissatisfied not only when they suffer from deprivation, but also when they are notably and unjustifiably discriminated against: recall reference group theory. Epidemiology confirms this finding: morbidity and mortality increase with economic inequality. Second, inequality is objectively undesirable because sociology has shown that social cohesion increases with social participation and decreases with social exclusion. Finally, equity is desirable because political science has shown that a deeply divided society is plagued by conflict and crime, and is therefore politically unstable as well as deficient in security.

In short, there is solid scientific evidence to back up political programs that pursue equity. Obviously, the same evidence disqualifies the inegalitarian agenda of fascists and neoconservatives (or neoliberals).

In sum, although science exudes neither morals nor ideology, it offers a solid foundation for both.

CONCLUSION

Basic science is losing the glamour it enjoyed half a century ago in North America, as shown by the declining enrollment in scientific careers. Presumably, the main causes of this decline are the rise of religious fundamentalism, the spread of postmodern nonsense, and the legitimate fear of the monsters that technology can engender unless it is controlled.

Regrettably, philosophy, or rather pseudophilosophy, has contributed to both postmodernism and to the double confusion of science with technology, and the latter with industry and government. For example, Jürgen Habermas fused science together with technology, and declared that "it," which the social constructivists call "technoscience," is the ideology of late capitalism. Obviously, these writers do not realize that technologists design artifacts—good, bad, or indifferent—whereas scientists just try to find objective truths, only very few of which can be used by technologists.

Take, for instance, modern genetics. This basic science has deepened and unified biology, as well as becoming the basis of genetic engineering. We all know that this technology, like all technologies, is ambivalent. For example, it has produced high yield cereals, the cultivation of which has had two effects. On the one hand it has increased sensationally the production of cereals; on the other it has ruined the farmers who are too poor to buy those seeds, the fertilizers, and the water necessary to cultivate them. Another unfortunate and unanticipated by-product of genetics it that it has inspired genetic determinism, the ridiculous if popular doctrine that the organism is only a gene carrier, and that genome is destiny (see, e.g., Lewontin 2000).

The concept of objective (or factual) truth is central in all walks of life, not only in science and technology. But of course truth never comes alone: it is always flanked by work and love—of self, others, nature, ideas, beauty, good works, or what have you. The search for truth requires the love of it as well as hard work. Work without truth is either inefficient or exploitative; and without love work is drudgery. In turn, love without truth is deceitful; and it is unsustainable without work. Here, then, is a secular substitute for the old Holy Trinity: *Truth, Work, Love.* Maybe we secular humanists should adopt it along with the slogan that the French Enlightenment gave us: *Liberty, Equality, Fraternity.*

REFERENCES

Black, Edwin. "From Long Island to Auschwitz." *Seed* 1, no. 8 (2003): 84–91, 124–25.

Bronowski, Jacques. *Science and Human Values.* New York: Harper, 1959.

Bunge, Mario. *Treatise on Basic Philosophy.* Vol. 8, *Ethics.* Dordrecht: D. Reidel, 1989.

———. *Emergence and Convergence: Qualitative Novelty and the Unity of Knowledge.* Toronto: University of Toronto Press, 2003.

———. *Chasing Reality: Strife over Realism.* Toronto: University of Toronto Press, 2006.

Cornwell, John. *Hitler's Scientists.* New York: Viking, 2003.

Heilbron, J. L. *The Dilemmas of an Upright Man.* Berkeley: University of California Press, 1986.

Lazarsfeld, Paul F., and Anthony R. Oberschall. "Max Weber and Empirical Social Research." *American Sociological Review* 30 (1965): 185–99.

Lewontin, Richard. *It Ain't Necessarily So*. New York: New York Review of Books, 2000.

Merton, Robert K. *The Sociology of Science*. Chicago: University of Chicago Press, 1973.

BIOETHICS AND STEM CELL RESEARCH

PART

I

3

STEM CELL RESEARCH
An Approach to Bioethics
Based on Scientific Naturalism

RONALD A. LINDSAY

INTRODUCTION

The moral status of the embryo has been the topic of vigorous debate in recent years, motivated principally by the promise of new therapies that may be derived from embryonic stem cell research. The following article was prepared in July 2006, at the time that the US Senate was debating legislation that would have loosened restrictions on stem cell research. This legislation was ultimately approved by Congress, only to be vetoed by President Bush. Although it was drafted at the time of the Senate debate, this article remains highly relevant. Moreover, it illustrates on several different levels the relationship between science and ethics, including the effect that a proper understanding of embryonic development can have on our views about the morality of stem cell research. For example, the article maintains that some of the arguments against stem cell research "are unpersuasive in part because they are premised on a misunderstanding of the relevant facts." Note that the Center for Inquiry, a nonprofit think tank, adopted this article as its position paper on the funding of stem cell research.

An earlier version of this article appeared on the Center for Inquiry Web site, July 2006.

METHOD IN BIOETHICS

Before discussing the moral implications of embryonic stem cell research, a few words about methodology are appropriate. Method in bioethics is critical. We cannot hope to achieve a consensus on disputed moral issues if there is no agreement, at least in general terms, about the procedures we should use in addressing and resolving moral disputes.

To begin, we believe it is important to acknowledge that the dispute over embryonic stem cell research is difficult to resolve in part because it raises novel questions. Our ancestors did not address ethical quandaries arising out of stem cell research for the obvious reason that such research was not a possibility for them. The status of human embryos and the protection they are entitled to, if any, is a problem of recent origin, so we should not be altogether surprised if there are differences of opinion about the treatment of embryos. This acknowledgment is important because many find uncertainty and doubt about moral questions deeply disquieting and troubling. There is always a temptation to remove such doubts through an unreflective and dogmatic application of norms and principles that may be widely accepted but which were developed to address different situations. This explains at least some of the appeal of the position that the embryo has the same moral status as a human person[1] and that stem cell research, as presently carried out, unjustifiably "kills" the embryo. If that were correct, we could avoid the ethical debate over stem cell research and simply state that it is morally wrong—as morally wrong as subjecting an adult human to harmful experimentation without her consent.

But we should resist the temptation to resort to dogma and vague and uninformative principles such as "the sanctity of life." One indispensable component of secular bioethics is free inquiry. We cannot approach novel moral questions with preset limits on acceptable answers. Dogma is not very helpful in any human endeavor. It has no utility in bioethical inquiry.

We need to recognize that moral concepts reflect the circumstances in which we live and our moral code has been developed to deal with the sort of contingencies that normally arise. We must be at least open to the possibility that moral norms, such as the prohibition on unjustified killing, that are universally accepted because they have proven necessary for the peaceful coexistence and cooperation of the members of a human community may not be applicable, or applicable in the same way, to groups of cells that resemble members of human communities only insofar as they have a similar genetic composition.

In addition, our moral arguments must be grounded in an accurate understanding of the available scientific evidence. We are not suggesting that we can deduce our values from facts. "Is" does not imply "ought." However, even though facts do not dictate our choices, they do circumscribe them. A number of arguments that have been advanced in the debates over stem cell research are unpersuasive in part because they are premised on a misunderstanding of the relevant facts.

As just indicated, ethics must make use of, but it is not equivalent to, science. Nonetheless, although there are key distinctions between ethical and scientific inquiry, some aspects of sound ethical inquiry are analogous to scientific inquiry. In science, hypotheses are continually tested and then modified or rejected as a result of experimental evidence. Similarly, in ethics, our moral judgments should continually be tested for adequacy by considering their practical implications.

Many moral philosophers utilize what is sometimes referred to as the method of reflective equilibrium. This approach is also referred to as the coherence model of justification. Whatever its label, the method seeks to test our initial moral judgments by detailing and examining the consequences of adhering to these judgments. One then tries to systematize the judgments and their consequences in a set of general moral principles that can explain and account for these judgments. These principles are themselves tested against our background theories, both moral and nonmoral. Judgments and principles that cannot be rendered consistent with each other and our background theories will need to be modified or discarded. Moreover, in this method, the testing and process of justification works in the other direction as well, that is, theories and principles are evaluated against our considered moral judgments to determine whether our more general commitments may require adjustments (hence the derivation of the term "reflective equilibrium"). Although not universally accepted, many bioethicists do follow this method (Beauchamp and Childress 2001; DeGrazia 1996) and it has the virtue of forcing us to examine critically many of our moral beliefs by considering their consequences and their consistency with our other beliefs. As we will see, this approach is very helpful in evaluating the claim that the embryo is the equivalent of a human person.

Finally, it is important that we do not lose sight of the fact that morality is a practical enterprise with certain widely shared objectives. Moral norms help us achieve a less painful, more desirable existence, by among other things, helping to provide security to the members of a community, ameliorating harmful conditions, and, in general, facilitating cooperation in achieving shared or complementary goals. We need to understand the rationale of our moral norms if we are to apply them successfully. In deciding whether the embryo is entitled to equal moral consideration with autonomous humans, we need to ask ourselves whether such treatment serves the objectives of morality. Unfortunately, this is a question that few have paused to consider in the debate over embryonic stem cell research.

SCIENTIFIC BACKGROUND FOR STEM CELL RESEARCH

As indicated, a basic understanding of the science of stem cells and embryonic development is necessary before discussing the ethical implications of stem cell research.

Stem cells are unspecialized cells that have the capacity to produce more stem cells and also to produce cells that are differentiated, for example, liver cells or neurons. Stem cells are present in all stages of an organism, including the embryonic, fetal, and adult stages (National Institutes of Health 2006; President's Council on Bioethics 2004; Weissman 2002).

However, embryonic stem cells have properties that are different from fetal or adult stem cells. In the early embryo (to around the five-day stage), each cell is totipotent, that is, under the appropriate conditions each cell could develop into a complete, individual organism. After five days, the embryo becomes a blastocyst, consisting of an outer sphere that can develop into membranes such as the placenta and an inner cell mass that can develop into a fetus. The cells of the inner mass are pluripotent, meaning they develop into any cell type in the body, but they are no longer totipotent. Embryonic stem cells from the inner mass of the blastocyst stage are currently the primary source of stem cells for research. One reason they are used in research is that they are considered to be more promising for work on most research projects than fetal stem cells and adult stem cells (National Institutes of Health 2006; President's Council on Bioethics 2004).

One problem with adult stem cells is that they do not appear to have the same potential to proliferate under research conditions as embryonic stem cells. Embryonic stem cells can proliferate for a year or more in the laboratory without differentiating, but to date scientists have been unsuccessful in obtaining similar results with adult stem cells. Moreover, adult stem cells are, at best, multipotent or multisomatic rather than pluripotent. Finally, and most important, it is still unclear whether true transdifferentiation can occur with adult stem cells, that is, it is unclear whether adult stem cells have the ability to develop into many different types of tissue as opposed to developing into different types of cells of similar tissue (Weissman 2002). For example, bone marrow stem cells can give rise to bone cells and other types of connective tissue, but do not appear capable of differentiating into other sorts of tissue.

Fetal stem cells appear to have pluripotent capacities, but these cells are at a later stage of development, which creates difficulties in using them for research. Moreover, there are ethical objections to using fetal stem cells in research as well, so it is doubtful whether there is any advantage to using them in research instead of embryonic stem cells.

In addition to understanding the differences between embryonic stem cells and other stem cells, it is also important to understand the basics of embryonic development before evaluating the ethics of stem cell research. Prior to gastrulation (when the so-called primitive streak, the precursor to the spinal cord, appears), it is questionable whether the embryo can be considered an individualized entity. That is because until gastrulation, the embryo may develop into one or more individuals. At least arguably, a nonindividuated embryo has yet to acquire a determinate identity (DeGrazia 2006; Steinbock 2006; Green 2002).

Finally, it is important to understand the potential sources of embryos for research and the processes by which embryos can be stimulated into providing stem cells. There are two principal potential sources for embryos, namely embryos produced as a result of in vitro fertilization (or IVF) which, for whatever reason, are regarded as "spare" embryos that will not be implanted in a uterus and embryos produced through somatic cell nuclear transfer (or SCNT) (McHugh 2004; Weissman 2002).

With embryos produced in IVF, the inner cell mass is separated from the outer sphere of cells and then cultured on a plate of "feeder" cells that will maintain the stem cells through a supply of nutrients. At this time, these feeder cells are typically mouse embryonic stem cells. After the cells of the inner cell mass begin to proliferate, they are removed and plated into fresh culture dishes and, eventually, if the process is successful, an embryonic stem cell line will be established.

The SCNT procedure is different in this important aspect: SCNT is accomplished by culturing the nucleus of a somatic cell and then transferring this nucleus into an enucleated ovum. This new cell is then stimulated to divide and, when the procedure works, the cell will develop into a blastocyst with the genotype of the somatic cell donor but with the mitochondrial DNA of the ovum. After development of the blastocyst, the inner cell mass is isolated and cultured in a manner similar to that used for embryos produced via IVF.[2]

Whatever the source of the embryo, under currently proven procedures, the use of the embryo in research will prevent its cells from differentiating and, without differentiation, the embryo will not be able to develop into an adult human. Some refer to the isolation of the embryo's inner cell mass and use of embryonic stem cells in research as "killing" the embryo. Whether that precise terminology is appropriate, the moral objections to embryonic stem cell research are based on the interference with the embryo's possible development that this research entails.

Before turning to address the moral implications of embryonic stem cell research, we note that after this paper was drafted, researchers announced that a procedure had been used in which a stem cell line was developed from the cells of a blastomere, which is an embryo at a very early (eight-cell) stage (Klimanskaya et al. 2006). These researchers suggested that this procedure could obviate the controversy over stem cell research because when one of the cells of a blastomere is removed for preimplantation genetic diagnosis (a procedure commonly used in connection with IVF), the remaining cells of the blastomere have not been prevented from maturing and differentiating into a fetus and then an infant. In other words, the embryo is not "killed." However, it is too early to determine what effect this new procedure will have on the debate over stem cell research. To begin, researchers have not been successful so far in developing a stem cell line from the cells of a blastomere without halting the maturation of the remaining cells. In the research in question, several cells were removed from the blastomere, and this process did prevent the embryo from maturing further. Developing a stem cell line from just one cell of a blastomere is a theoretical possibility but, as of now, not a reality. More importantly, those who believe the embryo has the status of a human person have already stated that they would object to such a procedure because of its potential for harming the embryo, whether or not it actually precludes maturation of the embryo (O'Brien 2006). Therefore, there does not appear to be a way to avoid addressing the moral status of the embryo in evaluating the morality of embryonic stem cell research.

MORAL IMPLICATIONS OF STEM CELL RESEARCH

Benefits of Stem Cell Research

The intense interest in stem cell research reflects the potential for developing important, indeed revolutionary, therapies as a result of this research. If stem cells can be reliably directed to differentiate into specific cell types, there is the possibility of developing replacement tissues for millions of Americans who suffer from debilitating diseases and disabilities, including Parkinson's and

Alzheimer's diseases, diabetes, heart disease, liver disease, and spinal cord injury, to name just a few. Although there is no certainty that such therapies could be developed, the research to date appears promising. For example, dopamine-producing neurons generated from mouse embryonic stem cells have proved functional in animals, thus indicating there is a realistic possibility that similar results could be reproduced in humans, with beneficial consequences to those suffering from Parkinson's (Kim et al. 2002). Even more dramatic results were obtained recently via an experiment conducted by researchers at Johns Hopkins University. These researchers were able to use neurons derived from embryonic stem cells to restore motor function in paralyzed rats (Deshpande et al. 2006).

The moral imperative to pursue research with such potentially beneficial consequences seems clear. Alleviation of suffering and restoration of health are important goals even if only one individual is benefited. If millions of individuals may be benefited, stem cell research assumes critical importance and warrants substantial support from federal funding.

The Position That Embryos Are Entitled to the Same Rights as Human Persons

However, there are some who believe that embryos deserve the full range of rights provided to human persons and that removing from an embryo that possibility of developing the capacities and properties characteristic of human persons is morally equivalent to killing an adult human. Those who hold this view maintain we should not "harm" embryos by utilizing them in stem cell research, just as we do not kill adult humans for research purposes.

An essential premise of this position is that even though the embryo does not currently possess the capacities and properties of human persons, it possesses the potential to develop these capacities and properties, and this potential is sufficient to provide it with the moral status of a human person. On this view, an embryo is merely a human person at an early stage of development. Another essential premise of this position—but one that is not always acknowledged—is that the embryo is already an individual. A necessary condition for possessing moral rights is individual identity. As the President's Council on Bioethics recognizes, "individuality is essential to human personhood and capacity for moral status" (President's Council on Bioethics 2004, 79). We do not grant moral rights to mere groupings of cells, even if they are genetically unique.

The argument that the embryo is entitled to the same rights as human persons has been most clearly articulated and ably defended by Professors Robert George and Alfonso Gomez-Lobo, two members of the President's Council on

Bioethics. In a statement that appears in the council's 2002 report titled *Human Cloning and Human Dignity*, Professors George and Gomez-Lobo assert that:

> A human embryo is a whole living member of the species *Homo sapiens* in the earliest stage of his or her natural development. . . . The embryonic, fetal, infant . . . stages are stages in the development of a determinate and enduring entity—a human being—who comes into existence as a single cell organism and develops, if all goes well, into adulthood many years later.
>
> Human embryos possess the epigenetic primordia for self-directed growth into adulthood, with their determinateness and identity fully intact. The adult human being that is now you or me is the same human being who, at an earlier stage of his or her life, was an adolescent, and before that a child, an infant, a fetus and an embryo. . . .
>
> Since human beings are intrinsically valuable and deserving of full moral respect in virtue of what they are, it follows that they are intrinsically valuable from the point at which they come into being. Even in the embryonic stage of our lives, each of us was a human being and, as such, worthy of concern and protection. Embryonic human beings . . . should be accorded the status of inviolability recognized for human beings in other developmental stages. (President's Council on Bioethics 2002, 294–301)

While this position enjoys some support both among the general public and scholars, and therefore is entitled to serious consideration, it is fundamentally flawed. This position is in tension with the accepted scientific understanding of embryonic development, is based on a controversial metaphysical position, conflicts with many of our moral judgments, and ultimately is unsupported by a credible theory of moral status. The position that embryos are entitled to the same moral status as human persons is untenable. Accordingly, there is no significant moral impediment to embryonic stem cell research.[3]

Objection to the View That the Embryo Is Equivalent to a Human Person: The Early Embryo Is Not an Individual

Until gastrulation, an embryo can divide into two or more parts, each of which, given appropriate conditions, might develop into separate human beings. This is the phenomenon known as "twinning" (although division into three or four separate parts is also possible). The phenomenon of twinning establishes that there is not one determinate individual from the moment of conception; adult humans are *not* numerically identical with a previously existing zygote or embryo. If that were true, then each of a pair of twins would be numerically identical with the same embryo. This is a logically incoherent position. If A and

B are separate individuals, they cannot both be identical with a previously existing entity, C.

Many of those who contend that embryos are entitled to the same rights as human persons are aware of the twinning phenomenon but they discount its significance. First, they maintain that this phenomenon does not affect those embryos that do not separate. Second, even for those embryos that undergo twinning, they maintain that this process does not undermine the claim that there was at least one individual from the moment of conception. In the words of the 2002 majority report of the President's Council on Bioethics: "The fact that where 'John' alone once was there are now both 'John' and 'Jim' does not call into question the presence of 'John' at the outset" (177).

This reasoning is unpersuasive. Addressing first the situation where twinning does occur, if "John" was there from the beginning and "Jim" originated later, this implies that at least some twins (and triplets, etc.) have different points of origin. This anomaly creates insuperable difficulties for a view that insists all human persons come into existence at the moment of conception. Are some twins not human?

More importantly, the assertion that "John" is present from the outset—that is, there is at least one individual present from the moment of conception—is nothing more than a dogmatic claim masquerading as scientific fact. There is no scientific evidence to establish the presence of a "John." What the science of embryonic development shows is that the early embryo consists of a grouping of cells with a genetic composition similar to the genetic composition of adult humans and that, after a period of time, these cells begin to differentiate and to organize themselves into a unified organism. Prior to gastrulation, there is no certainty that these cells will differentiate and organize nor is there any certainty that these cells will become one, two, or more individuals. In the words of the Human Embryo Research Panel, the cells of an early embryo do not form part "of a coherent, organized, individual" (HERP 1994, 9). The phenomenon of twinning confirms that the early embryo is not a unified, organized, determinate individual. To insist otherwise is to maintain—without any supporting evidence—that there must be some occult organizing principles that we have not yet been able to detect. Effectively, the position that there simply must be a determinate individual from the moment of conception is a restatement of ancient ensoulment views in modern dress.[4]

Objection to the View That the Embryo Is Equivalent to a Human Person:
The "Potential" of the Embryo Does Not Make It a Human Person

The fact that the early embryo is not an individual has obvious implications for the argument that the embryo is entitled to protection because it possesses the potential to develop capacities and properties characteristic of human persons. We cannot refer meaningfully to the potential of the embryo if it is not yet an individual.

However, even leaving the phenomenon of twinning aside, the argument from the potential of the embryo is not cogent for several reasons. The possibility that an embryo might develop into a human person does not obviate the fact that it has not yet acquired the capacities and properties of a person. An embryo is no more a human person than an acorn is an oak tree. Not only do embryos lack consciousness and awareness, but they do not have experiences of any kind, even of the most rudimentary sort. As already indicated, they have not even undergone cell differentiation.

Those who oppose embryonic research often try to minimize the gap between potential and actual possession of the characteristics of a human person by suggesting that the embryo's path of development is inevitable. They assert that the embryo has the same genetic composition as the human person it will become and these genes provide it with the intrinsic capability of developing into that human person. But this suggestion overlooks the important role that extrinsic conditions play in embryonic and fetal development. Those who claim full moral status for the embryo seem to regard gestation within a woman's uterus as an inconsequential and incidental detail. Obviously, it is not. The embryo must be provided with the appropriate conditions for development to occur. The embryo does not have the capability of expressing its "potential" on its own.

Recognition of this fact has special relevance in the context of the debate over stem cell research because of the two possible sources of embryonic stem cells, namely spare embryos from IVF procedures and embryos created from SCNT. In neither case are the embryos being removed from conditions that might permit their development. The spare embryos from IVF procedures have not been and will not be implanted in a uterus; instead, they will either be stored for an indefinite period or discarded. Therefore, they have no prospect of developing into a human person. Their potential is no more than a theoretical construct.

The lack of any real potential to develop into a human person is even clearer in the case of embryos that might be created through SCNT. These embryos will be created with the specific intention of being used solely for research. Therefore, unless they are misappropriated by some pro-embryo activist and covertly implanted in a uterus they have absolutely no chance of developing into a human person. It is misleading to speak of the potential of embryos to become human persons when the likelihood of such an event approaches zero.

Furthermore, the creation of embryos through SCNT shows that the argument from potential proves too much. Through SCNT, a somatic cell is allowed to express its potential to be transformed into an embryo that is latent in its genes but has been suppressed. If gene-based potential to develop into a human person is sufficient to provide an entity with full moral status, then each somatic cell in a human person's body has the same moral status as the person herself. This conclusion constitutes a *reductio ad absurdum* of the argument from potential; among other things, it would make even standard organ donation morally unacceptable.

Objection to the View That the Embryo Is Equivalent to a Human Person: The Unacceptable Consequences of This View

The conclusion that all the cells in a person's body possess the same moral rights as the person herself is just one of the unacceptable conclusions that follow from granting embryos the status of human persons. These unacceptable consequences demonstrate that granting full moral status to the embryo is not compatible with widely accepted moral norms and principles.

One important fact about embryonic development that is often overlooked is that between two-thirds and four-fifths of all embryos that are generated through standard sexual reproduction are spontaneously aborted (President's Council on Bioethics 2004). If embryos have the same status as human persons, this is a horrible tragedy and public health crisis that requires immediate and sustained attention. Up to 80 percent of humanity is at risk of dying suddenly. Not only should we abandon stem cell research, but we should reroute the vast majority of our research dollars from projects such as cancer research into programs to help prevent this staggering loss of human life. How can we have been so morally obtuse that we have failed to heed the silent cry of the millions of embryos that "die" each year?

Interestingly, none of the opponents of embryonic stem cell research have called for research programs that might increase the odds of embryo survival. Their failure to address this issue is puzzling if the embryo deserves the same moral respect as human persons. Consider that great strides have been made in reducing infant mortality in the last century. Why do the opponents of embryonic stem cell research not demand that similar efforts be made to improve the survival rate of embryos?

Similarly, IVF would appear to be morally objectionable regardless of whether some embryos produced by this procedure are used in research. Those who utilize IVF intentionally create many embryos that they know will be discarded eventually. How can we accept a process that consigns entities that supposedly have the status of human persons to the rubbish bin? Hypotheticals can sometimes prove useful in testing our moral judgments. Consider what our moral reaction would be if we had a process that generated not embryos but infants at a developmental stage of about six months. Would we regard this process as morally acceptable if the vast majority of infants so generated were thrown away? Presumably not. Indeed, many would find such a process repugnant. But if embryos have the same status as human persons, then a similarly repugnant result is produced by current IVF procedures.

Finally, it is worth noting that the focus of the current controversy over stem cell research is whether it should be federally funded, not whether it should be banned entirely (although there are some who have called for a ban). That we are even debating the wisdom of federal funding demonstrates that most of us do not consider the embryo to have the same status as a human person. We do not debate the pros and cons of federal funding of research that would destroy adult humans.

Consideration of these implications of the position that embryos are entitled to the same rights as human persons demonstrates that this position cannot be reconciled with widely accepted moral norms and principles. Of course, this does not "prove" that this position is morally unsound. It is always open to advocates of this position to argue that our accepted moral norms and principles are in need of radical reform. However, to date no such call for a moral revolution has issued from those who regard embryos as the equivalent of human persons.

Objection to the View That the Embryo Is Equivalent to a Human Person: The Failure to Provide an Adequate Theory of Moral Status

In our last objection, we note that those who insist that the embryo has the same moral status as a human person fail to articulate an adequate theory of moral status. In other words, they fail to identify which capacities or properties, intrinsic or relational, qualify an entity for moral respect. For example, is it rationality, the capacity for moral agency, sentience, social relationships, or some combination of these that constitutes a necessary or sufficient condition for moral status?

The defenders of full moral status for the embryo typically rely solely on the assertion that humanity entitles one to full moral status and that the embryo is fully human in light of its genetic composition (President's Council on Bioethics 2002, 294–301). There are several problems with this claim, however.

To begin, if humanity is a necessary condition for moral status, then this would preclude granting moral status both to nonhuman animals and to extraterrestrials that exhibit capacities such as rationality or moral agency. Without further argument, this would appear to be an arbitrary exclusion. Certainly, such entities appear to have interests (including the desire to be free from pain or distress) similar to human interests that are fostered or protected by our moral norms.

If humanity is a sufficient but not a necessary condition for moral status, then what is it about humanity that entitles one to moral status? No explanation is offered by those opposed to embryonic stem cell research other than the biological criterion of human genetic composition. However, unless a rationale is provided that explains *why* human genetic composition is so critical, then the insistence that genetic humanity is the key to moral status is mere question-begging.

Furthermore, insistence that genetic humanity is the key to moral status has disturbing implications. It is often overlooked that not all embryos, fetuses, or children produced by human parents have the same number of chromosomes. Humans typically have 23 pairs of (or 46) chromosomes. However, some embryos, fetuses, and children have extra chromosomes. Cells that have an irregular number of chromosomes are called aneuploid. Most embryos with aneuploid aberrations are spontaneously aborted, but some can survive. Down syndrome children, for example, have an extra chromosome 21. If genetic composition is what is critical for being a true human and enjoying full moral status, what do we say about Down syndrome children or children with other aberrant chromosomal composition? If they are entitled to full moral status, then genetic composition cannot be the sole determinant of moral status, but if it is not the sole determinant, what other factors are relevant and how would these other factors affect the status of embryos? To date, no proponent of the view that embryos are entitled to full moral status has confronted or answered these questions. But without answers to these questions, the claim that the embryo is equivalent to a human person cannot be adequately supported.

Critics might say that it is incumbent upon those who defend embryonic stem cell research to provide their own theory of moral status. We accept the validity of this point. Although it is not possible to provide anything resembling a thorough and definitive argument for a theory of moral status within the confines of this article, we will provide the following outline of the elements of such a theory: We maintain that the scope of morality, which is a set of practices that ultimately relies on reason instead of force, should presumptively include all beings who are capable of reasoning and, therefore, capable of being influenced by moral norms. (This provides the underlying rationale for the intuition that rationality or moral agency is important for moral status.) Moreover, we should not lose sight of the fact that morality has objectives, one of which is to ensure the survival of the moral community, including oneself and one's loved ones, which, for most of us, includes our children. Our children embody our hopes and aspirations and assuming a moral community has a desire to survive for more than one generation, its children are the key to its survival. So children who are wanted and intentionally gestated are entitled to the protection of our moral norms even when they are too young to be capable of reasoning. However, embryos that are designated for research use are, by definition, not entities that are, or have the potential to become, children and members of the moral community. Nor do they possess consciousness or rationality or any of the other characteristics that might entitle an entity of membership in the moral community.[5] Accordingly, the fact that their genetic composition may be similar to members of the moral community does not, by itself, entitle these entities to the protections of our moral norms.

The claim that an embryo is somehow entitled to the full panoply of human rights is completely novel and is unsupported scientifically, philosophically, historically, or culturally. As indicated by the foregoing arguments, the merits of this claim are highly dubious. This claim simply has not been supported adequately by rational argument or empirical evidence and must be rejected until such time as better arguments might be made.

CONCLUSION

The primary objection to government funding of embryonic stem cell research is that the embryo is inviolable because it has the same moral status as a human person. While this position is maintained by a number of persons, including some respected scholars and scientists, this position cannot withstand critical scrutiny. For the reasons set forth in this essay, the early embryo lacks moral status and there is no moral barrier to its use in research, especially research that can produce immense benefits for millions of ill, injured, and suffering persons. Embryonic stem cell research merits the financial support of the federal government.

NOTES

1. We use the term "human person" to designate an entity who presumptively has full moral status and is entitled to the full complement of moral rights. There are debates within ethics and bioethics whether "human being," "person," or "moral agent" is the appropriate category for the assignment of moral rights. In addition, of course, there are those who maintain that all sentient beings (that is, both humans and non-human animals) are entitled to equal moral consideration. Resolution of these controversies lies outside the scope of this article. In using the category "human person," we simply acknowledge the reality that most humans are recognized as having moral rights and that these rights are often associated with certain capacities, such as consciousness and rationality. Use of this term does not exclude the possibility that embryos might be entitled to the full complement of moral rights as well, whether or not they can be appropriately characterized as human persons. In short, we are using neutral terminology that allows the moral status of embryos to be resolved by argument, not semantics. By contrast, some of those who oppose embryonic stem cell research limit themselves to asserting that the embryo has the genes of a human, that humans are entitled to moral rights, and that, therefore, embryos are entitled to moral rights. This is tantamount to trying to resolve a moral dispute through stipulation.

2. It is important to note that to date SCNT has not been successfully used to generate a human embryo, at least not in any independently confirmed experiment. However, researchers at various universities have recently committed to begin experiments with SCNT to create human embryonic stem cell lines, using private funding (Harvard University 2006).

3. In focusing on the argument that the embryo cannot be used in research because it is equivalent to a human person, we are not ignoring the fact that there are other possible objections to embryonic stem cell research, including whether it can be appropriately regulated or will inevitably lead to even more troubling scientific research, such as cloning for reproductive purposes (the so-called slippery slope argument). However, we believe it is fair to say that the most prominent and widely accepted objection to embryonic stem cell research (certainly it was the one emphasized by President Bush in his veto message) is that it harms embryos.

4. The justification for granting moral status to the embryo based on ensoulment has been itself subject to significant debate over time and among theologians. Prevailing Christian doctrine for the period from the fifth to the seventeenth centuries was that of "delayed ensoulment," because a soul was presumed to need a separate human body. Abortion was thus tolerated, consistent with Old Testament principles that punished abortion with a fine.

5. Some, especially those who argue in favor of moral rights for nonhuman animals, maintain that sentience is sufficient to entitle an entity to moral status. We do not need to take a position on this particular issue as it is undisputed that the embryo is not sentient.

REFERENCES

Beauchamp, Tom L., and James F. Childress. *Principles of Biomedical Ethics*. 5th ed. New York: Oxford University Press, 2001.

DeGrazia, David. "Moral Status, Human Identity, and Early Embryos: A Critique of the President's Approach." *Journal of Law, Medicine & Ethics* 34 (2006): 49–57.

———. *Taking Animals Seriously: Mental Life and Moral Status*. New York: Cambridge University Press, 1996.

Deshpande, Deepa, et al. "Recovery from Paralysis in Adult Rats Using Embryonic Stem Cells." *Annals of Neurology* 60 (2006): 22–34.

Green, Ronald M. *The Human Embryo Research Debates*. New York: Oxford University Press, 2002.

Harvard University. *Approval Granted for Harvard Stem Cell Institute Researchers to Attempt Creation of Disease-Specific Embryonic Stem Cell Lines*. 2006. Available at http:www.news.harvard.edu/gazette/daily/2006/06/06-stemcell.html (accessed July 21, 2006).

Human Embryo Research Panel, National Institutes of Health. *Report of the Human Embryo Research Panel*. Vol. 1. Bethesda, MD: NIH, 1994.

Kim, J-H., et al. "Dopamine Neurons Derived from Embryonic Stem Cell Function in an Animal Model of Parkinson's Disease." *Nature* 418 (2002): 50–56.

Klimanskaya, Irina, et al. "Human Embryonic Stem Cell Lines Developed from Single Blastomeres." *Nature* (2006). Available at http://www.nature.com (accessed August 27, 2006).

McHugh, Paul R. "Zygote and 'Clonote': The Ethical Use of Embryonic Stem Cells." *New England Journal of Medicine* 351 (2004): 209–11.

National Institutes of Health. *Stem Cell Basics*. 2006. Available at http://stemcells.nih.gov/info/basics (accessed July 13, 2006).

O'Brien, Nancy F. "Pro-Life Official Dismisses New Stem-Cell Announcement as a Sham." *Catholic News Service*. 2006. Available at http://www.catholicnews.com/data/stories/cns/0604840.htm (accessed August 27, 2006).

President's Council on Bioethics. *Monitoring Stem Cell Research*. 2004. Available at http://www.bioethics.gov/reports (accessed July 17, 2006).

———. *Human Cloning and Human Dignity*. New York: Public Affairs, 2002.

President's Remarks on Stem Cell Research Policy. 2006. Available at http://www.whitehouse.gov/news/releases/2006/07/print/20060719-3.html (accessed July 23, 2006).

Steinbock, Bonnie. "The Morality of Killing Human Embryos." *Journal of Law, Medicine & Ethics* 34 (2006): 26–34.

Weissman, Irving L. "Stem Cells—Scientific, Medical and Political Issues." *New England Journal of Medicine* 346 (2002): 1576–79.

4

ATTACK OF THE ANTI-CLONERS
Biogenetic Engineering and Self-Improvement

ARTHUR CAPLAN

FREE INQUIRY: What would you say are the three biggest issues that bioethicists will be grappling with in the first half of the twenty-first century?

ARTHUR CAPLAN: I think the biggest issues will be, first, genetic engineering: How far can we go in designing plants, animals, and our own descendants? Second, what will we discover to be the limits of altering our brains and bodies, as we learn to use artificial organs, nanotechnology, and brain implants to repair disease, live longer, and improve our own abilities and capacities? And third, artificial birth: does it make sense to allow people to have children biologically if they can have healthier and safer children by creating them completely outside a human body?

FI: What is the ethical position of Leon Kass, chair of President Bush's Council on Bioethics, and how does it differ from your own? You have written that this council will "rely on religious rather than secular principles" and will reflect the president's own conservative Christian approach. What leads you to think this will be the case?

CAPLAN: This is precisely what did happen. The majority of the council argues that human life cannot be treated as a commodity, that it is wrong to

Originally published as "Arthur Caplan on the Future of Bioethics," *Free Inquiry* 23, no. 1 (Winter 2002/2003): 28–29.

"manufacture life," and that human life including cloned embryos has the same dignity and moral worth as a person from the moment of its creation. They know they cannot argue explicitly for these positions on religious grounds, so they have tried to present them as secular arguments. The problem is that the secular case for these positions is neither consistent nor coherent.

Leon Kass has tried to develop an "ethics of revulsion" to guide our policies on cloning and stem cell research. But this is simply moral intuitionism with a different face. As is well known in the history of ethics, moral intuitionism is as much a reflection of culture and historical time period as it is a secure base of moral insight. The ethics of revulsion simply cannot be used to obtain consensus, since our intuitions about cloning and the biological revolution are not clear. In addition, intuition has proven to be a miserably inaccurate guide to moral insight in the past—think of Nazi eugenics, Soviet gulags, the Taliban, and any number of ethnic and racial wars, all of which have been based on feelings of revulsion that one group has for another or against the views of nonbelievers.

FI: What is the difference between "therapeutic" and "reproductive" cloning? Do you think there is a significant ethical distinction between the two?

CAPLAN: Therapeutic cloning is the process wherein embryos are cloned and then destroyed to obtain stem cells for research. Reproductive cloning is the creation of cloned embryos to make babies. The latter is not at all safe at present given the results of animal cloning and absolutely should not be permitted unless and until animal studies show safer results. Therapeutic cloning is a useful avenue of research to pursue, and unless one holds that an embryo clone in a dish is of such value that it cannot be destroyed in the pursuit of research to cure diseases, then I see no reason why it would be unethical not to undertake therapeutic cloning.

FI: Is it true that therapeutic cloning research could produce cures or treatments for such diseases as Alzheimer's, Parkinson's, and diabetes? If so, what might be a realistic time frame for such results?

CAPLAN: No one has a clue. The research is in its earliest stages and it is impossible to tell at present where it might lead.

FI: What are the ethical arguments against therapeutic cloning, and do these essentially boil down to religious arguments about the sacredness of nature?

CAPLAN: They essentially boil down to seeing the embryo, cloned or not, as a full-fledged moral agent and person from the moment of its creation. This makes no sense scientifically since we know that many embryos cannot develop at all, that no embryo can develop unless it is placed inside a human womb, that an embryo in a dish is at most a potential life, and that no cloned embryo has shown the potential to become a human being. The religious view that hold that all embryos are persons, or even potential persons, does not square with the facts.

FI: Can therapeutic cloning actually be prohibited?

CAPLAN: Sure. Easily. It can be outlawed and no funds made available to do the work. However some countries such as China, India, and the United Kingdom have indicated they will do this type of research, so a worldwide ban is not likely.

FI: What are your views regarding so-called designer babies? Will the twenty-first century mark the return of a type of eugenics, and if so, is this something to be worried about? What might an ethically sound eugenics policy involve?

CAPLAN: We already engage in designer-baby technology now. That is what amniocentesis, preimplantation genetic testing of embryos, and chorionic villus sampling are all about—avoiding unwanted genes either by not implanting certain embryos or aborting fetuses.

My view is that it is a good thing to try to improve the abilities and capacities of your children. This is why we create schools and summer camps and tennis programs. Every major religion sees it as a parental duty to try and improve the lot of one's offspring. So I am not worried about attempts to use genetics to make healthier children. I would oppose forced genetic choices—penalties on people who decided not to use genetic medicine—or any genetic choice that would make a child worse off then he or she otherwise would have been. So I oppose narrowing a child's options and abilities through genetic selection or engineering.

FI: Is genetic enhancement another issue to be feared, or can it be handled in an ethically responsible way?

CAPLAN: I think it can be handled in a responsible way. But having done extensive research on Nazi racial eugenics, I am not sure we have created public policy that can ensure against future abuse.

FI: What, if any, restrictions should there be on life-extension research? Should humans be content with a "four-score and ten" time frame or will the human lifespan continue to expand? And given the fact that most of the world still doesn't have adequate health care, will the emphasis on life extension in highly developed countries just widen the already existing gap between nations?

CAPLAN: I think there is no reason not to try and extend our lifespan. We have been doing this with agriculture, public health, better housing, and medicine since the days of the Babylonians. We live much longer today than did the ancient Greeks, and I do not hear anyone suggesting that this is an unfortunate or immoral situation! I think that we need to ensure fair access to the benefits of all biomedical research, but that is a different issue from whether it is moral to seek to delay the debilities of aging or to try and live longer.

FI: Finally, are the ethical implications of the Human Genome Project— for example, the possibility that people will have their health insurance coverage based upon their genetic predispositions to certain diseases—being adequately addressed by our society? If not, what might be done to make society in general more "ethically literate" on this subject?

CAPLAN: No, they are not being adequately addressed. The threat of the misuse of genetic information is still very real. We do not have stringent enough requirements for the accuracy of genetic tests, availability of counseling, access to testing for the poor and uninsured, protection of confidentiality and privacy, or limits on how the public and private sectors can use genetic information.

We have undertaken a project on high school bioethics to try and increase literacy among young people on these subjects. But it is almost impossible to get foundations and other funders to put money into this crucial area. Many people fret that our society is not educated about the biotech revolution, but we spend far more time teaching kids how to make change than teaching them about their genes. And in some parts of our country, topics such as genetics and evolution are not even presented in textbooks or in science classes!

FURTHER READINGS BY ARTHUR CAPLAN

"Attack of the Anti-Cloners." *Free Inquiry* 23, no. 1 (Winter 2002/2003): 30.
"Mapping Morality: The Rights and Wrongs of Genomics." In *The Genomics Revolution*, edited by M. Yudell and R. DeSalle, 189–94. Joseph Henry Press, 2002.
"NAS Cloning Hearing." *Science* 294 (2001): 1651.
"Cloning Human Embryos." *Western Journal of Medicine* 176 (2002): 78–79.
"Protecting Subjects' Interests in Genetics Research." *American Journal of Human Genetics* 70 (2002): 965–71 (with J. F. Merz, D. Magnus, and M. K. Cho).
"What Is Morally Wrong with Eugenics?" In *Controlling Our Destinies*, edited by P. R. Sloan, 209–23. Notre Dame University Press, 2000.
Also see "Breaking Bioethics" on the health page of MSNBC.com, featuring several columns by Caplan on cloning and related topics.

5

FREEDOM OF SCIENTIFIC RESEARCH

PAUL KURTZ

History records the continuing efforts to censor free inquiry and scientific research. We are all too familiar with the attempts by theologians to prohibit free thought. Obstacles were placed in the way of each new development in science—usually in the name of God and in opposition to "blasphemy" and "heresy." Galileo was condemned for contesting the orthodox theistic view of the universe; Darwin, for his dangerous theory of evolution; and Freud, for his novel interpretations of human nature. In the long struggle between religion and science, higher religious "truths" were called on to restrict the range of scientific investigation.

Similar calls for censorship have been made in the name of politics, economics, and ideology. Vested interests have often opposed new ideas that are considered seditious to the established order. Since the time of Socrates, we have been familiar with the repression of inquiry for political ends. In our time, Nazi racist theories prohibited non-Aryan physics and social science, Stalinism banned those scientific theories that ignored dialectical materialism, and Lysenkoism exorcised genetic theories that contradicted its environmentalist dogma.

Excerpted from "The Ethics of Free Inquiry," *The Ethics of Teaching and Scientific Research*, by Sidney Hook, Paul Kurtz, and Miro Todorovich (Amherst, NY: Prometheus Books, 1977). Reprinted by permission.

Today there are similar efforts to limit scientific research, but now they are made primarily on ethical grounds.

In the conflict between free inquiry and censorship, science presupposes conditions of freedom that may themselves be justified on ethical grounds. The arguments are basically utilitarian in character: we ought to be committed to free inquiry because of long-range consequences for the common good. No one can predict what scientists may discover, or the therapeutic uses that these findings may have for humankind. Once the door to inquiry is closed, we are never certain what criteria will prevail or when the door will be slammed shut again. A society that does not allow freedom of its intellectuals, writers, artists, and scientists will eventually stagnate and die. Creativity is the source of vitality and life. Thus, both science and an open society presuppose the right to knowledge and the free use thereof.

Recently, however, these assumptions have come under heavy attack. Indeed, there has been a frontal assault on the scientific enterprise itself. Many people have become profoundly disillusioned with the promise of science. Science is held responsible for many serious problems in the contemporary world. Atomic physics gave us nuclear power and thermonuclear weapons. Biology and chemistry provided the means to wage biochemical warfare. Although scientific research has had immense positive results, it has also resulted in pollution, ecological destruction, and resource depletion. Thus the first indictment raised against science concerns haphazard technological growth. The fear of technology—fed by the popular media—often considers the scientist to be an amoral Frankenstein, fanatically dedicated to research that may be dangerous to society's basic welfare. The only way to guard society from these destructive tendencies, it is said, it to tame the scientist and police his research and the consequences of it.

The disenchantment with science has assumed other forms. The "counterculture" had rejected the logico-empirical method, and sought to expand the range of consciousness by means of psychedelic drugs. The counterculture had questioned the rationale for pure research and academic freedom, and sought to politicize the academy and judge it by aesthetic or moral criteria. Attendant to the counterculture, a whole series of cults of unreason proliferated—from the importation of Asian sects to the revival of astrology, the occult, exorcism, belief in reincarnation, magic, and spiritualism. In the quest for meaning, rigorous standards of evidence are considered too limiting to the imagination; even where scientific authority is sought, science fiction and speculative audacity reign. There is widespread belief in unidentified flying objects, extraterrestrial visitations, and doomsday prophecies. The realm of the paranormal, from telekinesis to faith healing and psychic surgery, has expanded.

In this broader context of the growth of irrationalism and obscurantism, the attack on scientific research must be appraised. It is one thing to raise serious doubt about the abuses of scientific technology in contemporary society—this is a meaningful and important concern. It is another thing to extend this indictment to the possibility of free scientific research.

Regarding technology, the results of scientific research obviously are used by industry and fulfill ancillary economic, political, and military purposes. In a democratic society, it is not the scientist alone who should judge the efficacy of a technological application. The entire society should decide, through debate, the costs and hazards of the applications of scientific knowledge. Hence, a society may decide to curtail certain products if they are considered noxious to the public health. It is industry that is being restricted here, not science. If cyclamates or artificial coloring are found to be carcinogenic or if fluorocarbon sprays do destroy the stratospheric ozone layer, their production can be prohibited. Insofar as technological applications have social consequences, society itself should evaluate and determine the uses of these applications by open discussion and the legislative process.

That is not at issue. What is at issue is the ensuing indictment not of technology *but of scientific research itself.* This has taken many forms in recent years. We are told that there are certain things that should not be researched because of possible misuses, or should be made illegal (such as fetal research, cloning, therapeutic stem cell research, or genetic engineering).

Again, this indictment of science is made basically on ethical grounds. In some circles this has reached a kind of moral hysteria. It involves a sweeping denunciation of the "high priests" of medicine and psychiatry, a suspicion of psychologists, geneticists, biologists, and other scientists. This ethical critique is not much different from earlier calls for censorship, and religious and political criteria are usually accompanied by a moral bias. Science was "wicked" because it contradicted religious pieties or because it opposed the prevailing political shibboleths. Whatever the grounds, all such calls for censorship involve the intrusion of extrinsic criteria on scientific research.

We cannot object to ethical evaluation by society of the effects of technology—for the goal here is no longer truth *per se* but practice. What is at stake is whether ethical objections should be taken as decisive in the area of pure research. Matters are complicated, for there is no absolute dualism between theory and practice; and all theoretical constructs have a practical impact, since thoughts are related to human conduct, interests, and purposes. Although there is no sharp distinction in kind, there is one of degree—for some theories do not seek directly to change the world.

In the area of knowledge and truth, I submit, *scientists ought, on utilitarian grounds, to be allowed to inquire as they see fit and to publish their results without the imposition of external standards of judgment as to the ethical worth of their investigations.*

Some scientific theories, however, can be tested only by experiment. Here is the rub. For in the act of inquiry, there may be a direct modification of the subject matter; this may be negative and harmful. I can best illustrate this by reference to the field of genetic research. Recent discoveries in recombinant E. coli DNA research in molecular biology are significant, but there is apprehension that a new and virulent strain of virus may be formed that will be resistant to medical treatment. If unleashed, even accidentally, such artificially created strains can be greatly hazardous to human life. Should such research be allowed to continue? The pure quest for truth is one thing; but if in testing one's hypothesis a highly noxious fallout can occur, should we permit it? The fears expressed by people in the greater Cambridge-Boston area about the possible dangers inherent in such research proposed at Harvard may have been justifiable. Some people think that such research need not be dangerous and that objections are based on a fear of the unknown. In any case, the issue was at least arguable. The opposition to embryonic stem cell research with blastocysts is based on a moral–theological premise that life begins at conception or with the first division of a cell in a petri dish. This effort has no place in the scientific laboratory.

Clearly a commitment to free scientific inquiry cannot be taken as an absolute. No right is absolute, not even the right to free inquiry. There may be some situations in which one would want to limit the actual experiments performed to test theories, because they may be too dangerous.

If that is the case, one should not therefore move to the other extreme and question each and every claim to free inquiry or judge it on extrinsic ethical grounds—as many people increasingly seem ready to do today. Scientists should not be kept continually on the defensive to justify their inquiries.

I would suggest that the right to free inquiry should be taken as a *prima facie* general principle, which we ought to respect save in exceptional cases. If we are to make an exception to the principle, this would depend on the possibilities of extraordinary dangers to life and limb. The general principle is justified on ethical grounds because of the proven value of knowledge to humanity.

Since some forms of moral opposition can become as tyrannical or fanatical as religious or ideological objections in destroying free inquiry, I would suggest that *the burden of proof always be placed on those who would limit inquiry.* It is the exception to the principle that needs justification, not the principle itself.

The best safeguard against the undermining of scientific research is an informed, intelligent public. The larger task facing scientists is to help educate the public about the nature of the scientific method and the roles of science and research in human progress. We have recently failed to accomplish this task, and the rising tide of subjectivism is due in part to a failure of people to appreciate the character of scientific intelligence in understanding nature. The assault on scientific research likewise is symptomatic of a failure by the broader public to appreciate how society has benefited from the untrammeled search for knowledge.

The freedom of scientific inquiry ultimately depends upon a public enlightenment that must be nurtured not only in the schools but also through every medium of communication in society. The task is heavy and unremitting and sometimes like the labors of Sisyphus. But it must be shouldered by all who have faith in human freedom furthered by the arts of intelligence.

6

STEM CELL RESEARCH
The Failure of Bioethics

DON MARQUIS

In recent years the issue of human embryonic stem cell (hereafter HESC) research has engendered fierce debate. Some object to HESC research because they say it involves taking a human life. Others argue that its prospective benefits are so huge that not to pursue it would be immoral. It is unreasonable to think that such a controversy will be resolved by journalists or politicians or, for that matter, by patients who hope for a cure from some dreadful disease.

However, it does seem reasonable that practitioners of academic bioethics should be able to help us clarify this issue. Presumably academics have the proper interests and education to think clearly about bioethics controversies. Academic essays provide an opportunity for careful examination of relevant arguments. Since leading bioethics and medical journals have devoted whole recent issues or parts of recent issues to this controversy,[1] examining this literature should shed considerable light on the HESC controversy.

Such an expectation, in this reader's experience, will be disappointed. It is amazing how much of the HESC bioethics literature confines itself to describing the science underlying the dispute, or to giving historical accounts of the committees that have reported on this issue, or to surveying the dispute in general terms rather than closely analyzing the arguments that bear on the

From *Free Inquiry* 23, no. 1 (Winter 2002/2003): 40–44.

central ethical issues.[2] The arguments that are offered are typically presented in a cursory way. Indeed, often they are more suggested than presented. Arguments that deserve critical scrutiny are quickly set out as if any rational reader would regard them as obviously sound.

No doubt there are many explanations for this. One, however, may have particular relevance to the HESC issue. Obtaining HESCs requires the destruction (or *disaggregation*, to use the sanitized term) of human embryos.[3] Whether such embryo destruction is morally permissible is (or should be) at the heart of the debate over the morality of HESC research. This has led many to expect that to a great extent, the stem cell controversy will mirror the abortion controversy. If one believes there are good arguments for the moral permissibility of fetal destruction, then many of the same arguments can apply to embryo destruction. If one believes that destroying a fetus destroys a human life with full moral status, then presumably the same arguments can apply to embryos. When these considerations are combined with the fact that most partisans on both sides of the abortion dispute seem to consider their positions so obviously true that only cursory argument in defense of them is needed, we may have a plausible explanation for the superficial nature of the HESC discussion.

The purpose of this essay is to provide evidence for the claims made in the above two paragraphs. Consider first the major arguments for the view that HESC research should be banned, or at any rate not funded. Richard Doerflinger has defended this view on the grounds that it is incompatible with a Catholic viewpoint.[4] Gilbert Meilaender has defended the view on more general religious grounds.[5] There are obvious problems with such defenses. Religious views are essentially matters of faith, and it is widely thought that there are no objective grounds for preferring one variety of religious faith to others. The fact that there are so many varieties of Christianity and of Islam and, I suppose, of many other religions of which I know little, is evidence for this. Accordingly, in the absence of a great deal of convincing argument that has not yet seen the light of day, particular religious considerations cannot establish the wrongness of HESC research. Such religious views count as no more than comforting opinions, like preferences in furniture or food, and we are left with no reason whatsoever to accept them as binding on the rest of us, or for that matter, even binding on their proponents.

No doubt, the weakness of the religious arguments has suggested to some proponents of HESC research that defending their position requires only a wave at some nonreligious arguments. This may count, therefore, as another reason arguments concerning HESC research seem less than compelling.

The letter that invited this article stated that many readers of this publication hold a view that, if it were true, might furnish a good argument in favor of HESC research. According to the editor, many *Free Inquiry* readers "support untrammeled freedom in scientific research." Yet to accept this slogan entails endorsement of the Tuskegee studies of the natural course of syphilis, or the notorious Willowbrook experiments in which retarded children were deliberately given hepatitis in order to study how that disease progressed, or the Nazi hypothermia experiments on Jews. However, there is a consensus among decent persons of all political and religious persuasions that these studies were profoundly immoral. Thus such an "untrammeled freedom" argument is plainly unsound.

Another argument for HESC research is based on the hope that it might provide cures, or at least reasonably successful treatments, for Alzheimer's disease, spinal cord injuries, muscular dystrophy, diabetes, and other diseases. This prospective benefits argument, although often offered in popular or political discussion, is as hopeless as the untrammeled freedom argument. The Tuskegee, Willowbrook, and Nazi studies were wrong, not because they were bad or useless science, but because the human subjects in them were treated inhumanely. Basic interests of those subjects were sacrificed without their consent for the ends of the research. There is now a strong consensus, both in society and in academic bioethics, that this is wrong even when the research clearly will promote the common good. In short, conformity with a respect for human subjects (RHS) principle is a necessary condition of morally permissible research, whatever its benefits.[6]

Just how should this RHS principle be formulated and qualified? Here is an issue that can provide a clear framework for analysis of the HESC dispute. Critics of HESC research claim in essence that it violates the principle of respect for human subjects. One can make at least a presumptive defense of the truth of this claim in the absence of any appeal to religion. Destroyed human embryos clearly belonged to our species. Therefore, they were human in one clear sense. Furthermore, the embryos in such research are clearly subjects, that is, the subjects of research. Thus, as the more thoughtful proponents of HESC research at least tacitly realize, arguments in favor of such research must appeal, not to an *unrestricted* or *unqualified*, RHS principle, but to a *restricted* or *qualified*, version. The case for HESC research requires the defense of a restricted version of the RHS principle that, on the one hand, does not include embryos and, on the other hand, includes those human subjects whose need for protection is uncontroversial.

How might such a case be made? Some authors have suggested that embryo destruction is permissible because embryos are not moral agents.[7] This in turn suggests a respect principle restricted to human subjects who are also moral agents. Plainly this will not do, since it is agreed by all decent people that scientific research that involves the destruction of two-year-olds is immoral, even though two-year-olds are not moral agents. It is worth noting, in this connection, that those retarded children who were deliberately infected with hepatitis in the Willowbrook experiments were not moral agents either.

Other authors have suggested that HESC research is morally permissible because embryos are not persons.[8] This is tantamount to claiming that the respect principle should be restricted to persons. A relevant meaning of *person* uses the term to refer to a cluster of psychological characteristics that human beings typically possess and animals do not.[9] But this restriction on the RHS principle is rejected by almost everyone. Infants clearly are not persons in this sense, and yet we believe that research that causes the destruction of infants is immoral.

One proponent of HESC research has offered a response to this objection. Carson Strong has defended the view that, although infants are not persons in virtue of any intrinsic property, good reasons exist for *conferring* the right to life on them because of the consequences for persons of doing so. Treating infants with love and concern will have good consequences for the persons they grow up to be. It will also have good consequences for other persons who may be affected adversely by those human beings who were treated badly when they were infants. Furthermore, treating some infants as expendable might lead us to lack concern for infants we intend to keep.[10] According to Strong these considerations, combined with the fact that infants "are *viable*, *sentient*, have the *potential to become self-conscious*, have been *born*, and are *similar in appearance* to the paradigm of human persons" are "significant enough to warrant conferring upon infants serious moral standing including a right to life."[11]

Strong claims that, on a moral theory in which only persons have full moral status in and of themselves, our conferral of full moral status on infants is mandated. This is hard to believe. All of the reasons Strong cites for treating infants with love and concern apply as well to fetuses. Yet many believe that killing a fetus a woman does not intend to keep is perfectly compatible with love and concern for a fetus she does intend to keep. Strong might protest that this objection does not take account of the fact that infants are viable, sentient, have been born, and are like paradigm humans in appearance, whereas fetuses are not. The trouble with Strong's view is that he argues that none of the more plausible of these factors is sufficient to underwrite full moral status. Given that, why should we assume that collectively they are of much help? Strong offers no argument here, only assertion.[12] Thus, we are left with good reason for thinking that restricting the RHS principle to persons is far too narrow.

Some have suggested that the destruction of embryos is justified because embryos are not capable of sentience, that is, they lack the capacity for thoughts, feelings, or experiences.[13] For this argument to go through, the respect principle must be restricted to individuals with a capacity for consciousness. Embryos lack present capacity for consciousness. So do temporarily unconscious adults. We all agree that research on temporarily unconscious adults that causes their deaths is immoral. Hence, the present capacity for consciousness restriction on the RHS principle is untenable.

This problem with temporarily unconscious adults can be fixed by adopting an RHS principle that excludes only those in whom the absence of consciousness is *irreversible*. Because it is reasonable to think that a subject whose absence of consciousness is irreversible cannot be harmed in any morally significant way by his or her destruction, there is a good deal to be said for this change. However, an embryo's lack of consciousness is not irreversible. In the proper environment embryos may develop mental capacities like our own. On this interpretation, a respect principle restricted to those with the capacity for consciousness (or a first cousin) might be defensible, but it does not exclude embryos.

One might attempt to deal with both of these problems by claiming that the RHS principle should be restricted to those who have in the *past* exhibited the capacity for consciousness. Critics of HESC research should respond that, instead, the RHS principle should be restricted to those who could in the future exhibit the capacity for consciousness. How should we resolve this disagreement? Society endorses medicine's concern with *prognosis*. In view of this, critics of HESC research seem to have the more defensible view.

An argument often given in defense of HESC research is that an embryo "is not clearly even an *individual*,"[14] that at the embryo stage, "it is doubtful one can speak of individuality."[15] Carol Tauer has reported that a consensus of the National Institutes of Health Human Embryo Research Panel favoring HESC research found that the embryo is not "a distinct individual," that it lacks "developmental individuation" and thus lacks full moral status.[16] Ronald Green has made essentially the same argument.[17] Restricting the RHS principle to individuals certainly seems reasonable. But why should we suppose that embryos are not individuals?

Here is a reason for supposing that they are. One can count them. One can unambiguously refer to one embryo, and then to a second, and then to a third. So it seems that embryos are indeed individuals and that restricting the RHS principle to individuals does not succeed in excluding embryos from its scope. Supporters of HESC research will protest that embryos are not individuals because of the possibility of twinning. [See Berit Brogaard's "Stem Cell Research and the Moral Status of the Human Embryo" in *Free Inquiry* 23, no. 1 (Winter 2002/2003) for an extended defense of the twinning argument.— *Eds*] But why should one suppose that this is a reason that embryos are not individuals? One amoeba can split into two. This should not tempt us to claim that it was not the case that there was one individual amoeba before the splitting. Indeed, how could one understand what *splitting into two* is unless the amoeba were an individual before the split? But unless one understands what splitting into two is, one cannot understand at all what it is for an embryo to twin. Therefore, the individuality restriction, although defensible, seems not to be helpful to the proponent of embryonic stem cell research.

Supporters of HESC research have also made the argument that:

> If an embryo is maintained outside a woman's body and those who provided the gametes for it have not decided to permit its development in a womb, it is not effectively a state in the early development of a person. Put differently, an extracorporeal embryo—whether used in research, discarded, or kept frozen—is simply not a precursor to any ongoing personal narrative.[18]

For this claim to do the work its proponents want it to do, the RHS principle must exclude cases where *we* fail to provide a human subject with an environment in which it can develop into a person. Thus such a restriction allows research on infants in a neonatal intensive care unit that results in their destruction or, for that matter, on any abandoned infant whatsoever. Accordingly, such a restricted version of the principle is too narrow.

Jeffrey Spike has argued that HESC research is morally permissible because it is not the case that embryos can develop independently.[19] This will hardly do, for the restriction on the RHS principle that is needed to make Spike's argument go through would allow unethical research on the disabled.

Spike has also defended HESC research on the grounds that "biologically if every one of those embryos was put into a woman, perhaps 10 or 20 percent would survive to birth." This won't do either. Research on patients with cancer in which the survival rate is only 10 to 20 percent is not exempt from the RHS principle.

This concludes my survey of the arguments that human embryo destruction is morally permissible, or, alternatively, that the principle of respect for human research subjects should be restricted so that embryos are excluded. What has been surveyed is not a pretty picture. In spite of the vast amounts of ink that academic bioethicists have spilled over the HESC issue, and in spite of the apparent sentiment among so many of them that HESC research should proceed, the crucial arguments offered to support this view are both sketchy and subject to all sorts of fairly obvious difficulties. Perhaps there are no arguments that can justify proceeding with HESC research. But that would oblige academic bioethicists to acknowledge the fact, not to pretend that this unpleasant little difficulty does not exist.

It is possible to imagine objections to the preceding analysis. For example, one might say that embryos cannot possibly be included in the RHS principle because that principle concerns the basic interests of human subjects—and embryos, lacking the capacity for consciousness, cannot have interests at all.[20] The argument for the latter claim is that whatever lacks the capacity for consciousness cannot take an interest in anything and what cannot take an interest in anything cannot have interests.[21] This objection is subject to a number of difficulties. The notion of what is in one's interest should not be too tightly associated with what one takes an interest in. Not everything that people take an interest in is in their (best) interest and not everything that is in people's best interest is what they take an interest in. Smokers and drug addicts are obvious examples. Furthermore, this objection cannot account for acting in the best interest of a temporarily unconscious adult or an infant.

Someone also might object to the preceding analysis on the grounds that respect for an individual is compatible with destroying her.[22] It would follow that my interpretation of respect for human subjects principle is too strong. However, whether or not such a notion of respect is possible is beside the point. The respect for human subjects principle used in standard medical research ethics does not permit harming human subjects without their consent if that harm can be anticipated.

One might also object to my analysis on the grounds that it holds proponents of HESC research to standards that are overly strict. Meyer and Nelson say:

> Our goal, however, is not to provide a knock-down argument about the moral status of the embryo, but to show how one systematic, reasonable view on moral status in general can be used to defend the moral propriety of destroying embryos that truly deserve respect.[23]

Meyer and Nelson refer to Mary Anne Warren's "developmental view" of human moral status.[24] Other defenders of stem cell research also have appealed to her view.[25] Warren is best known for her view that abortion is morally permissible because fetuses lack full moral status.[26] Warren's developmental view is indeed widely regarded as reasonable—precisely to those who consider abortion morally permissible on the grounds that fetuses lack full moral status because they are only developing human beings and not yet persons. If one holds this, then, of course, one will hold that a human being at the very earliest stages of development lacks moral standing. The triviality of this move boggles the mind. It has all the force of John Paul II's defense of his views of the morality of abortion and euthanasia in terms of—well—his own moral theology.[27] What is required for the success of the Meyer-Nelson point is a criterion for the reasonableness of a view that can be accepted by any rational person.

An adequate analysis of Warren's developmental view is far beyond the scope of this essay. In my view, a theory such as hers that bases full moral standing on moral agency cannot account even for the moral standing of adolescents, much less younger human beings, without some backing and filling and other moves that are utterly arbitrary. If proponents of HESC research are willing to tolerate arbitrariness, then they should not object to what they perceive as the arbitrariness of religious perspectives.

Another objection to the preceding analysis might be that the RHS principle includes embryos only if the embryo's status as a potential human being gives it the same moral status as an actual human being.[28] It is clearly not wrong to destroy isolated human cells. The only difference between a zygote and some arbitrary skin cell is that the zygote is a potential human being. And why should we suppose that being a merely potential human being is sufficient to underwrite full moral status?

The critic of HESC research can reply by holding that embryos are *actual* human beings. They are *very, very young* human beings. Not all human beings look like middle-aged professors. It seems doubtful that the ordinary notion of actual human being is sufficiently precise to underwrite either this objection or the response to it.

Another objection to my analysis might concern its strategy. I considered candidate restrictions on an RHS principle individually, and argued that each is indefensible or does not exclude embryos. One might argue that each of those qualities (except for individuality) should be considered to be "candidate sufficient conditions" for full moral standing. One might go on to argue that since embryos meet none of the candidate sufficient conditions for full moral standing, then there is no reason to think that they have moral standing. And if there is no reason to think that they have moral standing, then HESC research is morally permissible.

The trouble with this objection is that in order for it to be successful, one would have to show that all of the candidate sufficient conditions for full moral standing had been considered. In the first place, this has not been done. In the second place, it is easy to think of candidates for full moral standing that proponents of HESC research have not considered.

Another objection to the preceding analysis is that I have presupposed that morality must be objective in a way that it cannot possibly be, and that therefore I have held the defenders of HESC research to impossibly high standards. Such a critic might argue that morality is a social construct, that it is not based on some natural property or other of individuals.[29] This objection opens a very large can of worms. One problem with a somewhat subjectivist conception of morality is showing that it does not permit too much; that in the course of showing that research on human embryos is morally permissible, it does not also show that practices that seem clearly immoral are also morally permissible. That is a difficult, and to my knowledge, not successfully attempted task.

*   *   *

Thus far, this essay has endorsed no positive thesis. It has been concerned almost exclusively with criticizing the arguments of others. Can something positive and nonreligious be said in favor of banning human embryonic stem research? Here's a suggestion for an argument: Failing to respect the basic interests of ordinary human beings for the purpose of scientific research is wrong. Age discrimination is morally wrong. When we were very, very young, we were mere embryos. Therefore, destruction of human embryos for the purposes of scientific research is wrong.

Carson Strong would object to this argument on the grounds that embryos do not *become* self-conscious beings, they only *produce* beings that are capable of self-consciousness. His reason for this claim is that the embryo that was your precursor was also the precursor of the placenta that supported you.[30] Such an argument appears to require the assumption that an entity cannot shed some of its parts and remain self-identical. However, this seems false: consider amputees.

I would not pretend that the preceding suggestion for an argument is anything more than that. Furthermore, even I find the claim that embryos deserve the same moral respect as adult human beings counterintuitive. Nevertheless, because I think that on issues like this, the moral intuitions of others are not authoritative, it would be outrageous for me to believe that my own intuitions are more authoritative. I'm inclined to think that some argument or other concerned with individuality might be successful in showing that HESC research is permissible. However, I used to think that arguments concerned with the individuality issue were much better than they actually are, so I have no confidence at all in this conjecture. Furthermore, the dismal failure of the arguments of so many who think that HESC research is morally permissible suggests that

HESC research is not morally permissible. Of course, this conclusion could be shown to be false by only one good argument from HESC proponents.

NOTES

1. Here are some leading examples. *JAMA* 284, no. 24 (December, 2000); *Hastings Center Report* 31, no. 1 (January/February 2001); *Kennedy Institute of Ethics Journal* 9, no. 2 (1999); *American Journal of Bioethics* 2, no. 1 (2002); *Journal of Medicine and Philosophy* 22, no. 5 (October 1997).

2. A recent issue of *American Journal of Bioethics* (2, no. 2) devoted to the stem cell issue is especially noteworthy in this respect.

3. This wonderful term is found in Robert P. Lanza, Arthur L. Caplan, Lee M. Silver, Jose B. Cibelli, Michael D. West, and Ronald M. Green, "The Ethical Validity of Using Nuclear Transfer in Human Transplantation," *JAMA* 284, no. 24 (December 27, 2000): 3175–79. I shall henceforth refer to this essay as "Caplan."

4. Richard Doerflinger, "The Ethics of Funding Embryonic Stem Cell Research: A Catholic Viewpoint," *Kennedy Institute of Ethics Journal* 9, no. 2: 137–50. Doerflinger does offer some nonreligious considerations, but these are so cursorily presented that it is unclear exactly what they are. See p. 139.

5. Gilbert Meilaender, "The Point of a Ban, Or, How to Think about Stem Cell Research," *Hastings Center Report* 31, no. 1 (January–February, 2001): 9–15.

6. I assume that some authors who appear to reject this principle, such as Glenn McGee and Arthur Caplan, "The Ethics and Politics of Small Sacrifices in Stem Cell Research," *Kennedy Institute of Ethics Journal* 9, no. 2 (1999): 151–58 and Ronald M. Green, "Determining Moral Status," *American Journal of Bioethics* 2, no. 1 (2002): 20–30 are instead committed to qualification of the principle.

7. This is suggested in Michael J. Meyer and Lawrence J. Nelson, "Respecting What We Destroy: Reflection on Human Embryo Research," *Hastings Center Report* 31, no. 1 (January–February 2001): 18.

8. Ibid. Carson Strong seems to hold this view. See his "The Moral Status of Preembryos, Embryos, Fetuses, and Infants," *Journal of Medicine and Philosophy* 22, no. 5 (October 1997): 457–78.

9. Dan Brock uses the term this way in *Life and Death* (Cambridge: Cambridge University Press, 1993), p. 372. Others do also.

10. These arguments can be found, as Strong notes, in S. I. Benn "Abortion, Infanticide and Respect for Persons," and Joel Feinberg "Potentiality, Development and Rights." Both are in Joel Feinberg, ed., *The Problem of Abortion*, 2nd ed. (Belmont, CA: Wadsworth, 1984). See Strong, "The Moral Status of Preembryos, Embryos, Fetuses, and Infants," p. 464.

11. Strong, "The Moral Status of Preembryos, Embryos, Fetuses, and Infants," p. 468.

12. Ibid.

13. This argument can be found both in Caplan, p. 3177 and Meyer and Nelson, "Respecting What We Destroy," p. 18.

14. Meyer and Nelson, "Respecting What We Destroy," p. 18.

15. Caplan, p. 3177.

16. Carol Tauer, "Embryo Research and Public Policy," *Journal of Medicine and Public Policy* 22, no. 5 (October 1997): 430.

17. Ronald Green also gives this argument. See "Determining Moral Status," p. 22.

18. Meyer and Nelson, "Respecting What We Destroy," p. 18.

19. Jeffrey Spike, "Bush and Stem Cell Research: An Ethically Confused Policy," *American Journal of Bioethics* 2, no. 1 (2002): 45.

20. Carson Strong would endorse this principle. See Strong, "The Moral Status of Preembryos, Embryos, Fetuses, and Infants," p. 467.

21. This line of argument can be found in Bonnie Steinbuck, *Life Before Birth: The Moral and Legal Status of Embryos and Fetuses* (New York: Oxford University Press, 1992).

22. Meyer and Nelson, "Respecting What We Destroy," p. 19.

23. Ibid., p. 18.

24. Mary Anne Warren, *Moral Status: Obligations to Persons and Other Living Things* (Oxford: Clarendon Press, 1997).

25. Eric Juengst and Michael Fossel, "The Ethics of Embryonic Stem Cells—Now and Forever, Cells Without End," *JAMA* 284, no. 24 (December 27, 2000): 3180–84.

26. Mary Anne Warren, "On the Moral and Legal Status of Abortion," *Monist* 57, no. 1 (January 1973): 43–61. This essay has been widely reprinted.

27. See John Paul II, *Evangelium Vitae* (Boston: Daughter of St. Paul, 1995)

28. Caplan, p. 3177.

29. Green, "Determining Moral Status," pp. 20–30.

30. Strong, "The Moral Status of Preembryos, Embryos, Fetuses, and Infants," p. 460. This argument originally is due to Steven Buckle, "Arguing from Potential," *Bioethics* 2 (1988): 227–53.

7

EVERYBODY MUST GET CLONED
Ideological Objections Do Not Hold Up

DAVID J. TRIGGLE

In contrast to the Bob Dylan original, "Everybody Must Get Cloned" seems unlikely to serve as a national anthem for this decade. This failure reflects yet another triumph for metaphoric morality over significant science and human health.

In reality, the human cloning debate has less to do with a race of look-alikes, a team of superathletes, or even replacement cells and genes than it does with the far broader clash of cultures that, particularly in the United States, includes abortion, assisted suicide, birth control and family planning, evolution, religion in public spaces, and sex education. On one side, James D. Watson, Nobel laureate and author of *The Double Helix*, asks, "If we could make better human beings by knowing how to add genes, why shouldn't we?"[1] On the other side, Leon Kass, head of the President's Council on Bioethics, claims that "we can see all too clearly where the train is headed, and we do not like its destination."[2]

Both Kass and Francis Fukuyama subscribe to a thesis that "there is a natural functioning to the whole organism that has been determined by the requirements of the species' evolutionary history, one that is not simply an arbitrary social construction."[3] On first reading this thesis appears plausible, even resonant, but it is transparently false. Humankind has been interfering

From *Free Inquiry* 23, no. 1 (Winter 2002/2003): 32–33

with its evolutionary history ever since striding out of Africa: antibiotics, artificial insemination, Caesarian birth, contraception, in vitro fertilization, radiation therapy, sanitation and clean water, and surgery are just a handful of the
roadblocks that we have thrown in the way of "natural functioning." Presumably, neither Kass nor Fukuyama want to ban all of these now widely accepted
and publicly demanded practices . . . or do they?

Indeed, according to physicist Stephen Hawking, we may need extensive
genetic modification simply to stay competitive with emerging intelligent
machines and computers. "We must follow this road if we want biological systems to remain superior to electronic ones."[4]

Cloning and its attendant issues deserve a hearing independent of any argument that the technology and its uses are, no matter what the apparent benefit or
value, the final "slippery slope" for humankind. But this is not the hearing provided by the Kass-led President's Council on Bioethics, whose report is now
available.[5] The commission argued unanimously to ban reproductive cloning,
but split sharply on research cloning, where a majority favored a four-year moratorium while expressing support in principle for cloning for purposes of biomedical research. Cynics may say this decision was politically crafted so as to
follow—or at least not directly contradict—the views of Kass and President
[George W.] Bush, who have announced their opposition to any form of cloning.[6]

To be sure, there are excellent scientific and technological reasons not to
practice reproductive cloning at this time. It is inefficient; it is likely (and perhaps even certain at the present state of the technology) to be dangerous to the
clone, with the production of physical abnormalities and/or a shortened life
span associated with aberrant gene expression and regulation;[7] finally, the use
of any clone for "spare parts" is likely not to meet with approval by the clone.
In any event, the Brave New World scenario of creating defined worker groups,
usually of the militant or menial classes, through cloning is much more readily
achieved through societal conditioning and programming. For example, fundamentalist religions have no difficulty in producing religious zealots and suicide
bombers; the United States has been extremely successful in creating a new
underclass through the application of punitive drug laws directed almost exclusively against urban minorities. As for asexual reproduction, it is no fun; furthermore, Muller's ratchet hypothesis argues that sex purges the system of
deleterious mutations.[8] However, if gene loss from the Y chromosome continues at its historic rate, men will become extinct over the next five to ten million years: asexual cloning may then become necessary.[9] Ironically, this consideration should commend cloning to the fundamentalist religions that see sex
as a dirty, sinful, and nasty prerequisite for procreation.

Meanwhile, the only arguments that can be advanced against research cloning are blatantly ideological. One extreme position holds that all embryonic stem cell research or use involves the destruction of human life, and thus must be banned because it sacrifices one individual for the sake of the treatment of another individual's disease. Clearly, such a position would also ban abortion under any circumstance including rape and incest. Others argue that the use of "spare" embryos left over from fertility clinics is appropriate, but refuse to countenance the deliberate construction of embryos solely for research purposes. This is the same moral trap President Bush walked into on August 9, 2001, when he stated, "I have concluded that we should allow federal funds to be allowed for research on these existing stem cell lines, where the life and death decision has already been made." If it is immoral to create the stem cells in the first place, then surely it must be immoral to use them no matter how laudable the purpose. Additionally, why the distinction between the two kinds of embryos? As Michael Sandel, a member of the President's Council on Bioethics, observed, "Opponents of research cloning cannot have it both ways. They cannot endorse the creation and use of excess embryos from fertility clinics and at the same time complain that creating embryos for regenerative medicine is exploitative."[10]

Another argument holds that only federal funds should be withheld from research cloning programs. If it is immoral for federal funds to be used to develop new cell lines, why is it moral for private funds to be used? Nothing in recent months suggests that the private sector is more moral than the public sector.

For anti-cloning ideologues, the debate ultimately turns upon our definitions of life and its value. President Bush himself observed, "I also believe that life is a sacred gift from our creator. I worry about a culture that devalues life. . . ." Religious leaders have not been reticent in sharing God's views on life and its meaning. Georgetown University professor Edmund Pellegrino sums up the position of many conservative Protestant and Catholic groups in these words: "Upon conception, the biological and ontological individuality of a human being is established."[11]

Reasonable as the proposed four-year moratorium on research cloning may appear at first reading, since the opposition to cloning is dominantly if not exclusively theologically based, nothing is likely to change during the moratorium period. Hence, the moratorium serves little useful purpose: no secular-religious compromise is likely ever to be reached on this subject, since by definition dogma does not change. Furthermore, any decision to ban the use of federal funds for these purposes is foolish, since it will leave this critical area solely in the hands of for-profit fertility clinics[12] and the private biotechnology industry.[13] This, of all the new technologies, is not one to leave to Adam Smith's invisible hand. Those who favor doing so as a "market approach" cannot have read Adam Smith: had they done so, they would not have missed his observation, "People of the same trade seldom meet together, even for merriment and diversion, but the conversation ends in some conspiracy against the public. . . ."[14] Far better that we have a governmental statutory authority, along the lines of Britain's Human Fertilization and Embryology Authority, set the tone.[15]

In setting proper standards for cloning research, the non-dogmatic, non-ideological criterion should be to protect sentient life expressed in a suitably complex multicellular structure. The small collection of cells constituting the blastocyst is clearly not sentient. Therefore, ideological considerations aside, there should be no principled objection to the continued study of research cloning with human embryonic stem cells. Of course, patients are the ultimate bottom line. Daniel Perry estimates that as many as 12.5 million Americans suffer diseases or disorders that might be aided by stem cell research.[16] This number is likely to increase with our aging population. They will not be a silent majority.

NOTES

1. J. D. Watson, in "Engineering the Human Germline, A Symposium" (http://www.ess.ucla.edu/huge), published as *Engineering the Human Germline: An Exploration of the Science and Ethics of Altering the Genes We Pass to Our Children*, ed. G. Stock and J. Campbell (New York: Oxford University Press, 2000).

2. Leon R. Kass, "Preventing a Brave New World: Why We Should Ban Human Cloning Now," *New Republic*, May 17, 2001; "The Wisdom of Repugnance," *New Republic*, June 2, 1997, pp. 17–26.

3. Francis Fukuyama, *Our Posthuman Future: Consequences of the Biotechnology Revolution* (New York: Farrar, Strauss, and Giroux, 2001).

4. N. P. Walsh, "Alter Our DNA or Robots Will Take Over, Warns Hawking," *Observer* (London), September 2, 2001.

5. http://www.bioethics.gov/cloningreport/.

6. Ironically, at the very time that the Commission was announcing its proposed moratorium, two very important papers concerning therapeutic applications of clonal technology appeared. The first is J.-H. Kim, J. M. Auerbach, J. A. Rodriguez-Gomez, et al., "Dopamine Neurons Derived from Embryonic Stem Cells Function in an Animal Model of Parkinson's Disease," *Nature* 418 (2002): 50–56. The second: Y. Jang, B. N. Jahagirdar, R. L. Reinhardt, et al., "Pluripotency of Mesenchymal Stem Cells Derived from Adult Marrow," *Nature* 418 (2002): 41–49.

7. D. Humphereys, K. Eggan, H. Akutsu, et al., "Abnormal Gene Expression in

Cloned Mice Derived from Embryonic Stem Cell and Cumulus Cell Nuclei," *Proceedings of the National Academy of Sciences of the USA 99* (2002): 12889–894.

8. H. J. Muller, *Mutation Research* 1 (1964): 2–9. See also discussion in Olivia Judson, *Dr. Tatiana's Sex Advice to All Creation* (New York: Metropolitan Books, 2002).

9. D. Fox, "The Descent of Man," *New Scientist* (August 24, 2002): 28–33.

10. M. J. Sandel, "The Anti-Cloning Conundrum," *New York Times*, May 28, 2002.

11. E. D. Pellegrino, National Bioethics Advisory Commission, *Ethical Issues in Human Stem Cell Research*, vol. 3, Religious Perspectives, 2000.

12. Ronald Green, *The Human Embryo Research Debates: Bioethics in the Vortex of Controversy* (Oxford, UK: Oxford University Press, 2001).

13. D. J. Triggle, "Stemming the Tide," *Pharmaceutical News* 8 (2001):1 (from which portions of this article have been adapted).

14. Adam Smith, *The Wealth of Nations*, ed. E. Cannan (New York: Modern Library, 1994), orig. ed. 1776.

15. *The Human Fertilisation and Embryology Authority*, http://www.hfea.gov.uk.

16. D. Perry, "Patients' Voices: The Powerful Sound in the Stem Cell Debate," *Science* 287 (1999): 1423.

THE EMBRYO IN STEM CELL RESEARCH AND ABORTION

8

THE MORAL STATUS OF THE HUMAN EMBRYO
The Twinning Argument

BERIT BROGAARD

Recent scientific advances in research involving stem cells derived from human embryos have sparked considerable ethical debate concerning the moral status of the human embryo. Scientists believe that research using stem cells might eventually help us cure diseases such as Alzheimer's, Parkinson's, juvenile diabetes, spinal cord injury, and diseases of main organs. Stem cells apparently have the capacity to transform themselves into specific organ tissues. In the future, researchers may be able to use stem cells to develop, for example, liver cells that could cure someone with a malfunctioning liver. Because human embryonic stem cells have the potential to develop into all of the tissues in the human body, stem cells from human embryos are believed to have a greater potential to produce these results than stem cells from adult cells, umbilical cords, or the human placenta.

For research, embryonic stem cells are isolated from human blastocysts—embryos at around day four in the fetal development. In the course of obtaining stem cells from a living human blastocyst, the blastocyst is destroyed. For that reason, the main ethical challenge associated with stem cell research has to do with whether blastocysts have any moral status. There are two main arguments *for* the view that blastocysts have moral status. One relies on the claim that, if the embryo under favorable circumstances would be identical to the human

Originally published as "The Moral Status of the Human Embryo: The Twinning Argument," *Free Inquiry* 23, no. 1 (Winter 2002/2003): 45–48.

being as it would exist after birth, then it already has the same moral status as a human being after birth. The other relies on the claim that the embryo is entitled to protection because from the moment of conception it is a potential human being, even if it would not be identical to the future human being under favorable circumstances. The second of these arguments will not concern me here.[1] My focus is on the argument that the embryo has moral status because under favorable circumstances it would be identical to the human being that would exist after birth. I shall argue that the premise is false.

The most important argument against this claim, I believe, is the twinning argument.[2] The twinning argument, in its simplest form, is familiar: prior to gastrulation (the critical developmental step at which the embryo's three major germ layers, or tissue type divisions, form), the embryo is susceptible to twinning. Accordingly, it has the potential to develop into several human beings. Since the process of becoming *a* human being has not yet ended, the pre-gastrular embryo is not a human being.[3] Unfortunately, the twinning argument in its simplest form is flawed. The premise that if an entity is potentially two, it cannot be one is false. As the American Civil War teaches us, there are cases where identity is inherited even though an entity is susceptible to twinning. The United States in the period immediately prior to the Civil War was actually one but potentially two.[4] But, I will now argue, even though there are clear cases of individuals susceptible to twinning that persist over time, there are empirical grounds for denying that an embryo susceptible to twinning can be transtemporally identical to a future human being.

To make a case for the proposal that an embryo susceptible to twinning cannot be identical to a future human being, I shall first consider the possible scenarios under which twinning might occur. Second, for each possible scenario I shall determine whether there are empirical grounds for thinking that human embryonic twinning occurs under that scenario. Finally, for each possible scenario I shall determine whether it is conceivable that the pre-gastrular embryo under favorable circumstances is identical to the human being as it exists after birth. As we will see, according to the scenario under which embryonic twinning is known to occur, it is impossible that the pre-gastrular embryo is identical to a future human being.

HOW SHALL WE UNDERSTAND TWINNING?

First, one may hold that twinning is a form of cloning. On this view, the embryo would, in some pre-gastrular phase, be such that a process of forming new human individuals can still occur via budding. When budding occurs, a part of one individual substance becomes detached and forms a new individual substance in its own right, while the original substance continues to exist. Similar scenarios are known from the vegetable kingdom, where a cutting from one plant may be planted in the soil to result in a new plant without the original plant ceasing to exist as a separate individual. Budding does not entail the destruction of the entity that buds off the new individual. So, if embryonic twinning occurs via budding, the view that the pre-gastrular embryo under favorable circumstances would be transtemporally identical to the future human being is credible. Unfortunately, however, human development is nothing like that of plants. When a cutting is taken from a fully developed plant we have an original organism and a part that develops into a separate individual. We do not have one cell, or mass of cells, which divides into two. But this is exactly what we have in the case of embryos that undergo twinning.

Second, in light of the above considerations, one may hold that twinning occurs via fission.[5] When an entity (for example, an amoeba) undergoes fission, the entity reduplicates itself. New parts are formed that then split apart to lead separate existences. When fission occurs, the entity that undergoes fission is destroyed. This claim rests on the conceptual thesis that one individual cannot be identical to two individuals. Think of a log that is split into two for burning in the fireplace. One may find it quite natural to think that one log is identical with two logs given that their time frames are different. However, identity over time, like all other sorts of identity, is transitive. That is to say, if John-as-a-baby is identical to John-as-a-child, and John-as-a-child is identical to John-as-an-adult, then John-as-a-baby is identical to John-as-an-adult. Identity over time is also symmetric: if John-as-a-child is identical to John-as-an-adult, then John-as-an-adult is identical to John-as-a-child. Compare *identity* to love, which is neither transitive nor symmetric. From the fact that John loves Mary, and Mary loves Peter, it does not follow that John loves Peter. And from the fact that John loves Mary, it does not follow that Mary loves John. Since identity is both transitive and symmetric, if the one log were identical to the two logs, the two logs would be identical to each other. But they are not. We just said they were two, not one.

Of course, one may say that the one log is identical to the two logs taken together. But if this is so, then spatial connectedness does not matter in defining what a log is. That is, something can be a log even if its parts are spatially separated. In the case of an embryo, spatial separation may not matter either. But the two embryos that would result from the splitting of a single embryo would under normal circumstances develop into two human beings. So if the single embryo were identical to the two embryos taken together, then the single embryo would be identical to two adult human beings, which cannot be the case. Alternatively, one but not the other of the twins would be identical to the ancestor entity. But there is no property in virtue of which one but not the other twin could be said to be identical to the ancestor entity. So, if human embryonic twinning occurs via fission, an embryo that results from a twinning process begins to exist when the twinning process is completed.

But the fact that an embryo ceases to exist when twinning occurs does not rule out the possibility that an embryo that does not undergo twinning is identical to a future human being. So, one may hold the view that, when twinning occurs, the embryo begins to exist when the twinning process is completed, but, when twinning does not occur, the embryo begins to exist at the time of conception. Since we do not know whether a blastocyst would undergo twinning under favorable circumstances, we do not know whether it would be identical to a future human being under favorable circumstances. And since we do not know whether the blastocyst has moral status, destruction of the blastocyst is not justified.

The aforementioned theory entails that I could not have been a twin if I am not in fact a twin. For if twinning had occurred to me, I would have ceased to exist, and two new human individuals, that are not identical to me, would have come into existence. It may seem counterintuitive that I could not have been a twin. But no objection to the possibility that a pre-gastrular embryo—as twinning fails to occur—is identical to a future human being is to be found here. It is simply a conceptual fact that individuals susceptible to twinning via fission could not have been twins.

As it turns out, however, human embryos do not undergo twinning via fission. The reason is that the cells—and sums of cells—in the pre-gastrular embryo are totipotent: each of them has the potential to develop into a complete human being. The parts of an amoeba or a virus, by contrast, do not have the potential to develop into a new organism. New parts are formed which then split apart to lead separate existences. When the pre-gastrular embryo undergoes twinning, the bits destined to become a human being split into two halves without any foregoing reduplication.[6]

Recent embryonic research has given rise to skepticism about the view that the embryo is a featureless orb of cells prior to gastrulation. It has been shown that the mammalian body plan begins to be laid down already from the moment of conception.[7] A body axis is present, and there is already a clear division between bits destined to become the placenta (etc.) and bits destined to become the future human being, even at the two-cell zygote stage. Despite the existence of traits that appear to narrow down cell fate, the fact is that pre-gastrular embryos are susceptible to twinning. Even though the cells become biased toward producing certain tissues, those biases are not irrevocable. So the new data do not dispute the claim that the cells destined to become a human being are *totipotent*. After all, the pre-gastrular embryo does not have the kind of structure that would prevent it from separating into parts that can each produce a complete human being.

SEPARATION AS THE WAY TWINNING OCCURS

This leads us to the third way in which twinning can occur. On this scenario, the embryo is already not one but two (or more) entities, both of which would survive, should twinning occur, to form two independent embryos. That is, the embryo is, in some pre-gastrular phase, such that a process of forming new human individuals can still occur via separation. Separation is distinct from fission in that two or more entities are joined together as one entity, and at some point the relations conjoining the parts of this entity are disrupted in such a way that the previously attached individuals continue as separate new substances. In the case where twinning does not occur, one may hold one of the following views: one of the two parts of the embryo is under favorable circumstances transtemporally identical to the human being that exists after birth. Alternatively, one may hold that both parts of the embryo in favorable circumstances are identical to the human being.

The first of these alternatives implies a peculiar process under which—as twinning fails to occur—one human being would absorb into itself another entity that is of exactly analogous form and structure. But more important, it leaves open the question as to what might make it true that one but not the other half of the total embryo as it exists prior to gastrulation should be the human being that exists after birth.

On the second alternative, an embryo that does not undergo twinning consists of several parts that in favorable circumstances are jointly identical to the future human being. To show that this alternative is not possible either, I need to employ the notion of being identical to a human being whose possibility was never realized. The notion of being identical to all sorts of possible human beings is not strange at all. If I had not left my hometown I would not have gone to Buffalo nor have married Joe. If I had gone to Ohio State University instead of the University at Buffalo, I would have met Joe earlier than I actually did. These conditionals are not true of anyone else but me, and they are true of me. So, I am identical to a possible person that was never actualized, given my decision to leave my hometown and attend the University at Buffalo. Notice, however, that for each possible scenario there is only one possible human being to which I am identical, never two or three. So I am identical to just one possible human being in the possible situation in which I go to Ohio State University instead of the University at Buffalo. That is, I am identical to the possible human being (in that possible situation) with whom I share most of my qualities in common, including the quality of having originated from particular sperm and egg cells.

I can now turn to my argument that the second alternative is not possible either. Call the two halves of the embryo prior to gastrulation when twinning is still possible A and B. Even though twinning does not in fact occur, there is a possible situation in which A and B separate and continue as separate human beings. The actual human being that exists after birth is transtemporally identical to the actual sum of A and B. But the actual sum of A and B is identical to the possible sum of A and B. The possible sum of A and B, on the other hand, is identical to the possible sum of the two possible human beings. By transitivity, it follows that an actual human being is identical to two possible human beings that are both located in one and the same possible situation. But one human being cannot be identical to two possible human beings that are both located in one and the same possible situation. So the second alternative is not possible either.

An opponent may now object that the bundle of cells constituting the embryo is a whole, and that spatial separation of the two halves of a bundle is enough to destroy the whole. So, even for the case of twinning by separation, the loosely connected bundle of cells is a whole that ceases to exist if twinning occurs. But then the possible sum of A and B is not identical to the two possible human beings. So, the aforementioned transitivity of identity is averted.

What counts against this proposal is that the parts of the pre-gastrular embryo destined to become the human being and the parts destined to become the placenta are not spatially separated. If we suppose the degree of spatial separation between two entities x and y determines whether x is identical to a future individual z while y is identical to a future individual v, the parts of the embryo destined to become the human being would in every case fail to be identical to the human being.

Perhaps the objection is rather this: that there are cases where separation happens because the internal relations among certain parts of a whole cease to obtain, resulting in a split along the line where the former internal relations no longer hold. Even if we think of the pre-split thing as consisting of two parts, it is still one whole thing (and not a mere collection of parts). Because of the nature of identity, the original entity cannot be identical to both of the resultant entities.

The problem with this proposal is that the cells in the early embryo form a mere mass, being kept together spatially by an outer membrane. There is no causal interaction between the cells. They are separate bodies, which adhere to each other through their sticky surfaces and which have at this point only the bare capacity for dividing. In view of that, there is no reason to think that the entire bundle of cells, but not any one part of it, has some property in virtue of which it is identical to some potential human being. If each of the parts with a potential to become a complete human being is identical to a potential human being, the inference goes through.

In sum, human embryonic twinning occurs via separation. But if twinning occurs via separation, an embryo susceptible to twinning cannot be transtemporally identical to a future human being. Hence, if blastocysts are worth protecting, it is not because of their prospective identity to entities that we already know are worth protecting.[8]

NOTES

1. Singer and Dawson have discussed this argument in P. Singer and K. Dawson, "IVF Technology and the Argument from Potential," *Philosophy and Public Affairs* 17 (1988): 87–104. See also J. Feinberg, "Abortion," in *Matters of Life and Death: New Introductory Essays in Moral Philosophy*, 2nd ed., ed. Tom Regan (New York: Random House, 1980, 1986), p. 267; and D. Hershenov, "The Problem of Potentiality," *Public Affairs Quarterly* 13 (1999): 255–71.

2. In "Sixteen Days" (*Journal of Medicine and Philosophy* 28 [2003]: 45–78) Barry Smith and I argue that the pre-gastrular human embryo is not a human being. In this note I develop a new version of the twinning argument that is in many ways stronger than the twinning argument presented there. For discussion of the simple version of the twinning argument, see N. M. Ford, *When Did I Begin? Conception of the Human Individual in History, Philosophy, and Science* (Cambridge and New York: Cambridge University Press, 1988).

3. L. C. Becker, "Human Being: The Boundaries of the Concept," *Philosophy and Public Affairs* 4 (1975): 340.

4. Most likely, when we say that the United States is potentially two, we mean that a part of the United States could have become detached and formed a new country in its own right while the United States would have continued to exist.

5. W. Quinn, "Abortion: Identity and Loss," *Philosophy and Public Affairs* 13 (1984): 27.

6. Of course, as any horticulturalist knows, many plants can be bisected with the

bisected parts developing into complete plants of the same species. Similarly, *Planaria* are noted for their great ability to regenerate missing body parts. Chop a planarian into two pieces and each piece will develop the missing parts and become a separate planarian; the head of one (or the left side) is identical to the corresponding part of the original; the tail of the other (or the right side) is identical to the tail of the original. If the bisection of plants and flatworms is a form of twinning by fission, then we have to go carefully to distinguish what we are saying about human twinning. For if plants and flatworms, both of which have parts that are totipotent, can undergo twinning by fission, then what reason do we have for thinking that human embryos, which have parts that are totipotent, do not undergo twinning by fission? Granted. However, these cases appear to be cases of twinning by separation (see below). After all, if I can cut a flatworm into two pieces that can both survive, then it would seem that each part of the flatworm that can survive on its own is identical to a potential flatworm. But this means that flatworms and plants the parts of which can continue to exist as separate entities are not individuals in the sense in which human beings are individuals. Rather, they are collections of parts that could survive on their own under the right circumstances.

7. "Your Destiny, From Day One," *Nature Science Update*, July 8, 2002.

8. Thanks to Judy Crane, John Danley, David Hershenov, Richard Hull, Joe Salerno, Ron Sandler, and Rob Ware for helpful comments.

9

TOWARD RESOLVING THE ABORTION AND EMBRYONIC STEM CELL DEBATES
A Scientific and Philosophical Update

RICHARD T. HULL
AND ELAINE M. HULL

INTRODUCTION

Anyone listening to the campaign and subsequent speeches of President George W. Bush will know that the debates over abortion and fetal stem cells continue to rage. The tension for social policy of both the abortion and the embryonic stem cell issues is acute. On the one hand, the interests of women and chronically ill adults push toward liberal abortion policies and the use and even purposeful creation of human embryos in developing treatments employing embryonic stem cells. On the other hand, the political pressure for pro-life policies as representative of the highest values of our nation pushes us toward reduction and elimination of abortion and the use of embryonic stem cells. Add to this the contamination of existing cell lines permitted to be used under President Bush's August 2001 policy allowing research on then-existing stem cell lines, and the conflict becomes excruciatingly acute.

A notable feature of the debates on both issues is the stark absence of attempts to find common ground between the divided sides, and of reference to current scientific knowledge about embryonic development.

We propose today to attempt a move toward common ground by reviewing the current understanding of the physiology of human reproduction and

From a paper presented at a conference on Science and Ethics in Toronto, Ontario, in 2004. Published in *CSER Review* 1, no. 2.

applying the metaphysical foundations of biology to the earliest period of human development: the first sixteen days.

We believe that, understood in the terms of scientific fact, prevention or disruption of a fertilized ovum's implantation during this period of just over two weeks cannot be scientifically characterized as the destruction of a human life. We also believe that human embryonic stem cell research does not involve destruction of human lives, and that the deliberate fertilization of human eggs with human sperm for the purpose of obtaining fetal stem cells does not involve the creation and destruction of human lives. It follows from our argumentation that "Plan B" morning-after pills, as well as devices that prevent implantation of pre-embryo materials in the uterus, are not reasonably characterized as abortive agents in the sense found to be morally troublesome by conservatives, and that research on early human stem cells should, within limits, be morally permissible even in conservative thought.

If we are successful in our argumentation, a rational removal of claims of human destruction from the discussions of abortion, stem cell research, and pharmaceutical practices should result. Just perhaps, if the facts can be accepted by all sides, we can move in the direction of resolving elements of these heated debates through the application of science and reason.

CONSERVATIVE OBJECTIONS

There are three conservative claims that the position we defend must consider. The first is that the penetration of the sperm into the ovum constitutes the "moment" of fertilization and conception, at which point a single, genetically individual human being has come into existence. The second is that the product of fertilization is genetically identical with the infant that would be born if the natural course of gestation were not interrupted. And the third is that anything genetically identical with a human infant is itself that human being (or a part of it), appearances to the contrary.

From these claims, conservatives derive such conclusions as: Contraception measures that prevent implantation involve the killing of human beings; Early abortion involves killing of human beings; Creation of fertilized ova as sources for stem cells is creation of individual human beings to be exploited and ultimately killed without their consent. These powerful conclusions thus classify medical and research procedures as of a kind with acts of homicide and slavery; individuals who uncritically accept these conclusions, and the claims from which they derive, understandably feel outrage at those practices.

So in order to search for common ground, the three basic claims of the conservative view must be examined. We proposed to do so by applying current scientific understanding of the event and process of fertilization and development. We will show that it is scientifically indefensible to classify the immediate products of fertilization, and of cell division during the first two weeks after fertilization, as human organisms. The scientific view entails regarding those products as pre-organisms that are accurately characterized by reference to their many potentials.

THE PROCESS OF FERTILIZATION

The claim that fertilization takes place as the sperm penetrates the ovum and releases its genetic material goes hand in hand with the claim that genetic identity is fixed at this point for the duration of the resulting individual's life. These claims rest on several scientifically demonstrable errors.

We will omit the details of the history of our first actor, the sperm. Let it suffice to note that it takes about sixty days after the last mitosis for the sperm to become fully functional. It can be stored in the epididymis for some time before being ejaculated.

By contrast, what we call a woman's eggs, or her ova, have been kept in incomplete readiness for fertilization (called "prophase") before the first meiotic division for ten to fifty years.

In this earliest phase, the oocyte's chromosomes have been duplicated and are lined up with like maternal and paternal chromosomes adjacent to each other. The luteinizing hormone surge before ovulation breaks gap junctions through which granulosa cells have been telling the oocyte not to divide. As a result, the first meiotic division occurs just before ovulation. This process produces two sets of chromosomes, randomly mixed from the maternal and paternal chromosomes. One of these resultant sets of chromosomes "inherits" all of the cytoplasm of the oocyte; the other becomes a tiny polar body. But neither of the products of the first meiotic division is yet capable of joining the sperm's genetic material. The polar body never will have such capability, and another meiotic division has to occur in the set of chromosomes that received all the cytoplasm before the chromosomes from the sperm can join those from what we call the ovum, or egg.

Fertilization takes place in four discrete steps. In the first step, sperm in an ejaculate, each containing a single set of the male's chromosomes, move up the fallopian tube to the vicinity of the oocyte. As they are swimming up the female's reproductive tract, they begin a process known as capacitation. In this second step, the sperm are stripped of proteins that have masked them to protect them from attack by the female's defense mechanisms. This reorganization of the sperms' membranes exposes receptors that recognize the sugar molecules of the oocyte's outer covering, the zona pellucida. That recognition elicits the acrosome reaction: holes appear in the forward end of the sperm's membrane through which enzymes are released that can drill through the oocyte's zona pellucida. Sperm attach themselves to this outer covering of the oocyte and begin efforts to penetrate to the interior.

Once a single sperm has penetrated the zona pellucida, the third step occurs: the outer membranes of both sperm and oocyte fuse, setting off the cortical reaction, which hardens the zona pellucida, rendering the oocyte impervious to any additional sperm penetration. (This process is not always perfectly effective: should two or more sperm enter, a lethal condition is created called polyspermy.)

At this point, the nucleus of the sperm enters the cytoplasm of the oocyte. This in turn triggers a developmental process in the oocyte so that it completes a second meiotic division. Again, one set of the oocyte's chromosomes "inherits" the cytoplasm; the other forms another polar body that is usually ultimately discarded.

The two replicated sets of chromosomes from the oocyte are not necessarily identical, because of a process called crossing over in which parts of the replicated chromosomes from the woman's father cross over to become parts of the chromosomes from the woman's mother, and vice versa.

After this division, the mitochondria of the sperm and the membrane around its genetic material degrade, and the sperm's chromosomes and those of one set of the chromosomes of the oocyte come together. Only when this point is reached is fertilization complete.

Now, one might argue on the conservative side that we have only replaced a supposed "point of fertilization" with a process, the end of which is the point at which the future human has its genetic identity fixed forever. But the problem of this way of thinking is that the phrase "the future human" is not yet appropriate. For the fertilized ovum has several potential futures, only some of which involve one or more possible human beings. We need to discuss this set of possibilities with an analogy to make it clearer.

AN ANALOGY TO HELP US THINK ABOUT POTENTIALITY

Consider the oak tree's seed, the acorn, the product of the union of the equivalent of oak sperm and oak egg. An individual acorn is a potential oak. It is also a potential meal for a squirrel or a bear or a wild pig. It is part of a potential meal for humans; wild foods enthusiasts like Euell Gibbons (*Stalking the Wild Asparagus*) recommend boiling the acorn, then roasting it, and then grinding it up into a meal with other acorns to be added to flour to make bread dough. Many acorns decay and become part of the forest humus we call soil. So, the acorn has the potential for several possible outcomes; realizing any one of these potentials depends on intervening conditions and events, only some of which involve human intervention. Until some sets of these conditions and events occur and determine the individual acorn's future, its potentials are only possibilities. And, the possibility of any given acorn to "become" an oak tree is very small. We will return to this point in a moment.

Similarly, the fertilized human ovum has several potentials. It may become implanted in a woman's uterus and develop into an embryo that then may become a fetus that eventually may be born as a human infant. It may split one or more times and give rise to identical siblings: twins or triplets. Any of those potentials depend on the fertilized ovum or the subsequent bundle of dividing, unspecialized cells that we call the blastocyst ending up implanted in a receptive uterus; absent that implanting, the fertilized ovum's potential to give rise to one or more human infants won't be realized—at least, won't be realized naturally (at least until an artificial womb is perfected).

The fertilized human ovum also has, thanks to various technological developments, other potentials: to give rise to lines of stem cells that may in the future have their developmental potentials directed so as to give rise to some specific organ or tissue. Even if it is implanted in a uterus, it has many other potentials, only a few of which will be realized: to be a phenotypic female but a genetic male; to be born with various deformations, as happened with offspring of women given thalidomide during the early stages of pregnancy to control nausea; to develop an Rh factor reaction to the mother's blood and be born in need of a total transfusion. But the most likely potential is to spontaneously abort. By analogy with the acorn, **the fertilized ovum has many possibilities, the realization of which depends on whether it is and what happens around and in it in subsequent days and weeks.**

So, one might well argue that the fertilized ovum is only potentially a baby, just as the acorn is only potentially an oak tree. But even here, the "is" suggests that its identity is set by its particular actual future state. Perhaps it is more accurate to say that **the fertilized ovum has the potential to give rise to a baby, and that this is just one of the many potentialities that it has.**

Still, it is tempting to say that the potential to give rise to a human baby is the dominant, "natural" one. It is useful to consider the success rate of fertilized ova starting pregnancies. First, over 50 percent of fertilized ova simply pass out of the body without initiating a pregnancy. Second, about 31 percent of all pregnancies, defined as the implantation of the product of fertilization into the wall of some uterus, do not continue to term but end in spontaneous abortions. So the probability a particular fertilized ovum in its natural situation will give rise to a human being is about 51 percent of 69 percent, substantially smaller than its potential not to give rise to a human infant. For every 100 naturally fertilized ova, no more than 49 of them will implant; of those 49, only 34 will naturally result in births. The statistics for pregnancies of women over age thirty-five are even more severe: in them, 75 percent of all fertilized ova and 31 percent of all implanted embryos are lost.[1]

Hence, the likely future for a given fertilized human ovum, if the process of fertilization is "natural" and not interrupted by human actions, is *not* to give rise to a human being. Similarly, most acorns never give rise to oak saplings, but end up either as food for squirrels and other animals or as decaying humus on a forest floor. The likelihood of any fertilized ovum giving rise to a baby is thus only about one in three. **Given these statistics, it strains credulity to identify a fertilized ovum with some future human person**; all we can say is that **the potential of the fertilized ovum to give rise to a human being is about half as likely to be realized as not.**

Now, the conservative might find in these statistics grounds for much sadness. For, if the individual human being dates from the completion of fertilization, the failure of most of those humans to implant and come to term is a very serious medical challenge. We think conservatives ought to support vigorously research into the processes of fertilization, implantation, and gestation in order to improve the chances of each fertilized ovum to be successful in implanting and coming to full term. From the conservative's point of view, the toll in human lives of the natural failures of implantation and successful gestation to term far outweighs the toll in human lives of deliberate disruptions and abortions of pregnancies. But let us return to the central argument.

If the conservative is convinced by the facts that we don't have an individual until the process of fertilization yields a cell with a full set of chromosomes, and that process of fertilization takes most much of a full day, when the fertilization process is complete, don't we have an entity that is genetically continuous with one or perhaps two or three future children? And, since implantation in the uterus doesn't occur for five to six days, aren't all contra-conceptive measures that prevent or disrupt implantation ones that deny to one or more future humans the chance to survive? Aren't they tantamount to abortive measures? We thus must examine the claim that genetic identity determines individuality, and that the individual dates from the point when the process of fertilization is completed: these are implied by the claim that human life dates from fertilization.

GENETIC IDENTITY DOES NOT DETERMINE INDIVIDUALITY

On conservative religious views, what individuates the human organism is the attachment of the soul to a unique developing individual. The history of Judeo-Christian thought on this issue is very interesting: we shall not review it here other than to note that the doctrine of the soul is a doctrine of a unique, non-replicable something, one of which belongs to every human being. Christian thinkers, when they have attended to the facts of biology, have typically conceded that the point at which twinning is no longer possible is the earliest point at which ensoulment can occur. For, if the multiplying bundle of cells has a soul from the end point of the process of fertilization, but splits after fertilization to form two or more developing bundles of cells, very difficult questions arise. Which twin gets the soul? Is one of a pair of identical twins soulless? Does the soul divide in these cases? And, if one of the twins can get a new soul at the point of twinning, why not both? Is the original soul destroyed at the point of twinning? And so on.[2]

The point at which twinning ceases to be a possibility thus seems to many scientifically reflective religious thinkers to be the point of individuation, the point from which a distinct human individual dates. For, **prior to the point when twins can no longer develop from the bundle of replicating cells, we do not clearly have a single individual who can be plausibly and reliably identified with a single future child**. That point in the developmental process is rather far along.

Individuation occurs only after the original fertilized ovum cleaves into two cells, called blastomeres, which undergo mitosis and cytokinesis together, producing a series of stages of 2, 4, 8, then 16 cells. These cells become progressively smaller than their precursors as they still fit inside the original zona pellucida of the ovum. This process takes about three days. After reaching the 16-cell stage, the blastomeres form tight junctions in a process called compaction, giving rise to the morula (Latin for "mulberry" because of how it looks). Everything is still inside the zona pellucida: there is no new cytoplasm and no interaction with "outside" structures. The morula is simply floating through the fallopian tube and into the uterus. Each of the cells of the morula is totipotent. This means that each blastomere cell is undifferentiated and each remains capable, if properly manipulated, of giving rise to a full human being.

The morula undergoes initial differentiation during the next several days, with an outer layer of cells beginning to differentiate into placental material, and the remaining cells clustering at the center of the embryo. A fluid-filled void appears at the center of the embryo, now termed a "blastocyst." This cluster of cells has been traveling down one of the fallopian tubes toward the uterus. At about six days of development, the blastocyst reaches the uterus, and implantation begins. The zona pellucida breaks, and the blastocyst affixes to the uterine wall.

Cell division continues another eight days, but chiefly only differentiation into cells that will give rise to the placenta that will attach to the uterine wall and will give rise to structures that permit the mother's blood to carry O_2 and nutrients that will support the embryo. The next distinctive events occur at about two weeks of gestational age. At this time, the implanted embryo still consists of a disk of undifferentiated cells, surrounded by early placental material. Within this embryonic disk, a small cluster of cells forms an organizing center that soon becomes a line down the disk's middle, the so-called primitive streak. This marks the beginning of the process known as "gastrulation." Gastrulation is a process in which the embryo begins constructing the specialized tissues and organs that constitute a human organism.

So, individuation into a single human organism does not occur until after the fourteenth day with the beginning of gastrulation and the appearance of the primitive streak. Only at this point do all of the cells of the blastocyst lose their totipotency and begin becoming committed to specialized roles. Until that process of cellular differentiation begins, the blastocyst is more a community of possible individuals held together by a gelatinous membrane.

TWINNING AND FUSION

Additional problems remain for any attempt to date the individual human organism's existence from the point of genetic identity's being fixed by fertilization. Separate and genetically distinct morulas that might have gone on to become fraternal twins sometimes fuse during early development to form a single blastocyst. Further, the polar body, usually discarded after fertilization of the oocyte containing the cytoplasm, is itself sometimes fertilized by another sperm and then fuses with the morula.

The biological term for an individual that is the product of such fusion is "chimera." The resulting individual humans may be hermaphrodites if they have both sex chromosomes: literally part male and part female. But they may have inherited the same pair of sex-determining chromosomes; those individuals can go through their entire lives without realizing they are chimeras. Occasionally this fact emerges when it is determined they have two distinct blood types, or when testing for a familial genetic disorder shows that some of their cells have the mutation and others lack it.[3]

In sum, **the genetic uniqueness of the morula cells does not insure individuation**. The possibilities of both twinning and fusion must be laid to rest before an individual can properly be said to have come into existence. Those possibilities cease with the onset of the process of gastrulation. This process begins at about the fourteenth day after fertilization is complete. A massive migration of cells takes place within the blastocyst during the process of gastrulation, and cellular specialization begins in such a manner that the origins of the cranial axis, dorsal and ventral sides, can be identified only after this point. In this process, some of the cells of the blastocyst are destined not to be part of the future human, but give rise to the placenta.

Now the boundaries of a discrete, coherent organism have been formed; biology calls this entity the embryo. None of the cells is totipotent any more; each will be pluripotent in that, depending upon its relationship to other cells, it can give rise ultimately to the specialized cells of blood, bone, tissue, organs.

A human being is, biologically speaking, a human organism. Completion of gastrulation is the point of the emergence of the features of an organism: possession of a continuous external boundary, internal connection of its parts so that events transpiring within it constitute either cyclic sequences (digestion, respiration, elimination, and the like) or a range of allowed values (temperature, fluid pressure) outside of which the entity will die.[4] Gastrulation marks the emergence of the very early human organism out of the precursor morula cluster of totipotent cells.

The process of gastrulation takes a couple of days, so, we conclude that **the earliest point from which the unique individual human organism may reasonably be dated is sixteen days after the process of fertilization is complete**.

CONSEQUENCES FOR ETHICS AND SOCIAL POLICY

The consequences of the scientific understanding of the processes between fertilization and cellular specialization outlined above are considerable.

First, **physical and chemical measures that prevent the implantation of the cluster of pre-embryonic cells in the lining of the uterus do not involve destruction of any human beings,** since all such preventives—from the Lippes loop to the morning-after pill—act during the days and weeks before gastrulation begins.

Second, **chemical and surgical procedures that cause the lining of the uterus to slough off after implantation do not destroy any human beings, provided they occur within the first sixteen days after fertilization**.

Third, **discard of frozen embryos does not constitute destruction of any human beings**, since embryos are frozen well in advance of gastrulation, so that spare embryos whose parents do not want them to be implanted are not orphaned humans with any rights to be born.

Fourth, **embryos that are used to generate stem cell lines**, whether in the group accepted by President Bush's executive order (all of which we now know are impure because of contamination with certain mouse proteins) or sources of future embryonic stem cell lines in California or some other country, **are not human beings that have been sacrificed to human purposes**.

Finally, while the cloning of human beings is one possible technology that we may well want to avoid, **cloning human cells for medical purposes should not be objected to on the grounds that it involves the destruction of any human being**.

CONCLUSION

We hope that careful reflection on the biology of human development in its early stages may bring the opponents in the culture wars over abortion and stem cell research to a better understanding of the facts underlying those procedures, and perhaps allow design of mutually acceptable practices and policies that reflect shared moral orderings of alternatives. Perhaps science can help us agree that prevention of unwanted pregnancy is better than abortion, early abortion within the first two weeks after fertilization is better than late abortion, and the medical use of human tissues that don't involve destruction of individuals is better than uses that would involve such destruction.

Underlying our hope is a clear and positive view of the methods of the sciences and critical inquiry. The value of the sciences as background knowledge for our cultural and moral conflicts cannot be over emphasized: too often the scientific facts are not what lead our debates of public issues.

NOTES

1. J. A. Mcfalls, "The Risks of Reproductive Impairment in the Later Years of Childbearing," *Annual Review of Sociology* 16 (1990): 491–519.

2. For a sustained effort to deal with many of these issues, see Rose Koch-Hershenov, "Totipotency, Twinning, and Ensoulment at Fertilization," *Journal of Medicine and Philosophy* 31, no. 2 (April 2006): 139–64.

3. "Roger Hartfield, "Sons I Gave Birth to Are Unrelated to Me," United Kingdom, Telegraph.co.UK, November 13, 2003, http://www.telegraph.co.uk/news/ main.jhtml?xml=/news/2003/11/13/nivf113.xml&sSheet=/news/2003/11/13/ixhome .html; also see Henry T. Greely, "Defining Chimeras . . . and Chimeric Concerns," *American Journal of Bioethics* 3, no. 3 (Summer 2003): 17–20.

4. Barry Smith and Berit Brogaard, "Sixteen Days," *Journal of Medicine and Philosophy* 28 (2003): 45–78; also see Daniel Cohnitz, and Barry Smith, "Assessing Ontologies: The Question of Its Ethical Significance," in *Persons: An Interdisciplinary Approach*, ed. E. Runggaldier and C. Kanzian (Vienna: Hoelder-Pichler-Tempsky und Österreichischer Bundesverlag, 2003), pp. 243–59.

10
PARALLELS BETWEEN THE ETHICS OF EMBRYONIC STEM CELL RESEARCH AND ABORTION

MARIN GILLIS

A number of bioethicists are concerned with the relationship between the ethics of abortion and stem cell research, especially insofar as this relationship extends to public policy concerning stem cell research.[1] Many maintain that analogies between the two debates should not be drawn and that to do so is to be held in the jaws of US abortion politics, that is, in the loud and public fight between pro-life and pro-choice advocates. Not surprisingly, folks who do not want to press the relationship usually support embryonic stem cell research, or at least, they think that this research should not be regarded as impermissible for the same reasons abortion is regarded as impermissible.

I agree that one part of this legacy of abortion politics in the stem cell debate is misleading: namely, the claim that the crucial moral issue in stem cell research, like abortion, is a decision over the independent moral status of the embryo. But I disagree that as a result there are no parallels between the moral issues in abortion and embryonic stem cell research. I offer that it is important to see that some arguments in the abortion debate are analogous to those in stem cell research, even if one does not maintain that destructive embryo research is inherently wrong, because one may risk not understanding why women may be harmed in stem cell research unless one does.

The parallel between the ethics of destructive embryo research and abortion may be drawn in the following way: abortion and stem cell research are both morally wrong because an embryo or fetus is a moral patient with full (or potentially full) moral standing, that is, it is morally considerable as a person. And it is innocent. Thus it is intrinsically wrong to kill it. Moreover, to value it just as a source of cells is to value it only instrumentally. And as it is morally unacceptable to treat a person as a means only, so, too, is it morally unacceptable to treat an aborted fetus or an embryo as a means only.

But this construal of the analogy applies only to one side of each of the abortion and stem cell debates. That is, while those against abortion and against stem cell research may use similar argumentation—any action that destroys an embryo or fetus is inherently wrong owing to this entity's full moral status— one of the most important arguments in support of abortion is a woman's right to terminate her pregnancy. And this justification does not seem to be relevant to the proposal that it is not morally wrong to use embryos in stem cell research and therapy. The analogy between the ethics of the two issues will necessarily be incomplete as long as only one side is being taken into account. Therefore, the two debates ought not to be considered parallel.

To be sure, one justification for a woman's right to terminate her pregnancy is that the embryo or fetus has no inherent value; therefore no moral harm is done to it if one deliberately destroys it. In this way we might seem to have both sides of the stem cell debate, for and against, covered by the arguments for and against abortion. Because the embryo or fetus has no intrinsic moral value, using its remains for medical research and therapy is not morally wrong, nor is killing it. Consequently, the analogy is complete and debates are parallel.

However, suppose that the moral issue in the abortion debate is not over whether the embryo or fetus is a moral person, but rather as a dilemma involving the competing rights of an embryo or fetus and a pregnant woman. If one considers the abortion debate thus, two points may be seen to emerge. First, one will represent the abortion debate in fairer terms, which is a good thing to do if one is interested in the truth and/or women's rights. Second, one will see that the moral debate over stem cell research and abortion are not parallel. This consideration and the two points that follow from it form the basis of the view that it is misleading and even false to draw parallels between the ethics of abortion and the ethics of destructive embryonic research. In the following I present the case for this view.

In abortion, a pregnancy, an event in a woman's body, is terminated. By contrast, in embryonic stem cell research, an embryo, not inside a woman's body but developing in a petri dish, is destroyed. It seems that one should not see the latter as parallel to the abortion debate because there are no autonomy issues regarding women's rights over their own bodies to consider. There is no challenge to a woman's authority over her body in stem cell research.[2]

The location of the growing embryo is relevant to the claim that stem cell research should not be seen through the lens of the abortion debate. And this point is key to the claim that the difference between destructive embryonic research and the abortion debates is that only the latter involves a conflict with the autonomy rights of the rights of women. And it allows for another reason why the two debates ought not to be considered analogous.

If location is the key to the moral difference, then the reason why it is wrong to terminate a pregnancy but not destroy an embryo is that once a pregnancy has begun, it is wrong to interfere with the embryo's natural process of growth. The wrong is not that an entity is not being respected in a manner that it ought to be but rather that a natural process is being interfered with. A developing embryo is in a petri dish and not in a woman's body. Thus the ontology of the *ex utero* being embryo shifts from that of a *potential* human being to that of a *possible* human being.[3] It is impossible for the embryo in the petri dish to become a baby without serious technological intervention; whereas a developing embryo in a woman's body has the potential to become a baby. In embryonic stem cell research, there is no natural process to interfere with. Left on its own, the petri embryo will wither and die; left on its own, it will "go nowhere."[4] But an abortion interferes in a natural process; it terminates a pregnancy in a woman's body.

This kind of argumentation supporting the view that there is no parallel between the two debates moves away from the ethical consideration of moral standing of the embryo or fetus. It construes the abortion debate as a conflict between the following propositions: A woman has a right to control her body, and it is wrong to interfere with a natural process once it has started. Since it seems that neither of these propositions is relevant in the stem cell debate, one's abortion views cannot be seen to influence one's views on embryonic stem cell research and therapy. It also supports the common intuition that one can maintain an antiabortion position but support IVF and destructive embryonic stem cell research if the source of the stem cell line is unused embryos from IVF treatments; "the current tolerance of IVF would make no sense if the moral status of the embryo were crucial."[5]

That the ethics of abortion and destructive embryonic research ought not to be seen as analogous is not only to show that there is one side of the abortion debate that has no parallel in the stem cell debate, namely the right of a woman to make her own reproductive choices. It does not only claim that the analogy between the two debates is misleading because it is incomplete. There is a stronger claim that there are *no* parallels between the ethics of abortion and stem cell research. This stronger claim emerges if we regard what is at issue for pro-life advocates in abortion not as concern for the intrinsic value of the embryo, but rather that interference in the natural process of pregnancy is wrong. One sees the point of this strategy. It makes the location of the embryo in question the essential difference in the two debates: either in a woman's womb or outside of a woman's womb. Arguments used by pro-life abortion advocates are thus irrelevant to the ethics of destructive *ex utero* em

bryonic stem cell research since there is no natural process that risks being interfered with. Analogously, arguments used by pro-choice advocates are also irrelevant since there are no women's autonomy issues in *ex utero* destructive embryo research. Here is a supportive position of destructive embryonic stem cell research that may be consistently maintained by a person who is pro-life. It makes the pro-choice view irrelevant, and it even renders the feminist position that is supportive of a women's right to abortion, but critical of destructive embryonic research, incoherent. Abortion politics is happily out of the stem cell debate.

In critical response, I would like to draw attention to two issues. First, that the pro-life position is or ought to be underpinned by the principle that to interfere in a pregnancy is wrong, and that consequently one need not have to rely on the claim that the embryo/fetus has full moral or potentially full moral standing. And second, that of the question of the relation between women's autonomy and agency and the products of her reproductive labor, for example, her pregnancy, embryos, and eggs. I will address only the second.

Suppose the most uncontroversial source of embryonic stem cell lines is leftover embryos from IVF procedures. There may seem to be nothing morally wrong with destroying these embryos if it is held that (1) they have no inherent moral standing and (2) because IVF is more or less universally accepted, then so, too, are the processes and products that emerge with this technology. But this latter claim has to be false. The technology of IVF is relevant to the stem cell debate because it is the surplus embryos from this procedure that has enabled stem cell research to get started and to continue. However, just because IVF technology seems to be accepted does not mean that it ought to be or that everything associated with the technology is morally acceptable. Perhaps we now wish that we had done some things differently since the technology first started to be effective thirty years ago. In addition, it could be, though, that the good of generating embryos in IVF resides in the intention behind IVF, namely, the generation of a child.[6] And if this is granted, then it could be thought that these extra embryos are humans waiting to be born, not leftover tissue from a previous and altogether different medical procedure.

Women's involvement in embryonic stem cell research comes from their involvement in IVF. Because of the way IVF works, there are more fertilized eggs *in vitro* than would be needed by one potential gestating woman at one time. Because of the existence of embryo-freezing techniques and the difficulties of freezing ova, embryos that are not immediately needed for treatment are frozen. During the initial stage of IVF,[7] a woman is given leuprolide acetate (Lupron™), a drug that shuts down her ovaries. This drug has a host of side effects and is not approved by the FDA for multiple-egg extraction procedures although it is approved for other specific uses.[8] Then she is given high doses of a hormone called FSH, follicle-stimulating hormone.[9] Later, more hormones are induced into the woman's system in order to encourage implantation. These drugs can cause a reaction called Ovarian Hyperstimulation Syndrome (OHSS), which may appear in mild, moderate, or severe forms. It has caused death.[10] No long-term research has been conducted to determine the extent of all the risks involved, and hormone treatments associated with other procedures have proven dangerous to women in the past.[11]

In addition to these health risks, there are other mental health risks that women and their partners may suffer due to IVF treatment. Instead of exploring other options for a family, IVF offers what seems to be the only hope to a basic human desire if not a basic human right: a biological child. The actual percentage of successful births resulting from IVF is low. The average success rate for both Canada and the United States is approximately 20 percent.[12] Almost all women undergoing IVF go through multiple treatments before pregnancy occurs, if it ever does. For these women, the sense of inadequacy and loss that makes the medical route so appealing in the first place is reinforced with each failure. However, it is not possible to deal with this sense of loss and suffering if the woman still desires to "undo the loss." And here lies one of the major issues with IVF: there is no logical stopping point. As Berthelot reports, "Failure does not provide any reason to believe that success will not occur with the next attempt."[13]

Finally, there is a question concerning whether this therapy ought to be considered an enhancement because infertility is not universally considered a disease of the woman who undergoes the procedure.[14] For example, a couple's infertility may be attributed to male factor infertility, in a heterosexual couple; and, a single woman or a woman in a same-sex partnership desiring to be pregnant requires assisted reproduction, IVF being the most common, in order to conceive. Therefore, a woman who undergoes IVF treatment may herself be reproductively healthy. One could also hold the view that most female infertility may be a social construct; a position that gains support in light of the billion-dollar IVF industry in the United States,[15] that most women in hetero-sexual infertile couples would be willing to adopt a child,[16] and that having a biological child is considered necessary in order for a woman to realize her potential as a successful woman.[17]

In the end, even if one considers women's infertility a disease of the woman who undergoes the treatment, therapy for IVF is time-consuming, invasive, and potentially harmful, costly, and most likely unsuccessful. And a woman gives her voluntary informed consent to undergo it.

I offer that the ethics of stem cell research parallel the ethics of abortion because in both, women may be harmed for the same reason; namely, when her reproductive materials and reproductive labor are regarded as absolutely independent of her agency. In both issues, women are not respected as agents when ova, embryos, and fetuses, regardless of their location, are considerable as absolutely independent of her body and her volition.

The focus on the possible harm stem cell research and therapy may cause to women should lead one to a reexamination of women-centered arguments regarding the ethics of abortion. Indeed it is difficult, if not impossible, as the view I have examined earlier reveals, to understand what specific harms to women are risked in stem cell research if we do not. The view that abortion should be permitted on the grounds that woman has a right to control her pregnancy does not exhaust woman-centered positions on abortion. Nor does it completely capture the normative force of a position that is representative of women's experience in infertility, pregnancy, abortion, and childbirth. This defense of abortion rights "does not meet the needs, interests, and intuitions of many of the women concerned . . . a [better] ethics demands that moral discussions of abortion be more broadly defined than they have been in most philosophic discussions."[18] I will outline a few general considerations in the ethics of abortion through the lens of women's experience.

To maintain a fetus's life does not only mean that one does not kill it, as in not aborting it, it means that it has to be in the body of another person who has to sustain it for a number of months. To gestate a fetus requires considerable emotional and psychological investments and potentially large sacrifices on the part of the woman who gestates it. And it is not that the gestating woman is a fetal container or a baby machine, one whose value to the pregnancy is to keep the fetus growing.[19] In a pregnancy, the woman herself experiences the growing of the fetus in her body. This relationship requires a high degree of intimacy for a number of months.[20]

Moreover, philosophers point out that even if one as a right to life that cashes out into a right not to be killed, a right to life that involves the intimate support of another is an obligation beyond this right.[21] The abortion decision is better not thought of as a conflict of rights between two separate individuals, but rather, as a question of whether the pregnant women's pregnancy is a voluntary or involuntary intimacy. In this way, the moral harm in not allowing a woman to have an abortion if she wants it is that she would be in a situation of forced intimacy and no one should be forced into unwilling intimacy.[22]

There is a philosophical tension over what it is to be a human person that is brought out in the discussion of the morality of abortion through the lens of women's experience. It is the tension between a person's volitional capacity and her bodily existence. On the one hand, pregnancy involves a number of decisions made by the pregnant woman. The embryo or fetus may flourish more or less or die as a result of the pregnant woman's decisions, that is, her agency. There is thus volitional work in pregnancy. On the other hand, pregnancy involves biological processes over which the pregnant woman has no control. Philosophically, we tend to regard biological processes as being ontologically and morally distinct from volitional processes; we can be held morally responsible for the latter but not the former. But the morality of abortion when looked at from women's perspective reveals that what is done naturally, that is, biologically, "may be falsely distinguished from what is done volitionally."[23] The phenomenon of pregnancy clearly reveals that human beings are embodied agents. While the concept and philosophical implications of embodied agency needs to be worked out to general philosophical satisfaction, it will not become the subject of argument or speculation here.[24]

To conclude, consideration of women's reproductive autonomy is relevant in the ethic debate over destructive embryo stem cell research. A woman may be particularly affected by this research analogously to how she may be harmed in abortion. In either case a woman is wronged if her autonomy and agency is not respected with regard to: (1) her reproductive capacities, which include volitional activities; or (2) the products of her reproductive labor, namely, her embryos. Embryos and fetuses are not simply happened upon in the world. One does not bump into a fetus unless one bumps into a pregnant woman. And one does not bump into an *ex utero* embryo unless somewhere in the world a woman has gone through a multiple egg extraction treatment or an abortion.[25]

To claim that the consideration of women's autonomy is irrelevant to the consideration of embryos does not hold up. If we consider where these embryos come from, the rights of women may not seem as irrelevant to the moral debate over destructive embryo research as the view I have outlined above maintains. Embryos that lie in petri dishes are generated by human beings through a considerable amount of technological intervention that importantly involves the agency and bodies of women. Women are involved in stem cell research because embryonic cell lines are made from parts of her body that are subject to her control (e.g., ova stimulation). Therefore, she as an agent is relevant in the ethics of stem cell research and she must be respected in the generation of embryos, as in IVF, as well as their use.

NOTES

1. See authors in Suzanne Holland, et al., eds., *The Human Embryonic Stem Cell Debate: Science, Ethics, and Public Policy* (Cambridge, MA: MIT Press, 2001), for example. Laurie Zoloth, "Jordan's Banks," *American Journal of Bioethics* 2 (Winter 2002): 3–11. The most well-developed case for this view I have encountered is Robert Wachbroit's "Stem Cell Research and the Legacy of Abortion," in *Genetic Prospects: Essays on Biotechnology, Ethics and Pubic Policy*, ed. Verna Gehring (Oxford: Rowman and Littlefield, 2003): 75–84. I will regard the argumentation in this article as representative of the view.

2. Ibid., 78.

3. Ibid., 77.

4. Ibid.

5. Ibid., 79.

6. George Annas and Sherman Elias, "The Politics of Human Embryo Research: Avoiding Ethical Gridlock," *New England Journal of Medicine* 554 (1996): 1331.

7. For information on the risks associated with multi-egg extraction see The State of New York, "Becoming an Egg Donor," online at: http://www.health.state.ny.us/nysdoh/infertility/eggdonor.htm.

8. Endometriosis and fibroid-associated anemia.

9. W. Gifford-Jones, "Several Approaches to Deal with Infertility," *Financial Post* (June 6/8, 1998): R14.

10. M. M. Budev, "Ovarian Hyperstimulation Syndrome," *Critical Care Medicine* 33, Suppl 10 (2005): S301–306. "Although the prevalence of the severe form of OHSS is small, it is important to remember that OHSS is usually an iatrogenic complication of a nonvital treatment that has the potential for a fatal outcome."

11. E.g., estrogen therapy. See: A. D. Lyerly, et al., "The Ethics of Aggregation and Hormone Replacement Therapy," *Health Care Analysis* 9, no. 2 (2001): 187–211.

There is evidence of a link between the use of these hormones and the development of cancer in women who have undergone the IVF process. (E. Bartholet, "Adoption Rights and Reproductive Wrongs," in *Power and Decision: The Social Control of Reproduction*, ed. Gita Sen and Rachel C. Snow [Cambridge, MA: Harvard University Press, 1994], p. 194.) Ovarian cancer has a multifactor etiology (many contributing causes, not just one) and is the most fatal gynecologic disease. Researchers have observed an increased risk of disease in women who never become pregnant. (H. A.

Risch, et al., "Parity, Contraception, Infertility, and the Risk of Epithelial Ovarian Cancer," *American Journal of Epidemiology* 140 [1994]: 585–97.) It is suggested that the increased risk with infertility treatment is due to the use of fertility drugs (see A. S. Whittemore, et al., [Collaborative Ovarian Cancer Group] "Characteristics Relating to Ovarian Cancer Risk: Collaborative analysis of 12 US Case-control Studies. II. Invasive Epithelial Ovarian Cancers in White Women," *Journal of Epidemiology* 136 [1992]: 1184–1203; B. Kallen, et al., "In Vitro Fertilisation in Sweden: Obstetric Characteristics, Maternal Morbidity and Mortality," *British Journal of Gynecology* 112, no. 11 [2005]: 1529–35), although this claim is yet unresolved because of contrary evidence suggested by other studies. (For example, see: B. J. Mosgaard, et al., "Infertility, Fertility Drugs, and Invasive Ovarian Cancer: A Case-control Study," *Fertility and Sterility* 67 [1997]: 1005–12. No association was found between the use of fertility drugs and ovarian cancer in this study.)

12. For women between the ages of twenty-one and thirty-four, this number rises to about 25 percent. However, for those women over the age of forty-seven, the rate falls dramatically. See the CDC (US) reports, online at: http://www.cdc.gov/ART/; J. Gunby, et. al., "Assisted Reproductive Technologies (ART) in Canada: 2001 Results from the Canadian ART Register," *Fertility and Sterility* 84, no. 32 (2005): 590–99.

13. Bertholet, "Adoption Rights and Reproductive Wrongs," p. 193; L. S. Williams, "It's Going to Work for Me: Responses to Failures of IVF," *Birth* 15 (1988): 153–56.

14. See: J Elizabeth Heitman, "Social and Ethical Aspects of In-vitro Fertilization," *International Journal of Technology Assessment in Health Care* 15 (1999): 22–35; Judith Lorber, "The Dynamics of Marital Bargaining in Male Infertility," *Gender and Society* 7 (1993): 32–49; C. Shattuck and K. K. Schwarz, "Walking the Line between Feminism and Infertility: Implications for Nursing, Medicine, and Patient Care," *Health Care for Women International* 12, no. 3 (1991): 331–39; Sue Sherwin, *No Longer Patient* (Philadelphia: Temple University Press, 1992).

15. Deborah Spar, *The Baby Business: How Money, Science, and Politics Drive the Commerce of Conception* (Cambridge, MA: Harvard Business School Press, 2006).

16. Judith Lorber, "Choice, Gift, or Patriarchal Bargain: Women's Consent to *In Vitro* Fertilization in Aale Infertility," in *Feminist Perspectives in Medical Ethics*, ed. Becky Holmes and Laura Purdy (Bloomington: Indiana University Press, 1992), pp. 169–80.

17. N. Pfeffer, "Artificial Insemination, *In Vitro* Fertilization and the Stigma of Infertility," in *Reproductive Technologies: Gender, Motherhood, and Medicine*, ed. M. Stanworth (Minneapolis: University of Minneapolis Press, 1987).

18. Susan Sherwin, "Abortion through a Feminist Ethics Lens," *Dialogue* 30 (1991): 327.

19. Mary Mahowald argues that this view constitutes the fallacy of considering an object as if it exists without a context. As women's bodies are not acknowledged as belonging to female subjects and agents, then women's being in the discussion is that of mute matter. But as the life of a developing embryo or fetus cannot be divorced from

the life a pregnant woman, a consideration of the former can never take place in the absence of consideration of the latter. (Mary B. Mahowald, "Fetal Tissue Transplantation and Women," in *The Beginning of Human Life*, ed. Fritz K. Beller and Robert F. Weir [Dordrecht: Kluwer Academic Publishers, 1994], pp. 225–32.)

20. Margaret Olivia Little, "Abortion, Intimacy, and the Duty to Gestate," *Ethical Theory and Moral Practice* 2 (1999): 297.

21. Judith Jarvis Thomson, "A Defense of Abortion," *Philosophy and Public Affairs* 1 (1971): 47–66.

22. Little, "Abortion, Intimacy, and the Duty to Gestate," p. 296.

23. Susan Dodds, "Women, Commodification and Embryonic Stem-Cell Research," in, *Biomedical Ethics Reviews: Stem Cell Research*, ed. James Humber and Robert F. Almeder (Totowa, NJ: Humana Press, 2004), pp. 151–74.

24. One such attempt is: Margaret Urban Walker, *Moral Understandings: A Feminist Study in Ethics* (New York: Routledge, 1998). She notes the tension in the two projects of woman-centered ethics and describes it as a conflict between need to improve the lot of the oppressed (justice issue) as well as the interest to mine women's experiences for an understanding of a better model of ethics (embodiment).

For example, see the following collections: Verna Gehring, ed., *Genetic Prospects: Essays on Biotechnology, Ethics and Pubic Policy* (Oxford: Rowman and Littlefield, 2003); Robert Weir, et al., eds., *Genes and Human Self Knowledge* (Iowa City: University of Iowa Press, 1994).

25. This includes IVF, ova extraction for creating cloned embryos or lab embryos, and fetal oocytes that are extracted from fetal tissues after abortion.

EUTHANASIA AND ASSISTED SUICIDE

PART

III

11
THE RIGHT TO PRIVACY

PAUL KURTZ

I

Medical ethics is a relatively new interdisciplinary field of inquiry, which developed as a specialty in the early 1970s. It is now a fairly mature field involving doctors, nurses, hospital administrators, and healthcare professionals working in cooperation with philosophers, ethicists, religionists, lawyers, and the general public.

In one sense, medical ethics emerged because of the great advances in scientific medical research and the moral problems that often ensued as a result. This is especially true of the newer forms of technology, which enabled doctors to keep patients alive beyond the time that they might ordinarily have died. With these breakthroughs, questions of euthanasia and assisted suicide often become urgent. Many patients and their families do not wish to prolong an agonizing and painful death. There are constant pleas to doctors to hasten the process of dying and thereby reduce unnecessary suffering.

Before the emergence of medical ethics, doctors were placed on a pedestal. They were unquestioned authority figures who made the final decisions. But their judgments are now questioned and others have become involved.

Profound questions of which ethical principles and values ought to apply are constantly raised. Empirical facts are surely relevant: the circumstances surrounding the case, including a diagnosis of the patient's condition, and a prognosis of the probability of recovery. The ethical inquirers need to ask: Is death inevitable? Will it involve intolerable suffering? Can this be mitigated by palliative drugs? What is the quality of life likely to be? Also present are the values and principles that doctors and patients cherish. But perhaps the most important question is *who* shall ultimately decide: the state, the courts, the church, doctors, or the patient? This is today a heated controversy, where religious advocates insist that it is *never* right to terminate a life, whereas humanists disagree and wish to defend passive or active euthanasia under certain circumstances.

It is clear that much of the debate rests upon a central ethical principle: the importance for healthcare professionals to respect the wishes of the patient and especially his or her *autonomy*. In recent years this has become known as *informed consent*, which is intrinsic to a more general principle of the "right to privacy."

One may ask, what is the justification of "the right to privacy"? Many would argue on both deontological and utilitarian grounds: first, the right to privacy is implied by the principle of autonomy that every individual should be considered an end in himself, responsible for his or her own life—this is often interpreted as a basic deontological principle; and second, on utilitarian grounds, the right to privacy is tested by consequential reduction of suffering. What this means is that in a situation where a moral choice is demanded, pre-existing ethical values and principles, the facts of the case, and the consequences of pursuing various forms of treatment, including allowing the patient to die, are relevant to the process of ethical inquiry.

II

I submit that the right to privacy is a newly gained *prima facie* general ethical principle. People were not aware of its authenticity, say, two or three centuries ago. I submit that the right to privacy is a human right. It asserts that society should respect the right of an individual to control his or her own personal life. The zones of privacy that society should not intrude upon without good reason are a person's body, possessions, beliefs, values, actions, and associations insofar as these pertain to his or her own private sphere of interest and conduct. The right to privacy follows from the value we place on individual autonomy, that is, freedom of voluntary choice and the recognition of the importance of individual responsibility. The right to privacy is not unlimited, and society has the authority under certain conditions to restrict it, depending upon considerations of the common good. Nonetheless, it stands as a *general* principle that we ought to respect unless there are overriding considerations to the contrary. I disagree with those libertarians who want to make it an absolute right. Nevertheless, this right is so central to ethics that we consider it deontological. It ought to prevail unless there are overriding reasons to make an exception.

I think that we can defend euthanasia on other ethical grounds. For example, we have a duty to reduce unnecessary suffering if we can and this may apply to individuals separate from the right to free choice. Nonetheless, the right to privacy implies that a person should have control over his or her own body, nutrition, and health, and in the treatment of one's illnesses, he should be consulted if possible. This entails a principle of self-determination in regard to questions that emerge in the context of medical treatment. It applies to euthanasia. Individuals who are gravely ill and dying should have the right to refuse treatment and even to be assisted in easing suffering and hastening death.

This kind of free-choice euthanasia applies only to adults. Where do you draw the line? When does a person become an adult? Surely it is before the age of twenty-one; perhaps it even applies to late adolescence, but primarily to adults. It also applies to disabled persons, too, who are adults. I am excluding children or infants from this discussion. The movement for voluntary euthanasia obviously does not mean voluntary choice by a child or an infant. That is a separate and distinct issue that I cannot treat here, though there are important moral questions that have emerged concerning infanticide and that have to be carefully discussed. But I am focusing only upon adults in this essay.

Voluntary euthanasia implies that the adults are competent, able to make choices, and rational. Now, what is the meaning of the concept of rationality? This is a key question. But we are talking about the decision of a coherent person that is the result of a reflective judgment, and not a product of a hasty decision based upon the immediacy of pain.

Euthanasia thus involves informed consent. The patient should be fully informed in any medical context as far as possible so that he or she is capable of understanding his or her condition and the options and the consequences of alternative treatments. I do not like the term *patient*, but I would prefer *active person* who is being treated and is involved in a decision of what to do. The term *patient* suggests a paternalistic approach, where others decide what to do for him, but the term *active person* suggests active participation by the person in his own healthcare. Consent then does not mean passive acquiescence.

An essential part of the movement for voluntary euthanasia is the insistence that the choice to end one's life should follow from reflection made over a period of time. Therefore a living will becomes crucial. I think most of the states now recognize the validity of a living will. The decision to opt for euthanasia ought to follow from a long-standing intention of a person that under certain conditions he or she does not want to have his or her life prolonged and possibly wishes to hasten its termination.

Another salient point is that voluntary euthanasia applies only to dying persons, that is, only to people with terminal illnesses or injuries that are terminal. It doesn't apply to everyone in all circumstances. In my view, you cannot apply euthanasia unless you have a case where the process of dying has already set in. Here, in the judgment of the dying person, the quality of life is so impaired and so undermined that the person decides that he or she does not want to go on living and suffering and, having weighed the options, decides to die.

These considerations apply, of course, to *passive* euthanasia. It is difficult to understand how anyone could be opposed to passive euthanasia. I suppose that in the debate today virtually everyone supports some form of passive euthanasia. What this means is that no extraordinary means should be used to keep a person who objects alive who would otherwise die.

In my judgment it also should apply to *active* euthanasia. Here is the crux of the controversy today. What does active euthanasia mean? If a person is dying or has a terminal illness and if he or she wishes to have some assistance in hastening the end of his life, then you can raise the question of whether a pluralistic and democratic society, which allows options or choices, should allow that person's request to be fulfilled. This can be done either by increasing the dosage of morphine or by removing feeding tubes and other life-sustaining systems. Where to draw the line between active and passive euthanasia is often difficult to say. But clearly at one end of the scale, active euthanasia means that if someone is already dying and pleads for help to die with peace and dignity, then we have a moral obligation—and perhaps a legal right—to acknowledge that voluntary choice.

As I see it, it would be better if all of these matters were kept private, within the family, and were left to individuals to decide for themselves in consultation with their physicians. Both passive and active euthanasia have been going on from time immemorial. The problem has been exacerbated recently because many people who normally would have died were, because of the power of modern science and technology, kept alive beyond the time that would have been possible in the past. It is the tremendous progress of modern science that has led to these moral problems. The real question is not whether we should let the person die but whether we should keep the person alive in one sense. In either case we are intervening in natural processes, as I think we can and should do. Nonetheless, it would be better if this were a private matter.

But since there may be misuses and abuses, society has to be concerned that people's rights are not abused and that there are not violations of the right to live. Therefore there is a need for legal protections, which must be worked out by democratic means.

What about the obligations of others? We're talking about those individuals within our community who do not believe in euthanasia and are opposed to it. Some individuals believe that suffering has some spiritual merit and that suicide is a sin, and they are profoundly offended by any effort to terminate a life. Of course, euthanasia does not apply to them. That would be involuntary euthanasia, which I would strenuously oppose. All that voluntary euthanasia recognizes is that there are tens of millions of people who, after a deliberative process, have decided that they want to terminate their lives, actively or passively. The question is whether their rights should be recognized. From the standpoint of the bystander, what are the principles that should guide that person? Let me emphasize an earlier point that nothing that I have said is absolute. There are only general guidelines, and it may be that in certain cases you would want to override autonomy. One can think of moral dilemmas in which this may be the most meaningful option. I am prepared to admit that. But, if you decide to limit autonomy, you have to give a *good reason*. In other words, it seems to me that we have a prima facie obligation to recognize and respect the autonomy of those persons who, after a reflective decision, have opted for voluntary active euthanasia. If you are going to deny them that right, then you have to make a strong case. There may be some cases concerning disabled or handicapped persons where this may apply, where coercion from those around them has applied undue pressure, where the decision is not reflective, or where other pressing factors may pertain. Euthanasia has to be a freely chosen option on the part of the person.

From the standpoint of the bystander, it seems to me that there is still another ethical principle that is relevant, and that is the principle of *beneficence*. This suggests that loving members of the family, relatives, friends, and even doctors and lawyers who know the person have some sense of compassion and mercy. There is a deep, Christian principle of Christ's commandment to "love thy neighbour" (Mark 12:31) and to be merciful to those who suffer. If there is a plea from someone whom you know to help him to die with dignity, then that entails a kind of prima facie moral duty. That is a very powerful moral obligation in human society and should be considered within the context of a moral dilemma that a person is facing.

Another moral principle that should be taken into consideration is *nonmalfeasance*. We ought not to harm those persons whom we love or those people whose care we are entrusted with. This means that we ought to be concerned primarily with what will benefit the person. It is not always to the benefit of the active patient to be kept alive at all costs. You may be doing good to the active patient to help him die and thus not harm him by prolonging his agony. In other words, if you keep someone alive against his will who might otherwise die with some dignity, you may be hurting him and inflicting cruel and unnecessary harm on him. That is immoral. Here then is a double-edged prima facie principle of beneficence and of nonmalfeasance: and it has emerged as a "common moral decency."

There may be cases in which an individual opts for euthanasia, while his relatives or his community oppose his decision as unreasonable. In such a case you have an obligation to try to persuade that individual to act otherwise. If you have a person who insists that he or she does not want to be kept alive and you think that the person is mistaken and hasn't examined all of the options, or that he or she is reacting emotionally, then you have a duty to try to persuade the person that there is still some quality to life and that he or she ought not to exit so rapidly. And you ought to try to prevail. But if, in the last analysis, the active person who is suffering does not agree and insists that he still wants to die, then I submit that we ought to respect that demand for dignity. We need not ourselves wish to help that person to die, and if in own inner conscience we cannot, we should at least not prohibit or prevent him from dying, thus imposing our will upon him. In a clash of wills, it is the person who must voluntarily decide whether life is still meaningful, or whether he or she wants to die gracefully and with as much dignity as one can muster.

12

EUTHANASIA, UNNECESSARY SUFFERING, AND THE PROPER AIMS OF MEDICINE

JOHN SHOOK

It does not require any prolonged exposure to the debates over euthanasia to grasp that a large portion of the effort expended by disputants amounts to arguing over definitions. Ordinarily, terminological disputes are a good sign of healthy philosophical argument, so long as they contribute to a deeper understanding of the issues, and diminish the chances that opposed sides are really arguing past each other. My reading of recent work on euthanasia does not give me such confidence, however. I have become persuaded that the term "euthanasia" and its notorious types, "active" and "passive," have largely lost their argumentative utility.

The mania displayed by the many disputants for continuing to use these terms suggests that they remain useful only as rhetorical weapons to covertly advance predetermined moral or legal agendas. The field of medical science should therefore no longer feel well served by the bioethical debate over the morality of types of euthanasia. Genuine inquiry into the appropriate values of medicine is too obstructed by outdated and biased terminology. The critical examination of the ethical principles of medicine requires a fresh analysis of the realities of euthanasia.

I therefore propose abandoning the simplistic categories of "active" and "passive" euthanasia in favor of newly minted terms created by consulting a Latin dictionary: "clementhanasia," "cosmothanasia," and "imperothanasia." To test their argumentative value, an ongoing debate generated by James

Rachels and Bonnie Steinbock is analyzed.[1] Rachels's two primary conclusions are defended: the act of removing life support is just as much an act of homicide as giving a lethal injection, and the prevention of unnecessary suffering is not a primary aim of the medical profession. Steinbock's reply to Rachels does not affect these conclusions; indeed, her views actually support them. Steinbock thus fails to show that the American Medical Association does not inconsistently reject doctors intentionally killing patients while approving the withdrawal of life support. However, Steinbock's own primary conclusion is also defended: the AMA's permission to remove futile treatment is not inconsistent with its rejection of *mercy* killing. This essay concludes by clarifying and criticizing the AMA's long-standing position on euthanasia using the new terminology proposed here.

WITHDRAWAL EUTHANASIA IS HOMICIDE

Before we turn to the terminological issues, one presupposition required by this essay's treatment of these issues must be defended. This tenet is that an act of withdrawal euthanasia, typically treated as a specific type of passive euthanasia, is an act of homicide. The medical field has not taken a consistent position on this question, and philosophical progress here remains elusive. Many medical professionals, along with the American Medical Association, are more comfortable with the alternative view that the withdrawal of vital medical support that results in the patient's death is not any sort of killing, but merely "letting nature take its course."

Rachels defends the tenet that an act of withdrawal euthanasia is an act of homicide, but his defense proceeds in a very unusual direction. His defense requires us to first agree that the moral qualities of passive euthanasia are not significantly different from those of active euthanasia. Rachels asks to compare the moral evil of Smith, who deliberately drowns his cousin, with that of Jones, who stands by and allows his cousin to die by "accident." Taking for granted that the reader should agree with Rachels that Smith and Jones are equally morally evil, Rachels takes this as primary evidence of passive euthanasia's status as an act of killing. However, I am not so sure that I can easily agree, and when asked, my medical ethics classes are usually about evenly divided over this question. The root of this disagreement apparently lies, upon questioning, in my students' appeal to their understanding of the law. If both Smith and Jones were brought to trial, and all the facts of the case were before the jury, in the US legal system it is most likely that only Smith could be convicted and punished for murder. This is so, because it would be difficult for a prosecutor to even claim that Jones committed an act of homicide, since it is highly questionable whether Jones directly or indirectly was a cause of his cousin's death. I do not presume to resolve such questions, but the cause of reasonable disagreement with Rachels's own intuitions on the equivalent moral guilt of Smith and Jones is obvious.

Rachels's efforts to assimilate the moral qualities of passive euthanasia to those of active euthanasia are thus trebly confusing. First, it is doubtful whether our moral intuitions about Smith and Jones must coincide with Rachels's. Second, the case of Jones is not sufficiently analogous to the withdrawal of life support, the concern of the AMA, but rather to the *withholding* of life support. Withholding euthanasia is a type of euthanasia which neither Rachels nor the AMA nor Steinbock really consider to be as significant a moral question as active or withdrawal euthanasia. Third, if Rachels wants to show that the AMA inconsistently decries killing while countenancing withdrawal of life support, he should not appeal to their dubious moral equivalence, but rather to their common status as simple homicides. A homicide, following criminal law in the United States, is that act of a person which is a significant and proximate cause, directly or indirectly, of the death of another person. The nature of this person's intent behind doing this act is irrelevant to the question of whether it should be categorized as homicide, although it is quite relevant to whether the act is an act of murder as well.

It will be objected that since withdrawal euthanasia is one type of passive euthanasia, and that passive euthanasia must by definition be not really an action at all but only a nonaction, then withdrawal euthanasia could not be an act of homicide—it is not even an act at all! This objection seems to be specifically saying, for example, that when the artificial respiration machine is switched off to halt the flow of oxygen through an air tube that goes into the patient's trachea, or a feeding tube is pulled from a patient's body, whoever is responsible for these events performs an action to a machine or a tube, but does not perform any action to the patient, much less an act of homicide.

The appropriate response to this objection is to ask, what primarily caused the lack of oxygen in the patient's lungs, or caused the lack of nutrition in the patient's stomach, if not the person who performed the switching or pulling? I cannot follow a line of argument inferring that such a person could not be the primary cause of the absence of oxygen in the patient's lungs from the admitted premise that this person was the only cause of the machine halting the flow of oxygen through the air tube. Nor can I follow a line of argument inferring that such a person could not be a primary cause of the patient's death from the admitted premise that this person was the primary cause of the absence of oxygen in the patient's lungs. But perhaps this objection is instead claiming that a person could be a primary cause of the patient's death yet does not perform an act of killing, since an act of killing must be the only cause of death. Where the flow of oxygen is halted, or nutrition is halted, such halting is but one of the causes of death; there are many others, such as the body's vital need for oxygen or for nutrition. After all, if the patient didn't need oxygen so badly, the halting of oxygen through the air tube would not have been able to contribute to the patient's death! However, it is simply not the case that an action cannot be a killing unless it is the only cause of death; if it were so, then a pyromaniac could justifiably claim that his action of setting a house on fire could not be the killing of the child inside, since the house contained oxygen to support the fire.

The withdrawal of life support is an act of homicide because the withdrawal is a significant cause of the patient's hastened death. It need not be the only cause, of course, but neither is it an insignificant cause. The opposed view, that the only significant cause of death in the case of the withdrawal of life support is the disease/injury which created the need for life support, is unreasonable. To prove that this is so, let us examine a hypothetical case in which Smith withdraws the life support of another person. Suppose Smith is a new member of a criminal gang, and must now prove his worthiness by passing a test: killing Doe, a leader of a rival gang, within the next twenty-four hours. Since Doe is on life support in a hospital, making a slow recovery from a mysterious disease, Smith sneaks into Doe's room and aims his pistol at the unconscious Doe. Just then Smith notices all of the tubes and wires attaching Doe's body to large machines at the bedside, and has a flash of inspiration: instead of making more noise and leaving bullets at the scene of the crime, he could use his gloved hand to detach all of tubes and wires! Smith does so, and he watches as the last breaths heave out of the dying Doe. Satisfied that Doe is dead after five minutes, he then executes his getaway plan by jumping out of the hospital room window. Alas for Smith, he forgot that the room was on the third floor; security easily catches him as he tries to limp away from the hospital with a broken leg. Smith's trial is now at hand. All the pertinent facts are known, but Smith's defense attorney is confident that he can get his client off on the lesser charge of breaking and entering. The attorney will simply explain to the judge that Smith cannot be prosecuted for murder, much less homicide, because Smith was not a significant cause of Doe's death—only Doe's disease killed Doe! Granted, Smith pulled all the tubes and wires from Doe's body, but the cause of death according to the coroner was the disease, not Smith.

I hope, and expect, that this attorney's interesting defense would never succeed, and that Smith's trial would proceed. Of course Smith was a significant cause of death: if Smith had not withdrawn Doe's life support, Doe's disease would not have been able to contribute to Doe's death on that fateful day. Smith committed an act of homicide, and this is the case whether or not Doe's disease would have otherwise killed him later on, and even if it was certain that Doe would have actually died later that same day. The Smith example proves that an act of withdrawal of life support is a homicide, just as if Smith had instead shot Doe to death. When a doctor withdraws life support from a patient, which hastens the patient's death, from reasoning by analogy, that doctor performs an act of homicide on that patient. Objections to drawing such an analogy fall into four possible categories. First, the doctor's intentions behind withdrawal are presumably quite dissimilar from Smith's intentions. Second, the doctor's action may be very praiseworthy while Smith's action is only reprehensible. Third, it could be claimed that doctors cannot by definition kill patients. Fourth, in the Smith case Doe would likely have survived his hospital visit if not for Smith, since Doe was on the road to full recovery, but a doctor who withdraws futile life support should do so only when the patient will soon die anyway.

The first objection is irrelevant, since as explained above, the nature of the intent behind an act does not affect the question of whether it is a homicide. A person can commit a homicide for all sorts of reasons besides trying to profit from another's death. Negligent homicides happen all the time, and prison executioners surely perform homicides in the performance of their duties. The intent of the doctor bears only on the question of the moral status of withdrawal, not on the bare fact of whether a homicide occurs. This reply to the first objection also satisfies the second objection. As for the third objection, it asks us to define "doctor" so that a real doctor would never under any circumstances kill a patient. This notion is defeated by the unfortunate incidents of gross medical malpractice. The fourth objection is defeated by considering the hypothetical Smith further. Even if it were certain that Doe would have actually died later that same day from D, Smith's defense attorney could not, and should not, be able to persuade a judge that Doe's inevitable death precludes the possibility that Smith was a significant cause of Doe's actual death. The attorney's defense amounts to the claim that in some real sense, at the time Smith was pulling out Doe's tubes and wires, Doe was already dead from the disease, preventing Smith from being a cause of Doe's death. Aside from completely lacking any proper legal standing, this defense asks us to unreasonably confound common sense and the legal understanding of the "time of death."

One oft-mentioned version of objection four is worded as follows: the withdrawal of futile life support is not homicide, because the doctor only removes an artificial medical barrier to the patient's natural death. This objection could be understood in four different ways. In its first sense, this objection portrays the doctor's action to withdraw life support as no cause of anything at all, and certainly not a cause of the patient's death. This sense has already been refuted above. In its second sense, this objection portrays withdrawal as an action performed on the patient, not as a cause of the patient's death, but rather as a cause contributing to nature's ability to cause the patient's death. This portrayal of withdrawal also portends a major and unreasonable violation of common sense and legal theory, as shown by the Smith case. The fact that a coroner would not list the doctor's withdrawal is but professional courtesy. In its third sense, this objection portrays withdrawal as an action performed on the patient, not as a killing of the patient, but rather as the hastening of the patient's death. This sense likewise violates common sense and legal theory, since the definition of homicide does not recognize any valid difference between killing and hastening death. An alleged murderer is not released when it is discovered that his victim would have died later that day, or later that hour. In its fourth sense, this objection portrays withdrawal as an action performed on the patient, not as the cause of the hastening of the patient's death, but only as causing the patient to die sooner than the patient would have, had the life support not been withdrawn. This distinction eludes me completely; I think these descriptions are equivalent.

RACHELS'S DISPUTE WITH THE AMA

Since withdrawal euthanasia is an act of homicide, Rachels is right to accuse the AMA of both denouncing and defending the killing of a patient by a doctor. Let us be reminded of the AMA's 1973 statement to which Rachels refers:

> The intentional termination of the life of one human being by another—mercy killing—is contrary to that for which the medical profession stands and is contrary to the policy of the American Medical Association.
> The cessation of the employment of extraordinary means to prolong the life of the body when there is irrefutable evidence that biological death is immanent is the decision of the patient and/or his immediate family. The advice and judgment of the physician should be freely available to the patient and/or his immediate family.[2]

Aside from the fact that the AMA offers a poor definition of mercy killing (Smith terminated Doe's life but that act was hardly motivated by mercy), in this 1973 statement the AMA does presume that the withdrawal of medical treatment is not the termination of a human life by another. That is to say, the AMA presumes that withdrawal is not homicide, and hence not any sort of euthanasia. The current version of this AMA statement more clearly takes this position: "Euthanasia is the administration of a lethal agent by another person to a patient for the purpose of relieving the patient's intolerable and incurable suffering" (see the full AMA statement on euthanasia as an appendix to this essay). The AMA's current position defines euthanasia quite narrowly, even more narrowly than the bioethics field, for suspicious ends. The AMA's presumptions about the withdrawal of medical treatment and euthanasia are false and only serve to disguise dogmatic moral and legal agendas, as I have argued.

However, Rachels uses this point to step up to a larger claim: that the withdrawal of futile medical treatment is *mercy* killing. This larger claim is rightly challenged by Steinbock, but she does not successfully find a counterexample case of withdrawal. Unfortunately, the manner in which Steinbock goes about her argument portrays the issue as one of whether the withdrawal of life support is even a matter of euthanasia at all. She tries to defend the AMA, not by directly arguing that withdrawal is not killing (and good thing, too) but rather by arguing that the AMA's approval of the withdrawal of futile life support is not designed to approve a doctor's use of withdrawal as the *means* of preventing unnecessary suffering. While Steinbock is able to show that Rachels wrongly supposed that the AMA's statement must be understand as giving such approval, Steinbock tacitly gives the reader the misleading impression that euthanasia must be defined as the use of the patient's hastened death as the means of preventing unnecessary suffering. Such a definition is very unhelpful indeed, as we will see below. Still, Steinbock cannot be entirely blamed for this confusion, since Rachels says nothing to dispel the notion that this definition is Rachels's own, and says much to support this notion. Rachels is most interested of course to expose the AMA's statement as ample evidence of the AMA's failure to place patient comfort ahead of prolonging life, caused by the medical profession's cowardly fear of prosecution for homicide and murder. Rachels successfully exposes this failure by pointing out that if the medical profession were really motivated to prevent unnecessary suffering in cases where further treatment could but temporarily prolong life, then only the AMA's false belief that withdrawal is not homicide would stand in the way of its approval of active euthanasia over withdrawal euthanasia. If the AMA were to realize that both active and withdrawal euthanasias were homicides, then it

could proceed to the next question: which sort of homicide is in the best interests of the patient? Rachels's plea for active euthanasia, as often being the most
effective way to prevent unnecessary suffering, only makes sense at this stage.
By portraying active euthanasia as a means to accomplish such prevention,
however, Rachels leads the reader to similarly see withdrawal euthanasia as the
use of the patient's death to prevent unnecessary suffering. From Rachels, then,
we are drawn to the view that mercy killing is always an act of causing the
patient's death in order to prevent unnecessary suffrage. It is precisely on this
point that Steinbock aims her reply. Is it really true, she asks, that a doctor's
withdrawal of futile life support is always a matter of the doctor using the
patient's death as a means to prevent unnecessary suffering?

Steinbock, like the AMA, apparently is unwilling to countenance the
notion that withdrawal is homicide, that withdrawal is *killing*, but instead of
trying to argue that point directly, she instead argues that the AMA actually
approves of cases where the motivation is not one of *merciful* killing. There are
at least two kinds of cases, Steinbock says, where a doctor may permissibly
withdraw medical treatment without performing an act of merciful killing (and
hence an act of euthanasia). In the first, the doctor withdraws treatment only
because that is the patient's wish. In the second, the doctor withdraws treatment only because continued treatment prolongs the patient's life for no sufficiently worthy gain. In the first case, Steinbock (successfully) argues that it
could be the case that the doctor does not withdraw treatment because the
patient is suffering unnecessarily, but rather because the doctor believes that
she has the duty to respect this patient's wish to have treatment withdrawn.
Even if that may be the case, Steinbock cannot prove that this case is not mercy
killing, because she only argues that the motivation can be other than one of
mercy. In this case, Steinbock does not argue that this withdrawal is not killing.
As will be explained in the third section, Steinbock does actually have here a
counterexample to Rachel's view that a doctor's withdrawal of futile life support is a case of mercy killing, but she fails to use it carefully.

In the second case, where anticancer treatment is withdrawn, the motivation of the doctor is indeed merciful. However, Steinbock simply declares,
without detailed argument, that although the act of withdrawal does hasten the
patient's death, the act is not a homicide. Her own wording must be consulted:

> The decision here to cease anti-cancer treatment cannot be construed as a
> decision that the patient die, or as the intentional termination of life. It is a
> decision to provide the most appropriate treatment for the patient at that time.
> Rachels suggests that the point of the cessation of treatment is the intentional
> termination of life. But here the point of discontinued treatment is not to bring

about the patient's death but to avoid treatment that will cause more discomfort than the cancer and has little hope of benefiting the patient.[3]

Steinbock is claiming, without argument, that an act that hastens a person's death is not also an act of intentionally terminating that person's life. Granted, the very terms themselves suggestively inspire agreement with Steinbock. The word "termination" hardly seems fit to describe the consequences to a cancellation of cancer treatment. If so, then the proper perspective on Steinbock's proposed counterexample is not to agree with Steinbock that withdrawals are not homicides, but to get past terminological fog and get to the root of the question we must ask: Is the doctor's act of cessation of life-prolonging treatment an act of homicide; an act of directly or indirectly causing the hastening of the patient's death? The answer, in light of the Smith case above, is surely yes, since if the doctor had not done this act, in the absence of other factors, the patient would not have died sooner. Now, I am well aware that counterfactuals deserve their notorious reputation for starting arguments rather than ending them. Nevertheless, we have exposed one of the essential questions that must be faced in the euthanasia debate, no thanks to either Rachels or Steinbock. Lacking an argument to support her claim that the withdrawal of futile treatment is not the intentional hastening of the patient's death, Steinbock's second case ends up much as her first case did, remaining a case of merciful *killing*.

Because neither of Steinbock's cases successfully refute Rachels's claim that the withdrawal of futile medical treatment is mercy killing, she fails to defend the AMA's position that it completely repudiates euthanasia in any form. Therefore, she is powerless to defend the AMA against Rachels's moral condemnation of the medical profession's failure to place the prevention of unnecessary suffering as the priority over the mere prolongation of life for it own sake. Indeed, her first case can only impact Rachels's argument if it construes the doctor's motivation as something other than the desire to prevent unnecessary suffering. The overall impression of the collision between these two articles is that despite appearances, they actually do not manage to intersect much at all. The problem is largely terminological, and the remedy must likewise be terminological.

CLEMENTHANASIA

The linguistic heritage of "clementhanasia" represents the effort to return to the fundamental basis of euthanasia: that euthanasia is, aside from all other connotations, an act of mercy killing. Giving us our English word "clemency," the Latin term "clement" means roughly "mercy." Joining this term with "thanasia," meaning "death," creates the term "clementhanasia": an act of "merciful killing." Person Q performs an act of clementhanasia A on person P if and only if all three criteria below are met. No one can perform an act of clementhanasia on themselves; suicide and assisted suicide are not considered in this essay.

> A is an intentional act of homicide by delivering to P's body a lethal agent ("infusio-clementhanasia"), or
> A is an intentional act of homicide by removing a medical treatment from P ("recipio-clementhasia"), or
> A is an intentional act of homicide by cutting off food, water, or air for P ("fames-clementhanasia").
> Q's reasons for doing A essentially and primarily involve the belief that unnecessary suffering for P should be prevented.

Criterion one offers the traditional distinctions because they do reflect moral distinctions that many feel ought to be made. The order of their listing is not designed to show any moral preference. Clementhanasia by means of lethal agent becomes "infusio-clementhanasia" because "infusion" roughly indicates an insertion or injection. Clementhanasia by means of withdrawing medical treatment becomes "recipio-clementhanasia," since "recipio" means roughly to "take back." Clementhanasia by means of cutting off the supply of the basic needs of food, water, or air becomes "fames-clementhanasia" because "fames" means "starvation."

The notion of a "lethal agent" is supposed to be understood as broadly as possible, covering anything entering the patient's body which sufficiently interferes with its natural functions to cause death. An injection of potassium chloride is a paradigm example, as is the cruder but no less deadly bullet fired from a pistol at close range. Criterion one rules out two other traditional kinds of euthanasia. First, it rules out what has been traditionally called "withholding" euthanasia, in which Q refrains from doing some action that would have prolonged P's life. This type of euthanasia is problematic for many reasons. It is difficult to classify as an action at all. Furthermore, it typically involves the rationale of "allowing nature to take its course." This rationale portrays people as under an obligation to not interfere with human destiny, which is profoundly opposed to the spirit of clementhanasia: that there are some circumstances where people should undertake responsibility for the manner of another's death. Perhaps "withholding euthanasia" is a misnomer altogether. Refusing to interfere with nature's course should instead be called "cosmothanasia": death by nature. Second, criterion one rules out those in positions of influence or authority from performing clementhanasia. Person Q may suggest or persuade or command or give permission to another person R, who then performs clementhanasia, but if R does so, Q does not therefore also perform clementhanasia.

Criterion one requires that P's death must be a consequence of action A. P cannot by definition survive an act of clementhanasia performed on her, and there cannot be some other intervening circumstances that are the actual cause of P's hastened death. Criterion one does not require that Q knows that A will hasten P's death, since that stronger requirement amounts to adding that Q must justifiably believe that A will hasten P's death. This is too strong a requirement. Q might act on a false belief about P's medical condition yet still manage to hasten P's death by doing action A because, unbeknownst to Q, P's real medical condition made him very susceptible to A. In such a case, Q still managed to perform clementhanasia on P. Another interesting aspect of criterion two is that only "hastening death" is required, not "killing." Why, in light of my strenuous efforts to categorize hastening death as killing, do I sidestep this issue? The careful choice of words here is motivated by two considerations. First, my strenuous efforts may well be insufficient. Although killing is evidently a matter of hastening death, some readers may still balk at the reverse claim. Second, "hastening" death is a matter of degree (for how much time was the patient's life shortened?), while "killing" is not. Since the degree of hastening is quite likely a valid and important moral factor, the definition of clementhanasia should not obscure it. One further fact about the wording of criterion two should be highlighted: it does not require that Q intends to commit an act of homicide on P, nor does it require that Q's purpose in doing A must be to hasten P's death. Far too much purely verbal wrangling over "intending" has considerably clouded euthanasia debates. One side argues that a doctor, knowing the fatal consequences of withdrawal, must thereby intend the patient's death, while the other side argues that merely foreseeing the fatal consequences of withdrawal cannot imply that a doctor intends those consequences. Far too much moral weight is placed on ordinary vague English words here. One side uses "Q intends to do A" to mean that "Q knows that a description of his actions could include A." The other side uses "Q intends to do A" to mean that "Q by his actions primarily desires A to happen." There is just no right answer here, since in ordinary language the term "intends" and its synonyms easily cover both usages. The pragmatic answer to this problem is to define clementhanasia so that the essential nature of euthanasia is unobscured: the way that a doctor goes about preventing unnecessary suffering requires the trade-off of shortened life.

Criterion three is designed to also avoid the prevalent wrangling over the question of the exact nature of Q's intentions while performing A. It instead casts the issue as a question of how Q would sincerely account for doing A. It is largely this criterion that applies to Steinbock's attempt to carve out two cases of hastening a patient's death that fail to be acts of euthanasia. The first case supposes that the doctor performs action A, a withdrawal of treatment, which hastens P's death, because the doctor believes that she is under an overriding obligation to respect P's wish to have that treatment removed. On Steinbock's telling of this story, a crucial matter has been left out: why does the doctor believe that she is under this overriding obligation? Perhaps this doctor believes that a patient's wish to not be treated always overrides any other considerations. We are indeed left to read this case in this way; on this reading the doctor does not perform an act of clementhanasia. Since the doctor is not motivated by mercy, but by the command of the patient, the doctor's action should instead be called "imperothanasia": a "commanded death." However, it is quite possible that this doctor instead believes that this obligation is overriding in this particular case only because of this patient's present condition. For example, suppose the doctor believes that this particular patient has the right to refuse treatment because she believes that any person ought to have the right to refuse treatment in circumstances where continued treatment would only prolong suffering. If this were indeed the case, then criterion three applies, and the doctor would be performing an act of clementhanasia.

The second case offered by Steinbock describes the doctor's motivation behind withdrawing treatment as a desire to prevent unnecessary suffering, not as a desire to hasten the patient's death in order to prevent unnecessary suffering. Steinbock understands Rachels, as explained above, to be defining euthanasia in such a way as to require that the doctor intends to use the patient's death as the means of preventing unnecessary suffering. My definition of clementhanasia contains no such requirement. Steinbock's doctor correctly believes that the withdrawal of treatment will hasten the patient's death; thus criterion two is satisfied. Criterion three is satisfied because the doctor's reason for withdrawing treatment essentially involves the belief that unnecessary suffering for P should be prevented. Thus Steinbock's second case is an act of withdrawal clementhanasia.

In a similar way my definition of clementhanasia easily handles the oft-discussed case of the doctor who gives accelerated doses of morphine to a terminally ill patient in order to "keep him comfortable." Here, the doctor gives repeated heavy doses of morphine in the full knowledge that in addition to pre-venting pain, the morphine will hasten P's death by suppressing the patient's breathing. While this doctor can sincerely claim that the morphine doses were only intended to secure the patient's comfort, and not to directly cause the patient's death, this doctor's action easily meets all three criteria for active clementhanasia. It does not meet the typical criteria for euthanasia, since euthanasia is widely understood to require both that the doctor use the patient's death to prevent suffering, and that the doctor primarily intends by the action to kill the patient. In this morphine case, the doctor is using the morphine to relieve the suffering, not to kill the patient. While morphine also acts as a lethal agent, killing the patient hours later, the doctor can sincerely claim that this death was a foreseen but unintended consequence of the morphine doses. The definition of clementhanasia reveals some essential moral questions which euthanasia obscures: are there any circumstances in which a shortened life is a morally acceptable trade-off for less suffering, and if so, when in those cir-cumstances does another person have a moral duty to shorten someone's life to prevent her suffering?

UNDERSTANDING THE AMA'S STAND ON EUTHANASIA

In this essay, many sorts of actions that have at one time or another been taken to be acts of euthanasia are re-sorted into three categories: clementhanasia, cos-mothanasia, and imperothanasia. For convenience, let us set down their defin-itions together.

> Person Q performs an act of clementhanasia A on person P if and only if Q's act A is an act of homicide.

> (a) If A is the injection of a lethal agent into P, then "infuso-clemen-thanasia" occurs.
> (b) If A is the withdrawal of a medical treatment from P, then "recipio-clementhanasia" occurs
> (c) If A is the stoppage of the supply of food, water, or air for P, then "fames-clementhanasia" occurs.

> Q's reasons for doing A essentially and primarily involve the belief that unnecessary suffering for P should be prevented.

Person Q allows cosmothanasia to occur to person P if and only if Q correctly believes that P will be killed, if no human intervention occurs, by natural cause(s) N.

Q correctly believes that he is in a position to perform action(s) A which would counteract N and forestall P's death.

Q intentionally does not perform A.

Q's reasons for not doing A essentially and primarily involve the belief that unnecessary suffering for P should be prevented.

Person Q performs an act of imperothanasia A on person P if and only if Q's act A is an act of homicide.

(a) If A is the injection of a lethal agent into P, then "infuso-imperothanasia" occurs.

(b) If A is the withdrawal of a medical treatment from P, then "recipio-imperothanasia" occurs

(c) If A is the stoppage of the supply of food, water, or air for P, then "fames-imperothanasia" occurs.

Q believes that P has expressed a wish to have his death hastened in circumstances C describing P's present condition.

Q's reasons for doing A essentially and primarily involve the belief that P's expression of a wish to have his death hastened in these circumstances C creates for Q an overriding obligation to perform A.

The AMA's stand on euthanasia can now be rephrased using these terms. The AMA rejects infusio-clementhanasia, while apparently approving in some cases withdrawal clementhanasia, cosmothanasia, and imperothanasia. The AMA now has little choice over permitting doctors to withhold or withdraw vital care in the current legal climate, which can empower competent patients or legal guardians to refuse medical treatment. The current AMA statement on euthanasia gestures toward this legal reality by mentioning patient autonomy: "Patients near the end of life must continue to receive emotional support, comfort care, adequate pain control, respect for patient autonomy, and good communication" (see appendix).

In order for the AMA to avoid Rachels's argument that by permitting only withdrawal it fails to consistently show adequate concern for patient suffering, it must simply point out that Rachels has falsely assumed that it is in *any* case primarily motivated by patient suffering. Steinbock fails to show that the AMA does sometimes encourage concern for patient suffering, because her second case rashly assumes (falsely) that such withdrawal is not a homicide. Without that case, Steinbock can only defend the AMA from Rachels's charge of inconsistency by raising a case of imperothanasia, but in such a case the doctor is not asked to be primarily motivated by a concern for the patient's suffering, but only by a respect for the patient's legal right to refuse medical treatment. Nor can the AMA's approval of cosmothanasia be construed as a primary concern for patient suffering, since such a concern would morally justify the immediate relief of infusio-clementhanasia, not the lingering suffering of cosmothanasia. While the AMA does not have an inconsistent position on the priority of preventing unnecessary suffering, it does contradict itself by authorizing homicide by withdrawal while forbidding homicide by more active means, like lethal injection. The AMA's only logical recourse, if it wishes to forbid doctors to perform homicides, is to forbid withdrawal as well. Such an explicit stand against both clementhanasia and imperothanasia would relieve the AMA from logical contradiction, but at the heavy price of exposing its fundamental doctrine that any amount of suffering is always medically justified by extended life.

In conclusion, the AMA does not believe that the medical profession should place the efficient relief of patient suffering ahead of the priority of extending life. It does permit imperothanasia only because it has been legally required to do so, as the result of recent legal battles over patient's rights. If the medical profession wants to continue its twentieth-century obsession with postponing death at all costs, and if its definition of medical care cannot include the efficient prevention of suffering when amelioration or cure is no longer possible, then the euthanasia debate should now shift to a different question: Under what circumstances should a patient be released from medical care to the care of professionals trained to perform clementhanasia?

APPENDIX

The AMA Code of Ethics Statement on Euthanasia

E-2.21 Euthanasia

Euthanasia is the administration of a lethal agent by another person to a patient for the purpose of relieving the patient's intolerable and incurable suffering. It is understandable, though tragic, that some patients in extreme duress—such as those suffering from a terminal, painful, debilitating illness—may come to decide that death is preferable to life. However, permitting physicians to engage in euthanasia would ultimately cause more harm than good. Euthanasia is fundamentally incompatible with the physician's role as healer, would be difficult or impossible to control, and would pose serious societal risks. The involvement of physicians in euthanasia heightens the significance of its ethical prohibition. The physician who performs euthanasia assumes unique responsibility for the act of ending the patient's life. Euthanasia could also readily be extended to incompetent patients and other vulnerable populations. Instead of engaging in euthanasia, physicians must aggressively respond to the needs of patients at the end of life. Patients should not be abandoned once it is determined that cure is impossible. Patients near the end of life must continue to receive emotional support, comfort care, adequate pain control, respect for patient autonomy, and good communication.

Issued June 1994 based on the report "Decisions Near the End of Life," adopted June 1991 (*Journal of the American Medical Association* 267 (1992): 2229–33); updated June 1996.

(Available online through the AMA's Web site for its Code of Medical Ethics at http://www.ama-assn.org/ama/pub/category/14330.html)

NOTES

1. James Rachels, "Active and Passive Euthanasia," *New England Journal of Medicine* 292 (1975): 78–80. References are to its reprinting in *Killing and Letting Die*, 2nd ed., ed. Bonnie Steinbock and Alastair Norcross (New York: Fordham University Press, 1994), pp. 112–19. Bonnie Steinbock, "The Intentional Termination of Life," *Ethics in Science and Medicine* 6 (1979): 59–64. References are to its reprinting in *Killing and Letting Die*, 2nd ed., pp. 120–30.
   2. Rachels, "Active and Passive Euthanasia," pp. 112–13.
   3. Steinbock, "The Intentional Termination of Life," p. 124.

ORGAN TRANSPLANTS, SEXUALITY, AND HUMAN ENHANCEMENT

13

PERSONAL AUTONOMY, ORGAN SALES, AND THE ARGUMENTS FROM MARKET COERCION

JAMES STACEY TAYLOR

I t is well known that there is a significant shortage of organs available for transplantation. Indeed, figures show that eighteen people on the waiting list for organs die each day in the United States alone.[1] Recent scientific advances have, however, made a promising solution to this shortage possible: to allow markets in transplantable human organs. Such markets have been made possible not only by advances in organ transplantation technology that enable organs from one person to be transplanted into the body of another. They have also—and more recently—become possible as the result of the development of new immunosuppressive drugs, such as OKT-3 and cyclosporine A, that have expanded the pool of persons from whom a person needing an organ can receive one to include persons unrelated to the potential recipient. Moreover, advances in surgical techniques (such as laproscopic surgery) have also made the removal of an organ much less invasive and much less dangerous for the organ provider, thus removing barriers to satisfying persons' desires to sell their organs. However, it is not only advances in biomedical science that have made markets in human organs possible. It is often overlooked, for example, that the ease of international travel has made it possible for "transplant tourism" to take place, with persons from wealthy countries

A shorter version of this work was presented at the Conference on Global Bioethics, "Is There a Global Bioethics?" IHEU–Appignani Center for Bioethics at the United Nations, New York City, April 2006.

143

traveling to poorer countries to purchase transplant organs.[2] Developments in communications technology have similarly facilitated the growth of this market, with potential buyers, sellers, and middlemen using the Internet to facilitate trade.

Yet despite the potential that markets have for solving the shortage of human transplant organs, this way of solving the shortage has been vigorously opposed. The reasons for this opposition are numerous. Many persons hold that such markets are simply too repugnant to be allowed,[3] or object to them out of their suspicion of both science and scientists.[4] Others hold that allowing such markets would illegitimately commodify the human body,[5] while yet others believe that such markets would lead to a reduction in both the number and quality of organs procured.[6] Yet although these complaints are common among those who oppose allowing markets in transplantable human organs, one of the most widespread objections offered against such markets is that they will subject those who would be the typical vendors in them—the poor—to coercion or force.[7] Given this, the proponents of this objection claim, since coercing or forcing a person into performing a certain action (such as the sale of a kidney) would compromise her autonomy, and since respect for autonomy is a fundamental moral value within the West, markets for transplantable human organs should continue to be prohibited.

Despite the popularity of this objection to markets in human organs I will argue that it is mistaken—in all of its forms. To achieve this I will first address the "canonical" version of this argument: the Argument from Economic Coercion. Having shown that this version of the argument is mistaken I will then turn to three other variants of this argument: the Argument from Economic Oppression, the Argument from Economic Force, and the Argument from Inculcated Desires. I will show that each of these antimarket arguments is mistaken.

INITIAL CAVEATS

Prior to addressing the Argument from Economic Coercion and its cognates, some initial caveats are in order. First, I will address only the issue of whether or not markets in human kidneys should be allowed. Kidneys are both paired and nonrenewable, and so fall somewhere between hearts and whole livers on one hand, and renewable or plentiful human biological materials such as blood, plasma, semen, and ova on the other. Second, I will focus on defending a "current" market in human kidneys; that is, one in which a person can sell a kidney for removal while she is still alive. This is because this is the type of market that is typically the target of those who offer antimarket arguments based on their alleged coerciveness. Third, I will understand a person to be autonomous with respect to her actions if it is she, and not another agent, who is directing those actions. This is an account of "autonomy" that is acceptable to autonomy theorists of all stripes.[8] Finally, I will address only the question of whether markets should be allowed to procure transplantable human organs, separating this from the question of whether markets should also be used to distribute the organs thus procured.

THE ARGUMENT FROM ECONOMIC COERCION

In its canonical form the Argument from Economic Coercion is simple, elegant, and persuasive. Its proponents begin by noting that the only persons who are likely to sell their kidneys would be the desperate poor—and that they would only do so grudgingly. As such, they claim, allowing markets for kidneys would enable the economic desperation of the poor to *coerce* them into selling their kidneys. (Note that the claim is not that those who offer the poor the option of selling their kidneys would coerce them into doing so, but that by making this offer they would enable their situation to do so.) The proponents of this argument then note that if a person is coerced into performing a certain act then she will suffer from a diminution in her autonomy with respect to it. Thus, since allowing markets in human kidneys enables coercion to take place, and since coercion is inimical to autonomy, respect for autonomy should support the continued prohibition of such markets.[9]

Despite its simplicity, elegance, and persuasiveness, the Argument from Economic Coercion is fundamentally flawed, for its proponents misunderstand the nature of the relationship between autonomy and coercion. To see this, let us consider a classic case in which a person's autonomy is compromised by her being coerced into performing an action: a person is coerced by a highwayman into handing over her money to save her life. In this case we might be beset by two conflicting intuitions. On one hand, we might think that, despite the highwayman's threats, the person who was subject to coercion suffered from no diminution in her autonomy. After all, we might think, she chose to hand over her wallet; she could have tried to resist or else simply ignored his demands. On the other hand, however, we usually think that a person who performed an action only because she was threatened with a penalty if she did not do so is a paradigm case of someone whose autonomy has been compromised. We can, however, reconcile these apparently conflicting intuitions by distinguishing between a person's autonomy with respect to her choices, and a person's autonomy with respect to her actions. The person who was coerced by the highwayman seems to have retained her autonomy with respect to her choices. After all, it is she, and not he, who decides how she is to respond to her threat. (This accords with our first intuition, above, that the highwayman's victim suffers from no diminution in her autonomy as a result of being subject to coercion; she suffers from no diminution in her autonomy *with respect to her choices*.) However, in responding to his threat she decided to perform the action that he commanded her to do. Moreover, in so doing she would not be satisfying a desire merely to hand over her wallet to avoid being killed; she would be satisfying an open-ended desire to perform (within certain parameters) *whatever actions the highwayman would require of her* to save her life. As such, the person who was coerced by the highwayman would cede control of her actions (within certain parameters) to him. Since it would thus be he, and not she, who was controlling her actions, she would suffer from a diminution in her autonomy with respect to them to the extent that this was so. (This accords with our second intuition, above, that the highwayman's victim did suffer from a diminution in her autonomy as a result of being subject to coercion; she suffered from a diminution in her autonomy *with respect to her actions*.) A person who is successfully coerced into performing an action will thus suffer from a diminution in her autonomy with respect to it, to the extent that her performance of it is directed by the other agent to whom she has ceded control.

With this account of the relationship between autonomy and coercion in hand, it is clear why the antimarket Argument from Economic Coercion fails. The proponents of this argument hold that a person will be coerced by her economic situation into selling a kidney. However, as the above account of how subjecting a person to coercion compromises her autonomy makes clear, a person who is coerced into performing certain actions will suffer from a diminution in her autonomy with respect to them as a result of ceding control over the acts that she performs to her coercer. As such, a necessary condition for a person to suffer from a diminution in her autonomy as a result of being subject to coercion is that she be coerced *by an agent to whom she can cede control*. Thus, since a person's economic situation is not something to which she can cede control—it is not something that can determine her actions for her—a person cannot be coerced by the economic situation in which she finds herself. The Argument from Economic Coercion thus fails.

THE ARGUMENTS FROM ECONOMIC OPPRESSION
AND FROM ECONOMIC FORCE

Although the canonical form of the Argument from Economic Coercion is mistaken, there are variants of it that are unaffected by the above argument. Accepting that a person's economic situation cannot itself coerce, the defenders of this form of antimarket argument have developed alternative criticisms of the view that markets in transplantable human kidneys should be allowed. The proponents of one of these alternative arguments, which could be termed the Argument from Economic Oppression, hold that insofar as the dire economic circumstances of potential vendors are deliberately sustained by others with the intention of forcing them to sell their kidneys, the potential vendors *are* subject to the control of other agents. As such, the proponents of this argument claim, to the extent that this is so, the potential vendors *do* suffer from a diminution in their autonomy with respect to their vending actions. Thus, they conclude, respect for autonomy requires that markets in human kidneys continue to be prohibited.[10] By contrast, the proponents of what might be termed the Argument from Economic Force concede that the class of potential kidney vendors are *not* subject to the control of others, and so are not subject to coercion. However, they claim that the mere fact that such persons are not subject to coercion does not mean that their autonomy with respect to their vending actions is not compromised. This is because, they argue, persons who sell their kidneys, while not *coerced* into doing so by others, are still *forced* into selling out of economic necessity. Thus, since a person's being forced into performing an action compromises her autonomy with respect to it, and since allowing markets for human transplant kidneys would enable persons to be forced into selling them, they conclude that respect for autonomy should militate against allowing such markets.

Let us first consider the Argument from Economic Oppression. It is undeniable that certain groups or individuals have deliberately worked to sustain the economic impoverishment of others. The development of the sharecropping system in the American South and the current practice of making loans to illegal immigrants to wealthy nations and then charging them interest rates that ensure that they can never be free of the debt they have incurred are clear examples of this. It is thus true, as Paul Hughes notes, that "collective economic agents sometimes intend to control (and coerce) the people whose economic situations are directly affected by their decisions."[11] But does this show that the proponents of the Argument from Economic Oppression are right to hold that markets in transplantable human kidneys should be prohibited to protect the autonomy of the would-be vendors? It does not—and it does not show this *even if* it is true that the would-be vendors are subject to such economic oppression. To see why this is so, let us assume that the would-be kidney vendors are subject to economic oppression; that is, that others are intentionally sustaining their economic impoverishment with the aim of ensuring that they continue to perform actions (such as selling their kidneys) that benefit their oppressors. Insofar as the oppressors are manipulating the economic situation of those they are oppressing to manipulate them into performing these actions, and are successful in this, it is they, and not the oppressed, who are directing the actions of the oppressed, and so to the extent that this is so the oppressed suffer from a diminution of their autonomy with respect to them. However, this does not show that respect for the autonomy of the oppressed should lead one to advocate the prohibition of markets in human kidneys. Even if the would-be kidney vendors are economically oppressed in this way, their oppressors are able only to manipulate their situation to be one in which they are led to accept certain types of unappealing economic activity, such as working in sweatshops, becoming sex workers, or selling their kidneys. The oppressors of the would-be kidney vendors cannot control which type of unappealing employment they accept, or even which beneficiary of their oppression they will deal with once they have decided upon a particular type of economic activity. As such, even if the oppressed persons suffer from a diminution of their autonomy at the hands of their oppressors, they are still able to exercise their autonomy within the limits that their oppressors have imposed upon them. Thus, if steps are taken to restrict their options within these limits still further—by, for example, prohibiting them from becoming sex workers, or selling their kidneys—this will only serve to restrict still further their ability to exercise their autonomy. Hence, even though the proponents of the Argument from Economic Oppression are right to note that respect for autonomy should move one who is genuinely concerned with personal autonomy to work to eliminate the economic oppression that they rightly recognize exists, they are mistaken to think that this argument also supports the continued prohibition of markets in transplantable human kidneys. Instead, it supports allowing them.

A similar response can be offered to the Argument from Economic Force. The proponents of this argument note that in certain circumstances it is plausible to say that a person's autonomy with respect to her actions is compromised owing to the exigencies of her situation, even if she is not coerced into acting by another agent. For example, to borrow an example from Aristotle, the proponents of this argument might note that it would be plausible to say that a ship's captain who threw his cargo overboard during a storm to prevent his ship from sinking would suffer from diminished autonomy with respect to that action since he was forced by his circumstances to perform it.[12] There is, however, an important disanalogy between the circumstances of the Aristotelian sea captain and the potential kidney vendor: the latter have considerably more choices available to them than does the former. The evidence for this claim is readily available. Of the persons within the economic class of actual kidney vendors (i.e., those who could be considered to be potential kidney vendors), only a very small minority of them actually sell their kidneys. The persons within this class thus clearly have options other than kidney selling available to them—and many of them choose to pursue these other options rather than sell their kidneys. Rather than being forced into performing one particular action, as Aristotle's sea captain was, then, the members of the class of potential kidney vendors have a *range* of possible actions open to them. As such, they are able to exercise their autonomy by choosing between the possible actions that are available to them. To restrict the range of options that are available to them still further by prohibiting them from selling their kidneys would thus not enhance their ability to exercise their autonomy, but, instead, diminish it. Thus, like the proponents of the Argument from Economic Oppression, if the proponents of the Argument from Economic Force are genuinely concerned about the autonomy of potential kidney vendors they should favor allowing markets in human transplant kidneys, rather than oppose them.

THE ARGUMENT FROM INCULCATED DESIRES

The final variant of the Argument from Economic Coercion, which we might term the Argument from Inculcated Desires, has become popular with certain prominent critics of both markets and scientific advance from the radical Left. The basis of this argument is the contention that recent advances in biotechnology that have the potential to commodify things that previously could not, practically, be commodified (such as kidneys, or surrogate pregnancy) have been developed primarily to enrich the scientific community (and, presumably, their sponsors). Nancy Scheper-Hughes, for example, writes that "global capitalism and advanced biotechnology have released new medically incited 'tastes' (a New Age gourmet capitalism, perhaps) for human bodies . . . for the skin and bones, flesh and blood, tissue, marrow and genetic material of 'the other.'"[13] Scheper-Hughes goes on to claim that the shortage of transplantable organs is itself artificial, writing that "the very idea of organ 'scarcity' is what Ivan Illich would call an artificially created need, invented by transplant technicians and dangled before the eyes of an ever expanding sick, aging, and dying population."[14] Similarly, in her book *Women as Wombs: Reproductive Technologies and the Battle over Women's Freedom*, Janice Raymond criticizes "the liberal consumer movement that supports new reproductive technologies and contracts.... The new reproductive technologies represent an appropriation made by scientific experts of the female body, depoliticizing reproduction and motherhood by recasting these roles as fundamental instincts that must be satisfied."[15]

The variant of the Argument from Economic Coercion that is offered by both Scheper-Hughes and Raymond seems to be that the current demand for organs and reproductive technologies (such as commercial surrogate pregnancy or the purchase of ova) has been manufactured by those who have developed the relevant transplantation and reproductive technologies. Since this is so, the proponents of this argument continue, the desires that persons now have to secure (for example) transplant kidneys, or ova, have been artificially inculcated into them by those who have developed (and who control) the technology that could satisfy them. As it is intrinsically unpleasant to have one's desires unsatisfied, the persons into whom these desires have been inculcated are pressured by their possession of them into satisfying them. Since the persons who inculcated these desires into them did so both knowing that this would be the case and intending that they would thus be led to satisfy them, these persons have, through the inculcation of these desires into others, taken action to ensure that the persons into whom they were inculcated would perform the actions that the inculcators desired them to perform. Insofar as the possessors of these desires perform the actions that those who inculcated them into them wished them to perform, and did so as a result of the inculcation of these desires, it is the inculcators, and not the possessors of the inculcated desires, who are directing their actions. To the extent that this is so, then, the possessors of the inculcated desires would suffer from a diminution in their autonomy with respect to the actions that they would perform to satisfy these desires. Thus, if we are truly to respect autonomy, we should prohibit, rather than allow, the combination of the development of transplant and reproductive technologies together with their commercialization, for this would undermine the inculcation of these autonomy-compromising desires.[16]

This is a subtle argument (despite the rhetoric that often accompanies its presentation) and there is something that is importantly right about it—although this does not mean that its antimarket conclusion should be accepted. Before turning to outline the insight contained within this argument, however, we should first note that its proponents are mistaken both to claim that the shortage of transplantable organs is an "artificial" shortage (Scheper-Hughes) that need not concern us, and that recent improvements in organ transplantation technology and recent developments in reproductive technologies have inculcated new desires within persons. Scheper-Hughes is right to note that the shortage of transplantable organs is artificial insofar as it is a product of the development of organ transplantation, for, trivially, were organ transplantation impossible there would be no shortage of transplantable organs. (There would be zero demand, and zero supply.) However, that the shortage of transplantable organs is artificial in this way does not show, as Scheper-Hughes appears to believe, that it is not a real *medical* shortage of organs, just as the fact that vaccines are artificial does not show that a shortage of them would not pose real medical difficulties and would thus need to be remedied. The proponents of the Argument from Inculcated Desires are also mistaken to believe that the desires for transplant organs and the desire to become a mother are not real desires that persons have. It is clear, for example, that many women (and men) genuinely do desire to become parents, and that this is not a desire that has been inculcated into them by "scientific experts" in conjunction with the "liberal consumer movement." Similarly, although persons would be unlikely to desire to receive a transplant organ unless they were aware that this was possible, such desires are not inculcated into them by the scientific community. Instead, they are simply instantiations of their (quite natural) desires to restore their health, avoid their suffering, and increase their longevity.

Given that the desires to receive transplant organs, or to conceive children, are not inculcated into persons by those who have developed the technological means to satisfy them, the antimarket Argument from Inculcated Desires fails, for it depended for its success upon it being true that these desires were deliberately inculcated into persons by those who possessed the means to satisfy them—at a price. Despite this, however, it must be acknowledged that this antimarket argument does contain a kernel of truth—albeit one that seems to have been overlooked by its proponents. This kernel is that in making offers to persons (for example, to provide them with a transplant kidney at a certain price), one is acting in such a way that would, if the offers are accepted, lead the persons to whom they are made to have their autonomy with respect to their actions diminished. To see this, consider again the case of the highwayman that was discussed above. In that case it was argued that the highwayman's coercion of his victim diminished her autonomy with respect to her actions insofar as she decided to cede control over them to him. Similarly, a person who is seeking a particular good or service (such as a transplant kidney) would, like the highwayman's victim, be willing to perform any action within certain parameters to receive it. (The parameters would be more or less broad depending on how great the person's desire for the good or service in question was.) Like the victim of the highwayman, then, the seeker of a good or a service would be willing to cede control over her actions to the offerer of such goods or services; she would be willing to have her actions directed by him to secure the good in question. Thus, when a person agrees to (for example) a "transplant tourism" package to secure a transplant kidney, she has acted upon her desire to cede a certain degree of control over her actions (e.g., to write out a check for an amount that he specifies) to secure the good that she desires.[17]

Given this, if we hold autonomy to be valuable, should we advocate for the prohibition of markets in human kidneys on the basis that offering persons such kidneys would, if the offer was accepted, lead to the compromise of their autonomy with respect to the actions that they performed to secure it? We should not—for two reasons. If we were to prohibit markets in human kidneys on this basis, we would need to prohibit *all* situations in which offers are made and accepted. And this result that is clearly a reductio ad absurdum of any attempt to use the fact that offers, like threats, can compromise a person's autonomy to oppose a kidney market. Drawing on this, we should also recognize that even though offers might lead to a person's autonomy being compromised, this does not in itself give us reason to restrict them, for her acceptance of such offers might confer benefits upon her that outweigh the compromise of her autonomy. Indeed, if we believe that autonomy is primarily of instrumental value insofar as it enables persons to direct their own actions in an effort to secure their own well-being, we should expect that a person's autonomy would be commensurable with her well-being in this way. As such, then, it should come as no surprise that allowing a person to give up some of her autonomy to secure something that she considers to be more valuable to her is a trade-off that even a respecter of autonomy should allow.

CONCLUSION

From the above discussion it is clear that none of the extant variants of the Argument from Economic Coercion are successful in showing that markets in human transplant kidneys should be prohibited. Moreover, since prohibiting such markets would be to coerce persons into not buying and selling kidneys, it appears that if we are truly concerned with personal autonomy (and even if we believe it only to have primarily instrumental value), we should allow kidney markets, not prohibit them.[18]

NOTES

1. US Department of Health and Human Services, Donate Life, http://www.organdonor.gov/ (accessed May 1, 2006).

2. Nancy Scheper-Hughes, "Commodity Fetishism in Organs Trafficking," *Body & Society* 7 (2001): 45–50.

3. See, for example, John B. Dossetor and V. Manickavel, "Commercialization: The Buying and Selling of Kidneys," in *Ethical Problems in Dialysis and Transplantation*, ed. C. M. Kjellstrand and J. B. Dossetor (Dordrecht: Kluwer Academic Publishers, 1992), p. 71.

4. See, for example, Janet Raymond, *Women as Wombs: Reproductive Technologies and the Battle over Women's Freedom* (New York: Harper San Francisco, 1994).

5. Bob Brecher, "The Kidney Trade, or, the Customer Is Always Wrong," *Journal of Medical Ethics* 16 (1990): 120–23.

6. See, for example, G. M. Abouna et al., "The Negative Impact of Paid Organ Donation," in *Organ Replacement Therapy: Ethics, Justice, Commerce*, ed. W. Land and J. B. Dossetor (New York: Springer-Verlag, 1991): 164–72.

7. See, for example, Dossetor and Manickavel, "Commercialization," p. 63.

8. For an outline of recent accounts of personal autonomy, see James Stacey Taylor, introduction, in *Personal Autonomy: New Essays*, ed. James Stacey Taylor (Cambridge: Cambridge University Press, 2005), pp. 1–29.

9. The canonical form of the Argument from Economic Coercion—and a more elaborate version of the following response to it—are outlined in James Stacey Taylor, *Stakes and Kidneys: Why Markets in Human Body Parts Are Morally Imperative* (Aldershot, UK: Ashgate 2005), chapter 3.

10. Examples of this argument have been offered by Paul Hughes, "A Review of James Stacey Taylor, *Stakes and Kidneys: Why Markets in Human Body Parts Are Morally Imperative*," *American Journal of Bioethics* 6 (2006): p. 94; and T. L. Zutlevics, "Markets and the Needy: Organ Sales or Aid?" *Journal of Applied Philosophy* 18 (2001): 297–302.

11. Hughes, "A Review," p. 94.

12. Aristotle, *Nicomachean Ethics*, trans. W. D. Ross (Oxford: Clarendon Press, 1908), bk. III, chap. 1.

13. Scheper-Hughes, "Commodity Fetishism," p. 54.

14. Nancy Scheper-Hughes, "The End of the Body," in *Taking Sides: Clashing Views on Controversial Economic Issues*, ed. Thomas R. Swartz and Frank J. Bonello (McGraw-Hill, 2003), p. 111.

15. Raymond, *Women as Wombs*, pp. xii, xix. Quoted by Veronique Campion-Vincent, *Organ Theft Legends* (Jackson: University Press of Mississippi, 2005), p. 101.

16. Note that as it is reconstructed here, the proponents of this argument need not be committed to the stronger conclusion that transplant and reproductive technologies should be prohibited outright. This is because one might hold that if technological development occurs *absent* its commercialization, then the developers of this tech-

nology would *not* be developing it with the intention that others desire it, and thus would not be developing it with the intention of controlling which actions these others would perform in order to gain access to it (e.g., pay for it). Thus, the proponents of this argument are not necessarily opposed to advances within biomedical technology, but only to these advances coupled with the intention to control the actions of others.

17. That persons cede control over their actions in this way is typically masked when they accept offers since the actions that they must perform are typically specified in advance (e.g., on price tags) and they can then choose whether or not to perform them. But this need not be the case. Imagine, for example, a store which has a pricing policy of requiring its customers to perform the actions that its managers request to secure the goods they desire. Such a store would still be the functional equivalent of a more conventional store with set prices with respect to the effects that its offers would have on its customers' autonomy, but its offers would be clearly akin (at least with respect to its effects on its customers' autonomy) to the threats made by the high-wayman.

18. An earlier version of this paper was presented at the conference "Is There a Global Bioethics?" in New York City that was organized by the IHEU-Appignani Center for Bioethics. I thank my audience on that occasion for their stimulating comments, and Ana Lita for encouraging me to develop this paper further.

14

SEX, MEDICINE, AND ETHICS
Some Quandaries

VERN L. BULLOUGH

M edicine traditionally has been regarded as both an art and a science. Although in the past it has been more art than science, it increasingly has relied upon science. As it relies more on science, it has had to discard many traditional ideas, and in the process ethical answers to medical issues in the past also have to be discarded or reinterpreted. This has to be a continuing ongoing process because science itself is continually being modified as new data emerge. It is simple to say that the basis of medical ethics should be to do no harm, but the new medical ethics demands that patients also be involved in the decision making, and what constitutes harm becomes ever more difficult to determine. I would like to illustrate this from some examples in my own research on sex and gender issues as well as on contraception.

A good place to start is with the penis of the newborn boy. Should he or should he not be circumcised? In the United States circumcision became widely adopted in the late nineteenth and early twentieth centuries. Though there are obviously religious reasons for circumcision in Judaism and Islam, it was Saint Paul's message that non-Jewish converts to Christianity did not have to be circumcised, which had been the tradition in much of the Christian past. In light of this statement, how did so many Americans (there were almost no circumcisions in the European countries) come to be circumcised in the twen-

Originally published as "Religion, Sex and Science: Some Historical Quandaries," *Journal of Sex Education and Therapy* 26, no. 4 (2001): 254–59.

tieth century? Several reasons have been advanced but the dominant one was the almost hysterical fear that Americans of the late nineteenth century had about the dangers of masturbation. Masturbation was believed to lead to insanity and by its weakening of the body make diseases such as pneumonia, tuberculosis, and dozens of others more likely. This belief was widespread and was only challenged by the discovery of bacteria as a causal factor in disease. Obviously since it had so many dangerous consequences, masturbation was a habit that had to be stopped and ways to do so were many and varied, including girdles to prevent children from touching their genitals. It was far better, however, to adopt preventive measures and a key element in this campaign was circumcision of young male infants. The argument went that the necessity for the mother to pull back the foreskin in order to cleanse the penis led to an early implantation in the infant of the sensuousness of his organ and encouraged him to play more with his penis than he would if there was no foreskin and the crown was less sensitive. The solution was to circumcise male infants, a practice advocated by a wide variety of authorities. Even though the association of masturbation and disease was gradually undermined at the beginning of the twentieth century, circumcision had already been institutionalized in American life. A custom, once started, is difficult to change and the medical community was slow to speak out against circumcision. Many simply rationalized that it was not harmful and was not particularly traumatic (debatable), and they were certainly happy to pick up a few extra dollars (later much more) for doing the operation. It was not until the 1950s that it began to be argued, that the male orgasm was more intense in the uncircumcised male than in the circumcised, that challenges began to be raised. (By the way, this argument is a difficult if not impossible one to answer.) In the meantime, other reasons were put forward to justify it. Some argued that infant circumcision prevented phimosis, a condition making urination painful and, in the adult, intercourse somewhat difficult since the tightness makes it difficult to be drawn back. Such a condition is easily fixed by minor surgery and is comparatively rare. The ethical question, however, is does this statistically unusual condition justify circumcising all males? There is a similar condition in the female, an adhering clitoris (*labial phimosis*), but this is easily correctable as an adult and no one is willing to remove the clitoris or labia in the girl child. The American Pediatric Association finally went on record opposing circumcision several decades ago, but later modified the statement because of strong opposition from some parents. The result has been a decision to leave it as an option for parents rather than trying to eliminate it. The support of many of those advocating continued circumcision was not for any medical reason, but because some thought the circumcised penis looked better. Others did not want their child's penis to look different than that of the father, while still others feared that circumcision was so much the norm that their uncircumcised child might receive unwelcome attention from his peer group. Should this decision be made by the parents or should the child himself or the adult male be left to decide? This leaves it a very real ethical problem for the pediatrician since if the decision is to be left to the parents, he/she needs to explain all the options and possible results before proceeding. Is this enough or should he make strong recommendations to not have their boy child circumcised?

Another issue with strong ethical implications is how to deal with infants who have ambiguous genitalia. In the past, probably most were classified as males. Once chromosome tests could be given after 1956 there was often an attempt to do surgery to the infant to conform to chromosomal sex, but there is more to sexual identity than chromosomes. Much of these attempts in the 1960s to do radical interventionist surgery come out of the research of John Money, one of the founders of modern gender study. He felt that infants under two (sometimes he said three) were very pliable on gender identity, and physicians should make strong early efforts for a child's sex to be identified as either male or female so the necessary adjustment to gender behavior could take place as early as possible. The result was early and often drastic surgery on children with ambiguous genitalia. As indicated, however, we have increasingly found that there are more biological factors involved in intersex infants than chromosomes, and many of these other factors might have programmed the child's development in different ways, and early surgical intervention made it much more difficult to intervene later when sexual identity was more established. Moreover, Money's ideas initially were based on his study of hermaphrodites and there were many variables that he could not easily assess. What he wanted was to have a real-life case, which he found in a person known in the literature as John-Joan. This case involved two identical twins, who because they seemingly had some pain when they urinated (they had phimosis), their parents, on the advice of their physician, sent the boys to be circumcised at about seven months. The circumcision was to be done by a cautery gun to burn off the foreskin. Unfortunately, as the first twin was being circumcised, there was a short in the gun, which resulted in burning the boy's penis to a crisp. The parents were beside themselves and for a year or so hunted for a solution for the boy without a penis. Physicians told them that there was little that could be done until puberty and even then the result would not lead to a realistic penis. Some advised raising the child as a girl. The parents sought out Money for advice, and after consulting with him, they decided to raise the child as a girl.

The boy's testicles were removed and just before he was two he was given a girl's name and was raised as one. The conversion ultimately proved unsuccessful and in his teens he resumed male clothes and roles even though he lacked penis and testicles. Unfortunately, the failed results were not conveyed to the public until more than twenty years later. Even before the failed results were conveyed to the public, there was considerable debate in the sex community about radical intervention in cases of children with ambiguous genitalia. Leading the demands for a change in practice was the Intersex Society, many of whose members had been arbitrarily changed when they were young children and were in full-scale rebellion about what medicine had done to them. The society argued, that except for minor corrective surgery, no major surgery should be performed until the child was able to decide. As the increasing number of negative results of early sexual surgery finally reached the public and as agitation increased, the failure of the John-Joan case finally was made public. A full-scale reconsideration of procedures began. For the most part, radical surgery has been less and less frequently performed. This is another of the medical dilemmas in which ethical issues remain unclear. The problem is that parents of intersex children themselves are in a quandary. Most parents are unprepared for the answer we don't know when someone asked them whether their baby is a boy or a girl. Children themselves are often taunted by other children where there is ambiguity. What should the ethical position be? I am not certain. I would certainly advise minor corrective surgery, if possible, but radical surgery I guess has to depend on the ability of the parents to deal with ambiguity. Part of the difficulty in the John-Joan case is that the parents could not really cope with any of the solutions they were offered. I am not certain that I could have coped any better. The intersexed children just emphasize the quandary facing ethical decisions.

Let me give you an even more complicated one. The case of transsexual surgery. The possibility of such surgery emphasizes just what modern medicine can do and how new problems arise. Such surgery is dependent on developments in the last decades of the nineteenth century, which grew out of the use of anesthesia and the establishment of aseptic techniques. Surgery became a major part of medical intervention. As new challenges appeared, surgeons attempted to find a surgical solution. Corrective surgery for sexual ambiguity began and there were in fact even some sex changes done in Germany in the 1920s and 1930s on an experimental basis by Magnus Hirschfeld. It is not always clear, however, whether the subjects were hermaphrodites or not. Though removal of testes and penis has a long history, the result was eunuchs, not sex changes. Women had also had ovariectomies, hysterectomies, as well as breast removal for various reasons, but this did not make them men. The major factor in making such changes theoretically possible was the discovery of hormones and the ability to manufacture them. These developments had occurred by the 1950s. In the case of men wanting to change sex, there was still another development: effective electrolysis for hair removal, which also became available about the same time.

Theoretically, medicine then by the end of the 1940s could help someone alter their sex, but the question was, should they do it? The issue came to public attention with the Christine Jorgensen case in 1952, when a Danish endocrinologist, Christian Hamburger, recommended surgical removal of Jorgensen's penis and testicles and massive hormone therapy. Jorgensen became a sensation when her story was released and the Hearst papers, for example, ran her story in four different weekend issues of their weekly magazine. Hamburger was besieged by applicants who he generally turned away, although he had to take one, who, after being turned down, cut off his own penis and testicles in a hotel room nearby. Still, just because someone wants some optional surgery, should it be given? It is a debate that continues in the medical profession. At first some university centers established centers to consider such surgery with teams of psychiatrists, surgeons, endocrinologists, psychologists, and others, and though it was clear that such changes could be done, most universities soon closed their programs, and individual entrepreneurial surgeons came to dominate the field, at least in the United States. Psychiatric opinion remains divided with some arguing that the surgery is only contributing to the patient's psychopathology and not curing it. The result in the United States is that a handful of surgeons perform the operations on a fairly large number of patients. The leading American surgeon in the twentieth century was Stanley Biber, who, before his semiretirement in 2000 from his practice in Trinidad, Colorado, had operated on approximately ten thousand patients. On the whole those who went through sexual transformation seem content with their change in life, while a small minority do not.

What are the ethical problems involved? Should the patient's desire to change sex be fulfilled? In spite of public acceptance of sex change, there is a real division in the medical community. Some feel that by doing such surgery, physicians are contributing to imprisoning would-be transsexuals in their crazy dream and closing the path of wisdom to them. What they need, it is argued, is psychotherapy and not surgery (Chiland 2002, 165) Where should the ethicist stand on such issues? Chiland, for example, says that the transsexual phenomenon "is surely a product of our technology-based individualistic culture, a token of its contradictions, and disease of our culture" (Chiland 2003, 2). She feels that despite the fact that medical developments offer "the possibility of sex conversion does not impel transsexuals to make their request" and in fact "imprison them in their crazy dream and closes the path of wisdom to them" (Chiland 2002, 165).

But if we can justify such surgery, where do we stop? In the sex field there are a lot of psychopathologies that demand surgical intervention. For example, there is a paraphilia called apotemnophilia, in which the person becomes fix-ated on carrying out a self-contrived amputation or obtaining one in a hospital. Because someone wants a leg or arm amputated, should we do it? This is a real fixation and not a made-up one. In the days when transsexual surgery was in its beginning stage, there was a problem of getting surgeons. Many who oper-ated on the borderline of medicine entered the field including a certain John Leonard Brown who, unfortunately, I helped persuade to engage in transsexual surgery. It soon appeared that he would operate on anyone who had money for anything, no questions asked. For those who did not have money for trans-sexual surgery, he offered them a discount for every patient they recruited, and if they recruited enough paying customers, he would do it free. Unfortunately, he was not a particularly good surgeon, and when hospitals barred him from access to their surgical units he began operating anywhere, including at least one time on a kitchen table under very unsanitary conditions. At least once when an anesthetist was not available, he alleged operated without giving it. He lost his license to practice in California, and I found he had lost it earlier in Hawaii and Alaska. Still he continued to operate on his ever-willing patients, eventually setting up in Tijuana, Mexico. In 1998, he operated on a seventy-nine-year-old man who had hired him to amputate his leg to satisfy a sexual fetish. The patient died and Brown was convicted of murder and sent to jail. By his own count he had performed six hundred transsexual surgeries and many other kinds of volunteer surgery such as his leg amputation (Ciotti 2000). Can we distinguish between transsexualism and amputation of other limbs? This is an ethical dilemma. I have been in favor of transsexual surgery, but I have opposed optional surgery for those pathologies that involve amputation of other limbs. Is this consistent? Can I parse my ethical dilemma?

In fact, wherever one turns in the sex-related medical area, one faces new ethical dilemmas. Birth control is an especially slippery slope. Often simply doing a tubal ligation or inserting an IUD, prescribing a birth control pill, or applying a patch, involves an ethical decision. Some Catholic hospital chains have taken over previously secular hospitals and have ordered physicians not to prescribe birth control pills. This leaves a physician in a tremendous dilemma. Does he leave the particular group and abandon his patients or does he act surreptitiously and on the side, or does he just refer them to a Planned Parenthood clinic or does he simply try to ignore what is going on? Increasingly we are past the age when an individual physician treated an individual patient. Instead we have a bureaucracy that be dealt with which raises all kinds of ethical issues which go beyond the individual physician.

One area where medical ethics has changed is sterilization. In the past, in many states, including California, sterilization was done regularly on poverty patients and on mentally deficient or mentally disabled patients, almost always without the consent of the patient. Much of this was done in the name of Eugenics and many states, including California, had laws encouraging sterilization. The governor of California in 2001 issued a public apology for these sterilizations done in the name of Eugenics, a procedure that many of our humanist pioneers advocated.

I observed what I felt was basically an unethical stance in China where, when I was visiting back in the 1980s, female sterilization was done by chemically scarring of the fallopian tube. Women who underwent such sterilizations after having had one child were promised all kinds of rewards including guaranteed college admission to their first child and significant (for China) monetary reimbursement. The procedure was done in an outpatient setting and involved almost an assembly line procure taking five minutes or so with one patient being prepared for the procedure, a second undergoing the procedure on one fallopian tube, and a third on the other fallopian tube. It entailed opening the vaginal opening with a speculum and then inserting a catheter through the cervix into each fallopian tube duct and injecting an acid formulator. The acid would then result in severe scarring, thereby blocking the tube. The procedure was done without anesthetic since that would have involved time-consuming procedures. Physicians assured me it was painless, but watching the patients afterwards as they clutched their stomachs and bent over in pain indicated to me that this was not quite true. Some seemed to be in shock. I wrote up my experience in an American medical journal and also talked about it to others, indicating my belief that some anesthetic should be used. Surprisingly, or perhaps not so surprisingly, many of the people felt that the goal of curtailing population growth in China should overcome my concern for a woman who only had a comparatively brief period of pain. They believed that the dangers of overpopulation were so great that even criticism such as mine would lead to a curtailment of sterilization in China. Unfortunately, many of those who criticized me were nonbelievers, but hopefully not humanists.

Humanists have long been concerned with population growth and believe it poses a major threat to the survival of humanity. This is a legitimate concern and it is tied into a number of other issues that our freethought forebears in the minds of the current generation did not handle very well. There are no simple answers. Do we want someone who is barely able to take care of themselves and whose intelligence is that of a six- or eight-year-old to have a child? Or to make someone else pregnant? With today's injectables and implants, there are other options to sterilization, but how much say should the patient have in making such a decision? Unfortunately also, the profit motive for some of the drug companies is heavily involved and this complicates the whole question of ethical answers. For example, one of the major scandals took place in the manufacture of IUDs. Individuals and compacts, impressed by the success of the Lippes loop in the early 1960s, rushed to find a similar bonanza. The A. H. Robins Company, for example, bought the rights to the Dalkon shield, developed by a physician, Hugh Davis, and his business associates. They sold it to an eager company without doing any real testing although they claimed to have done so. It was not tested by Robins and there was no federal law at the time requiring such tests. It was made of the same material as the Lippes loop but it had several sharp pointed edges to distinguish it from its rival. Unfortunately these edges tended to increase the dangers of infection. By 1976 some seventeen deaths had been attributed to it, yet the company ignored the complaints and discounted the deaths until 1980 when it finally advised physicians using it to remove it. The subsequent lawsuits bankrupted the Robins Company, but it also raised the liability rate for use of IUDs, so much so that the Lippes loop, a cheap and inexpensive contraceptive, was forced to withdraw from the American market. The IUD, while used in many other countries, was unavailable for nearly twenty years. In the 1990s new forms, such as the copper IUD, have since become available on the American market. They are probably the most effective of all contraceptives but are still not widely used because of the Robins fiasco.

But profit itself is not necessarily enough if a company decides for various reasons to remove a fairly effective method of birth control from the market. A good example is what happened to the polyurethane sponge impregnated with a spermicide, 250 million of which under the name of "Today," were sold between 1983–95. It was not as effective as the IUD but it had a long history going back at least to biblical times and its commercial form, which included a spermicide, was widely used by younger women with an effective rate equivalent to that of the diaphragm. The safety and effectiveness of the sponge was certified by the FDA and its sale would indicate it was popular with large groups of women. Nonetheless, when the company that manufactured it, now called Wyeth, found it needed to upgrade the New Jersey factory where it was made, it decided it would be better business practice to simply quit manufacturing it and concentrate on the pill, which had a greater profit margin and which they also made. I hold this was a violation of ethics. The panic in some women which the withdrawal caused was immortalized in a 1995 episode of the television series *Seinfeld*, where Elaine, hearing of the decision to stop its manufacture, ran around New York seeking to find a supply of sponges, the contraceptive method she favored. As of this writing, however, a start-up company, Allendal Pharmaceuticals, was ultimately able to purchase the rights from Wyeth and has put them on the market again. Like the condom, the sponge does not require a prescription, an important issue for many would-be users since all the other barrier methods such as the cap or diaphragm require a physician's prescription.

Ethical issues on the behalf of businesses were also involved when the use of oral contraceptives or the "pill" was approved by the FDA in 1960. They were an instant moneymaker. One militant feminist, hostile to the drug industry, described the pill as giving the manufacturer a guaranteed customer for thirty or forty years of her life for preventing a disease (pregnancy), which could not be cured and which always demanded a replenishment with only a few interruptions for a planned pregnancy. The early pill, however, had severe drawbacks, which had not been anticipated, and a very receptive public was loath to discuss. The manufacturer, which had some inkling or problems, did not share them with the public at large. The problem was that the first pill, Enovid, included 10mg of progestin and 150 micrograms of estrogen, and had considerable side effects for many women. These were originally downplayed by the manufacturer and ignored by most segments of the medical community until militant feminists staged demonstrations against the manufacturer beginning in the late 1960s. Only then was the pill reformulated, which now are either low progestin pills (without estrogen) or combination pills, which include small mcg of estrogen.

Money issues also complicated the marketing of the morning-after pill. The company which held the patents to Mifepristone or RU 486, an abortifacient developed in France, fearful of a boycott of its other drug products by anti abortionists, abandoned its potential market in the United States. A special company had to be set up by devoted advocates to manufacture the pill and do the necessary tests for FDA approval, a procedure that withheld the pill from the market for many years. Even more ethically ambiguous was the decision of the by now numerous manufacturers of the pill to withhold its possible use as a morning after pill. Though it became widely known through the underground that most of the standard pills could be used as emergency contraceptives by tripling or quadrupling their dose after unprotected intercourse, it took a long time for this information to finally become more widely known. Was keeping it a secret ethical?

Ethical issues often become distorted in cases of medical controversy. An interesting example is another drug, usually called misoprostol, a prostaglandin pill to make sure the accumulated material involved in afterbirth is expelled by the uterus. Marketed as Cytotec, it has been approved as a treatment for gastric ulcers, and so worried was the manufacturer, Searle, that the drug might be associated with abortion that they issued a national letter to health providers stating that Cytotec was not approved for the inducing of labor or abortion even though they knew it was being widely used by obstetricians. In a sense Searle was technically correct, the drug had not been approved for inducement of labor but only because Searle had not asked for such approval. Is this ethical? The fear of a backlash clouds ethical responsibility wherever potential gain or loss of profits is involved.

If we move directly into the abortion area, the bioethical issues are compounded, at least at the present time, by the US government giving out misinformation. For example, the Centers for Disease Control, under pressure from the Bush administration, included a statement that abortion might be a causal factor in cervical cancer. This in spite of the fact that only one lone paper found a possibility that it might be a causal factor, something that more than two hundred other research papers denied. In fact, the one paper which did so had been seriously undermined by subsequent follow-up studies. Should deliberately false propaganda be a bioethical issue? I think it should. So should harmful actions by government. The US government, for example, has cut down on US monetary support of family planning in those states where abortion remains a viable option. Should the personal beliefs of a powerful official undermine basic human needs in a country or in a world that disagrees with his opinion?

Part of the difficulty is that scientific advances have made medicine so complex that literal bureaucracy of healers is necessary and if the illustrations I have given you from the sex field are any indication, attempting to arrive at what is an ethical decision is no easy matter. There are just too many gray areas and only by holding conferences such as this can we begin to understand just how complicated making an ethical decision is in today's world of wonderful medical advances.

REFERENCES

Bullough, Vern L. *Encyclopedia of Birth Control.* Santa Barbara, CA: ABC Clio, 2000.
———. "Masturbation: An Historical Overview." *Journal of Psychology and Human Sexuality* 13, nos. 2–3 (2002).
———. *Science in the Bedroom: A History of Sex Research.* New York: Basic Books, 1994.

Bullough, Vern L., and Bonnie Bullough. *Contraception: A Guide to Birth Control Methods*. Amherst, NY: Prometheus Books, 1997.

Ciotti, P. "Organ Grinder." *San Francisco Metropolitan*, March 2, 2000.

Hamburger, C., G. K. Stiriup, and E. Dahl-Iversen. "Transvestism, Hormonal, Psychiatric, and Surgical Treatment." *Journal of the American Medical Association* 152 (May 30, 1953): 391–96.

Money, John. *Love Maps*. Amherst, NY: Prometheus Books, 1986.

Money, John, and A. A. Ehrhardt. *Man, Woman, Boy, and Girl*. Baltimore: Johns Hopkins University Press, 1972.

15

FROM HUMAN-RACISM
TO PERSONHOOD
Humanism after Human Nature

JAMES HUGHES

Conflicts over who is and who is not a living human person are central to many of the conflicts in the US "culture wars." The religious right argues that fetuses and the brain dead have human dignity (souls) and a right to life. The Great Ape Project argues for a ban on experimentation on chimpanzees and gorillas on the grounds that they are persons with fundamental "human" rights. Technology critics like Langdon Winner (2002), Francis Fukuyama (2002), and Bill McKibben (2004) warn that humanity is threatened by an emergent posthumanity, while the National Science Foundation encourages the cross-fertilization of nanotechnology, biotechnology, and the information and cognitive sciences (NBIC) toward the goal of "improving human performance."

All these issues are connected as part of a broad political struggle between advocates and opponents of two basic humanist propositions. First, humanists believe that what is of value in human life is our capacity for thought, feeling, and conscience, our "personhood," and not our biological characteristics like our genders, race, or genomes. Second, humanists believe we should be free from superstitious taboos and religious authority in our free use of reason and science, that we should be able to freely use human powers to reach our fullest potentials. In previous eras the struggle over these propositions emancipated

Adapted and modified from "From Human-Racism to Personhood: Humanism after Human Nature," *Free Inquiry* 24, no. 4 (June/July 2004): 36–37.

slaves and gave women suffrage. The antihumanists insisted that women and Africans were biologically incapable of equality with white men, while the humanists insisted that women and Africans had the same capacities for thought and feeling, and therefore the same right to citizenship.

In the emerging biopolitics of the twenty-first century, the struggle will be to determine which kinds of life have rights and citizenship. For "human-racists" fetuses and the brain dead are vulnerable human beings facing slaughter. Champions of personhood see fetuses and the brain dead as pre- and postpersons, lives whose interests are trumped by the interests of existing persons, such as women wanting to control their bodies, the disabled and sick looking for therapies from stem cells, and families waiting to bury their dead. Advocates of personhood take seriously the claims of great apes and cetaceans to some rough moral parity with humanity on the basis of their cognitive complexity, while human-racists reject rights for nonhumans out of hand.

In this essay I will argue what may seem counterintuitive to some humanists: that humanism leads to the position that "humanness" or "human nature" is morally irrelevant, and that a transhuman respect for personhood should be central instead. Not only is the idea of a unitary human nature a meaningless concept, it is a product of the imperfect human cognition that generates the concepts of "soul" and "God." But as it is deployed today in biopolitical debates "human nature" is often a morally offensive concept whose purpose is to divide *Homo sapiens* from our evolutionary origins, our ape cousins, and our future.

UNHELPFUL ONTOLOGICAL CONCRETENESS IN HUMAN COGNITION

Central to the humanist tradition is a critical approach to the abstract concepts without empirical referents. Yet, ironically, it is precisely the capacity to posit such abstract concepts, such as spirits in the human body, in animals and in things, which distinguishes *Homo sapiens* from other species. As Dennett has argued, the concept of a human "soul" was a natural extension of our self-awareness, of our illusion of a unitary and continuous self-identity (Dennett 1992; Boyer 2001). This attribution of an abstract ontology to things has its uses, but these vitalist illusions can also trap us into positing identities that do not exist, of making inaccurate predictions, and persisting with dysfunctional and limiting beliefs.

Take for instance Leon Kass's grounding of his opposition to human enhancement in the existence of Platonic ideal types, including a unitary and inviolate human nature:

(Creatures) have their given species-specified natures: they are each and all of a given sort. Cockroaches and humans are equally bestowed but differently natured. To turn a man into a cockroach . . . would be dehumanizing. To try to turn a man into more than a man might be so as well. . . . We need a particular regard and respect for the special gift that is our own given nature. (Kass 2003)

Without ever clearly defining what this human nature is, Kass deploys the concept to both separate us from our continuity with other animals, and bar any improvement in our condition. When exactly does a man's evolution into cockroach violate his human nature? When does man become dehumanized in becoming more than human?

Few proponents of a distinctive and unitary human nature or soul attempt to answer these questions because they do not have a clear definition of human nature to begin with. They can't specify when hominids got human nature or a soul, or which specific transhuman modifications would rob us of this vitalist essence. They can't agree which aspects of the mind and behavior are part of the soul or human nature, and which are unnatural, or how parts of human nature might also be shared by other animals. Only after we have deconstructed their illusory theory of a human nature, can we begin a serious discussion of the qualities of the human condition worth preserving.

NO CLEAR DEFINITION

One clear problem with the idea of human nature is that, despite thousands of years of investigation, and intimate access to the subject of investigation, there is no agreement about what human nature is. Are we innately good, compassionate, altruistic, or evil, sinful, and selfish? Is moral striving a liberation of our true human nature from sinful influences or capitalism, or is moral behavior a persistent struggle of the good in human nature against its dark side? Or are we a blank slate, morally and behaviorally, or inscribed with all our personality traits, and even beliefs, at birth? Some writers identify human nature with the apparently distinctive human capacities for cognition, language, tool use, and the creation of meaning and categories, while others include physiology that we share with other species, such as mortality, limbically mediated emotions, and our genetic predispositions for altruism and aggression.

Cognitive neuroscience, ethology, and evolutionary psychology are attempting to specify the exact structure and epidemiology of human cognitive traits, and clarify which capacities and impulses are genetically innate and which are plastic or learned. These efforts continue to generate enormous insight, but they have also given some inappropriate succor to advocates of human nature and natural law—as if a tendency to genetic nepotism can be easily generalized to universal love for the children of God—even though these sciences simultaneously challenge the traditional understandings of free will, personal identity, and human exceptionalism.

Of course it is true that there are myriad genetic, hormonal, and physiological features that shape our desires, thoughts, and behavior, and some of which we share with most other human beings. But this constellation of influences fails as a theory of human nature on both analytical and normative grounds. It fails analytically because it posits a vague constellation of species-typical traits which had no clear beginning, are not actually species-specific, and are not clearly threatened by any specific enhancement. Normatively the argument fails because we are not morally bound by our genes.

NO CLEAR BEGINNING AND NO CLEAR BOUNDARY WITH OTHER SPECIES

There is no clear beginning for human nature or the human species. There was, we can assume, no day when all our hominid precursors gave birth to modern humans with opposable thumbs, hidden estrus, upright posture, language ability, abstract cognition, and tool use. These traits may have emerged abruptly in evolutionary time, but the periods were still tens or hundreds of thousand of years. Which of grandmothers or grandfathers would the defenders of human nature determine finally had "it," and were not just savage beasts like their parents? Our branch of the evolutionary tree shows continuous change, right up through the last fifteen thousand years (Philips 2006; Voight 2006). Without specifying which traits confer membership in humanity it is not clear whether our genetic differences from Pleistocene humans mean we share human nature with them or not. Did the recently discovered tool-using "hobbits" of Indonesia, *Homo florensis*, have human nature?

Similarly, we share with primates almost all the qualities that allegedly make us special: self-awareness, culture, language, and tool use. No, they aren't good at abstract reasoning or grammar, but then neither are small children, the demented, or the developmentally delayed, and yet they apparently have human nature.

Accepting that the things we value and attribute to human nature are actually shared continuously with nonhuman ancestors and contemporaneous species is not a devaluation of those traits, or of humanity. In fact it is only by affirming the value of reason, language, compassion, and culture making that we can build an ethical framework to guide human enhancement technologies.

NO CLEAR ENDING

Without a clear definition of human nature, or specification of the things of value, the opponents of human enhancement technology flounder in defining which enhancements cross the line. Francis Fukuyama and the President's Council on Bioethics see the line being crossed with Ritalin, antidepressants, antitrauma drugs, and preimplantation genetic diagnosis, while others focus further along on the advent of superintelligent immortals and human-animal hybrids. As David Reardon, an antiabortion activist who is promoting an amendment to the Missouri constitution to forbid human genetic engineering, cloning, and transhumanism, has said:

> Any ethic that fails to (1) define human nature, and (2) assign some value to protecting human nature, inherently lacks the ability to find any limits on the justifications that can be offered to alter or destroy human nature, human beings, or humanity. (Reardon 2005)

Reardon is, of course, completely wrong. Although human nature is being deployed to stop enhancement, the vague and chimerical concept provides no clear lines and policy conclusions. It is only when we let go of the notion of a unitary and inviolate human nature that we can turn to the challenge of delineating which features of embodied human existence are so important that we want to preserve them from technological modification, and which are so central that we want to encourage their enhancement and further evolution.

HUMAN NATURE IS NOT NORMATIVE

Even if we do have some clear set of evolved traits that were distinctively human, they are not normatively binding on us (Bayertz 2003). To the extent that we are born with impulses for aggression, racism, or selfishness, or limits on our capacity for wisdom, awe, or compassionate action, we may in fact be morally obliged to modify human nature (Savulescu 2005).

The boldest and most interesting defense of the naturalistic fallacy of a moral imperative of human nature comes from Francis Fukuyama. Fukuyama argues that human rights and social solidarity are grounded in a shared human nature. Any effort to tinker with human nature will erode social solidarity and lead to totalitarianism. But he explicitly refuses to define human nature, calling it simply "Factor X."

> Factor X cannot be reduced to the possession of moral choice, or reason, or language, or sociability, or sentience, or emotions, or consciousness, or any other quality that has been put forth as a ground for human dignity. It is all these qualities coming together in a human whole that make up factor X.

This argument for human nature as an ineffable gestalt is very convenient. If human nature were the sum of these features rather than their irreducible whole, then they might be individually improved, and human nature with them. If human nature was self-awareness, empathy, and the ability for abstract thought, for instance, then a green-skinned, four-armed transgenic could still be part of the Jeffersonian polity, and a superior citizen if she was smarter and more empathic.

But Fukuyama's Factor X is also a unique argument that the diversity of humanity must stay within its existing standard deviations from the mean of human traits. This allows Fukuyama to answer the challenge that a normative human nature excludes some existing humans who don't fit this ideal typical model, such as the disabled. Variation in intelligence, longevity, or morphology are OK, so long as we stay within our existing parameters of variation. Although our social unity can apparently still encompass conjoined twins, amputees, people born with fur or tails, and the developmentally delayed, mentally ill, and extremely smart, too many kids on Ritalin or too many 130-year-olds would apparently break the bell-curved social contract.

But if people four feet tall can feel solidarity with people seven feet tall, why can't the average person be six feet tall instead of five and a half? Why would everyone enjoying the happiness or intelligence experienced by the luckiest 1 percent of the population fracture humanity into racial subgroups? Certainly, the sudden adoption by a minority of superintelligence, immortality, and uploading would challenge existing understandings of shared citizenship, just as shared citizenship had to be forged across racial differences in the past. But human enhancement technologies pose no challenge to Fukuyama's normative standard deviation if all members of a society become more intelligent, long-lived, and beautiful, and gradually move the bell curve to the right.

For Fukuyama and the other bioconservatives this blurring of the line between ur-humans and posthumans is even more horrifying than the emergence of an entirely separate posthuman species. Since all good flows from the people of our race having pure Factor X, and race pride in the goodness of our shared Factor X, it must be protected from the complexities of a multiracial society and even more from race-mixing contamination.

THE INESCAPABLE RACISM OF THE HUMAN NATURE CONCEPT

The use of the concept of human nature today is, we see, inescapably racist, *human-racist*, with the same consequences for tyranny, violence, and suppression of human diversity as the ideology of European racism before it. The human-racists are more inclusive racists than their forebears, but racists nonetheless in their effort to ground solidarity in biological characteristics instead of shared recognition that another being has self-awareness, feelings, and thoughts like our own. We hear in the panicked demands to ban the mixing of human and animal DNA striking echoes of the demands to protect the purity of the white race from mongrelization. The root of this racialist anxiety was laid bare in Mary Douglas's work (1966); it is the taboo on the violation of categories, the ritual taboos against blurring of lines between male and female, white and black, animal and man, and man and the gods.

In fact, Yuval Levin, a staffer on the President's Council on Bioethics, explicitly embraced Douglas's analysis as the mission of "conservative bioethics" in the inaugural issue of the bioconservative journal *New Atlantis*. The goal of conservative bioethics, he says, is to defend the taboos which

> stand guard at the border crossings between the realm of the properly human and those of the beasts and the gods. When the boundaries are breached, when degradation or hubris is given expression, our stomachs recoil. (Levin 2003)

This alleged self-evident repugnance is the same rationale for bans on race mixing given by all racialists.

The irony is that human-racism is being promoted by some progressives precisely as a means to unify humanity through "species consciousness," just as white American identity was used to meld together Poles, Irish, and Italians, and pan-Arabism and pan-Africanism was promoted to transcend nationalism and tribalism.

The doctrine of a unifying human nature has also become an unquestioned assumption in human rights discourse. For instance the United Nations *Universal Declaration on the Human Genome and Human Rights* (UN General Assembly 1998) says:

The human genome underlies the fundamental unity of all members of the human family, as well as the recognition of their inherent dignity and diversity.

As with bans on miscegenation, human-racists demand bans on human enhancement technologies in order to protect the purity of the human race. President Bush called for a ban on human-animal hybrids in his 2006 State of the Union message, and Missouri has become the first US state to consider a ban on human-animal hybrids, cloning, human-genetic modification, and transhumanism. Bioethicists George Annas and Lori Andrews have been working with an international network of opponents of human enhancement towards an international treaty to make human genetic modification a "crime against humanity." Genetic enhancement, they say,

> can alter the essence of humanity itself (and thus threaten to change the foundation of human rights) by taking human evolution into our own hands and directing it toward the development of a new species, sometimes termed the 'posthuman.' . . . Membership in the human species is central to the meaning and enforcement of human rights. (Annas, Andrews, and Isasi 2002)

Again, like the white supremacists, Annas justifies the suppression of posthumanity on the grounds that they are destined to engage in race war to enslave or exterminate the pure humans:

> The posthuman will come to see us (the garden variety human) as an inferior subspecies without human rights to be enslaved or slaughtered preemptively. It is this potential for genocide based on genetic difference, that I have termed "genetic genocide," that makes species-altering genetic engineering a potential weapon of mass destruction. (Annas 2001)

THE VIOLENT POTENTIAL OF THE HUMAN RACISTS

Is it mere hyperbole to point to the similarity between the race war apocalypticism of the white supremacists and the species-extermination apocalypticism of the bioconservatives? Unfortunately not. Beyond the violence that would be done to human life, longevity, and well-being by attempts to ban any modification of our chimerical human nature, there is the actual violence that apocalyptic human-racism has already generated, and will generate. Theodore Kaczynski, aka "the Unabomber," waged a bombing campaign for *eighteen years* in the United States against scientists engaged in projects that he thought threatened human nature, principally through cybernetics and genetic engineering.

> Human nature has in the past put certain limits on the development of societies. People could be pushed only so far and no farther. But today this may be changing, because modern technology is developing way of modifying human beings . . . getting rid of industrial society will accomplish a great deal. It will relieve the worst of the pressure on nature so that the scars can begin to heal. It will remove the capacity of organized society to keep increasing its control over nature (including human nature). (Kaczynski 1995)

Bombers of abortion clinics are also soldiers in the human-racist effort. In the embryo rights belief system *all* bearers of the human genome have equal moral worth, just as *only* bearers of this human genome have worth. The Christian Right's "Manifesto on Biotechnology and Human Dignity," which calls for a ban on human genetic modification, makes clear the link they see between defense of the unborn and bans on human enhancement.

> The uniqueness of human nature is at stake. Human dignity is indivisible: the aged, the sick, the very young, those with genetic diseases—every human being is possessed of an equal dignity; any threat to the dignity of one is a threat to us all . . . at every stage of life and in every condition of dependency they are intrinsically valuable and deserving of full moral respect. (Manifesto on Biotechnology and Human Dignity)

HUMANISM NOT HUMAN-RACISM

The humanist tradition does not fetishize biological humanness, and human rights do not depend on biological similarity. As humanists facing the challenges of contemporary biotechnology, we need to embrace a *trans*-human understanding of humanist values, a humanism beyond human-racism.

The corollary of personhood as the basis of moral community is that the flowering of all persons is the goal of the humanist project. The transhumanist works toward the fullest flowering of each person's potential, freeing them from the domination of other people, ensuring they are educated, housed, and fed, and that they are empowered to control their own lives. John Stuart Mill said, "What more can be said of any condition of human affairs, than that it brings human beings themselves nearer to the best thing they can be?" Creating institutions to fulfill the promise of the Universal Declaration of Human Rights would be a great step towards this goal. But reaching our fullest potential also requires access to technology, from the printed word and electricity to vaccinations and birth control. With democracy and human rights we push back the social and economic constraints on our personhood. With technology we push back the natural constraints.

In the coming decades humanists and transhumanists need to wage a global campaign to radicalize the idea of human rights. We need to assert our rights to control our own bodies and brains, whether we choose to change our genders or medicate our brains. We need to assert that the measure of a society's fairness is how universally available we make the prerequisites for achieving our fullest potential. We need to defend the right to enhance ourselves—whether through education and exercise or genetic engineering and cybernetic implants. We need to extend these "human rights" and citizenship not only to all humans, regardless of nationality, but to all persons, ape, human, posthuman, or machine. We need to build the global institutions that can protect the rights of persons, and expand the freedoms they enjoy.

To the degree that we succeed in our campaign to clarify that rights are based on personhood not human-racism, and that fulfilling the potential of all persons should be our collective goal, we will fulfill the dreams of our humanist forebears.

REFERENCES

Anderson, Carl, et al. "Manifesto on Biotechnology and Human Dignity." 2003. http://www.cbc-network.org/redesigned/manifesto.php.

Annas, George. "Genism, Racism, and the Prospect of Genetic Genocide." Presented at the World Conference against Racism, 2001. http://www.thehumanfuture.org/commentaries/annas_genism.html.

Annas, George, Lori Andrews, and Rosario Isasi. 2002. "Protecting the Endangered Human: Toward an International Treaty Prohibiting Cloning and Inheritable Alterations." *American Journal of Law and Medicine* 28, nos. 2–3 (2002): 151–78.

Arnhart, Larry. "Human Nature Is Here to Stay." *New Atlantis*, no. 2 (Summer 2003): 65–78.

Bayertz, Kurt. "Human Nature: How Normative Might It Be?" *Journal of Medicine and Philosophy* 28, no. 2 (April 2003): 131–50.

Bostrom, Nick. "In Defence of Posthuman Dignity." *Bioethics* 19, no. 3 (2005): 202–14.

Dennett, Daniel. *Consciousness Explained*. N.p., Back Bay Books, 1992.

———. *The Intentional Stance*. Cambridge, MA: Bradford Books, 1987.

Douglas, Mary. *Purity and Danger: An Analysis of Concepts of Pollution and Taboo*. London: Routledge and Kegan Paul, 1966.

Fukuyama, Francis. 2002. *Our Posthuman Future: Consequences of the Biotechnology Revolution.* New York: Farrar, Strauss and Giroux, 2002.

Kaczynski, Theodore. "Unabomber Manifesto." 1995. http://www.thecourier.com/manifest.htm.

Kass, Leon. 2003. "Ageless Bodies, Happy Souls: Biotechnology and the Pursuit of Perfection." *New Atlantis* 1 (Spring 2003).

Levin, Yuval. 2003. "The Paradox of Conservative Bioethics." *New Atlantis* 1 (Spring 2003): 53–65.

McKibbern, Bill. *Enough: Staying Human in an Engineered Age.* N.p., Owl Books, 2004.

Philips, Melissa. 2006. " Many Human Genes Evolved Recently." *New Scientis.* (March 7). http://www.newscientist.com/channel/being-human/dn8812.html.

Pinker, Steven. "Can We Change Human Nature?" A talk presented at The Future of Human Nature, April 11–12, 2003.

Reardon, David. "Unenhanced Ethics." *PLOS Medicine* (2005). http://medicine.plosjournals.org/perlserv/?request=read-response&doi=10.1371/journal.pmed.0020121.

Savulescu, Julian. "New Breeds of Humans: The Moral Obligation to Enhance." *Ethics, Science and Moral Philosophy of Assisted Human Reproduction* 10, Suppl 1 (2005): 36–39.

United Nations General Assembly. *Universal Declaration on the Human Genome and Human Rights.* UN General Assembly, 1998.

Voight, B. F., S. Kudaravalli, X. Wen, and J. K. Pritchard. "A Map of Recent Positive Selection in the Human Genome." *PLoS Biology* 4, no. 3 (2006): e72. http://biology.plosjournals.org/perlserv/?request=get-document&doi=10.1371/journal.pbio.0040072.

Winner, Langdon. "Are Humans Obsolete?" *Hedgehog Review* (Fall 2002). http://www.virginia.edu/iasc/hh/THRtoc4-3.html.

DETERRENCE AND CAPITAL PUNISHMENT

PART V

16

GETTING TOUGH ON CRIME
What Does It Mean?

RICHARD TAYLOR

Growing criticism of our criminal justice system focuses on the death penalty. Every poll shows that Americans favor it, but there is also an increasing realization that innocent people are sometimes put to death. When it was found that thirteen people on death row in Illinois had been wrongfully convicted, Governor George Ryan, a conservative Republican who favors the death penalty, felt constrained to suspend all executions.

The issue was dramatically brought to a head in Chicago in 1996, when four men on death row were exonerated by DNA evidence of the crime for which they had been jointly convicted. Two of them barely escaped execution, and eventually three other men, not previously suspected, were convicted of that crime.

Often, to be sure, convictions result from mere technical errors in the trial process, as when defense lawyers are found to have slept through the trial, but, in the past twenty-five years, eighty-seven persons have been freed from death row, not on technicalities, but on the basis of *evidence* showing that they could not have been guilty. Today condemned persons are increasingly set free by DNA evidence, which, when it is available, is conclusive. One wonders how many innocent people were judicially put to death before today's DNA techniques were developed. We shall never know, because those cases are closed, and no district attorney wants to see them reopened.

From *Free Inquiry* 21, no. 3 (Summer 2001): 32–33.

Failures associated with the death penalty are, however, only one aspect of a flaw that pervades the entire criminal justice system. That has to do with how we have been conditioned, primarily by a long religious tradition, to think of punishment as payment of a debt. The wrongdoer must pay by suffering, and the degree of suffering must be proportionate to the evil done. This is why Americans are so fond of the death penalty. Those guilty of particularly brutish crimes are said to *deserve* it. Sins must be atoned for, and the formula for redemption is suffering. The victims of crime, it is thought, are somehow *entitled* to this. Indeed, in the case of a capital crime, the family members are invited to come and watch the condemned get killed. The nourishment of this base emotion, which is sheer vengeance, is then dignified by describing it as "closure."

This way of viewing capital punishment is, among Western industrialized nations, almost uniquely American. As more and more people are put to death here, fewer and fewer are executed in Europe, and indeed, the abolition of the death penalty has now become a condition for membership in the European Union. Some countries even refuse to extradite to America those charged with capital offenses.

This desire to make offenders pay has not reduced crime. On the contrary, the prison population has quintupled in two decades, and half of it is now made up of nonviolent offenders such as drug users. Meanwhile, prosecuting attorneys as well as elected judges win office over better-qualified opponents on their promise to "get tough on crime," and fine judges are denied appointment to higher courts in the face of accusations that they are "soft" on crime.

But what, really, does it mean to get tough on crime? In the public mind it means simply imposing ever-harsher sentences, that is, getting tough on *criminals*. This has led not only to a dramatic increase in executions, but the imposition of increased suffering for lesser and even victimless crimes, such as drug use. Worst of all, it has led to draconian sentences even for children.

This assault upon children is something new. Children were, not long ago, kept out of the criminal justice system and dealt with in juvenile courts, where there was a chance for rehabilitation; but of late the laws have been changed to enable prosecutors to try them as adults—that is, as if they were adults. This has the effect of making prosecutors, never known for compassion, and not judges, the ones who determine the sentence, since heavy sentences are, under laws, mandatory for adults. How far can such a fiction be carried? Consider a white, middle-class housewife who kills her abusive husband. Suppose a prosecutor sought to have her tried as a black male, thinking he could thus get a stiffer sentence. The absurdity would leap up.

Since 1992, forty-five states have made it easier to prosecute juveniles as adults, sometimes with respect to children only ten years old. No thought here is given to rehabilitation, or to the fact that children have no clear notion of felony. They lack even a clear sense of human mortality, and are thus unable to really grasp the significance of killing someone. Thus a boy was sentenced to life without parole for the death of a playmate in circumstances that can be rationally viewed as accidental. The two were wrestling. He was twelve years old and, needless to say, black. Two weeks later a fifteen-year-old was given the same sentence by the same state, Florida.

The only explanation for such outrages is the felt need for vengeance. The offender must be made to pay. The propriety of this notion, of ancient origin, seems never to be questioned, at least in our society. Conservative religionists, who, strangely, equate this attitude with the idea of the sanctity of life, take it for granted, and the rest fall into line. A debt is owed and must be paid. The fact that no clear meaning can be given to the idea of a debt, in this sense, does not matter. The metaphor serves to cover what is really at work here. Two decades ago Canada officially repudiated this approach to the criminal justice, declaring that its mandate must be the reintegration into society of criminal offenders. As a result, the rate of recidivism in that country has been cut in half.

And this brings to light the overwhelming absurdity of the vengeance principle. Getting tough on crime, one would suppose, would involve taking steps to reduce crime. In fact, it produces the very opposite effect, by fostering crime.

Only a miniscule few, from the criminal population as a whole, are executed, and very few spend their lives in prison. Approximately six hundred thousand are released each year, and that number is growing. What, then, shall we expect of, let us suppose, a twenty-year-old black male who is released after serving time for selling cocaine to an undercover cop? He has no high school diploma, no valuable skills, and a prison record. What are his chances of getting any kind of job? Add to this that for years he has been treated as an outcast, and his only associations have been with criminals. He has, in effect, been groomed and trained for a life of crime—all in response to the policy of getting tough on crime. Some may want to think that at least he has been made to "pay his debt" to society, whatever that is supposed to mean—but in truth it is society that pays, and will continue to pay, dearly, for what it has done to him.

Nationwide, 40 percent of ex-prisoners end up back in prison within three years. When, however, some effort is made at rehabilitation, this figure is always reduced. In Texas, a state that is notoriously tough on offenders, 23 percent of those released are back in prison in two years, but the rate is reduced to 16 percent for those that are given some sort of job training.

Criminologists have found that what does not work in reducing crime is boot camps and threats. Boot camps are, of course, the epitome of getting tough on crime, as this is generally understood. Young offenders are subjected to the most strenuous activity and stringent discipline. And they have failed utterly, their graduates emerging more hardened than ever.

What has been found to be the single most effective antidote to crime on the part of released prisoners has been employment *before release*. Enlightened companies have in some cases sought out employees within the prison population, especially those who have exhibited a desire to "go straight" and, most important, have been given training to that end. Getting tough on crime, and its only meaningful sense, thus turns out to be the opposite of what has been assumed. It means, in effect, getting "soft" on offenders who might be saved, by giving them a sense of dignity, purpose, and hope rather than just paying them back for what they have done.

What shall we conclude?

First, that prison sentences and prison policies should never deprive a prisoner of all hope. Life sentences are often justified, simply by the danger of singularly violent and incorrigible felons being returned to society, but they should never be fixed in advance as being without possibility of parole. The possibility of rehabilitation, even when small, must be kept alive, not extinguished.

Second, juveniles should never be tried as if they were adults. They are in every case disturbed youths and usually from dysfunctional families. They offer the best hope of all for rehabilitation, even those whose crimes have been most shocking.

Third, job training should be the primary function of every prison system. Until it is, expressions like "correctional facility" will have no meaning. This will not, by itself, serve to rehabilitate, and will often fail utterly, but it is the best single step.

Fourth, as a corollary of this, prisoners should never be *denied* training and educational opportunities on the ground that they do not "deserve" them. Those who, for example, can profit from college-level courses should have them, even at the considerable expense of taxpayers.

Fifth, and perhaps most important, every effort should be made to provide employment *before* release, to those who show some promise, and government itself should provide incentives to businesses for hiring these convicts when they get out.

Would this approach solve everything? Certainly not. Some ex-prisoners, even promising ones, given every such break, will nevertheless revert to crime and, in some cases, violent crime. Then, of course, the cry will go up that we must "get tough on crime," and politicians will ride into office on that slogan.

Nothing is perfect. No reforms will eliminate recidivism. These policies would, however, greatly reduce it, as has been shown where they have been tried. The prevailing policy of misdirected toughness, on the other hand, far from reducing crime, has only exacerbated it.

17

CAPITAL PUNISHMENT AND HOMICIDE
Sociological Realities and Econometric Illusions

TED GOERTZEL

I have inquired for most of my adult life about studies that might show that the death penalty is a deterrent, and I have not seen any research that would substantiate that point.
> —Attorney General Janet Reno, January 20, 2000

All of the scientifically valid statistical studies— those that examine a period of years, and control for national trends—consistently show that capital punishment is a substantial deterrent.
> —Senator Orrin Hatch, October 16, 2002

It happens all too often. Each side in a policy debate quotes studies that support its point of view and denigrates those from the other side. The result is often that research evidence is not taken seriously by either side. This has led some researchers, especially in the social sciences, to throw up their hands in dismay and give up studying controversial topics. But why bother doing social science research at all if it is impossible to obtain accurate and trustworthy information about issues that matter to people?

From *Skeptical Inquirer* 28, no. 4 (July/August 2004): 23–27.

There are some questions that social scientists should be able to answer. Either executing people cuts the homicide rate or it does not. Or perhaps it does under certain conditions and not others. In any case, the data are readily available and researchers should be able to answer the question. Of course, this would not resolve the ethical issues surrounding the question, but that is another matter.

So who is right, Janet Reno or Orrin Hatch? And why can they not at least agree on what the data show? The problem is that each of them refers to bodies of research using different research methods. Janet Reno's statement correctly describes the results of studies that compare homicide trends in states and countries that practice capital punishment with those that do not. These studies consistently show that capital punishment has no effect on homicide rates. Orrin Hatch refers to studies that use econometric modeling. He is wrong, however, in stating that these studies all find that capital punishment deters homicide. In fact, some of them find a deterrent effect and some do not.

But this is not a matter of taste. It cannot be that capital punishment deters homicide for comparative researchers but not for econometricians. In fact, the comparative method has produced valid, useful, and consistent findings, while econometrics has failed in this and every similar area of research.

The first of the comparative studies of capital punishment was done by Thorsten Sellin in 1959. Sellin was a sociologist at the University of Pennsylvania and one of the pioneers of scientific criminology. He was a prime mover in setting up the government agencies that collect statistics on crime. His method involved two steps: "First, a comprehensive view of the subject which incorporated historical, sociological, psychological, and legal factors into the analysis in addition to the development of analytical models; and second, the establishment and utilization of statistics in the evaluation of crime" (Toccafundi 1996).

Sellin applied his combination of qualitative and quantitative methods in an exhaustive study of capital punishment in American states. He used every scrap of data that was available, together with his knowledge of the history, economy, and social structure of each state. He compared states to other states and examined changes in states over time. Every comparison he made led him to the "inevitable conclusion . . . that executions have no discernable effect on homicide rates" (Sellin 1959, 34).

Sellin's work has been replicated time and time again, as new data have become available, and all of the replications have confirmed his finding that capital punishment does not deter homicide (see Bailey and Peterson 1997, and Zimring and Hawkins 1986). These studies are an outstanding example of what statistician David Freedman (1991) calls "shoe leather" social research. The hard work is collecting the best available data, both quantitative and qualitative. Once the statistical data are collected, the analysis consists largely in displaying them in tables, graphs, and charts which are then interpreted in light of qualitative knowledge of the states in question. This research can be understood by people with only modest statistical background. This allows consumers of the research to make their own interpretations, drawing on their qualitative knowledge of the states in question.

Figure 1 is an example of the kind of chart Sellin prepared, using recent data. The graph compares homicide rates per 100,000 population in Texas, New York, and California. From 1982 to 2002, Texas executed 239 prisoners, California 10, and New York none. The trends in homicide statistics are very similar in all three states, all of which follow national trends. These states were chosen arbitrarily, but data for other states are readily available. If you prefer to compare Texas to Oklahoma, Arkansas, or New Mexico, the data are readily available in back issues of the *Statistical Abstract of the United States and Uniform Crime Reports*. The results will be much the same.

Hundreds of comparisons of this sort have been made, and they consistently show that the death penalty has no effect. There have also been international comparative studies. Archer and Gartner (1984) examined fourteen countries that abolished the death penalty and found that abolition did not cause an increase in homicide rates. This research has been convincing to most criminologists (Radelet and Akers n.d.; Fessenden 2000), which is why Janet Reno was told that there was no valid research linking capital punishment to homicide rates.

The studies that Orrin Hatch referred to use a very different methodology: econometrics, also known as multiple regression modeling, structural equation modeling, or path analysis. This involves constructing complex mathematical models on the assumption that the models mirror what happens in the real world. As I argued in a previous *Skeptical Inquirer* article (Goertzel 2002), this method has consistently failed to offer reliable and valid results in studies of social problems where the data are very limited. Its most successful use is in making predictions in areas where there is a large flow of data for testing. The econometric literature on capital punishment has been carefully reviewed by several prominent economists and found wanting. There is simply too little data and too many ways to manipulate it. In one careful review, McManus (1985, 417) found that: "There is much uncertainty as to the 'correct' empirical model that should be used to draw inferences, and each researcher typically tries dozens, perhaps hundreds, of specifications before selecting one or a few to report. Usually, and understandably, the ones selected for publication are those that make the strongest case for the researcher's prior hypothesis."

Models that find deterrence effects of capital punishment often rely on rather bizarre specifications. In a rigorous and comprehensive review Cameron (1994, 214) observed that "what emerges most strongly from this review is that obtaining a significant deterrent effect of executions seems to depend on adding a set of data with no executions to the time series and including an executing/non-executing dummy in the cross-section analysis . . . there is no clear justification for the latter practice."

In less technical language, the researchers included a set of years when there were no executions, then introduced a control variable to eliminate the nonexistent variance. The other day upon the stair, they saw some variance that wasn't there. It wasn't there again today, thank goodness their model scared it away. Not all the studies rely on this particular maneuver, but they all depend on techniques that demand too much from the available data.

Since there are so many ways to model inadequate data, McManus (1985, 425) was able to show that researchers whose prior beliefs led them to structure their models in different ways would obtain predictable conclusions: "The data analyzed are not sufficiently strong to lead researchers with different prior beliefs to reach a consensus regarding the deterrent effects of capital punishment. Right-winger, rational-maximizer, and eye-for-an-eye researchers will infer that punishment deters would-be murderers, but bleeding-heart and crime-of-passion researchers will infer that there is no significant deterrent effect."

THE MYTHICAL WORLD OF CETERIS PARIBUS

Econometricians inhabit the mythical land of Ceteris Paribus, a place where everything is constant except the variables they choose to write about. Ceteris Paribus has much in common with the mythical world of Flatland in Edwin Abbot's (1884) classic fairy tale. In Flatland everything moves along straight lines, flat plains, or rectangular boxes. In Flatland, statistical averages become mathematical laws. For example, it is true that, on the average, tall people weigh more than short people. But, in the real world, not every tall person weighs more than a shorter one. In Flatland knowing someone's height would be enough to tell you their precise weight, because both vary only on a straight line. In Flatland, if you plotted height and weight on a graph with height on one axis and weight on the other, all the points would fall on a straight line.

Of course, econometricians know that they don't live in Flatland. But the mathematics works much better when they pretend they do. So they adjust the data in one way or another to make it straighter (often by converting it to logarithms). Then they qualify their remarks, saying "capital punishment deters homicide, ceteris paribus." But when the real-world data diverge greatly from the straight lines of Flatland, this can lead to bizarre results.

Statistician Francis Anscombe (1973) demonstrated how bizarre the Flatland assumption can be. He plotted four graphs that have become known as Anscombe's Quartet. Each of the graphs shows the relationship between two variables. The graphs are very different, but for a resident of Flatland they are all the same. If we approximate them with a straight line (following a "linear regression equation") the lines are all the same (fig. 2). Only the first of Anscombe's four graphs is a reasonable candidate for a linear regression analysis, because a straight line is a reasonable approximation for the underlying pattern.

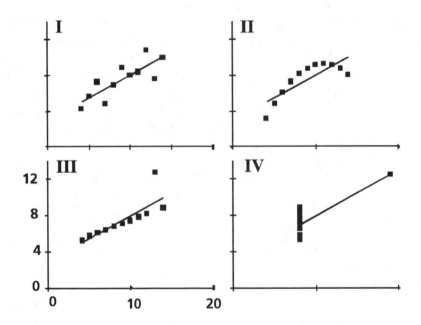

The data on capital punishment and homicide, when plotted in figure 3, look a lot like Anscombe's fourth quartet. Most of the states had no executions at all. One state, Texas, accounts for forty of the eighty-five executions in the year shown (the patterns for other years are quite similar). An exceptional case or "outlier" of this dimension completely dominates a multiple regression analysis. Any regression study will be primarily a comparison of Texas with everywhere else. Multiple regression is simply inappropriate with this data, no matter how hard the analyst tries to force the data into a linear pattern.

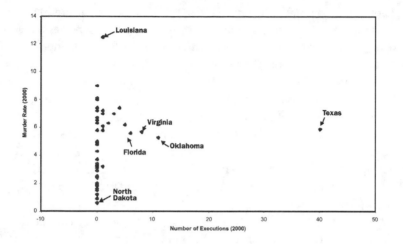

Unfortunately, econometricians continue to use multiple regression on capital punishment data and to generate results that are cited in congressional hearings. In recent examples, Mocan and Gittings (2001) concluded that each execution decreases the number of homicides by five or six while Dezhbaksh, Rubin, and Shepherd (2002) argued that each execution deters eighteen murders. Cloninger and Marchesini (2001) published a study finding that the Texas moratorium from March 1996 to April 1997 increased homicide rates, even though no increase can be seen in the graph (fig. 1). The moratorium simply increased homicide in comparison to what their econometric model said it would have otherwise been. Of all the econometric myths, the wildest is this: We know what would have been.

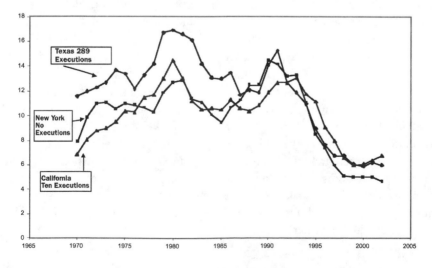

Cloninger and Marchesini concede that "studies such as the present one that rely on inductive statistical analysis cannot prove a given hypothesis correct." However, they argue that when a large number of such studies give the same result, this provides "robust evidence" which "causes any neutral observer pause." But if McManus is correct that econometricians are likely to specify models to fit their preconceptions, then if many of them reach the same conclusion it may just mean that they have the same bias. Actually, there are a variety of biases among econometricians, which is why there are almost as many on one side as on the other of this issue. In response to Ehrlich's (1975) initial econometric study, other econometricians using the same data included Yunker (1976), who found a stronger deterrent effect than Ehrlich, and Cloninger (1977), who supported his findings. But Bowers and Pierce (1975), Passel and Taylor (1977), and Hoenack and Weiler (1980) found no deterrence at all.

Econometricians often dismiss the kind of comparative research that Thorsten Sellin did as crude and unsophisticated when compared to their use of complex mathematical formulas. But mathematical complexity does not make for good social science. The goal of multiple regression is to convert messy sociological realities into math problems that can be resolved with the certainty of mathematical proof. Econometricians believe they can control for the myriad variables that affect homicide rates, just as a chemist eliminates impurities to see how two chemicals interact in their pure form. But they cannot convert the real world into a Flatland, so they use statistical adjustments to compensate. With these adjustments, they claim to answer the Ceteris Paribus question: If everything else were equal, what would the relationship between capital punishment and homicide be?

It would be handy for social scientists if we lived in a Flatland where everything else was equal and questions could be answered with a few calculations. But multivariate statistical analysis does not answer real-world questions such as, "Does Texas, with a high execution rate, have a lower homicide rate than similar states?" or "Did the homicide rate go down when Texas began executing people, compared to trends in other states that did not?" Instead, it answers the question, "If we use the latest, most sophisticated statistical methods to control for extraneous variables, can we say that the death penalty deters homicide rates other things being equal?" After decades of effort by many diligent researchers, we now know the answer to this question: There are many ways to adjust things statistically, and the answer will depend on which one is chosen. We also know that of the many possible ways to specify a regression model, each researcher is likely to prefer one that will give results consistent with his or her predispositions.

It is time to abandon the illusion that mathematics can convert the real world into the mythical land of Ceteris Paribus. Social science can provide valid and reliable results with methods that present the data with as little statistical manipulation as possible and interpret it in light of the best qualitative information available. The value of this research is shown by its success in demonstrating that capital punishment has not deterred homicide.

REFERENCES

Abbot, Edwin. *Flatland: A Romance of Many Dimensions.* 1884. http://www.alcyone .com/max/lit/flatland/. Accessed January 29, 2004.

Anscombe, Francis. "Graphs in Statistical Analysis." *American Statistician* 27 (1973): 17–21.

Archer, Dane, and Rosemary Gartner. "Homicide and the Death Penalty: A Cross-national Test of a Deterrence Hypothesis." In *Violence and Crime in Cross-National Perspective.* Edited by Dane Archer and Rosemary Gartner. New Haven, CT: Yale University Press, 1984.

Bailey, William, and Ruth Peterson. "Murder, Capital Punishment, and Deterrence: A Review of the Literature." In *The Death Penalty in America: Current Controversies.* Edited by Hugo Bedau. New York: Oxford University Press, 1997.

Bowers, W. J., and J. L. Pierce. "The Illusion of Deterrence in Isaac Ehrlich's Work on Capital Punishment." *Yale Law Journal* 85 (1975): 187–208.

Cameron, Samuel. "A Review of the Econometric Evidence on the Affects of Capital Punishment." *Journal of Socio-Economics* 23 (1994): 197–214.

Cloninger, Dale. "Deterrence and the Death Penalty: A Cross-sectional Analysis." *Journal of Behavioral Economics* 6 (1977): 87–107.

Dezhbaksh, Hashem, Paul Robin, and Joanna Shepherd. "Does Capital Punishment Have a Deterrent Effect? New Evidence from Post-moratorium Panel Data." *American Law and Economics Review* 5, no. 2 (2002): 344–76. http://aler.oup journals.org/cgi/content/abstract/5/2/344. Accessed January 12, 2004.

Ehrlich, Isaac. "The Deterrent Effect of Capital Punishment: A Question of Life and Death." *American Economic Review* 65 (1975): 397–417.

Fessenden, Ford. "Deadly Statistics: A Survey of Crime and Punishment." *New York Times*, September 22, 2000. http://www.nytimes.com/2000/09/22/national/ 22STUD.html?ex=1074747600&en=908c0021415e7e9a&ei=5070. Accessed January 20, 2004.

Freedman, David. "Statistical Models and Shoe Leather." *Sociological Methodology* 21 (1991): 291–313.

Goertzel, Ted. "Myths of Murder and Multiple Regression." *Skeptical Inquirer* 26, no. 1 (2002): 19–23.

Hatch, Orrin. Minority views, appended to the "report" of the Committee on the Judiciary of the United States Senate on The Innocence Protection Act of 2002, 107th Congress, Second Session, Report 107-315, Calendar No 731. 2002. http://frweb gate.access.gpo.gov/cgibin/getdoc.cgi?dbname=107_cong_reports&docid=f :sr315.107.pdf. Accessed January 12, 2004.

Hoenack, Stephen, and William Weiler. "A Structural Model of Murder Behavior and the Criminal Justice System." *American Economic Review* 70 (1980): 327–41.

McManus, Walter. "Estimates of the Deterrent Effect of Capital Punishment: The Importance of the Researcher's Prior Beliefs." *Journal of Political Economy* 93 (1985): 417–25.

Mocan, Naci, and Kaj Gittings. "Pardons, Executions and Homicide." *Working Paper 8639*. National Bureau of Economic Research, 2001. http://www.nber.org/papers/ w8639. Accessed January 12, 2004.

Passell, Peter, and John Taylor. "The Deterrent Effect of Capital Punishment: Another View." *American Economic Review* 67 (1977): 445.

Radelet, Michael, and Ronald Akers. "Deterrence and the Death Penalty: The View of Experts." N.d. http://sun.soci.niu.edu/~critcrim/dp/dppapers/mike.deterrence. Accessed January 23, 2004.

Reno, Janet. 2002. Quoted in Mocan and Gittings 2001.

Sellin, Thorsten. *The Death Penalty.* American Law Institute, Philadelphia, 1959.

Toccafundi, David. 1996. *The Sellin Collection at Penn.* 1996. http://www.library .upenn.edu/exhibits/pennhistory/library/sellin.html. Accessed January 24, 2004.

Yunker, James A. "Is the Death Penalty a Deterrent to Homicide? Some Time Series Evidence." *Journal of Behavioral Economics* 5 (1976): 45–81.

Zimring, Franklin, and Gordon Hawkins. *Capital Punishment and the American Agenda.* Cambridge: Cambridge University Press, 1986.

PSYCHIATRY AND PSYCHOTHERAPY

18
SECULAR HUMANISM AND "SCIENTIFIC PSYCHIATRY"

THOMAS SZASZ

My aim in this paper is to ask, is Secular Humanism compatible with so-called Scientific Psychiatry, and show that it is not.

The Web site of the Council for Secular Humanism states: "Secular humanists reject authoritarian beliefs. They affirm that we must take responsibility for our own lives and the communities and world in which we live. Secular humanism emphasizes reason and scientific inquiry, individual freedom and responsibility, human values and compassion, and the need for tolerance and cooperation."[1]

The term "psychiatry" refers to both the principles and practices of this ostensibly medical specialty. It is necessary to emphasize at the outset that, unlike typical medical practices based on consent, typical psychiatric practices rest on coercion. In a free society, most social relations between adults are consensual. Consensual relations—in business, medicine, religion, and psychiatry—pose no special legal or political problems. In contrast, coercive relations—one person authorized to use the power of the state to compel another person to do or abstain from an action of his choice—are inherently political and morally problematic. In my following remarks I address only those relations between psychiatrists and patients that are actually or potentially coercive. In the prevailing legal and polit-

From *Philosophy, Ethics, and Humanities in Medicine* 1, no. 5 (April 25, 2006).

ical climate (especially in the United States but by no means there alone), most psychiatric practices fall into this category.

It is not only the power but also the duty to coerce mental patients—to protect them from themselves and to protect society from them—that has always set psychiatrists apart from other medical practitioners. This is more true today than ever, but it is less obvious because it is better concealed.

When I was a medical student in Cincinnati in the early 1940s, there were no voluntary patients in Ohio state mental hospitals. A person could no more gain admission to a state mental hospital voluntarily than he could gain admission to a prison voluntarily. Individuals civilly committed to state mental hospitals were considered legally incompetent. In the old days of asylum psychiatry, the connection between mental illness and legal incompetence was unambiguous. If a person was mad enough to merit confinement in a madhouse, then he was incompetent. If he was not so confined, he was competent and safe from psychiatric coercion.

In the aftermath of World War II, partly as a result of the Nazi practice of exterminating mental patients, American social attitudes toward psychiatry and mental hospitals began to change. Erving Goffman's book, *Asylums*, and my book, *The Myth of Mental Illness*, both published in 1961, challenged the moral and legal legitimacy of psychiatric coercions, exemplified by involuntary confinement in a mental hospital.[2] Journalists compared state mental hospitals to concentration camps and called them "snake pits."

At this critical moment, so-called psychiatric drugs miraculously appeared. Politicians and the public quickly accepted the psychiatrists' claim that mental illnesses are brain diseases and that neuroleptic drugs are effective treatments for such diseases. Politicians and mental health professionals used this fiction as a peg on which to hang the complexly motivated program of emptying the state mental hospitals, misleadingly called "deinstitutionalization." In short, the three events characteristic of modern psychiatry—the "drug treatment" of mental illness, deinstitutionalization, and the conflation of mental illness and legal incompetence—occurred in tandem, each facilitating and supporting the others. At the same time, psychiatry—which had always been an arm of the coercive apparatus of the state—became more coercive and politicized. Politicians joined psychiatrists in authenticating and promoting the medical reality of "mental illnesses." The dual fictions—mental illnesses are brain diseases effectively treated with drugs—became dogma, and deviation from it heresy. Herewith a few examples.

In 1999, President William Clinton declared: "Mental illness can be accurately diagnosed, successfully treated, just as physical illness."[3] Tipper Gore,

President Clinton's Mental Health Advisor, emphasized: "One of the most widely believed and most damaging myths is that mental illness is not a physical disease. Nothing could be further from the truth."[4] First Lady Hillary Rodham Clinton explained: "The amygdala acts as a storehouse of emotional memories. And the memories it stores are especially vivid because they arrive in the amygdala with the neurochochemical and hormonal imprint that accompanies stress, anxiety, and other intense excitement. . . . We must . . . begin treating mental illness as the illness it is on a parity with other illnesses.[5] A White House Fact Sheet on Myths and Facts about Mental Illness declared: "Research in the last decade proves that mental illnesses are diagnosable disorders of the brain."[6]

With impressive naivete, then Surgeon General David Satcher concluded: "Just as things go wrong with the heart and kidneys and liver, so things go wrong with the brain."[7] The view that mental diseases stand in the same relation to brain diseases as, say, urinary problems stand in relation to kidney diseases is superficially attractive. The argument goes like this. The human body is a biological machine, composed of parts, called organs, such as the heart, the lung, and the liver. Each organ has a "natural function" and when this fails, we have a disease, such as coronary atherosclerosis, emphysema, hepatitis. If we define human problems as the symptoms of brain diseases, then they are brain diseases, even in the absence of any medically ascertainable evidence of brain disease. We can then treat mental diseases as if they were brain diseases.

The error in this reasoning is that if we add up all our body parts, the sum is obviously greater than its parts combined. A living human being is not merely a collection of organs, tissues, and cells; he is a person or moral agent. At this point the materialist-scientific approach to understanding and remedying its malfunctions breaks down. The pancreas may be said to have a natural function. But what is the natural function of the person? Theists and atheists have lungs and livers so similar that one may be transplanted into the body of another without altering his personal identity; but their beliefs and habits differ so profoundly that they often find it difficult or impossible to live with one another.

The truth is that the treatment of so-called mental diseases is no more successful today than it was in the past. Deinstitutionalization did not liberate mental patients. Some state mental hospitals inmates were transinstitutionalized, rehoused in parapsychiatric facilities, such as group homes and nursing homes. Others were imprisoned for offenses they were prone to commit, transforming prisons into the nation's largest mental hospitals. Still others became "street persons," living off their social security disability benefits. Most idle, indigent, unwanted persons continue to be incarcerated in mental hospitals—intermittently, committed several times a year, instead of once for decades.[8]

Most importantly, the powers of courts and mental health professionals were vastly expanded. Before World War II, they could control and forcibly "treat" only persons housed in mental hospitals. Armed with "outpatient commitment" laws, judges and psychiatrists can now control and forcibly "treat" persons living in the community.

The introduction of neuroleptic drugs into psychiatry created the illusion that mental illnesses, like medical illnesses, were "treatable" with drugs. Doubt about the benefits of long-term mental hospitalization was replaced by confidence in the effectiveness of outpatient chemotherapy for mental illness. This development greatly enlarged the number of persons classified as mentally ill, contributed to the false belief that legal competence is a psychiatric issue, and further confused the legal relations between psychiatrist and mental patient.

Today, a person whose behavior is socially deviant—especially if he has once been a "mental patient"—risks being considered incompetent. For example, if such a person kills himself or someone else, then, after the fact and simply because of his act, he is considered incompetent and his psychiatrist's treatment of him is likely to be judged to be "medically negligent": regarded as the patient's guardian, the psychiatrist is considered to have failed to fulfil his "duty to protect" his ward or "third parties" endangered by his ward. None of this was true as recently as the 1960s.[9]

To conduct arm-length relations with individuals we do not know, we must make certain presumptions about them. The automobile dealer presumes that his customer is legally competent and responsible for his purchase. The physician whose patient complains of blood in his stool presumes that the patient has a disease. The Anglo-American legal system presumes that a person accused of a crime is innocent until proven guilty, and competent until proven incompetent.

We are proud of our criminal justice system because it protects the accused from the power of the state, a power we distrust because its avowed aim is to harm the individual. Similarly, we are also proud of our mental health system, because it protects the mentally ill person from the dangers he poses to himself and others, a power we trust because its avowed aim is "therapeutic," not punitive.

Difficulties arise, however, once the power of the state to "help" goes beyond offering services (or money) and, instead, the state makes use of coercion. The justification for psychiatric coercion is further weakened by resting the requirement for commitment on "mental illness" and "dangerousness." There are no objective criteria for either mental illness or dangerousness. Thus, psychiatric determinations and declarations of their presence or absence are essentially oracular and rhetorical. Nevertheless, they fulfil a very important function: they instruct the listener to assume a desired attitude toward the "patient."[10]

Characterizing a door as brown or white is descriptive. Characterizing it as needing to be opened or closed is dispositive. Descriptive characterizations can be proved or disproved. Dispositive characterizations cannot, they can only be obeyed or disobeyed. The difference between the situation of the person accused of a crime and the situation of the person accused of mental illness is illuminating. The defendant has a right to deny his crime and disagree with his accusers. His insistence on his innocence is not interpreted as evidence of his guilt. The person diagnosed as mentally ill loses this right. His disagreement with the psychiatrist is interpreted as "lack of insight into his illness" or "denial of his illness." His insistence on his sanity is interpreted as evidence of his insanity.

Psychiatrists use the term "competent" as if they were identifying a "mental condition" in the designated person. That is why courts request the psychiatrist to examine defendants for competence, as if they were looking for and finding, or not finding, certain facts. Psychiatric "findings," however, especially in a forensic setting, are not facts but recommendations for a course of action toward the defendant.

Ironically, it is precisely because the American system of criminal justice is so intensely concerned with protecting innocent persons from punishment that it is especially vulnerable to corruption by excuses couched in terms of psychiatric disabilities and coercions justified as psychiatric treatments. The root of the problem lies largely in the concepts of mental illness and dangerousness, and partly in the doctrine of mens rea, sound mind.

The legal doctrine of mens rea, sound mind, which holds that unlawful behavior constitutes a crime only if it is committed by an actor who possesses a "guilty mind"—that is, whose "mind" can be held responsible (because it knows right from wrong), also works to strip the person incriminated as mentally ill of his rights. Since the Middle Ages and before, insane persons—perceived as similar to "wild beasts"—have been regarded as lacking mens rea. This is why "infants, idiots, and the insane"—in John Locke's famous phrase, repeated unchanged ever since—are not prosecuted or punished by the criminal law, but instead are restrained, as minors and as mad, by family courts and mental health laws.

Treating mentally ill persons as if they were like children fails to take into account the many obvious differences between them. Minority is an objectively defined (chronological) condition and a legal status. Mental illness is neither. Children are, by definition, under tutelage. Few mental patients are under tutelage and those that are, are in that status not because they are mentally ill but because they are declared to be legally incompetent.

I maintain that "mental illness" is not something the patient has, it is something he is. The modern psychiatrist is likely to view Lady Macbeth as insane, the victim of manic depressive psychosis, an illness that renders her not responsible for her crimes. Shakespeare viewed her as "Not so sick . . . as troubled with thick coming fancies," for which "more she needs the divine than the physician."[11] Ironically, today's Lady Macbeths, female and male alike, receive the ministrations of divines, albeit they are called "medical doctors" and are licensed physicians (or pseudo-physicians, called "mental health professionals"). I interpret this as a symptom of the transformation of the theocratic state into the therapeutic state.

In *Democracy in America*, Alexis de Tocqueville warned: "The species of oppression by which democratic nations are menaced is unlike anything that ever before existed in the world . . . Above this race of men [incessantly endeavoring to procure their petty and paltry pleasures] stands an immense and tutelary power, which takes upon itself alone to secure their gratifications and to watch over their fate. . . . For their happiness such a government willingly labors . . . provides for their security . . . facilitates their pleasures, manages their principal concerns. . . ."[12]

Did Tocqueville foresee the coming of pharmacracy, that is, government informed and legitimized not by gods (theocracy), social position (aristocracy), or popular sovereignty (democracy), but by medicine and its ideology that tends to define human problems as "diseases," curable by coercions defined as "treatments"? Evidence for the medicalization of every kind of undesirable behavior abounds.

I first proposed the term "pharmacracy" in 1974, to complete a triad of phrases to identify that we are in the process of a profound cultural transformation.[13] Prior to World War II, the American system of social controls rested on Christian moral values and was enforced by a judicial apparatus based on English common law, the Constitution, and the rule of law. Since then, our system of social controls has become increasingly dependent on the principles of a politicized medicine, and has been legitimized and enforced by a complex state apparatus that commingles the principles and practices of paternalistic "therapy," punitive psychiatry, collectivistic public health, and the criminal justice system.

To articulate this insight, in 1960 I proposed the phrase "myth of mental illness." The term was intended to lay bare that the phenomena we so label are neither mental nor illnesses, and that the measures used to remedy them are not treatments but efforts to tranquilize, pacify, and subdue the disturbing person.[14] In 1963, I proposed the term "therapeutic state" to identify the transformation of our dominant political ideology from a democratic welfare state legitimized by the rule of law into an autocratic therapeutic state legitimized by psychiatry as a branch of medicine.

Finally, in 1974, in Ceremonial Chemistry, I wrote: "Inasmuch as we have words to describe medicine as a healing art, but have none to describe it as a method of social control or political rule, we must first give it a name. I propose that we call it pharmacracy, from the Greek roots pharmakon, for 'medicine' or 'drug,' and kratein, for 'to rule' or 'to control.' . . . As theocracy is rule by God or priests, and democracy is rule by the people or the majority, so pharmacracy is rule by medicine or physicians."[15] In a theocracy, people perceive all manner of human problems as religious in nature, susceptible to religious remedies. Similarly, in a pharmacracy people perceive all manner of human problems as medical in nature, susceptible to medical remedies.

Perceptive writers—for example, Samuel Butler, Aldous Huxley, C. S. Lewis, and Adolfo Bioy Casares—foresaw this trend and described some of the features of the therapeutic state and the pharmacratic controls that characterize it. In his satirical dystopia, Erewhon (1872), Butler wrote: "As I have already said, these [persons we regard as criminals], though not judicially punishable, are recognized as requiring correction. Accordingly, there exists a class of men trained in soul-craft, whom they call straighteners, as nearly as I can translate a word which literally means 'one who bends back the crooked.' . . . Indeed, the straighteners have gone so far as to give names from the hypothetical language (as taught at the College of Unreason) to all known forms of mental indisposition, and to classify them according to a system of their own, which, though I could not understand it. . . ."[16]

In Erewhon Revisited (1901), Butler presciently debunked the now virtually unchallenged poppycock that psychotropic drugs "cure" bad behavior. He wrote: "No more swearing. No more bad language of any kind. A lamb-like temper ensured in about twenty minutes, by a single does of one of our spiritual indigestion tabloids. In cases of all the more ordinary moral ailments, from simple lying to homicidal mania, in cases again of tendency to hatred, malice, and uncharitableness . . . our spiritual indigestion tabloids will afford unfailing and immediate relief."[17]

Toward the end of Brave New World (1932)—the world in which all conflicts and discomforts have been eliminated—the human remnant Huxley calls the Savage, and the dictator whom Huxley calls the Controller, Mustapha Mond, engage in the following dialogue: "We prefer to do things comfortably" [said the Controller]./"But I don't want comfort. I want God, I want poetry, I want real danger, I want freedom, I want goodness, I want sin."/"In fact, said Mustapha Mond, "you're claiming the right to be unhappy."/"All right, then," said the Savage defiantly, "I'm claiming the right to be unhappy."[18]

More recently, C. S. Lewis (1953/1970) warned: "Of all the tyrannies a tyranny sincerely exercised for the good of the victims may be the most oppressive. . . . To be 'cured' against one's will and cured of states which we may not even regard as disease is to be put on a level with those who have not yet reached the age of reason or those who never will; to be classed with infants, imbeciles, and domestic animals. For if crime and disease are to be regarded as the same thing, it follows that any state of mind which our masters choose to call 'disease' can be treated as a crime; and compulsorily cured. Even if the treatment is painful, even if it is life-long, even if it is fatal, that will be only a regrettable accident; the intention was purely therapeutic."[19]

In our own day (1986), Argentinean novelist Adolfo Bioy Casares observed: "Well then, maybe it would be worth mentioning the three periods of history. When man believed that happiness was dependent upon God, he killed for religious reasons. When he believed that happiness was dependent upon the form of government, he killed for political reasons. . . . After dreams that were too long, true nightmares . . . we arrived at the present period of history. Man woke up, discovered that which we always knew, that happiness is dependent upon health, and began to kill for therapeutic reasons. . . . It is medicine that has come to replace both religion and politics in our time."[20]

I have asserted that Secular Humanism is incompatible with the principles and practices of psychiatry. However, I do not speak for Secular Humanism. Those who do must decide whether that decision is well-founded or not. I ask only that the decision-makers keep in mind two things: (1) The paradigmatic practices of psychiatry are civil commitment and insanity defense—that is, depriving innocent persons of liberty and excusing guilty persons of their crimes—and that the consequences of both are confinement in institutions ostensibly devoted to the treatment of mental diseases. (2) *Black's Law Dictionary* states: "Every confinement of the person is an 'imprisonment,' whether it be in a common prison, or in private house, or in the stocks, or even by forcibly detaining one in the public streets."[21]

NOTES

1. http://secularhumanism.org/.

2. E. Goffman, *Asylums: Essays on the Social Situation of Mental Patients and Other Inmates*, (Garden City, NY: Doubleday Anchor, 1961); T. Szasz, in *The Myth of Mental Illness: Foundations of a Theory of Personal Conduct* (New York: Hoeber-Harper, 1961).

3. Quoted in Office of the Press Secretary of the President of the United States,

"Remarks by the President, the First Lady, the Vice President, and Mrs. Gore at White House Conference on Mental Health," Blackburn Auditorium, Howard University, Washington, DC; Arianna Online, 1158 26th Street, Suite #428, Santa Monica, CA 90403, e-mail: info@ariannaonline.com, Copyright ©1998 Christabella, Inc., June 7, 1999.

4. Quoted in Office of the Press Secretary of the President of the United States, "Remarks by the President, the First Lady, the Vice President, and Mrs. Gore at White House Conference on Mental Health," Blackburn Auditorium, Howard University, Washington, DC, June 7, 1999. In *New York Times* Internet edition. Arianna Online, 1158 26th Street, Suite #428, Santa Monica, CA 90403, e-mail: info@ariannaonline .com, Copyright © 1998 Christabella, Inc., June 7, 1999. Emphasis added.

5. Clinton HR: Office of the Press Secretary, The White House, ibid.

6. White House Press Office: "White House Fact Sheet on Myths and Facts about Mental Illness," June 5, 1999. "Myths and Facts about Mental Illness," in *New York Times* Internet edition, June 7, 1999, www.info@ariannaonline.com.

7. D. Satcher, quoted in "Satcher Discusses MH Issues Hurting Black Community," in *Psychiatric News* (October 15, 1999); emphasis added.

8. T. Szasz, *Cruel Compassion: The Psychiatric Control of Society's Unwanted* (1994; Syracuse, NY: Syracuse University Press, 1998).

9. T Szasz, *Liberation by Oppression: A Comparative Study of Slavery and Psychiatry* (New Brunswick, NJ: Transaction Publishers, 2002).

10. T. Szasz, *Insanity: The Idea and Its Consequences* (1987; Syracuse, NY: Syracuse University Press, 1997).

11. *Macbeth*, Act V, Scene iii, Lines 36–39.

12. A. de Tocqueville, *Democracy in America*, vol. 2, ed. Bradley Phillips (1835–40; New York: Vintage, 1945), p. 336.

13. T. Szasz, *Ceremonial Chemistry: The Ritual Persecution of Drugs, Addicts, and Pushers*, rev. ed. (1976; Syracuse, NY: Syracuse University Press, 2003).

14. T. Szasz, "The Myth of Mental Illness," *American Psychologist* 15 (1960): 113–18.

15. Szasz, *Ceremonial Chemistry*, p. 139.

16. S. Butler, *Erewhon, or: Over the Range* (1872; Harmondsworth: Penguin, n.d.), pp. 72, 74–75.

17. S. Butler, *Erewhon Revisited*, in *Erewhon and Erewhon Revisited* (1901; London: Everyman's Library J. M. Dent, 1947), p. 242.

18. A. Huxley, *Brave New World* (1932; New York: HarperPerennial, 1969), p. 246.

19. C. S. Lewis, *God in the Dock: Essays on Theology and Ethics*, ed. Hooper G. Walter (Grand Rapids, MI: William B. Eerdmans, 1970), pp. 292–93.

20. A. B. Casares, "Plans for an Escape to Carmelo," *New York Review of Books* 7: April 10, 1986.

21. H. C. Black, *Black's Law Dictionary*, 4th ed., rev. ed. (St. Paul, MN: West, 1968), p. 890.

19
WHAT'S THE PROBLEM?
A *Response to* Secular Humanism and Scientific Psychiatry

DEREK BOLTON

The sociology of psychiatry—the ways in which psychiatry is shaped by and shapes wider society and its values—is a matter of enormous importance, because psychiatry has major impacts of many people's lives, and it costs a lot of money. Important but neglected, with some brave exceptions, among whom Szasz has ranked among the best few for decades. One writer, on the other hand, especially one who wants to make a point, tends to pursue one point, and it is up to the reader to consider other points of view, pros and cons, problems which are not addressed as well as those which are solved. This present piece by Szasz is a cogent and provocative summary of much of what he has long argued, in the form of a proposal that secular humanism is incompatible with scientific psychiatry.

Szasz sketches the two players, citing the Web site of the Council for Secular Humanism as follows:

> Secular humanists reject authoritarian beliefs. They affirm that we must take responsibility for our own lives and the communities and world in which we live. Secular humanism emphasizes reason and scientific inquiry, individual freedom and responsibility, human values and compassion, and the need for tolerance and cooperation.

From *Philosophy, Ethics, and Humanities in Medicine* 1, no. 6 (April 25, 2006).

And then psychiatry is characterized like this:

> The term "psychiatry" refers to both the principles and practices of this ostensibly medical specialty. It is necessary to emphasize at the outset that, unlike typical medical practices based on consent, typical psychiatric practices rest on coercion.

I imagine the credo of secular humanism would attract a lot of well-wishers, at face value, give or take some interpretations in tricky cases of some of the key terms especially in the second quoted sentence; but anyway, generally fine sentiments. Psychiatry on the other hand gets off to a terrible start, what with having an ill-defined basis, medical but not really, and being typically coercive. Since secular humanism values freedom, among other things, and psychiatry operates by coercion, the answer to the question Szasz raises at the start whether they are compatible is just "no." The problem solves itself as soon as it is formulated, and the rest of the piece is an elaboration of the point.

Just the definitions of secular humanism on the one hand and psychiatry on the other shows up the strength of Szasz's conclusion clearly, but the easiness of it all signifies that hard problems are left invisible. What are the hard problems?

First, much of mental health services are provided to voluntary consumers who walk through the clinic door asking for treatment. What can the kind of position adopted by Szasz say about this? Perhaps that these people are victims of a delusion, of the same myth that defines psychiatry? Or that they wish to shirk responsibility for their feelings and behavior? Deluded or feckless they may be, but in any case apparently not responsibly seeking help for something reasonably called a "mental health problem." So for example, consider the case of a seventeen-year-old young man finding that he is continually having thoughts that his parents may have an accident, that to stop this happening he is convinced that he has to undo the thoughts by repeating what he was doing when he has them without having them, that this takes hours, gets in the way of revising for his state exams, seeing friends and sleeping, believes that this all makes no real sense, finds out on the Net that he has what is called OCD and that it is treatable (stoppable) by CBT, so goes looking for it. Is such a man deluded, feckless, or responsibly taking care of himself? Do we have to choose one of the first two options? Or can we go with the third? If the first two, what should the young man be doing in his predicament? Or is it, despite appearances, not a predicament at all? What should the therapist he contacts do? What does the position adopted by Szasz recommend we say and do in such a case? These are the day-to-day problems and questions that are apparently passed by in Szasz's critique of psychiatry. And abstract debates about such as individual freedom, and whether so-called mental health problems are or are not brain disorders, just get us to ignore them.

In the coercive case, what should be done instead? What should be done with a person—let us say a mother of two young children and a new baby to make the case a hard one—who has so-called postnatal depression and in this so-called depressed state expresses clear intent to kill herself, with attempts, and a clear choice not to have treatment? What should be done? Leave her to it?

These are the practical problems, in both kinds of case, voluntary treatment-seeking and coercive treatment, that keep people with the problems, their families, and the professionals, awake at night. We all need to know what we should do instead, if not follow the current arrangements. The credo of the Council for Secular Humanism was presumably not designed to get involved with these practical problems, and nor is Szasz's piece.

Behind all this it may be that the real issue is not about what are called mental health problems and its management, which would be why little is said about them, but about the role of the state. After introducing the definitions that make it clear that psychiatry is incompatible with the ideals of secular humanism, Szasz continues:

> In a free society, most social relations between adults are consensual. Consensual relations—in business, medicine, religion, and psychiatry—pose no special legal or political problems. In contrast, coercive relations—one person authorized to use the power of the state to compel another person to do or abstain from an action of his choice—are inherently political and morally problematic.

It is a secure and comfortable world in which consensual relations pose no special legal or political problems, in which these problems are raised only by a coercive state: one source of problems, which comes with its own built-in solution, curtailing the power of the state. But what here is said about consensual relations between two parties that spike a third—not an unusual position after all? Or are these consensual relations that damage a third party illegal, regulated by law, backed up by a coercive state, which would then not be so bad after all? How is the argument meant to run here? Apparently the state has to regulate the behavior of citizens and corporations in many ways, to make it work at all. There is after all no property without property law, no trade without contracts, nor indeed is there freedom to act without law which protects the individual against coercion by another.

Further, law itself rests on the notion of individual responsibility for action. This notion is fundamental to the kind of position adopted by Szasz, fundamental and unquestioned, secure and comfortable. But the assumption of individual responsibility only seems this way when we ignore all the many kinds of problematic cases in which it is questionable, problems that exercise the legislators and the courts, how to judge individual responsibility in cases involving such as corporate misdemeanors or war crimes, for example, or involving minors, the seriously physically ill, the state of people in altered/uncharacteristic states of consciousness for various reasons and causes, and of people with severe so-called mental health problems. If it is to be understood adequately, mental health law that warrants coercion has to be discussed in the context of problems such as these that interrogate the assumption of individual responsibility and freedom, not only in the assumption of free, autonomous, responsible, value-laden, and cooperative individuals managing things for themselves for the best.

20

THE ASSAULT ON SCIENTIFIC MENTAL HEALTH
Ethical Implications

SCOTT O. LILIENFELD

M y thesis in this chapter is straightforward: the field of mental health practice is in crisis. Specifically, I will argue that the allied fields of mental health—clinical psychology, psychiatry, social work, counseling psychology, educational psychology, psychiatric nursing, and occupational therapy, among others—are drifting progressively from their scientific moorings. Moreover, I will maintain that the steady erosion of the scientific underpinnings of mental health practice bears serious, if not dire, ethical implications for mental health clinicians and consumers alike.

FIRST, THE GOOD NEWS . . .

Lest this chapter come across as a sustained Jeremiad, let me begin with three pieces of good "news," although none is genuinely new. First, numerous meta-analyses (quantitative literature reviews) have demonstrated convincingly, skeptics aside (e.g., Dineen 1998), that psychotherapy works. A broad spectrum of therapeutic interventions, including behavioral therapy, cognitive-behavioral therapy, interpersonal therapy, and perhaps even some variants of brief psychodynamic therapy, are efficacious for mood disorders, anxiety disorders, eating disorders, and several other conditions (Chambless and Ollendick 2001; Wampold 2001). Moreover, the effects of these therapies generally exceed those of nonspecific (or "placebo") interventions, such as relaxation training or nondirective listening. Despite recent controversies regarding potential adverse side effects, including suicide (e.g., Healy and Whitaker 2003; Wallach and Kirsch 2003), there is also general agreement that some pharmacological agents, including selective serotonin reuptake inhibitors (e.g., Prozac, Zoloft) and antipsychotic agents (e.g., Risperdal), are efficacious for mood/anxiety disorders and psychotic disorders, respectively, although it seems likely that drug companies have sometimes overstated their efficacy. Second, several published surveys demonstrate that many and perhaps even most psychotherapists are basing their practices on solid scientific research (e.g., Freiheit, Vye, Swan, and Cady 2004). Third, there are numerous high-quality doctoral programs in clinical psychology and related fields that place a high premium on scientific training. Many of these programs, which adopt either a "scientist-practitioner" or "clinical science" model (McFall 1991), emphasize the integration of scientific findings with clinical practice.

NOW THE BAD NEWS . . . THE SCIENTIST-PRACTITIONER GAP

Despite the good news, on balance all is not well. The past several decades have witnessed a large and probably widening gulf between research on the causes and treatments of mental disorders, on the one hand, and everyday clinical practice, on the other. This gulf has been referred to, perhaps misleadingly, as the scientist-practitioner gap (Fox 1996; Tavris 2003). I say misleadingly because this phrase inadvertently implies that science is incompatible with clinical practice, which is the very misconception I wish to dispel.

There are at least four primary lines of evidence for the scientist-practitioner gap. First, surveys indicate that approximately 25 percent of psychotherapists in the United States and Great Britain regularly use suggestive techniques, such as hypnosis, guided imagery, journaling, and body work, to recover purported memories of child sexual abuse (Polusny and Folette 1996; Poole, Lindsay, Memon, and Bull 1995). These findings are worrisome given that these suggestive techniques have been found in numerous studies to be associated with a heightened risk for false memories, with no increase in the proportion of true memories (Lynn, Lock, Loftus, Krakow, and Lilienfeld 2003; Lynn, Lock, Myers, and Payne 1997).

Second, surveys also show that 30–40 percent of clinicians in the United States use the Rorschach Inkblot Test and human figure drawings (e.g., the Draw-A-Person Test) in their practice (Watkins et al. 1995), even though these measures have been found to be essentially useless for the substantial majority of clinical purposes for which they are put (for exceptions, see Wood, Nezworski, and Garb 2003 and Lilienfeld, Wood, and Garb 2001). Perhaps even more troublesome, an estimated 35 percent of psychologists who perform evaluations for child custody cases use the Rorschach, as do an estimated 31 percent of psychologists who evaluate children for possible neglect or abuse. Yet the Rorschach Inkblot Test has never been validated for either of these clinical purposes (Wood, Nezworski, Lilienfeld, and Garb 2003).

Third, a third or more of mental health professionals who work with children suspected of having been abused use anatomically detailed dolls (ADDs) as a means of detecting such abuse (Davey and Hill 1999; Hunsley, Lee, and Wood 2003). Yet numerous studies demonstrate that ADDs are of doubtful validity, especially when combined with suggestive questioning. In particular, ADDs yield high false-positive rates, especially among African American children. These high false-positive rates in part reflect the fact that many nonabused children engage in sexualized doll play (Koocher et al. 1995; Wolfner, Faust, and Dawes 1993).

Fourth, there is compelling evidence that the majority of clients do not receive scientifically supported treatments, and that the majority of therapists do not implement them. For example, the Surgeon General's (2000) report concluded that most clients with severe mental disorders do not receive scientifically based interventions. Moreover, a large-scale survey revealed that individuals in the general population with recent histories of panic attacks or severe depression more often availed themselves of complementary and alternative treatments of little or no documented efficacy (including energy therapy, acupuncture, and laughter therapy) than of scientifically supported treatments (Kessler et al. 2001).

These disquieting findings are paralleled by surveys of clinician's practices. Mussell et al. (2000) found that only a minority of therapists who treated clients with eating disorders administered scientifically supported interventions for these conditions, namely behavioral, cognitive-behavioral, and interpersonal therapies. Moreover, a recent survey of doctoral-level psychologists in Minnesota (Freiheit et al. 2004) found that between 17 percent and 21 percent of practitioners at least occasionally use eye-movement desensitization and reprocessing (EMDR) to treat OCD, panic disorder, or social phobia, even though EMDR has only been demonstrated to be efficacious for civilian posttraumatic stress disorder. Moreover, between 8 and 10 percent use energy therapies for anxiety disorders (which ostensibly manipulate patients' invisible "energy fields"), even though such treatments have no demonstrated efficacy for these conditions.

Disturbingly, there is preliminary evidence that the scientist-practitioner gap is growing. For example, Goisman, Warshaw, and Keller (1999) found that the proportion of clients with anxiety disorders who received behavioral or cognitive-behavioral treatments—which are the only interventions firmly established as efficacious for these conditions—either remained the same or decreased from 1991 to 1996. Yet over this five-year period, there was accumulating research evidence that these interventions were efficacious for anxiety disorders. Hence, in the anxiety disorders domain, there is a striking dissociation between research evidence and clinical practice. Surveys of treatment practices for other major psychological disorders are sorely needed.

A COMMUNICATION PROBLEM

To a substantial extent, the problem underpinning the scientist-practitioner gap is one of communication. Researchers in academic settings are spending less and less of their time speaking with clinicians, and vice versa.

In addition, perhaps because of the increasing pressures placed on clinicians by managed care and other bureaucratic demands, clinicians are spending little time keeping abreast of the research literature. For example, a survey by Beutler, Williams, and Wakefield (1993) revealed that only 28 percent of mental health professionals, including psychologists, psychiatrists, and social workers, read research articles. Moreover, only 30 percent of those who attend research conferences (who are themselves a minority of mental health professionals) attend research (as opposed to clinical) presentations. As a consequence, it is hardly surprising that many clinicians administer nonscientific interventions and assessment techniques, as they are not keeping themselves apprised of the current state of the scientific evidence.

Moreover, the American Psychological Association (APA), the world's largest organization of mental health professionals, has not helped matters. A distressingly large number of the continuing education (CE) courses sponsored by APA-approved providers promote psychological procedures based on either questionable science or blatant pseudoscience, including rebirthing, Jungian sandplay therapy, psychological theatre therapy, neurofeedback, and calligraphy therapy (Lilienfeld 1998). The APA has even refused to put an end to CE workshops on critical incident stress debriefing for individuals exposed to traumatic events, a technique that has been found to be ineffective and perhaps harmful in controlled studies (McNally, Bryant, and Ehlers 2003). The state of affairs at some state psychological organizations is scarcely better. The Georgia

Psychological Association has recently awarded CE credit for workshops on energy therapy, and the Minnesota Psychological Association has recently awarded CE credit for workshops on drumming meditation and canoeing (see Lilienfeld, Lynn, and Lohr 2003).

THE REACTION

Given these deeply troubling developments, one might have expected the reaction from scientifically minded mental health professionals to be one of profound concern, even indignation. Yet in most quarters of the Ivory Tower and clinical world the silence has been deafening.

For example, no recent president of the APA has made the scientist-practitioner gap a priority, and most have barely acknowledged its existence. At least one recent APA president has come close to denying its existence (Sternberg 2003). Some have gone even further, questioning whether clinicians bear an ethical responsibility to ground their practices in scientific evidence. For example, a recent president of the APA maintained that "psychologists do not have to apologize for their treatments. Nor is there an actual need to prove their effectiveness" (Fox 2001, pp. 1–2). The current president of the APA, Ronald Levant, has argued strongly against the movement toward empirically supported therapies (Levant 2004). This movement represents an effort to identify formal criteria for, and lists of, psychological treatments that have been shown to be efficacious in rigorously controlled studies (see Herbert 2000, and Westen, Morrison, and Thompson-Brenner, in press, for thoughtful discussions of the pros and cons of this movement). According to Levant, subjective clinical experience should be weighted equally in conjunction with scientific findings in reaching treatment decisions. Therefore, he maintains, lists of empirically supported therapies prematurely constrain clinicians' freedom to use their personal experience as a guide when selecting interventions. Yet Levant's position neglects decades of research demonstrating that clinical experience, although often enormously useful as a wellspring for hypothesis generation, is severely limited for testing hypotheses systematically (Beutler 2004; Dawes, Faust, and Meehl 1989; Garb 1998).

Moreover, the accreditation standards for clinical psychology training programs have progressively loosened in recent decades. In the not-so-distant past, these programs were often required to provide graduate students with standardized coursework in research methodology, psychometrics, statistics, descriptive psychopathology, psychotherapeutic outcome research, and the like. Nevertheless, current APA standards for accreditation encourage clinical programs to adopt their own training models and evaluate programs on the basis of how closely they adhere to these models. Although perhaps reflecting a well-intentioned effort on the part of APA to foster creativity on the part of training programs, this dilution of content requirements has had the unintended effect of weakening students' training in the science of clinical psychology (Lilienfeld et al. 2003).

Our field's collective failure to police itself has resulted in increased pressure from outside the field, such as from lawyers and managed-care companies. For example, most of the impetus to prevent therapists from using suggestive techniques to recover early memories of abuse and unearth supposed "alters" in patients with multiple personality disorder has come from the legal profession, not from the APA or other professional organizations (Grove and Barden 1999). As Meehl (1993) presciently observed over a decade ago:

> It is absurd, as well as arrogant, to pretend that acquiring a Ph.D. somehow immunizes me from the errors of sampling, perception, recording, retention, retrieval, and inference to which the human mind is subject. In earlier times, all introductory psychology courses devoted a lecture or two to the classic studies in the psychology of testimony, and one mark of a psychologist was hard-nosed skepticism about folk beliefs. It seems that quite a few clinical psychologists never got exposed to this basic feature of critical thinking. My teachers at Minnesota . . . shared what Bertrand Russell called the dominant passion of the true scientist—the passion not to be fooled and not to fool anybody else . . . all of them asked the two searching questions of positivism: "What do you mean? How do you know?" If we clinicians lose that passion and forget those questions, we are little more than be-doctored, well-paid soothsayers. I see disturbing signs that this is happening and I predict that, if we do not clean up our clinical act and provide our students with role models of scientific thinking, outsiders will do it for us. (pp. 728–29)

THE SEDUCTIVE APPEAL OF PSEUDOSCIENCE IN MENTAL HEALTH

The mental health field has been remarkably susceptible to fads (Beyerstein 2001; Dawes 1994; Kalal 1999). A highly conservative estimate places the number of psychotherapies at over five hundred (Eisner 2000), and this number is increasing on a yearly basis. Moreover, the substantial majority of these five-hundred-plus treatments have never been subjected to empirical scrutiny. A highly selective sampling of treatments for which no compelling (or in many cases, even suggestive) scientific support has been obtained include Thought

Field Therapy, Visual Kinesthetic Dissociation, rebirthing, reparenting, holding therapy, facilitated communication, sensory-motor integration therapy, angel therapy, laughter therapy, past-life regression therapy, nude marathon encounter therapy, orgone therapy, psychomotor patterning, Jungian sandplay therapy, Imago Relationship Therapy, dolphin-assisted therapy, and Neurolinguistic Programming (see Lilienfeld et al. 2003 and Singer and Lalich 1996 for discussions, and see Shannon 2002, for other examples). A number of these treatments, such as Thought Field Therapy and related energy therapies, are increasingly popular and are practiced by hundreds and perhaps thousands of clinicians.

Many of these treatments fall under the broad rubric of pseudoscience, meaning that they possess many of the superficial trappings of science but precious little of its substance (Herbert 2003; Lilienfeld et al. 2003; Ruscio 2002). Because many pseudoscientific treatments are understandably appealing to mental health consumers and practitioners alike, we must all remain vigilant in the face of their seductive charms.

For one thing, pseudoscientific treatments frequently offer "quick fixes" for intractable or chronic psychological problems. For example, many proponents of Neurolinguistic Programming purport to cure severe phobias in five minutes or less. Hence, such treatments inspire hope in desperate clients and frustrated therapists.

In addition, pseudoscientific treatments often cloak their assertions in the argot of well-established disciplines, such as neuroscience, thereby lending them an unearned cachet of scientific respectability. For example, advocates of EMDR speak of "neuro-nodes" and "neural valences" when attempting to account for the effects of this technique (see Shapiro 1995). Yet many of the neuroscience concepts used by EMDR proponents are largely devoid of substantive scientific content (Lohr, Tolin, and Lilienfeld 1998).

The popularity of many pseudoscientific treatments almost surely stems from the influence of confident and charismatic "gurus" who promise dramatic advances, if not miracle cures. For example, the title of a best-selling book on EMDR, cowritten by its founder, described this technique as a "breakthrough treatment" for anxiety (Shapiro and Forrest 1997). Although EMDR is clearly more efficacious than no treatment (Davidson and Parker 2001), there is not a shred of evidence that it represents a "breakthrough" or even an important innovation in anxiety disorders treatment. Moreover, many acolytes of faddish treatments resort to an "appeal to authority" when confronted with legitimate scientific criticisms, invoking the assertions of the developers of these treatments rather than scientific evidence.

Finally, as Beyerstein (1997) observed in an article that should be required reading for all mental health professionals, there is a plethora of reasons why even entirely bogus treatments can appear efficacious. These reasons include spontaneous remission (naturally occurring improvement), placebo effects (improvement due to the mere expectation of improvement), regression to the mean (the statistical tendency for more extreme scores to become less extreme on retesting), demand characteristics (the tendency of patients to behave in ways that confirm therapists' hypotheses), and initial misdiagnosis of the patient's condition. To Beyerstein's excellent list, I would add "effort justification," the phenomenon whereby individuals who invest a great deal of time and energy in a psychological treatment may feel a need to persuade themselves that this treatment was worth the trouble (Cooper and Axsom 1982).

WHY SHOULD WE CARE?

Some mental health professionals could argue that the concerns I have raised are much ado about nothing. For example, they could contend that many untested treatments are likely to prove innocuous at worst, and that some will almost certainly prove efficacious. Moreover, perhaps it's best to let sleeping dogs lie. Many psychotherapy fads will certainly pass, and many patently ineffective treatments will slowly but surely be relegated to the dustbin of pseudoscience. Nevertheless, there are at least four problems with this increasingly ubiquitous laissez-faire attitude toward untested and demonstrably inefficacious treatments.

First, individuals who expend a great deal of time and money in pursuit of unsubstantiated treatments will often be left with precious little of either. Moreover, these individuals may forgo the chance to obtain treatments of documented efficacy. Economists term this adverse side effect "opportunity cost."

Second, pseudoscientific treatments damage the credibility of clinical psychology and other mental health disciplines. Mental health consumers who receive suboptimal treatment or misguided advice may be less likely to turn to mental health professionals for much-needed psychological help.

Third, for reasons that remain poorly understood, some individuals tend to become worse following psychotherapy. The proportion of clients who experience such "deterioration effects" is not widely agreed on, but it appears to be in the neighborhood of 3–6 percent (Strupp, Hadley, and Gomez-Schwartz 1978). Surprisingly little research has examined the predictors of deterioration in psychotherapy (Garske and Anderson 2003).

Fourth, and closely related to the preceding point, there is increasing evidence from a variety of sources that certain forms of psychotherapy are directly harmful to patients, their family members, or both. For many decades, a widely accepted maxim in the psychotherapy outcome literature was that "doing something is always better than doing nothing." According to this maxim, a novel intervention can at worst prove harmless, so it rarely if ever hurts to experiment with an untested intervention.

Bolstering this maxim was the widely invoked "Dodo Bird Verdict" (Luborksy, Singer, and Luborsky 1975; Wampold et al. 1997), named after the Dodo Bird in Lewis Carroll's *Alice in Wonderland* who, following a race, declared pollyannishly that "all have won and all must have prizes." According to the Dodo Bird verdict, all psychotherapies are equally efficacious: there are five hundred or more winners, and all cross the finish line at the same time. Extending this logic, some proponents of the Dodo Bird verdict maintain that one need not be concerned about demonstrating the efficacy of a novel therapy given that it is bound to work as well as existing therapies.

Yet recent controlled trials and meta-analyses of controlled trials demonstrate convincingly that the Dodo Bird verdict is erroneous. For example, numerous studies indicate that behavioral and cognitive-behavioral therapies tend to be superior to other therapies for at least some anxiety disorders, including obsessive-compulsive disorder and generalized anxiety disorder. Moreover, the Dodo Bird verdict does not hold for childhood and adolescent psychiatric disorders, such as conduct disorder and depression, for which behavioral and cognitive-behavioral therapies again offer a decided edge over other therapies (Chambless and Ollendick 2001; Hunsley and Di Guilio 2002).

PSYCHOLOGICAL TREATMENTS TO AVOID

Even more damaging to the Dodo Bird verdict are findings demonstrating that certain therapies tend to be iatrogenic, that is, to make individuals worse. Indeed, in a recent chapter, we (Lilienfeld, Fowler, Lohr, and Lynn, in press) construct a provisional list of "Psychological Treatments to Avoid." Specifically, we identified psychological treatments that (a) have exhibited negative effect sizes in controlled clinical trials or that (b) have been demonstrated to be physically or psychologically harmful to clients, their family members, or both.

Our preliminary list of "Psychological Treatments to Avoid" includes the following eight interventions:

(1) *Critical incident stress debriefing*, which is a popular intervention for

victims of trauma that was used widely in New York City in the wake of the September 11 terrorist attacks. This method has been shown to be either ineffective or harmful in several controlled studies, perhaps because it impedes natural coping and recovery processes (Litz, Gray, Bryant, and Adler 2002; McNally et al. 2003).

(2) *Grief counseling*, which is regarded as virtually *de rigueur* in many quarters following the loss of loved ones. Yet there is reason to suspect that grief counseling may be detrimental among many individuals experiencing normal bereavement reactions. Neimeyer's (2000) meta-analysis of twenty-three studies of grief counseling suggested the possibility of slight positive effects for some clients, but also indicated that 38 percent of clients assigned to grief counseling conditions fared more poorly than clients assigned to control conditions.

(3) *Peer group interventions for conduct disorder*, which attempt to treat children and adolescents with behavioral problems by placing them in groups. Dishion, McCord, and Poulin (1999) found that quasi-experimental studies suggested that peer group interventions with conduct-disordered adolescents resulted in a worsening of antisocial behaviors. They conjectured that these iatrogenic effects were attributable to "deviancy training," that is, the vicarious reinforcement of adolescents' antisocial propensities by peer discussion.

(4) *Scared Straight and boot camp programs*, which attempt to treat conduct-disordered adolescents by means of a "get tough" approach that exposes them to the harsh consequences of a criminal lifestyle (Scared Straight programs) or military-style discipline (boot camp programs). Although intuitively appealing and politically popular, these programs are at best ineffective and perhaps iatrogenic (Peters, Thomas, and Zamberlan 1997; Petrosino and Turpin-Petrosino 2002).

(5) *Recovered memory techniques*, which as noted earlier comprise a variety of suggestive procedures, such as hypnosis, guided imagery, and journaling, to unearth purported memories of early trauma, and which have been shown in numerous laboratory studies to be associated with an elevated risk of confidently held false memories (Lynn et al. 2003).

(6) *Dissociative identity disorder (DID) oriented therapy*, which aims to uncover purported alter personalities in individuals with suspected DID, known formerly as multiple personality disorder. Like recovered memory techniques, such therapy relies heavily on suggestive procedures, including hypnosis and repeated prompting of ostensible indwelling identities. DID-oriented therapy results in an increased number of alters across the course of treatment, and there are good reasons to believe that such alters are being created rather

than discovered by clinicians (see Lilienfeld et al. 1999 and Spanos 1994 for discussions).

(7) *Attachment therapies*, which include rebirthing, reparenting, and holding therapies, and which are premised on the unsupported assumption that separation from one's biological parents produces enduring adverse effects in children, including bottled-up rage and antisocial behavior in the adoptive home. These therapies sometimes require extreme levels of physical restraint, and they have been linked to the deaths of several children, including Candace Newmaker, a ten-year-old girl smothered to death in Colorado by several therapists who were practicing a variant of rebirthing therapy. There is no research evidence that attachment therapies are efficacious (Mercer 2002).

(8) *Facilitated communication*, which is based on the entirely unsupported conjecture that autistic children's communication defects are attributable to motor, not cognitive, problems (Biklen 1990). Hence, with the aid of a facilitator who guides the child's hands, autistic children (and children with similar developmental disabilities) who are mute or severely language-impaired can purportedly produce communications using a computer keyboard or letter pad. Nevertheless, there is overwhelming evidence from controlled studies that the "facilitated communications" ostensibly produced by autistic children are unwittingly generated by facilitators themselves, who are guiding autistic children's hands over the keyboard (Herbert, Sharp, and Gaudiano 2002). The use of facilitated communication has resulted in numerous uncorroborated allegations of child sexual abuse against the parents of autistic children, in some cases leading to the removal of these children from parents' homes.

THE FACILITATED COMMUNICATION DEBACLE

The facilitated communication debacle underscores dramatically many of the hazards of unsubstantiated mental health treatments. This technique was remarkably popular in the early 1990s following its "importation" from Australia (Romanczyk, Arnstein, Soorya, and Gillis 2003). Numerous parents who were understandably desperate to find a means of communicating with their autistic children seized upon this technique as a miracle cure for their children's profound linguistic deficits. Facilitated communication was especially appealing to parents and practitioners because it implied that most autistic children are not mentally retarded, as virtually all psychologists and psychiatrists had believed, but rather motorically impaired. Remarkably, facilitated communication was disseminated far and wide before any rigorously controlled tests of its efficacy were undertaken (Herbert et al. 2002). As a consequence, the hopes of the parents of autistic children were first raised and then dashed in the cruelest fashion imaginable, and many parents found themselves separated from their children as a consequence of unsubstantiated allegations of abuse.

The tragic story of facilitated communication imparts at least two crucial lessons. First, it underscores why controlled tests of efficacy are required before treatments are promoted and marketed to the general public and practitioners. Second, it underscores the limitations of subjective clinical judgment and experience. Practitioners who enthusiastically embraced facilitated communication "saw" with their own eyes that this method worked. But they were the hapless victims of a diabolical illusion. The facilitated communication debacle reminds us that although informal clinical observations can be helpful in the context of discovery, they are extremely limited in the context of justification, that is, systematic hypothesis testing (Reichenbach 1938).

ETHICAL IMPLICATIONS

When mental health professionals administer treatment and assessment techniques that have clearly been shown to be ineffective or harmful, troubling ethical questions arise. Moreover, when these professionals administer techniques that are entirely untested, they bear an ethical obligation to inform their clients that these techniques are experimental.

The APA and other professional organizations (e.g., state and provincial licensing boards) must be willing to impose meaningful sanctions, including expulsion in extreme cases, on practitioners who provide clinical services that have consistently been shown to be ineffective or harmful in well-conducted scientific studies. Moreover, these organizations must be willing to impose sanctions on therapists who do not provide clients with full informed consent regarding the treatments they offer, including treatments that have never been subjected to controlled trials. From a libertarian perspective, one could justifiably argue that clients have every right to undergo untested interventions if they wish to. But in such cases, clients must be fully informed of the potential risks and benefits of, as well as of the absence of research evidence for, these treatments.

The APA Ethics Code offers guidance concerning practitioners' ethical responsibilities when administering unsubstantiated or untested techniques. For example, this code makes clear in several places (e.g., Rule 1.06) that psychologists must rely on the best available scientific knowledge when making professional judgments. Moreover, Rule 1.14 asserts that "psychologists [should] take reasonable steps to avoid harming their patients or clients, research participants, students, and others with whom they work, and to minimize harm where it is foreseeable and unavoidable." Yet the APA has been reluctant or unwilling to impose sanctions on practitioners who violate these rules, including practitioners who use suggestive practices to recover ostensible memories of early trauma, a practice that (a) unambiguously runs counter to scientific evidence and (b) has the potential to harm clients and their families. Ethical guidelines have little meaning if they are not enforced.

Scientific findings cannot dictate ethical decisions, but they can inform them. In the case of mental health practice, an accumulating body of research evidence affords invaluable guidance to clinicians for distinguishing techniques that are helpful from those that those that are ineffective or potentially harmful. The time is long past for professional organizations to hold clinicians accountable for neglecting such evidence. Relying on research evidence to inform one's choice of clinical interventions is both sound science and sound ethics.

REFERENCES

Beutler, L. E. "The Empirically Supported Treatments Movement: A Practitioner's Perspective." *Clinical Psychology: Science and Practice* 11 (2004): 225–29.

Beutler, L. E., R. E. Williams, and P. J. Wakefield. "Obstacles to Disseminating Applied Psychological Science." *Journal of Applied and Preventive Psychology* 2 (1993): 53–58.

Beyerstein, B. "Why Do Bogus Therapies Seem to Work?" *Skeptical Inquirer* 21 (1997): 29–34.

———. "Fringe Therapies: The Public at Risk." *Scientific Review of Alternative Medicine* 5 (2001): 5–13.

Biklen, D. "Communication Unbound: Autism and Praxis." *Harvard Educational Review* 60 (1990): 291–314.

Bottcher, J., and T. Isorena. *LEAD: A Boot Camp and Intensive Parole Program: An Implementation and Process Evaluation of the First Year.* NCJ 150513. Washington, DC: California Youth Authority and US Department of Justice, National Institute of Justice, 1994.

Chambless, D. L., and T. H. Ollendick. "Empirically Supported Psychological Interventions: Controversies and Evidence." *Annual Review of Psychology,* 52 (2001): 685–716.

Cooper, J., and D. Axsom, "Effort Justification in Psychotherapy." In *Integrations of Clinical and Social Psychology.* Edited by G. Weary and H. Mirels. New York: Oxford University Press, 1982.

Davey, R. I., and J. Hill. "The Variability of Practice in Interviews Used by Professionals to Investigate Child Sexual Abuse." *Child Abuse and Neglect* 23 (1999): 571–78.

Davidson, P. R., and K. C. H. Parker. "Eye Movement Desensitization and Reprocessing: A Meta-analysis." *Journal of Consulting and Clinical Psychology*, 69 (2001): 305–16.

Dawes, R. M. *House of Cards: Psychology and Psychotherapy Built on Myth*. New York: Free Press, 1994.

Dawes, R. M., D. Faust, and P. E. Meehl. "Clinical versus Actuarial Judgment." *Science* 243 (1989): 1668–74.

Dineen, T. "Psychotherapy: The Snake Oil of the 90s?" *Skeptic* 6 (1998): 54–63.

Dishion, T., J. McCord, and F. Poulin. "When Interventions Harm: Peer Groups and Problem Behavior." *American Psychologist* 54 (1999): 755–54.

Eisner, D. A. *The Death of Psychotherapy: From Freud to Alien Abductions*. Westport, CT: Praeger, 2000.

Fox, R. E. "Charlatanism, Scientism, and Psychology's Social Contract." *American Psychologist* 51: 777–84.

Fox, R. E. "The Dark Side of Evidence-based Treatment." *Practitioner Focus*. Winter 2001. http/www.apa.org/practice/pf/jan00/cappchair.html.

Freiheit, S. R., D. Vye, R. Swan, and M. Cady. "Cognitive-behavioral Therapy for Anxiety: Is Dissemination Working?" *Behavior Therapist*, 27 (2004): 25–32.

Garb, H. N. *Studying the Clinician: Judgment Research and Psychological Assessment*. Washington, DC: American Psychological Association, 1998.

Garske, J. P., and T. Anderson. "Toward a Science of Psychotherapy Research: Present Status and Evaluation." In Lilienfeld, Lynn, and Lohr, *Science and Pseudoscience in Clinical Psychology*, 145–75.

Goisman, R. M., M. G. Warshaw, and M. B. Keller. "Psychosocial Treatment Prescriptions for Generalized Anxiety Disorder, Social Phobia, and Panic Disorder, 1991–1996." *American Journal of Psychiatry* 156 (1999): 1819–21.

Grove, W. M., and R. C. Barden. "Protecting the Integrity of the Legal System: The Admissibility of Testimony from Mental Health Experts under Daubert/Kumho Analyses." *Psychology, Public Policy, and Law* 5 (1999): 224–42.

Healy, D., and C. Whitaker. "Antidepressant and Suicide: Risk-benefit Conundrums." *Journal of Psychiatry and Neuroscience* 28 (2003): 340–47.

Herbert, J. D. "Defining Empirically Supported Treatments: Pitfalls and Possible Solutions." *Behavior Therapist* 23 (2000): 13–122, 134.

Herbert, J. D., I. R. Sharp, and B. A. Gaudiano. "Separating Fact from Fiction in the Etiology and Treatment of Autism: A Scientific Review of the Evidence." *Scientific Review of Mental Health Practice* 1 (2002): 23–43.

Hunsley, J., C. M. Lee, and J. M. Wood. "Controversial and Questionable Assessment Techniques." In Lilienfeld, Lynn, and Lohr, *Science and Pseudoscience in Clinical Psychology*, 39–76

Kalal, D. M. "Critical Thinking in Clinical Practice: Pseudoscience, Fad Psychology, and the Behavior Therapist." *Behavior Therapist* 22 (1999): 81–84.

Kessler, R. C., J. Soukup, R. B. Davis, D. F. Foster, , S. A. Wilkey, T.J.L. van Rompay, et al. "The Use of Complementary and Alternative Treatments to Treat Anxiety and Depression in the United States." *American Journal of Psychiatry* 158 (2001): 289–94.

Koocher, G. P., G. S. Goodman, C. S. White, W. N. Friedrich, A. B. Sivan, and C. R. Reynolds. "Psychological Science and the Use of Anatomically Detailed Dolls in Child Sexual Abuse Assessments." *Psychological Bulletin* 118 (1995): 199–222.

Levant, R. F. "The Empirically Validated Treatments Movement: A Practitioner's Perspective." *Clinical Psychology: Science and Practice* 11 (2004): 219–24.

Lilienfeld, S. O. "Pseudoscience in Contemporary Clinical Psychology: What It Is and What We Can Do about It." *Clinical Psychologist* 51 (1998): 3–9.

Lilienfeld, S. O., and S. J. Lynn. "Dissociative Identity Disorder: Multiple Personalities, Multiple Controversies." In Lilienfeld, Lynn, and Lohr, *Science and Pseudoscience in Clinical Psychology*, 109–42.

Lilienfeld, S. O., S. J. Lynn, I. Kirsch, J. F. Chaves, T. R. Sarbin, G. K. Ganaway, and R. A. Powell. "Dissociative Identity Disorder and the Sociocognitive Model: Recalling the Lessons of the Past." *Psychological Bulletin* 125 (1999): 507–23.

Lilienfeld, S .O., S. J. Lynn, and J. M. Lohr, eds. *Science and Pseudoscience in Clinical Psychology*. New York: Guilford Press, 2003.

Lilienfeld, S. O., J. M. Wood, and H. N. Garb. "The Scientific Status of Projective Techniques." *Psychological Science in the Public Interest* 1 (2000): 27–66.

Lilienfeld, S. O., K. A. Fowler, J. M. Lohr, and S. J. Lynn. "Pseudoscience, Nonscience, and Nonsense in Clinical Psychology: Dangers and Remedies." In *Destructive Trends in Mental Health*. Edited by N. Cummings and R. Wright. New York: Taylor & Francis, in press.

Litz, B. T., M. J. Gray, R. A. Bryant, A. B. Adler. "Early Intervention for Trauma: Current Status and Future Directions." *Clinical Psychology: Science and Practice* 9 (2002): 112–34.

Lohr, J. M., K. A. Fowler, and S. O. Lilienfeld. "The Dissemination and Promotion of Pseudoscience in Clinical Psychology: The Challenge to Legitimate Clinical Science." *Clinical Psychologist* 55, no. 3 (2002): 4–9.

Lohr, J. M., Tolin, D. F., and S. O. Lilienfeld "Efficacy of Eye Movement Desensitization and Reprocessing: Implications for Behavior Therapy." *Behavior Therapy* 26 (1998): 123–56.

Luborsky, L., B. Singer, and E. Luborsky. "Comparative Studies of Psychotherapies: Is It True that "Everybody has won and all must have prizes?" *Archives of General Psychiatry* 32 (1975): 995–1008.

Lynn, S. J., T. G. Lock, E. F. Loftus, E. Krackow, and S. O. Lilienfeld. "The Remembrance of Things Past: Problematic Memory Recovery Techniques in Psychotherapy." In Lilienfeld, Lynn, and Lohr, *Science and Pseudoscience in Clinical Psychology*, 205–39.

Lynn, S. J., T. G. Lock, B. Myers, and D. G. Payne. "Recalling the Unrecallable: Should Hypnosis Be Used to Recover Memories in Psychotherapy?" *Current Directions in Psychological Science* 6 (1997): 79–83.

McFall, R. M. "Manifesto for a Science of Clinical Psychology." *Clinical Psychologist* 44 (1991): 75–88.

McNally, R. J., R. A. Bryant, and A. Ehlers. "Does Early Psychological Intervention Promote Recovery from Posttraumatic Stress?" *Psychological Science in the Public Interest* 4 (1997): 45–49.

Meehl, P. E. "Philosophy of Science: Help or Hindrance?" *Psychological Reports*, 72 (1993): 707–33.

Mercer, J. "Attachment Therapy: A Treatment without Empirical Support." *Scientific Review of Mental Health Practice* 1 (2002): 105–12.

Mussell, M. P., R. D. Crosby, S. J. Crowe, A. J. Kropke, C. B. Peterson, S. A. Wonderlic, and J. E. Mitchell. "Utilization of Empirically Supported Treatments for Individuals with Eating Disorders: A Survey of Psychologists." *International Journal of Eating Disorders* 27 (2000): 230–37.

Neimeyer, R. "Searching for the Meaning of Meaning: Grief Therapy and the Process of Reconstruction." *Death Studies* 24 (2000): 541–58.

Peters, M., D. Thomas, and C. Zamberlan. *Boot Camps for Juvenile Offenders.* Program Summary, NCJ 164258. Washington, DC: US Department of Justice, Office of Juvenile Justice and Delinquency Prevention, 1997.

Petrosino, A., and C. Turpin-Petrosino. "'Scared Straight' and Other Prison Tour Programs for Preventing Juvenile Delinquency." *Cochrane Library*, issue 4.

Polusny, M. A., and V. M. Folette. "Remembering Childhood Sexual Abuse: A National Survey of Psychologists' clinical Practices, Beliefs, and Personal Experiences." *Professional Psychology: Research and Practice* 27 (1996): 41–52.

Poole, D. A., D. S. Lindsay, A. Memon, and R. Bull. "Psychotherapists' Opinions, Practices, and Experiences with Memories of Incestuous Abuse." *Journal of Consulting and Clinical Psychology* 68 (1995): 426–37.

Reichenbach, H. *Experience and Prediction.* Chicago: University of Illinois Press, 1938.

Romanczyk, R. G., L. Arnstein, L. V. Soorya, and J. Gillis. "The Myriad of Controversial Treatments for Autism: A Critical Evaluation of Efficacy." In Lilienfeld, Lynn, and Lohr, *Science and Pseudoscience in Clinical Psychology*, 363–98.

Ruscio, J. *Clear Thinking with Psychology: Separating sense from Nonsense.* Pacific Grove, CA: Wadsworth, 2002.

Shannon, S., ed. *Handbook of Complementary and Alternative Therapies in Mental Health.* San Diego, CA: Academic Press, 2002.

Shapiro, F. *Eye Movement Desensitization and Reprocessing: Basic Protocols, Principles, and Procedures.* New York: Guilford Press, 1995.

Shapiro, F., and M. S. Forrest. *EMDR: The Breakthrough Therapy for Overcoming Anxiety, Stress, and Trauma.* New York: Basic Books, 1997.

Singer, M., and J. Lalich. *Crazy Therapies: What Are They? How Do They Work?* San Francisco: Jossey-Bass, 1996.

Spanos, N. P. "Multiple Identity Enactments and Multiple Personality Disorder: A Sociocognitive Perspective." *Psychological Bulletin* 116 (1994): 143–65.

Sternberg, R. J. "Analyzing the Relationship between Therapists and Research Psychologists." *Chronicle Review*, April 4, 2003.

Strupp, H. H., S. W. Hadley, and B. Gomez-Schwartz. *Psychotherapy for Better or Worse: The Problem of Negative Effects.* New York: Wiley, 1978.

Surgeon General. *Mental Health: A Report of the Surgeon General.* Washington, DC: Department of Health and Public Services, 2002.

Tavris, C. "The Widening Scientist-Practitioner Gap." In Lilienfeld, Lynn, and Lohr, *Science and Pseudoscience in Clinical Psychology*, ix–xvii.

Wallach, H., and I. Kirsch. "Herbal Treatments and Antidepressant Medication: Similar Data, Divergent Conclusions." In Lilienfeld, Lynn, and Lohr, *Science and Pseudoscience in Clinical Psychology*, 306–30.

Wampold, B. E. *The Great Psychotherapy Debate: Models, Methods, and Findings.* Mahwah, NJ: Erlbaum, 2001.

Wampold, B. E., G. W. Mondin, M. Moody, F. Stich, K. Benson, and H. Ahn. "A meta-analysis of Outcome Studies Comparing Bona Fide Psychotherapies: Empirically, 'All have won and all must have prizes.'" *Psychological Bulletin* 122 (1997): 203–15.

Watkins, C. E., V. L. Campbell, R. Nieberding, and R. Hallmark. "Contemporary Practice of Psychological Assessment by Clinical Psychologists." *Professional Psychology: Research and Practice* 26 (1995): 54–60.

Westen, D., C. Morrison, and H. Thompson-Brenner. "The Empirical Status of Empirically Supported Therapies: Assumptions, Methods, and Findings." *Psychological Bulletin* (in press).

Wolfner, G., D. Faust, and R. M. Dawes. "The Use of Anatomically Detailed Dolls in Sexual Abuse Evaluations: The State of the Science." *Applied and Preventive Psychology* 2 (1993): 1–11.

Wood, J. M., M. T. Nezworski, and N. N. Garb. "What's Right with the Rorschach?" *Scientific Review of Mental Health Practice* 2 (2003): 142–46.

Wood, J. M., M. T. Nezworski, S. O. Lilienfeld, and H. N. Garb. *What's Wrong with the Rorschach? Science Confronts the Controversial Inkblot Test.* San Francisco: Jossey-Bass, 2003.

21

FRINGE PSYCHOTHERAPIES
The Public at Risk

BARRY L. BEYERSTEIN

> **Knowledge consists in understanding the evidence that establishes the fact, not in the belief that it is a fact.**
> —Charles T. Spraling

From Hippocrates to the present, the first duty of the helping professions has been "Do no harm." Unfortunately, a widening gap between science and the further reaches of psychotherapy has allowed certain practices to flourish that have the potential to do much harm. Although the vast majority of counselors who engage in "talking therapies" continue to act responsibly, the profession has not always been as quick as it should be in curtailing fringe practitioners whose antics put the unsuspecting public at risk. At the outset, it must be said that although fringe practices such as "rebirthing" and Neurolinguistic Programming are based on what Richard Rosen[1] has aptly dubbed "psychobabble," most of them probably do little damage in the long run—providing we overlook the costs of pandering to the narcissistic irrationalism of society's more affluent worriers. Despite their absurd premises, these therapeutic outliers at least provide clients of a certain metaphysical bent with com-

From the *Scientific Review of Alternative Medicine* 5, no. 2 (Spring 2001): 5–13. Presented as a keynote address to the 2002 Annual Convention of the Canadian Psychological Association.

forting mythologies that explain why their lives are not as fulfilling as they had expected. Indirectly, these quaint rituals can supply existential support, emotional consolation, and even some useful spurs to change troublesome habits. Thus, on balance, psychotherapies founded on ill-conceived assumptions may still prove beneficial if they furnish needed reassurance in an atmosphere where clients can mull over solutions to their dissatisfactions in life.

That said, the dangers posed by fringe therapists arise principally in three ways. One is the potential for manipulation and fraud. Cultlike pseudotherapies can prey on the dependency needs of vulnerable people while extracting unconscionable sums of money. The nonsensical prattle of Scientology is but one example.[2,3,4] Other fringe operators have been known to victimize clients sexually as well as monetarily. All told, these victims could have been helped much more ethically, effectively, and cheaply by scientifically trained counselors who would target specific, tractable problems in their lives. Another concern is that inadequately trained therapists may fail to recognize early signs of serious psychopathologies that, left untreated, could prove disastrous. And finally, much hardship has been created, albeit often with the best of intentions, by ill-informed counselors who encourage their clients' delusions while claiming to "recover" repressed memories of childhood sexual abuse, ritual satanic abuse, or abduction by extraterrestrials.[5]

HOW DID THIS STATE OF AFFAIRS COME ABOUT?

As scientific psychology emerged from wholesale reliance on intuition and folk wisdom, its pioneers argued that the best way to train psychotherapists was the so-called scientist-practitioner model (also called the "Boulder model" after the Colorado campus whose psychology department was an early proponent). It was assumed that if therapists had a strong background in behavioral research, they would base their professional activities on a valid understanding of human memory, cognition, emotion, motivation, personality, and brain function. Sad to say, this linkage has become increasingly strained as an assortment of new players has been drawn into the lucrative therapeutic-industrial complex. The practice of psychotherapy is drifting further from its scientific underpinnings as a growing percentage of the therapeutic workforce is graduated from stand-alone schools of professional psychology and a variety of programs in schools of social work and nursing.

To make matters worse, a number of for-profit, nonaccredited diploma mills have sprung up, offering degrees of questionable quality to aspiring psychotherapists on the run. And with the growth of the "New Age" movement, the market has also been flooded by a growing cadre of therapists with little formal training but an immense investment in pop-psychology and "post modernist" psychobabble. In most jurisdictions, these entrepreneurs cannot call themselves psychologists or psychiatrists because licensing statutes restrict these titles to professionals with specified credentials and training. They can, however, offer their services (where local laws permit) by appropriating unreserved titles such as counselor, psychotherapist, psychoanalyst, sex therapist, pastoral counselor, Dianetics auditor (one of several pseudonyms for Scientology), New Age guide, relationship advisor, mental therapist, etc.

To the extent that many of these people are kind, empathetic individuals possessed of some common sense, they undoubtedly help more than a few troubled clients. This, of course, is all to the good and, as Dawes[6] points out, research shows that, for most everyday psychological difficulties, there is not much evidence that therapists with extensive professional training have greater rates of success than these sympathetic listeners armed with the conventional wisdom of the ages. The dangers arise, however, when their lack of training makes untutored advisors more likely to venture into the risky pursuits discussed below. There is also the possibility that bad advice could exacerbate rather than alleviate clients' complaints. The public is generally unaware of the fact that regulations in most jurisdictions governing who can perform psychotherapy are fairly weak. This invites increasing numbers of self-styled entrepreneurs whose training is of the "watch one, do one, teach one" variety. Unless he or she checks in advance, the average client arriving at the clinic door will have little way of knowing which brand of therapist the luck of the draw will provide.

The thinning of the bond between psychotherapy and empirical research is reflected in the fact that even the more respectable stand-alone professional schools generally offer a "Psy. D." (Doctor of Psychology) degree rather than the traditional PhD. The PhD is a research degree, requiring competence in experimental design and statistics and the ability to understand and criticize, if not actually contribute, to the scientific literature. In the scientist-practitioner model, critical thinking skills are honed as trainees acquire a grounding in the science of psychology at the postgraduate level before specializing in psychodiagnostics and psychotherapeutics. In this way, the need for impartial follow-ups to gauge the effectiveness of therapeutic techniques is impressed upon would-be providers. Most stand-alone professional psychology schools, catering to the demands of those eager to achieve professional status with less of this tedious exposure to the science of psychology, have reduced that portion of their curriculum in favor of an apprenticeship approach where particular therapeutic techniques are assimilated by rote. Even in many university-based clinical psychology programs that still require the methodology courses and research participation, there has been a growing tendency for clinical training to become isolated from other parts of their departments where the bulk of the theoretical and experimental work is done. One result of this estrangement has been that many clinical trainees leave these programs insufficiently committed to the idea that therapeutic interventions should be tied to research that supports their safety and effectiveness.

This failure to instill a self-critical attitude in many therapists-in-training was deplored by Paul Meehl,[7] a former president of the American Psychological Association, over a decade ago:

> When I was a student, there was at least one common factor present in all of the psychology faculty . . . namely, the general scientific commitment not to be fooled and not to fool anyone else. Some things have happened in the world of clinical practice that worry me in this respect. That skepsis, that passion not to be fooled and not to fool anyone else, does not seem to be as fundamental a part of all psychologists' mental equipment as it was a half century ago. One mark of a good psychologist is to be critical of evidence. . . . I have heard of some psychological testimony in court rooms locally in which this critical mentality appears to be largely absent.

At the highest levels of the profession, the erosion of the linkage between science and clinical practice was further aggravated in recent years when many research psychologists left the American Psychological Association (APA) to form the rival American Psychological Society. The defectors felt that the APA was undervaluing the scientific side of its mandate as it devoted more effort to lobbying and other professional issues primarily of concern to clinicians. Many also felt that the APA had been too timid in disciplining those of its members who engage in scientifically dubious practices. On several occasions, I have witnessed this reluctance to chastise peddlers of outlandish wares myself. My disappointments sprang from fruitless attempts to get various psychological associations to rein in their members who charge clients for scientifically discredited services such as subliminal audiotapes, graphology (handwriting analysis), dubious psychological tests, bogus therapy techniques, and various so-called *rejuvenation* techniques for recovering supposedly repressed memories. I continue to be appalled to see journals of various psychological associations with advertisements for courses carrying official continuing education credits for therapists that promote this kind of pseudoscience. The political will to sanction well-connected, dues-paying mavericks is obviously weak.

In the case of psychiatry, one would have hoped that, as a specialty of medicine, the basic science taught in the premedical curriculum, and medical training itself, would make practitioners less susceptible to pseudoscience. Unfortunately, many departures from science-based theories have been perpetrated by psychiatrists.[8] For example, there are well-known psychiatrists among those who advocate treating current maladjustments by encouraging patients to "re-live" mental trauma that supposedly occurred *in utero*, during birth, or even in previous incarnations.[1,9] There are others who still support the discredited views of "hidden memories" criticized below, and the most prominent advocate of the "alien abduction" hypothesis is John Mack, a professor of psychiatry at the Harvard Medical School.[10] Modern biologically oriented psychiatrists overwhelmingly reject such views, but many in the older generation of psychodynamically trained (i.e., Freudian) analysts cling to other diagnoses and therapies based on scientifically dubious rationales.[11]

Summarizing the foregoing trends, Lilienfeld,[12] a model for the hard-nosed scientist-practitioner, concluded that many cherished assumptions "taken for granted by most [clinicians] are little more than pseudoscientific beliefs built upon an edifice of myth and misconception." Let us now examine some of those myths.

PSYCHOTHERAPEUTIC FICTIONS

Mainstream psychotherapies are highly successful. Scientific understanding of how best to alleviate emotional distress and other problems of living has been steadily accumulating, but those who specialize in talk therapy still have much to be modest about. With respect to the effectiveness of psychotherapy in general, Dawes[6] summarized several meta-analyses of the therapy outcome literature. Meta-analysis is a mathematical technique for combining and differentially weighting the results of many individual studies in a way that can provide a more reliable estimate of the effects of the manipulation in question than simply tallying up the number of studies "for and against." As Hagen[13] points out, however, meta-analyses can be misleading, especially in the realm of psychotherapeutic outcome research. The conclusions drawn from a meta-analysis are only as sound as the studies that were included in it and the judgment of the reviewer who chooses and weights them. It is the contention of Epstein [in the *Scientific Review of Alternative Medicine* 5, no. 2 (Spring 2001)] that even the modest claims of therapeutic efficacy conceded by Dawes[6] Lilienfeld,[12] the *Consumer Reports* survey,[14] and others are overstated because the methodologies employed in most of the studies of therapeutic outcome suffer from substantial defects.

Be that as it may, Dawes[6] argues that when psychotherapists base their interventions on the reliable research at their disposal, there is reason to believe that recipients will be helped—though not to the extent that many assume and all would wish. While research shows that there is a tendency for psychological complaints to get better, even if they are not treated, and that there is a placebo effect with psychological interventions, just as with medical treatments, there is some evidence, that psychotherapy has more than just a placebo effect. The upshot is that the *process* of interacting with a sympathetic mentor in all but the most nonsensical psychotherapeutic settings can promote real, albeit often modest, improvements in emotional adjustment. While these data provide some comfort to treatment providers, the same studies consistently indicate that the effectiveness of treatment is unrelated to specific type of training the therapist has had or the length of time he or she has been practicing. Looking at the same data, Lilienfeld[11] concluded, "There is no compelling evidence that clients need to pay high-priced professionals to enact psychological change; relatively straightforward behavioral interventions implemented by para-professionals will often suffice."

Even if minimally trained therapists can do some good, there remains the danger that they will divert clients from treatments that would help them more. More worrisome is the possibility that their limited knowledge will lead them to apply risky procedures that can exacerbate existing conditions or even create serious problems of their own. When such malpractice occurs, these uncertified therapists have no professional associations and disciplinary boards to whom dissatisfied customers can turn. It is when therapeutic fads emerge from a research vacuum and treatments lack proper outcome evaluations to back them up that these safety concerns arise.

Clinical Judgment

One of the most prevalent misconceptions in the field of psychotherapy is that "clinical judgment" is a reliable basis for deriving predictions about clients' behavior (e.g., regarding recidivism, violence-proneness, etc., or even job suitability). In fact, the kind of reasoning involved in these judgments tends to be quite fallible.[15,16,17,18] As Dawes[6] concluded in his devastating review, predictions based on simple statistical formulas almost always outperform those based on the *ad hoc* reasoning touted as "clinical intuition." Research also indicates that increased experience or specialized training in the field is unlikely to improve a clinician's hit rate for such judgments. Dawes goes so far as to assert that the clinician's role in making these predictions should be restricted to gathering the raw data that researchers will use for deriving reliable statistical decision-making rules. Once these rules have been formulated, their strict application will produce far better predictions than therapists' subjective impressions.

Psychoanalysis

Psychoanalysis, the system invented by Freud and developed by followers such as Jung, Adler, Fromm, Reich, and Sullivan is almost synonymous with psychotherapy in the public mind. Its concepts are so ingrained in literature, cinema, and everyday discourse that most laypersons are surprised when they hear that psychoanalysis has been widely attacked as a nonfalsifiable pseudo-science.[11,19,20,21,22] Its detractors also point to its culture-bound and misogynistic views of personality, the excessive duration and cost of its treatments (weekly, over many years), and its poor track record in helping any but the mildest of psychological complaints. The psychoanalytic movement has also been largely responsible for perpetuating several popular misconceptions, discussed below. Among these dubious conjectures are: (a) that most psychological problems in adults stem from trauma or abuse in childhood, (b) that people are inevitably damaged, psychologically, by tragedies that befall them, (c) that the mind routinely "represses" memories of events that would be too disconcerting if allowed to enter awareness, and (d) that the mind, when traumatized, readily "splits" to form multiple, experientially isolated personalities.

The Trauma/Psychopathology Connection

With respect to the causes of emotional dysfunction, much personal and societal harm has resulted from the uncritical acceptance (among some therapists, as well as the public) of the assumption that most psychological problems stem from trauma or maltreatment early in life. In an excellent critique of this supposition, Pope[23] points out that, alongside those who *were* mistreated and *do* bear emotional scars in later life, there are many others who were abused as children but grew into surprisingly well-adjusted, high-achieving adults. On the other hand, there are many people who enjoyed a loving, supportive upbringing but nonetheless suffer great emotional torment as adults. The conjecture that psychopathology necessarily results from past trauma is easy to accept because it fits our intuition that horrible problems should have horrible causes and because clinical practice typically lacks the appropriate control groups for sorting out such causal attributions.[15,16,17,18] Once again, familiarity with scientific psychology would alert people to the fact that, as far as general happiness or unhappiness with one's lot in life is concerned, inherited constitutional factors account for more variance than one's objective situation.[24] Because abuse sometimes does lead to psychopathology, there is also a tendency to jump to the conclusion that mistreatment necessarily underlies most cases of maladjustment. Many unsuspecting persons, seeking help for vaguely focused problems of living, have stumbled upon recovery-obsessed therapists who assume (and sometimes aggressively suggest) that the cause of the client's unhappiness must lie in forgotten abuse at the hands of family, friends, satanic cults, or visitors from outer space. In their zeal to uncover this mistreatment, these counselors have been known to create false beliefs in their clients that they were victimized.[5,23,25,26]

In a related vein, concern has been raised about the growing number of doubtful diagnoses of Post-Traumatic Stress Disorder (PTSD).[27] With the aid of well-meaning therapists, many people are now seeking compensation for emotional difficulties supposedly caused by incidents that are little more than what used to be considered the vicissitudes of life. In fact, most people are far more resilient than is generally believed and this mounting number of questionable demands for compensation is beginning to threaten the solvency of some insurance plans. As with the aforementioned survivors of abusive childhoods, Bowman[18] has shown that there are substantial individual differences in how people react to major adversity in their lives. Once again, the problem arises from the lack of appropriate comparison groups for forming clinical judgments. Just as someone who spends too much time in the vicinity of the divorce courts might be hard-pressed to believe that anyone has a successful marriage, reliance on clinical experience alone can produce an inflated estimate of the likelihood that PTSD will follow a personal misfortune. According to Bowman,[18] many clinicians develop a faulty baseline for making such diagnoses because they typically see only a subset of those who survive catastrophic events, that is, the ones who subsequently seek help for protracted emotional disturbances. The rest, who overcome their horrific experiences in one way or another, get on with their lives and do not show up in therapists' offices, and hence in clinicians' subjective tallies. Consequently, therapists who do not read beyond their narrow professional specialties are in danger of developing unrealistically high expectations that emotional debility will follow a cataclysmic event. This, in turn, can foster an undue willingness to support those who claim to suffer PTSD after relatively mild incidents.

This inclination can be magnified if the therapist is insufficiently mindful of the base rate of similar symptoms in the population at large. In fact, the sorts of difficulties typically attributed to PTSD (mood swings, fatigue, headaches, rotating bodily pains, and difficulties with concentration, memory, sleep, digestion, etc.) are fairly prevalent in those who suffered no comparable trauma.[18,28] To assume automatically that the symptoms one sees are necessarily the result of past trauma is to commit the logical fallacy known as *post hoc, ergo propter hoc* ("after this, therefore because of this"). The trauma and symptoms may be causally connected, but not necessarily.

Multiple Personality

If proof were needed that conventionally trained psychotherapists can succumb to pseudoscientific thinking, a case in point would be the current diagnostic fad, "Multiple Personality Disorder" (MPD), also known as "Dissociative Identity Disorder."[8] The mere fact that a psychological syndrome could rocket from obscurity to near-epidemic proportions in a remarkably short interval should, in itself, raise suspicions of an iatrogenic component. The MPD fad could only have taken hold where proponents lacked a firm grasp of the relevant empirical literature and insurance carriers were willing to pay for the prolonged treatment proponents say is required. The modern advocates who revived the formerly discarded diagnosis of MPD seriously underestimated the power of social conditioning in conjunction with the high suggestibility of some individuals to *create* rather than *reveal* apparent multiple personalities. These misconceptions spread rapidly by way of plots in novels and movies, uncritical media reports, and an endless parade of "pop psychology" books aimed at the general public.[29]

The history of the MPD craze has been analyzed in a penetrating volume by the late Nicholas Spanos.[30] It shows how patients with a weakly developed sense of self can interpret the complex, ambiguous communications of therapists in ways that engage imaginal and other cognitive skills to create the subjective experience of as many "alternate" personalities as the therapist will unwittingly reward. In earlier times, these patients would probably have been diagnosed as suffering from hysteria. Like the excellent hypnotic subjects that they are, these "multiples" become totally absorbed in the personas they concoct, focusing on them one by one, as the setting demands.[31]

Unfortunately, Spanos did not live to see a revealing interview with Borch-Jacobsen[29] given by the Columbia psychiatrist Herbert Spiegel. In it, Spiegel revealed for the first time how, in the 1960s, a fellow psychiatrist, Cornelia Wilbur, essentially created the diagnostic category of MPD out of whole cloth.

A highly suggestible patient of Wilbur's, whom Spiegel felt was suffering from hysteria, was depicted instead by Wilbur as a "multiple personality." With the help of Flora Schreiber, a popular writer, Wilbur sensationalized the case in a resulting book, *Sybil*.[32] Predictably, it became a runaway best seller and highly popular movie. Although Spiegel declined Wilbur's offer of coauthorship, because he disbelieved her account, *Sybil* engendered a thriving cottage industry among therapists and self-diagnosed sufferers who believed its far-fetched speculations.

Passing familiarity with the work of T. X. Barber[33] and his colleagues on "fantasy-prone personalities"and other hypnosis-like phenomena[34] would have prompted a greater awareness that social conditioning and compliance with the implied suggestions of an authority figure can create not only "alternate personalities," but also vivid pseudomemories of abduction and sexual molestation by Satanic covens or space aliens. Although client sincerity is not at issue in these cases, there is no reason to believe these experiences are anything but constructions of their own minds.[35]

Ignorance of Research into the Nature of Memory and Social Influence: "Recovered" Memories of Childhood Abuse, Satanic Ritual Abuse, or Alien Abduction

Nonsensical beliefs cease to be merely amusing when pseudoscientific theories destroy the lives of innocent people. Ignorance of modern research in the areas of memory and interpersonal influence misguides the efforts of counselors who are persuaded by books such as Bass and Davis's *Courage to Heal*.[36] Neither author of this best-selling tome of the recovery movement has any psychological credentials, a fact they proudly proclaim along with their questionable practices for uncovering supposedly repressed memories of sexual abuse.

Sexual abuse of children is a social problem of greater magnitude than most professionals used to think. Nonetheless, in the belated rush to curtail this evil, the pendulum may have swung too far in the opposite direction, fomenting witch-hunts wherein unfounded accusations, based on allegedly "recovered" memories are automatically believed. As a result, jobs have been unfairly lost, reputations destroyed and family ties shattered. More than a few innocent people have been sent to jail and a few were even driven to suicide.[5,23,26,37,38] It is a concern that, as more of these false accusations become widely known, a backlash might develop that would threaten many of the salutary reforms achieved by those who have led the crusade against real, as opposed to imagined, sexual abuse. An organization has been founded for purposes of helping people who claim to be falsely accused in this way and promoting more scientific views of memory and psychopathology: The False Memory Syndrome Foundation: 3401 Market St., Ste. 130, Philadelphia, PA 19104-3315.

It is doubtful that the "hidden memory" craze could have gained the momentum it did if proponents in the "recovery movement" had been familiar with the relevant research on human memory. Many of their practices are predicated on outmoded views, such as the misconception that memory records every aspect of every experience, much like a videotape that is simply "replayed" verbatim when an event is recalled. In fact, memory is much more abbreviated, inferential, and reconstructive than it feels like when we experience it.[5,25,39] As a result, it is also much more prone to confabulation and error than many people believe.

Moreover, as with the credulous espousal of MPD, many in the recovery movement were also unaware of research on suggestibility and interpersonal influence that shows how easy it is to implant false memories, quite unintentionally, during therapy. This, in conjunction with the questionable views about the etiology of psychological distress discussed earlier, led many recovery-oriented counselors to use scientifically unsupportable techniques in ill-advised attempts to ferret out the memory traces they were sure must be hidden in their clients' minds.

Clients' denials of initial suggestions that they had been abused were often ignored because most therapists of this persuasion also subscribe to dubious notions of repression. That is, that traumatic memories are forcibly kept from awareness until they are "recovered" in therapy. It is supposed that a subconscious censor actively keeps troublesome memories out of consciousness until the barrier can be circumvented by special therapeutic techniques. This idea of "strong repression" is also derived from Freudian speculation that has never enjoyed much empirical support.[23,25,39,40] Unfortunately, much research shows that the methods advocated for breaking through the repressive wall are the very ones likely to create false memories. These risky "rejuvenation" techniques include hypnosis, guided imagination, role playing, dwelling on childhood photos and mementoes, and participation in exhortative "recovery group" sessions. Misuse of the much overrated technique of hypnosis in this regard has been widely documented.[30,31,41] The ability of subtle suggestions and probing techniques to create highly convincing pseudomemories has been demonstrated repeatedly. The initial comeback of many in the recovery movement was that only a few "bad apples" in the profession lead their clients in this fashion. However, a large-scale survey of relevant beliefs among doctorate-level psychotherapists disputes this.[42,43] The level of belief in the foregoing misconceptions was found to be very high. Similar pseudomemories can be created when therapists encourage clients' fantasies that they have been abducted and mistreated by extraterrestrials[44] or by underground satanic cults.[45]

A more pernicious side of this mutual delusion of patient and therapist is that many self-professed victims are led to believe that, in order for them to recover, some suspected (often innocent) abuser must pay. In the "satanic ritual abuse" version of this scenario, the abuse supposedly occurs during orgiastic rites of devil worship, sexual perversion, torture, and human sacrifice. Concerted efforts by law enforcement agencies around the world have failed to find any evidence that these allegedly pervasive satanic conspiracies exist.[45] This has not prevented charges being laid and convictions being obtained, however.[46] The fact that supporters of alleged victims of satanic abuse and extraterrestrial abduction firmly believe their "memories," despite the implausibility of such events, should give pause to therapists and prosecutors who accept virtually every patient "recollection" of abuse at face value.

From a purely practical standpoint, encouraging patients' to dwell on early traumas, even if they are undeniably real, is questionable in that there is little research to show that it helps victims get better. Instead of pressing patients to ruminate incessantly about tragedies from long ago (which may well exacerbate rather than alleviate their emotional distress), they would probably be better served by sympathetic, practically-oriented counselors who will help them pick up the pieces in the here-and-now and aid them in finding workable strategies for achieving a more satisfying future.[18]

Ignorance of Modern Brain Research

There are a variety of devices, exercises, and potions vigorously marketed by entrepreneurs who claim they can improve well-being and performance by "reprogramming" or improving the chemical efficiency of the brain. Most proponents have little or no understanding of modern neuroscience and offer even less evidence for their wares. Descriptions and critical reviews of these New Age sellers' claims can be found in the following references.[47,48] An example of how even well-trained professionals can fall prey to "neurobabble" and thus promote highly questionable therapies based on outdated notions about brain function is contained in the critical review by Hines in this issue of *SRAM*.

In a similar vein, questionable notions about brain biochemistry have spawned a large industry selling herbs and supplements that are alleged to have therapeutic effects for various neurological conditions and/or to improve brain function in normal people.[48] In [the *Scientific Review of Alternative Medicine* 5, no. 2 (Spring 2001)], Brue and colleagues report on a test of one such combination of products claimed to alleviate the symptoms of attention deficit hyperactivity disorder in children. While the authors find some reason to pursue further research with some components of the supplement cocktail they tested, the results offer little support for the supplement industry's claims in general.

OTHER QUESTIONABLE PRODUCTS
IN THE THERAPEUTIC MARKETPLACE

Space does not permit detailed critiques of the large number of scientifically-suspect practices vying for customers in the therapeutic marketplace. Here, I can only list a selection of currently fashionable pseudoscientific psychological products and provide references where the case against them is made in detail.

Aroma Therapy

Believers claim that the odors of certain "essential oils" have unique and lasting effects on various psychological problems.[49,50] There are many theoretical and practical difficulties with this notion.[51] In the current issue of *SRAM*, Sgoutas-Emch and colleagues present a well-controlled study that fails to support aroma therapists' claims to alleviate stress. These results are in line with those of the present author who also found (in a blinded study done with the encouragement of professional aroma therapists) no support for the contention of aroma therapists that there are uniquely arousing and sedating essential oils (Anderson and Beyerstein, in preparation).

Eye-Movement Desensitization and Reprocessing (EMDR) Therapy

Shapiro[52] has promoted the doubtful claim that back-and-forth eye-tracking of a therapist's finger while imagining traumatizing events from the past can cure patients of debilitating anxiety. Several reviews have raised strong doubts about Shapiro's claims.[53,54,55,56] Critics argue that Shapiro merely borrowed elements from existing cognitive-behavior therapies and added the superfluous ingredient of finger waving, with no scientific rationale or data to back up this highly improbable practice. When EMDR works with traumatized people, it is likely because of its overlap with validated treatments such as "cognitive restructuring"[57] where clients are repeatedly forced to experience traumatic memories, along with desirable thoughts, in order to extinguish their disturbing emotional reactions to recollections of distressing events.

Handwriting Analysis

The pseudoscience of graphology claims psychological traits and diagnoses can be derived from the analysis of handwriting. While no scientific case can be made for these claims, even more far-fetched assertions are made by "graphotherapists." The latter contend that undesirable psychological attributes can be eliminated by learning to remove the signs that indicate those traits from one's handwriting. Graphology firms routinely offer marital and psychological advice and consultations on hiring and promotion, the credit worthiness of borrowers, and the guilt or innocence of criminal defendants. Although the evidence against graphology is overwhelming,[58] advertisements continue to appear in journals directed at psychotherapists for graphology seminars that carry continuing education credit for licensed psychologists and psychiatrists. In some advertisements, the promoters promise to teach techniques for identifying secret drug abusers, philanderers, and both perpetrators and victims of sexual abuse from signs supposedly encoded in their handwriting.

Meditation as Psychotherapy

Marketing schemes such as Transcendental Meditation (TM) have profited handsomely from those seeking release from the psychological and physical ills attributed to the stresses of today's fast-paced lifestyles. Research papers from TM devotees, largely from the TM-owned Maharishi International University, have claimed special efficacy for the mental exercises prescribed by the TM organization. In addition to their claims of improved physical and psychological health, TM-ers assert that meditators can learn to levitate and that if one percent of the local population takes up TM, the crime rate in that locale will drop. As far as TM's psychological pretensions are concerned, outside evaluators with no personal stake in the outcome find that TM, or any other form of meditation, is no more efficacious than simple rest.[59,60]

Therapies that Encourage Clients to Recall Their Thoughts While In Utero, during Birth, or in Early Childhood

Rebirthing, Primal Scream Therapy, and Dianetics (Scientology) all assert that people can and should recall times in their lives when their brains and cognitive processes were too immature to lay down memories of the sort posited by these theorists.[1] As I have noted elsewhere,[9] our understanding of neural development makes such claims extremely unlikely. As discussed above, the idea that early trauma frequently leads to adult psychopathology is equally questionable. As we have also seen, clients in situations like this are capable of responding to suggestions that they are recalling such events, fooling themselves with pseudomemories of such early times before, during, or after birth.

Self-Help Psychotherapy Books

A spate of do-it-yourself therapy and self-improvement books also continues to sell well to an anxious public. The advice they offer runs the gamut from reasonable and useful to bizarre and unsupported.[61,62]

CONCLUSION

As long as people refuse to think critically and to put psychotherapy methods to hard-nosed empirical tests, bogus treatments will continue to flood the market. It continues to amaze me that many people who demand extensive, impartial evaluations of automobiles or televisions before making a purchase, will put themselves in the hands of psychotherapists with little or no prior investigation of their credentials, theoretical orientations, professional affiliations, or their records of successfully helping their clients in the past. For reasons I have summarized in an earlier edition of *SRAM*,[63] testimonials from satisfied customers are essentially useless in deciding the efficacy of both psychological and medical treatments.

For those who agree that advance screening of psychotherapists by potential consumers is at least as good an idea as checking the qualifications and achievements of would-be home renovation contractors, several sources come to mind. A good overview and critique of various fringe psychotherapies is contained in a special edition of the *International Journal of Mental Health*, edited by Loren Pankratz.[64] Another good source of such information is a volume by Gambrill.[62] A thought-provoking, if occasionally overly strident, critique from within the psychotherapy industry (by one who voluntarily left the profession because of concerns not unlike those voiced in this article) has been penned by Tana Dineen.[65] A thoroughly disillusioned Dineen attacks her former colleagues for making mental illnesses out of what used to be considered the normal hardships of life and for promulgating questionable treatments lacking in scientific rationales and proof of efficacy.

Potential consumers should also know that most state and provincial psychological and psychiatric associations maintain consumer advocacy and quality assurance boards to assist the public in this regard—even though, as we have seen, these organizations have not always been as ready to police their own as one would wish. For those with an on-ramp to the Information Superhighway, good discussions of the latest therapeutic fads by skeptical clinicians are obtainable at sscpnet@listserv. acns.nwu.edu. The abbreviation "sscp" stands for "Society for a Science of Clinical Psychology," a group of academics and clinicians dedicated to restoring a strong scientific basis for psychotherapy. And finally, it is a pleasure to announce that a new journal has recently been founded that will be dedicated to exposing junk science in psychotherapy. Under the editorship of Scott Lilienfeld, this companion to *SRAM*'s efforts in the biomedical field will be called *Scientific Review of Mental Health Practice*. In light of the transgressions discussed above, it should be apparent that this is a necessary corrective whose time is long overdue.

NOTE: The author would like to express his thanks to Drs. James Alcock, Scott Lilienfeld, and Gerald Rosen for their helpful comments on an earlier version of this paper. The conclusions expressed herein are, of course, those of the author.

REFERENCES

1. Rosen, R. D. *Psychobabble: Fast Talking in the Era of Feeling*. New York: Atheneum, 1978.

2. Evans, C. *Cults of Unreason*. New York: Farrar, Straus, and Giroux, 1973.

3. Miller, R. *Bare-faced Messiah: The True Story of L. Ron Hubbard*. Toronto, ON: Key-Porter Books, 1987.

4 Behar, R. "The Thriving Cult of Greed and Power." *Time*, May 6, 1991, pp. 50–57.

5. Baker, R., ed. *Child Sexual Abuse and False Memory Syndrome*. Amherst, NY: Prometheus Books, 1998.

6. Dawes, R. M. *House of Cards: Psychology and Psychotherapy Built on Myth*. New York: Free Press, 1994.

7. Meehl, P. "Psychology: Does Our Heterogenous Subject Matter Have Any Unity?" *Minnesota Psychologist* (Summer 1986): 4.

8. McHugh, P. "Psychiatric Misadventures." *American Scholar* (Autumn 1992): 498–510.

9. Beyerstein, B. L. "The Brain and Consciousness: Implications for Psi Phenomena." *Skeptical Inquirer* 12, no. 2 (1988): 163–73.

10. Mack, J. E. *Abduction: Human Encounters with Aliens*. New York: Scribner's, 1994.

11. Crews, F. "The Unknown Freud." *New York Review of Books* (November 18, 1993).

12. Lilienfeld, S. O. "Arguing from a Vacuum." *Skeptical Inquirer* 19, no. 1 (1995): 50–51.

13. Hagen, M. A. "Damaged Goods?" *Skeptical Inquirer* 25, no. 1 (2001): 54–59.

14. "Does Therapy Help?" *Consumer Reports*, November 1995, pp. 734–39.

15. Gilovich, T. *How We Know What Isn't So: The Fallibility of Human Reason in Everyday Life*. New York: Free Press/Macmillan, 1991.

16. Levy, D. A. *Tools of Critical Thinking: Metathoughts for Psychology*. Boston: Allyn and Bacon, 1997.

17. Chapman, L., and J. Chapman. "Illusory Correlation as an Obstacle to the Use of Valid Psychodiagnostic Signs." *Journal of Abnormal Psychology* 74, no. 3 (1969): 271–80.

18. Bowman, M. *Individual Differences in Posttraumatic Distress: Problems in the Adversity-distress Connection*. Hillsdale, NJ: Lawrence Erlbaum, 1997.

19. Grunbaum, A. *The Foundations of Psychoanalysis: A Philosophical Critique*. Berkeley: University of California Press, 1984.

20. Torrey, E. F. *The Freudian Fraud*. New York: Harper Collins, 1992.

21. Gray, P. "The Assault on Freud." *Time*, November 29, 1993, pp. 47–50.

22. Horgan, P. "Why Freud Isn't Dead." *Scientific American*, December, 1996: 106–11.

23. Pope, H. G., Jr. *Psychology Astray: Fallacies in Studies of "Repressed Memory" and Childhood Trauma*. Boca Raton, FL: Upton Books, 1997.

24. Lykken, D., and A. Tellegen. "Happiness Is a Stochastic Phenomenon." *Psychological Science* 7, no. 3 (1996): 186–89.

25. Loftus, E., and K. Ketcham. *The Myth of Repressed Memory*. New York: St. Martin's Press, 1994.

26. Baker, R. A. *Hidden Memories*. Amherst, NY: Prometheus Books, 1992.

27. Rosen, G. M. "Posttraumatic Stress Disorder, Pulp Fiction, and the Press." *Bulletin of the American Academy of Psychiatry and the Law* 24 (1996): 267–69.

28. Shorter, E. *From Paralysis to Fatigue: A History of Psychosomatic Medicine in the Modern Era*. New York: Free Press, 1992.

29. Borch-Jacobsen, M. "Sybil—The Making of a Disease: An Interview with Dr. Herbert Spiegel." *New York Review of Books* (April 24, 1997): 60–64.

30. Spanos N. P. *Multiple Identities and False Memories*. Washington, DC: American Psychological Association Press, 1996.

31. Piper, A. "Multiple Personality Disorder: Witchcraft Survives in the Twentieth Century." *Skeptical Inquirer* 22, no. 3 (1998): 44–50.

32. Schreiber, F. R. *Sybil*. New York: Regency, 1973.

33. Barber, T. X., and S. Wilson. "The Fantasy Prone Personality: Implications for Understanding Imagery, Hypnosis, and Parapsychological Phenomena." In *Imagery:*

Current Theory, Research and Application, ed. A. Sheikh, 340–87. New York: J. Wiley and Sons, 1983.

34. Baker, R. A. *They Call It Hypnosis*. Amherst, NY: Prometheus Books, 1990.

35. Clark, S., and E. Loftus. "The Construction of Space Alien Memories." *Psychological Inquiry* 7, no. 2 (1997): 140–43.

36. Bass, E., and L. Davis. *The Courage to Heal: A Guide for Women Survivors of Child Sexual Abuse*. New York: Harper and Row, 1988.

37. Crews, F. "The Revenge of the Repressed (Part 1)." *New York Review of Books* (November 17, 1994): 54–60.

38. Crews, F. "The Revenge of the Repressed (Part 2)." *New York Review of Books* (December 1, 1994): 49–58.

39. Lindsay, D. S., and J. D. Read. "Psychotherapy and Memories of Childhood Sexual Abuse: A Cognitive Perspective." *Applied Cognitive Psychology* 8 (1994): 281–338.

40. Holmes, D. "The Evidence for Repression: An Examination of Sixty Years of Research." In *Repression and Dissociation: Implications for Personality Theory, Psychopathology and Health*. Edited by J. Singer. Chicago: University of Chicago Press, 1990.

41. Yapko, M. "Suggestibility and Repressed Memories of Abuse: A Survey of Psychotherapists' Beliefs." *American Journal of Clinical Hypnosis* 36, no. 3 (1994): 163–11.

42. Poole. D. A., D. S. Lindsay, A. Memon, and R. Bull. "Psychotherapy and the Recovery of Memories of Childhood Sexual Abuse: U.S. and British Practitioners' Opinions, Practices, and Experiences." *Journal of Consulting and Clinical Psychology* 63, no. 3 (1995): 426–37.

43. Katz, Z. "Canadian Psychologists' Education, Trauma History, and the Recovery of Memories of Childhood Sexual Abuse." Doctoral Dissertation, Department of Psychology, Simon Fraser University, Burnaby, BC, 2000.

44. Klass, P. A. *UFO Abductions: A Dangerous Game*. Amherst, NY: Prometheus Books, 1989.

45. Hicks, R. D. "Police Pursuit of Satanic Crime." *Skeptical Inquirer* 14, no. 3 (1990): 276–86.

46. Wright, R. *Remembering Satan*. New York: Vintage Books, 1995.

47. Beyerstein, B. L. "Brainscams: Neuromythologies of the New Age." *International Journal of Mental Health* 19 (1990): 27–36.

48. Beyerstein, B. L. "Pseudoscience and the Brain: Tuners and Tonics for Aspiring Superhumans." In ed. *Mind-Myths: Exploring Everyday Mysteries of the Mind and Brain*, edited by S. Della Sala, 59–82. Chichester, UK: John Wiley and Sons, 1999.

49. Scholes, M. *Aromatherapy*. Aroma Press International. N.p., 1993.

50. McCutcheon, L. "What's that I Smell? The Claims of Aromatherapy." *Skeptical Inquirer* 20, no. 3 (1996): 35–37.

51. Lawless, H. "Effects of Odors on Mood and Behavior: Aromatherapy and Related Effects." In *The Human Sense of Smell*, edited by Laing et al., 361–87. Berlin: Springer-Verlag, 1991.

52. Shapiro, F. "Eye Movement Desensitization: A New Treatment for Post-traumatic Stress Disorder." *Journal of Behavior Therapy and Experimental Psychiatry* 20 (1989): 211–17.

53. Lilienfeld, S. O. "EMDR Treatment: Less than Meets the Eye?" *Skeptical Inquirer* 20, no. 1 (1996): 25–31.

54. Rosen, G. M. "A Note to EMDR Critics: What You Didn't See Is Only Part of What You Didn't Get." *Behavior Therapist* 16 (1993): 216.

55. Rosen, G. M. "Treatment Fidelity and Research on Eye Movement Desensitization and Reprocessing (EMDR)." *Journal of Anxiety Disorders* 13, nos. 1–2 (1999): 173–84.

56. Lohr, J. M., R. A. Kleinknecht, D. F. Tolin, and H. Richard. "The Empirical Status and the Clinical Application of Eye Movement Desensitization and Reprocessing." *Journal of Behavior Therapy and Experimental Psychiatry* 26, no. 4 (1995): 285–302.

57. Meichenbaum, D. "Examination of Model Characteristics and Reducing Avoidance Behavior." *Journal of Personality and Social Psychology* 17 (1971): 298–307.

58. Beyerstein, B., and D. Beyerstein, eds. *The Write Stuff—Evaluations of Graphology*. Amherst, NY: Prometheus Books, 1992.

59. West, M. A., ed. *The Psychology of Meditation*. Oxford, UK: Clarendon Press, 1987.

60. Blackmore, S. "Is Meditation Good for You?" *New Scientist* (July 6, 1991): 30–33.

61. Rosen, G. M. "Self-help Treatment Books and the Commercialization of Psychotherapy." *American Psychologist* 42, no. 1 (1987): 46–51.

62. Gambrill, E. *Critical Thinking in Clinical Practice*. San Francisco: Jossey-Bass, 1990.

63. Beyerstein, B. L. "Social and Judgmental Biases that Make Inert Treatments Seem to Work." *Scientific Review of Alternative Medicine* 3, no. 2 (1999): 20–33.

64. Pankratz, L., ed. "Unvalidated, Fringe, and Fraudulent Treatment of Mental Disorders." Special issue: *International Journal of Mental Health* 19, no. 3 (1990).

65. Dineen, T. *Manufacturing Victims: What the Psychology Industry Is Doing to People*. Montreal, QC: Robert Davies Publishing, PQ, 1996.

SCIENCE, RELIGION, AND ETHICS

22

SCIENCE AND RELIGION
No Irenics Here

FRED WILSON

ABSTRACT

There is a view, once again gaining favor, that science and religion are just different things and that they are compatible. But things are not, I propose, that simple. (Many) religions hold that values are objectively there, as part of the ontological structure of the universe. This position found philosophical expression in the philosophy of Plato and Aristotle (and their many successors through the ages). It holds that in order to understand things of this world it is necessary to transcend it to see how things "down here" fit into that objective value structure. Scientific understanding, in contrast, is wholly naturalistic, of this world "down here." It does yield casual understanding of things, and a method for resolving differences, in a way that religious/metaphysical positions never offered such a method. It thereby shows that that religious/metaphysical way of thinking is in fact fantasy. But further: it shows that to understand things one does not have to find some sort of objective value structure in which to place them. As for the values that we have, it shows that these are rooted in our psychology and our culture: so their only justification is not some fantastic absolute or objective standard, but only in how they serve human

From *Metaphysica: International Journal for Ontology & Metaphysics* 7, no. 2 (2006): 159.
Reprinted by permission of the editor.

well-being. There arc two consequences of the emergence of scientific ways of thinking: the first is that it frees us from the illusion of objective values, enabling us to look (paradoxically) objectively at our moral values and to evaluate them according to human standards; and the second is that it forces us to take responsibility for the values we act upon—no longer can we escape that responsibility by ascribing them to God or to an objective value structure in the universe ("natural law").

S tephen Jay Gould has argued[1] that there is science on the one hand and morality and religion on the other, and that these are nonoverlapping magisteria (NOMA): there is no logical conflict between them, they do different things: the one deals with matters of fact, the other deals with matters of value, of goodness and God.[2]

This sounds much like the fact-value distinction that is part and parcel of the scientific worldview. But things are not so simple. There are other worldviews. And in any case, morality is one thing, God and ultimate reality and meaning is another.

Many religions—certainly the religions of the Judeo-Christian-Islamic traditions—hold that values are objectively there, as part of the ontological structure of the universe. On this view, our value judgments are either true or false depending upon what are the objective values in the universe. "That must be bad because God has laid it down that way." So, no gay rights, no masturbation. "It's not up to me to decide, it is God's will, so I have to excise these people who go contrary to the natural order of things laid down by God." "The ultimate meaning of your life is determined by the will of God." Thus formulated, these are merely beliefs, or at best beliefs. To be more than that, they need a defense, some sort of philosophical defense. These doctrines found that philosophical defense in the metaphysics of Plato and Aristotle.

It begins with Socrates, dissatisfied with the explanations proposed by Anaxagoras for explaining ordinary events in the world. Socrates argued with Anaxagoras, so Plato records in the *Phaedo*.[3] The latter, Socrates declared, could not explain why he, Socrates, was about to drink the hemlock rather than escape to Thebes. The event—the observable event—of sitting in his cell is to be followed by another event; these events, which are given to us in our sensible experience of the world, are separable—the earlier does not, in itself, imply a later. Yet, why this event rather than that event follows the earlier needs an explanation, at least it does if we are to count things as rational, as having reasons. Anaxagoras argued that, in effect, people, like other animals, are skin and bones. But this does not explain: at best it leaves us acting like other animals, out of material self-interest: if Anaxagoras were right then he, Socrates, would flee prison for Thebes. Yet Socrates is about to do what the dog would not do, namely stay and drink the hemlock. He is doing this because (a) it is "for the best"—he is doing what he dutifully owes to Athens—, and (b) he is acting to bring about the best, so far as he can attain it. There is on the one hand the form of perfect human justice—the *a priori* form of human justice—*a priori*, because we have never experienced ideal morality in the ordinary world, only imitations that fall short of it, only mere approximations to it—, and there is, on the other hand, the striving which is Socrates: Socrates, as an active being, so moves his body as to imitate in the world of ordinary experience the ideal form of human justice. It is this striving to imitate the form that explains why Socrates sitting in prison is to be followed by his drinking the hemlock rather than by his running off to Thebes.[4]

Here are eight important points about this metaphysics:

- First, the explanation model proceeds in terms of unifying the events of ordinary experience. These events are separable, that is, logically separable. They come to be connected through the activity of an entity, something that Socrates refers to as his soul. The unification is thus a unification by an *entity*. Understanding ordinary events thus comes through our capacity to grasp the activity of this entity that unifies. Socrates being in prison will be followed by his drinking the hemlock and not by his running off to Thebes, because he as his soul strives in a way that connects the two events.

- Second, the activity has a certain form. This form is objectively there in the world. So is the soul. Both, however, are outside the world of ordinary experience; they transcend that world. So both are timeless, and in that sense immortal. Socrates makes clear that the immortality of the soul was the main conclusion that he wished to draw from his alternative explanation scheme.

- Third, the soul actively aims to imitate in its outward appearance an ideal form. The form thus enters as a crucial piece in the explanation. The form is the *reason* why things are as they are.

- Fourth, the form is also normative; it states not only what things are, but what they ought to be. In this way, values are built into the objective structure of the world. And explanation makes an appeal to values: there is no fact-value distinction. So there is only one magisterium, on this metaphysics.

- Fifth, if we call a pattern of behavior of some thing in the world a natural law just in case that it is there because of the form of that thing, then natural laws are not only patterns of how things *do* behave but also how they *ought* to behave: natural laws are both descriptive and normative.

- Sixth, understanding what is going on in the world of ordinary experience consists of an intuitive grasp of the form of the activity unifying things we experience. This intuition is a rational intuition since it is an intuition of the reasons for things. Human reason is the capacity to grasp the forms, the reasons for things. Since the forms are outside the world of ordinary experience, it turns out that in order to understand this world, one must transcend it; in order to discover the truth of something, the truth about what it is and what it ought to be, one must go outside the world we know in our everyday life, and grasp the forms of things.

- Seventh, the truth of things in the world of ordinary experience is to be found in the forms that explain why things are as they are. Thus, in order to discover the truth of this world, one must turn away from it, a realm of untruth, and turn to another, higher, realm of timeless perfection. This includes moral truth. For, the forms provide a criterion, an objective criterion, for the correctness or incorrectness of our value judgments.

- Eighth, since the natural laws are normative, and since there can be violations of norms—people sometimes do not do their duty—the metaphysics has to allow that natural laws have exceptions. These exceptions will have causes, but the causes will be objects external to the changing object; the latter will be changed by the external substances in ways that are contrary to the natural tendencies of its strivings. Besides natural change there is unnatural or violent change. The model is human behavior, just as the basic model finds its original application in Socrates' own case. But Aristotle extends the distinction to all things, all sorts of change.

Plato dealt mostly with the explanation of human behavior. Aristotle extended the model to the explanation of all change. He called the bearer of active powers "substances," and, details aside, this philosophy endured until the seventeenth century. It was assimilated into Christianity, and provided the metaphysical support needed by religious dogma and morality. This was the morality that inspired, among others, St. Dominic who, during the Albigensian crusade after the siege of Bézier, instructed the crusaders to burn all the inhabitants, Christians and Cathars alike, letting God draw the needed distinction later. That was in 1209: 20,000 slaughtered. St. Thomas allowed that it was entirely just that heretics be burned, so grievous was their sin. This was the natural order of things: the form of the good demanded it. It was God's will, disclosed to us when we grasped the reality of natural law.

Others of course found other things in the ideal form of justice. Not all that they found there was as evil as what St. Thomas found. One English defender of the cause of righteousness argued that it was part of the natural order of things that "thou shalt not expose thy privy parts in public."

It is evident that different people or different groups found different things amongst the forms. It is not so much that the value judgments reflected the forms and as the forms reflected the value judgments. The forms are in fact not objectively there, in the world, or, rather, outside the world but there. The forms are simply projections of the values of those who accept that they are there. They are value judgments disguised as objective fact. What the Platonic-Aristotelian metaphysics does is provide a rationale for values held on other grounds.

In the sixteenth and seventeenth centuries the powerful hold of these patterns on the minds of men and women came to be broken.

Galileo and William Harvey took the essential practical steps. For the Aristotelean, observation is not basic, what is needed is a rational intuition of the form of the substance changing—only that will give knowledge of which patterns are natural laws, and which are violations.

However, the forms are illusory, there are no such things. This judgment applies equally to the explanations of falling stones as it does to Socrates in prison. For Aristotle, free fall is the natural motion of earthy objects, other motions are unnatural. In particular, projectile motion is unnatural. But, on the model that means that it requires the action of an external substance to effect the change. This proved a stumbling block. It is evident that there is no external substance acting in projectile motion. Thinkers thought about it from Aristotle to Galileo, but could not solve the problem. Galileo changed the question. He said that he would not look for Aristotelian powers, that the natural/unnatural distinction has no cognitive content, and that one should look for exceptionless patterns in the behavior of changing things. He was able, through careful experimental work, to establish that free fall and projectile motion were simply two patterns falling under a more general pattern of change. Galileo succeeded in the cognitive task of finding exceptionless patterns, the Aristotelians failed in the cognitive task of intuiting the forms of things.

Two things are important here. One is the cognitive goal, that of finding exceptionless patterns. The second is the method of discovering these, the method of forming hypotheses as to what these patterns are, and testing them by observation and experiment, eliminating those that are false, retaining those that pass the tests.

Harvey effected in physiology a change parallel to that which Galileo made in physics. Instead of arguing about whether Galen or Aristotle is correct about the seat of the soul—the brain or the heart?—, Harvey established, through careful observation and experiment, that the heart circulates the blood. This, as a matter of fact, is the way things work, this is the pattern their behavior exemplifies. Harvey discovered what he did by looking at alternatives and then conducting experiments that eliminated all but the hypothesis that the heart has the effect of circulating the blood.

The philosophical names are Bacon and Locke—Bacon as the first to lay out in detail the logic of the experimental method, and Locke for stating clearly that the method of the new science was the only human reason that we have, and that we have no capacity, innate or otherwise, to penetrate to a realm of essences that is outside the world of ordinary experience but somehow defines the truth of that world. In fact, argued Locke, the world of the forms is a figment of our philosophical imagination. Just as moral content of the forms was a projection of the wishes and values of those defending the metaphysics, so also the natural-unnatural distinction in physics. Natural motions were those motions that one was inclined to see as Natural, and that inclination was transformed into a metaphysical truth; but there was no such objective basis for the distinction. The problem of projectile motion turned out to be a pseudo-problem, and therefore one incapable of solution. Galileo abandoned the pseudo-problem in favor of one that could be solved; Locke showed that it was indeed a pseudo-problem.

The cogency of the case made by Bacon and Locke was reinforced by the success of the new science in solving problems where the old metaphysics of forms had not. For two thousand years people had looked in vain for a solution to the problem of projectile motion; restating the problem as one of discovering patterns rather than the form of a substance, Galileo had a problem that could and was solved. The work of Galileo culminated in that of Newton who could calmly assert that "I shall demonstrate the frame of the system of the world." No Platonist, no Aristotelian, no rationalist, had ever been able to make that claim.

WHAT CAN BE SAID OF THE NEW SCIENCE?

- First, the explanation model established by Galileo proceeds in terms of unifying the events of ordinary experience. These events are separable, that is, logically separable. But where the older metaphysics of forms unifies by locating those events in a *timeless entity*, the new science unifies them by locating generalizations under which they fall—the new science unifies by means of a *timeless pattern*.

- Second, activity is not the model for explanation in the new science. Activity is simply one among the various kinds of processes in the world of ordinary experience. Activity is itself explained by being subsumed under a generalization, by locating it as part of a pattern.

- Third, there is no transcendent form, and therefore none that enters into any explanation of things in the world. The *reason* why things are as they are is given not by forms but by patterns.

- Fourth, the patterns that explain are descriptive, and in no way normative; they state only what things are, and not what they ought to be. Thus, on the scientific account of ordinary things, values—objective values—are not among the things in the world. And explanation makes no appeal to values: there is a sharp fact-value distinction. There are indeed two nonoverlapping magisteria (NOMA).

- Fifth, if we call a pattern of behavior a natural law just in case that it has passed the tests required by the scientific method, then natural laws are only patterns of how things *do* behave and in no way are patterns of how they *ought* to behave: natural laws are descriptive, not normative.

- Sixth, understanding what is going on in the world of ordinary experience consists of a grasp of the general patterns unifying things we experience. This grasp is acquired through the scientific method: we know a pattern just in case that it has passed the tests required by the scientific method. The patterns give the reasons for things, and human reason is the capacity to grasp these patterns The patterns are patterns of things *in* the world, so that in order to understand this world it is not necessary to transcend it. The truth about this world is discovered by examining this world and nothing else.

- Seventh, the truth of things in the world of ordinary experience is to be found in that world. But that world contains no objective values; whatever we say about these, it remains that we do not know them by observation and experiment. Science provides no criterion, no objective criterion, for the correctness or incorrectness of our value judgments. However, though there are no objective values, it does not follow that there are no values, that is, value judgments or valuings of things—of course there are. Thus, though there are no objective values in the world disclosed by science, there certainly are relative values. There is no ultimate meaning to life or to one's life, but there are subjective meanings.

- Eighth, again, though there are no objective values, there are valuings, the value judgments that people make. It is these that explain human behavior. It is valuings that do the explaining, or rather regularities about valuings and behavior that explain. So, if you wish to explain why Socrates did what he did, there is no need to invoke transcendent forms or objective values, what one needs to cite are the values in the sense of the value judgments that moved Socrates, and beyond that the patterns describing the social and cultural forces that so shaped Socrates that he had these values and not others, and including also the laws of learning that describe how these external forces came to mold Socrates' way of being.

Morality thus becomes, with the new empirical science, not something that is discovered in the world, not something that we rationally intuit; it is something that we find within ourselves, but put there by social forces, forces over which we have some control, and not by God over whom we have no control. Morality thus turns out to be something that we create, that is, we as social beings. In fact, we have a choice in the matter. We can, within limits at least, choose the values we are to live by. As for what we can't choose, then at the least we can accept those things as our fate in the world of fact. We can ask, what vision of the good do we have? Is it a good worth having? And we can ask whether it is an attainable good, and if it is, we can ask how we can best go about attaining it? The former are questions of value. Science will not help us answer those. But the others are questions of fact, and there science can tell us the answers to those questions.

In other words, while science cannot tell us what that the good is, it can describe the means that are available for attaining that good. Now, one of the things that it will tell us—this is common sense, but, then, science is but the long arm of common sense—is that most of the goods that we value can be attained only if we form with our fellows a stable society or community of persons. So science—common sense—tells us that we must develop shareable values and cooperative behavior. Indeed, it can tell us how better to develop a social order that can secure the goods that make life worth living. In other words, we can secure our vision of the good only if we have a moral and social order that promotes that end.

But we have options. The moral or social order, our moral and political values, is not something that is imposed upon us, it is something that we find within ourselves, and it is something that we can shape and develop.

It is therefore something for which we must take responsibility. Once we accept the framework of science, and of scientific reason, then we can no longer argue that our values are not of our doing, that they are somehow there, independently of us. No longer can we say of some odd rule—"thou shalt not shave"—or some rule that denies one a minor pleasure—"thou shalt not masturbate"—or some more dangerous rule—"thou shalt not be a cathar" or "thou shalt not suffer a witch to live"—no longer can we say that it is the natural law that this be so, or that it is God's will that it be so. If it is so, then it is because we want it to be so. Science frees us from the burden of objective values, but at the same time it gives us the responsibility for the values that we have, for the moral order in which we live, and for our vision of the good.

It is true that, if we disguise our values as matters of fact, their motive power is increased. Think of the ringing declaration that "we hold these truths to be self evident, that all men are created equal. . . ." But they achieve that power only by sacrificing their true nature, and, more importantly, only by giving up the opportunity for critical evaluation of these values: what is self-evident is not to be critically examined.

We see here wherein lies the power of the older metaphysics of forms. It provides a mechanism by which the mind can disguise its own values as objective matters of fact: one's own values or the values of one's own society find their place in the objective order of the universe. The forms are simply one's own values disguising themselves as objective fact, the metaphysics a means for effecting that disguise. But it is a disguise that allows us to ignore our responsibility for our values, and allows us to institute without critical examination both the silly and the nasty. The critical reason that is empirical science frees us from the burden of such values, and, more particularly, liberates us from moral irresponsibility.

To be sure, it has been suggested that science is empirical, but that there are other forms of cognition or whatever that take us to a world outside the world of science but no less legitimate, a world of forms and of objective values. Science, however, provides a critique that allows it to exclude such an idea. Recall the natural-unnatural distinction. Locke showed that the problem this created for projectile motion was a pseudo-problem. That same Lockean critique applies to anything based on the notion of a supposedly a priori form or nature. Locke argued that all those of our concepts that we have for describing matters of fact are derived from sense experience. All our ideas derive from impressions, as Hume was later to put it. The point is both factual and normative—factual because it turns out, upon systematic examination of our ideas, that the ones that have clear content are those derived from sense experience; and normative because we ought to use only those concepts, those ideas, that have clear content, and the only ideas that have clear content are those that derive from sense.

In effect we—this was Locke's thought—take the idea of science and turn it on our ideas themselves.[5] Use the "plain historical method" to uncover their origins, as Locke put it. Do a natural history of religion, as Hume would have it. When we have examined these concepts that are supposed to describe a non-empirical metaphysical reality, and have succeeded in explaining them genetically, it turns out that there is nothing there in those concepts: these ideas or rather, to reflect the normative point about the concepts that we ought to have, these pseudo-ideas or pseudo-concepts have content but none of it content that could be said to describe the world—insofar as there is content in these concepts, it derives from values and wishes—values and wishes that have disguised themselves as concepts describing objectively the world in which we live. By giving a natural history of these concepts, a genealogy in Nietzsche's sense, that is, a scientific or causal analysis of their this-worldly origins, they are revealed to be pseudo-concepts. In a world in which science provides the standard of rationality, it turns out that no one has the right to claim to have ideas that give access to some superior realm of forms or natures.

Now return to Gould's scheme. On this scheme we have nonoverlapping magisteria. There are facts, science, and there is morality. This distinction is accepted by the scientific worldview. But it is rejected by the old metaphysics of Plato and Aristotle, which thereby contributes to the illusion that values are objective and that we bear no responsibility for them. However, Gould places religion among the aspects of the magisterium contrasted to that of science— this other magisterium is of ethics and morality and, also, God and ultimate meaning. If ultimate meaning is nothing more than our vision of good, and if ethics and morality simply reflect the moral sensibilities that we in fact have, then all is satisfactory. But why include religion and God? In fact, once you have God placed among the value judgments, it turns out that this other magisterium involves many clearly apparent statements of fact, from "God exists" and "God is a jealous God and wants no others before him" on down. If these do reflect or embody values, then those values are disguised as statements of fact. That may, as we have seen, increase their motive power. But at the same time, it protects them from critical evaluation. Gould notwithstanding, God is an illusion, a projection of our own values upon the world freeing us for the need to defend our choices. He/she/it ought therefore to be exorcised from the magisterium of ethics. He/she/it has no place in the magisterium of science, neither has he/she/it a place in the magisterium of ethics and morality.

At least, he/she/it has no place in either if we are responsible knowers and doers.

NOTES

1. Stephen Jay Gould, *Rock of Ages: Science and Religion in the Fullness of Life* (New York: Ballantine Publishing Group, 1999). See also Michael Ruse, *Can a Darwinian be a Christian?* (Cambridge: Cambridge University Press, 2001).

2. Gould, *Rock of Ages*, p. 5.

3. See *Phaedo* [trans. G. M. A. Grube (Indianapolis, IN: Hackett, 1977)], 97c1ff.

4. For discussion of this argument against Anaxagoras, see R. Turnbull, "Aristotle's Debt to the 'Natural Philosophy' of the *Phaedo*," *Philosophical Quarterly* 8 (1963): 131–43; and G. Vlastos, "Reason and Causes in the *Phaedo*," *Philosophical Review* 78 (1969): 291–325. See also F. Wilson, *Socrates, Lucretius, Camus: Two Philosophical Traditions on Death* (Lewiston, NY: Mellen, 2002), pp. 97ff; and F. Wilson, "Socrates' Argument for Immortality: Socrates, Maritain, Grant and the Ontology of Morals," *Maritain Studies* 20 (2004): 3–26.

5. Cf. F. Wilson, "The Lockean Revolution in the Theory of Science," in, eds., *Early Modern Philosophy: Epistemology, Metaphysics and Politics*, ed. S. Tweyman and G. Moyal (New York: Caravan Press, 1986), pp. 65–97. Also F. Wilson, *The Logic and Methodology of Science in Early Modern Thought* (Toronto, ON: University of Toronto Press, 1999).

23

IS RELIGION COMPATIBLE WITH SCIENCE AND ETHICS?
A Critique of Stephen Jay Gould's Two Magisteria

PAUL KURTZ

I

We may ask, what is the relationship between science and religion and science and ethics? Succinctly, I argue that religion in the strong sense is neither compatible with either science or ethics. The answer to these questions, however, is contingent on what is meant by "religion." I wish to deal with theistic religion in its monotheistic forms, derived from the influence of Abraham, which considered God to be a person. These forms of religion claim to provide (1) a special kind of revealed truth, nonnatural and independent of science, (2) the authoritative source of morality, and (3) the divine judge of the political order. As such, religion is incompatible, not only with science, but also with humanistic ethics and democratic politics; and the historical conflict between these areas of human culture and religion will most likely continue. If on the other hand you hold that religious discourse is the functional equivalent of "existential poetry"—as I do—then religion and science are not necessarily incompatible. Religious conservatives may object to this functional analysis because they believe that theistic religion in the last analysis is absolutely True, Righteous, and Just. If this is the case then I submit that religion *is irreconcilable* with science, and much of ethics, and politics.

This paper was read at a special meeting on "Science and Religion" of the American Association for the Advancement of Science, February 18, 2005, Washington, DC.

Stephen Jay Gould proposed a compromise between the domains of religion and science. He maintains that "there are distinct magisteria and as such are compatible. The . . . magisterium of science covers the empirical realm: what is the universe made of (fact) and why does it work this way (theory)." He then goes on to distinguish this from "the magisterium of religion," which "extends over questions of ultimate meaning and moral virtue." He calls this the "nonoverlapping magisteria" or NOMA.[1] These two areas, he claims, are logically distinct.

I think that Gould's effort to accommodate both realms is profoundly mistaken. I should point out that I speak as a scientific naturalist and a skeptic, a position that Gould shared. I had worked with him on a variety of projects in defending science against antiscience. I think that Gould was so concerned about the attacks on science by creationists that he tried to develop a truce, in order to allow methodological naturalism to operate in evolutionary science.

Religion and science have conflicted historically, primarily because of different conceptions of *truth*. Science presupposes a number of methodological principles of inquiry and confirmation. Science requires free inquiry, critical thinking, and the willingness to question assumptions. A hypothesis or theory is justified by the evidence, its predictability, logical consistency, and mathematical coherence; and it depends upon replication and peer review. Religious claims to truth are based on appeals to authority, tradition, faith, mysticism, and revelations. Science is implicitly universal, attempting to transcend social-cultural bias, and it seeks to justify its principles objectively. Religions more often than not dispute the authority of *other* religious traditions; and they have often suppressed free inquiry—the house arrest of Galileo and the burning of Bruno at the stake visibly dramatized the conflict at the beginning of the modern era. Many great scientists, such as Newton, Halley, and Boyle, believed in both science and theology, but they recognized that while *doing* science occult causes should be rejected. For although God created the universe, "He also established invariant laws to run the universe without interference."[2]

Nonetheless, there has been a protracted battle sometimes reduced to *ad baculum* (appeals to force) and *ad vericundiam* (appeals to authority) to defend the power of a dominant religion, and this cannot be easily forgotten. The campaign against Darwin's theory of evolution still continues today, and it demonstrates this impasse. The current opposition to stem cell research in biogenetic engineering by many theists does so as well. We should not assume that the conflict between religion and science is a thing of the past. Occult, paranormal, or supernatural entities cannot be appealed to in order to resolve a scientific question, yet some disciples of religion dispute that claim. Methodological naturalism—that inquirers seek natural causes and explanations—is fundamental to the scientific outlook. So let us not blithely claim—as does Gould—that because the pope accepts the theory of evolution that this battle is over. Many Protestant, Orthodox, Jewish, and Islamic fundamentalists surely do *not* accept evolution. Moreover, the opposition to stem cell research upon embryos or oocytes is based on his belief that the "soul" is implanted at the moment of conception or in the first division of cells in vitro fertilization in a petri dish (blastocysts). The interpolation of the "soul" is surely an occult cause. Theists still hold that the human species is the "highest form" of life, and curries divine favor over the millions of other species that are extinct. Both of these postulates have no place in evolutionary science.

Science and religion would be compatible only if the advocates of religion no longer seek to censor or repress scientific research, or inject theological considerations, such as "intelligent design theory" into science.

Gould maintained that the proper function of religion is in the realm of morality and meaning; for he believes that science has *no* role to play in such "nonfactual" domains. I think that Gould is again here mistaken. He would leave these questions primarily to the authority of religious teachings. Yet religious traditions often differ violently on which moral imperatives to follow. Roman Catholic bishops are against capital punishment and divorce. Protestant fundamentalists are for capital punishment and liberal Protestants for divorce. Western Judaic Christian theologians support monogamy. Muslims are for polygamy. Different religions will go to war singing hymns to God or Allah or Jehovah and kill each other in the name of God. Many disciples of religion have opposed women's rights; others have defended them. So we ask: the magisterium of *which* denomination is legitimate? Similarly for the question of ultimate meaning and purpose, the belief in salvation and the afterlife. Will the Rapture save *only* Evangelicals and condemn everyone else to hellfire? Will heaven only be open to devout Muslims who believe in the revelations of Muhammad and are they empowered to embark upon the jihad? This may sound like strong language, but this is what is happening today, as in the past, and these are historical *facts*.

Indeed, scientists have played an important role in their critique of the religions of Revelations. Similarly, biblical and Qur'anic critics have used the tools of historical research, archeology, linguistics, anthropology, and psychology to examine the claims of Revelations; and they've often found these lacking in adequate corroboration. The issue of how the Bible and the Qur'an were written has led to considerable skepticism about their inerrant claims to truth. Similarly, science has cast doubt about the "soul" being separable from the body, that "discarnate entities" exist in some form after the death of the body, and that they can achieve immortality. These are matters of faith that have little or no evidential grounds.

In reference to morality, there is an important tradition of philosophical inquiry from Socrates, Plato, Aristotle, Spinoza, Kant, and Mill, down to the present—which contests the idea that ethics necessarily belongs under the magisterium of religious faith. Philosophical ethical inquiry seeks alternative principles and values. It is not the pursuit of salvation, but of individual happiness and social justice that is the purpose of ethical inquiry; that is, the secularized-naturalized form that ethics has taken since the Renaissance, the Enlightenment, and the democratic revolutions of the modern world. They resist ceding their ethical domain to the magisterium of religion, without protest.

Gould maintains that science deals with fact and not moral values, which are beyond the capacity of empirical research. This is a simplistic and demonstrably false claim; for the applied sciences attempt to provide guidelines in dealing with moral questions; and they have introduced *new* principles and prescriptions. Education, social psychology, psychiatry, and the policy sciences, such as economics, sociology, and political science, illustrate the use of science to resolve moral and social problems. Granted that we cannot simply deduce what "ought" to be the case from what "is." But at the very least we can frame or modify our value judgments in the light of factual considerations, including knowledge of the causes and consequences of alternative policies and means-ends evaluations.

A good illustration of this is the emergence of medical ethics in the last three decades, where medical researchers, doctors, lawyers, and philosophers have attempted to clarify and develop principles and values by which various treatments are evaluated. For example, the appeal to "the informed consent" of the patient is such a principle. Similarly for living wills indicating when not to resuscitate a patient and/or to hasten the dying process. Clearly, some religious traditions dispute these principles. Nonetheless, few in the field of medical ethics would concede that scientific knowledge is *not* relevant to decision making or that a religious magisterium should be given free rein to determine the result. Thus, I submit that there ought to be some kind of *separation* of religion and ethics, for rational considerations and scientific evaluations are often relevant to the resolution of ethical issues.

The question of homosexuality is especially relevant here. Is it "wicked" because it is contrary to God's laws, or does psychiatric and biological research indicate that homosexuality is fairly widely practiced, that it may be genetic, and thus cannot simply be considered unnatural or a disease. That the ancient view of humankind should prevail in such moral questions and that it is appropriate to defer to the magisterium of religious teachers alone is highly questionable. I grant of course that the great religions are the repository of moral wisdom. I deny that they are exclusively so and/or that they are infallible.

There is still a third area where religion conflicts, and that is within the domain of politics. Many ideological-theological disciples of theism have argued that the political order should be subsumed under the divine order. This is the case in the Muslim world, where *sharia* as revealed through the Qur'an and Hadith is taken as the fountainhead of law. This has often led to a demand for theocracy, the wedding of mosque and state. A similar conflict is being waged today in democratic societies between the secular and theocratic conceptions of the state. Secularists have called for strict separation of religion and state. Others hope to bridge the two, as in the United States today. Individual voters of course have the right in a pluralistic society to express their religious convictions in the public square; but *do* they have the right to impose their theological views on others or prevent free inquiry and dissent so essential for scientific research and investigation?

Incidentally, one may ask, under which magisterium does Stephen Jay Gould's own thesis fit? Is his book *The Rocks of Ages* to be interpreted as a scientific treatise—it is hardly that—or is it ethical and political? Is he developing a moral case for tolerance and a balanced doctrine of the mean? Or is he expressing his own convictions, which have no basis in fact to justify them? Are his arguments independent of the magisterium of religion? Interestingly, although Gould acknowledges the role of philosophy and rational inquiry in ethics, he virtually concedes ethics to faith and the magisterium of religion, but this would contradict his *own* recommendations that are not necessarily based upon religion, but represents his own views about the role of science. I have no objections to his taking a position, but does this not contradict his distinction between two magisteria? Is he prepared to add a third—"the magisterium of rationality"?[3]

II

If religion has been under retreat in the modern world in its contest with science, ethics, and politics—what remains for it? Does it have *any* function? Is there some basis for compatibility? I think that there is, though my solution may not be acceptable to traditional religionists.

What is the proper domain of religion? Is anything left to it? My answer is in the affirmative. I think that religion and science are compatible, given a functional interpretation of religion. Religions will continue with us in the fore-seeable future and will not easily wither away. No doubt my thesis is contro-versial: religious language, I submit, is not primarily descriptive; nor is it pre-scriptive. The descriptive and explanatory functions of language are within the domain of science; the prescriptive and normative are the function of ethics. Both of these domains, science and ethics, have a kind of autonomy. In one sense, each moral agent is able to render his or her own moral judgments. Sim-ilarly within the political domain, religionists do not have any special compe-tence. It should be left to every citizen of a democracy to express his or her political views.

If this is the case, what is appropriate for religiosities? The domain of the religious, I submit, is *evocative, expressive, emotive*. It presents aesthetic inspi-ration, moral poetry, performative ceremonial rituals, which act out and *dra-matize* the human condition and human interests, and seek to slake the thirst for meaning and purpose. Religion—at least the religions of revelation—deal in fictionalized tales, parables, narratives metaphors, stories, and myths; and they frame the divine in human form (anthropomorphic). They express the existen-tial yearnings of individuals endeavoring to cope with the world that they encounter and to find meaning in the face of death. Religious language in this sense is eschatological. Its primary function is to express *hope*. If science gives us truth, morality the good and the right, and politics justice, then religion is the realm of expectation and promise. Its main function is to overcome despair and hopelessness in response to human tragedy, adversity, and conflict—the brute, inexplicable, contingent, and fragile facts of the human condition. Under this interpretation religions are not primarily true, nor are they primarily good or right or even just; they are, if you will, evocative, attempting to transcend contrition, fear, anxiety, and remorse, providing balm for the aching heart—at least for many people, if not all.

I would add to this the fact that religious systems of thought and belief are products of the creative human imagination. They traffic in fantasy and fiction, taking the promises of long-forgotten historical figures and endowing them with eternal cosmic significance.

The role of creative imagination, fantasy, and fiction should not be dis-missed. These are among the most powerful expressions of human dreams and hopes, ideals, and longings. Who could have imagined that J. K. Rowling's Harry Potter series of fictionalized books would so inspire young people, or that so many humans would be entranced by fictionalized novels, movies, and plays. Religious narratives are similar to other powerful works of art, such as the operas of Verdi and Puccini, or the literature of Dante, the plays of Shakespeare and Molière, or the novels of Dostoyevsky and Balzac. The cathedral at Chartres or the skyscrapers of New York make bold statements of human aspiration. Thus religion is more like art than science. The creative religious imagination weaves tales of consolation and expectation. They are dramatic expressions of human longing, enabling humans to overcome grief and depression and escape from the tragedies of the world.

In the above interpretation of religion as dramatic existentialist poetry, science and religion are not necessarily incompatible, for they address different human interests and needs. But then religion cannot be taken as true, except in a metaphorical aesthetic sense.

A special challenge to naturalism emerges at this point. *Methodological naturalism* is the basic principle of the sciences; namely, that we should seek natural causal explanations for phenomena, testing these by the methods of science. *Scientific naturalism*, on the other hand, goes beyond this, because it rejects as nonevidential the postulation of occult metaphors, the invoking of divine spirits, ghosts, or souls to explain the universe; and it tries to deal in materialistic, physical-chemical, or nonreductive naturalistic explanations.

If this is the case, the great challenge to scientific naturalism is not in the area of truth but of hope, not of the good but of promise, not of the just but of expectation—in the light of the tragic character of the human condition. This is in stark contrast with the findings of neo-Darwinism, which recognizes that death is final, not simply the death of each individual but the possible extinction some day in the remote future of the human species itself. Evolutionists have discovered that millions of species have become extinct. Does not the same fate await the human species? Cosmological scientists indicate that at some point it seems likely that our sun will cool down, indeed, looking into the future, that a Big Crunch may overtake the entire universe. Others talk about a deep freeze.[4] Some star trekkers are inspired by science fiction. They say that one day perhaps we will leave the earth, inhabit other planets and galaxies. Nonetheless, at some point the death of the individual, our species, our planet and solar system seems likely.

What does this portend for the ultimate human condition? We live in an epoch where the dimensions of the universe have expanded enormously on the macro and on the micro level. We are talking about billions of light-years in dimension, and perhaps even multiverses. Much of this is based on speculative extrapolation. Nonetheless, we can ask, does the naturalistic picture provide sufficient consolation for the human spirit? The central issue for humans is the question of human *courage*. Can we live a full life in the face of ultimate human extinction? These are large-scale questions, yet they are central for the religious consciousness. Can scientific naturalism, insofar as it undermines theism, provide an alternative dramatic, poetic rendering of the human condition, offering hope and promise? Countless numbers of brave individuals can enjoy significant lives and even thrive, accepting the possible distant death of the species and our solar system. But apparently so many other humans cannot bear that thought. They crave immortality and religion satisfies their need. Many others do not stay awake nights worrying what will happen five billion years from now. They find life worthwhile for its own sake here and now, and they try to live as fully and richly as they can in a secular and naturalistic world.

NOTES

1. Stephen Jay Gould, *Rocks of Ages: Science and Religion in the Fullness of Life* (New York: Ballantine Books, 1999), p. 6.

2. Ibid., p. 21.

3. Gould recognizes the frailty of his argument when he says in a footnote: "I apologize to colleagues in philosophy and related fields for such an apparently cavalier 'brush off' of an old and difficult topic still subject to much discussion, and requiring considerable subtlety and nuancing to capture the ramifying complexities. I recognize that this claim for separation of the factual from the ethical has been controversial (and widely controverted) ever since David Hume drew an explicit distinction between 'is' and 'ought.' . . . I acknowledge the cogency of some classical objections to strict separation—particularly the emptiness of asserting an 'ought' for behaviors that have been proven physically impossible in the 'is' of nature. I also acknowledge that I have no expertise in current details of academic discussion (although I have tried to keep abreast of general developments). Finally, I confess that if an academic outsider made a similarly curt pronouncement about a subtle and troubling issue in my field of evolution or paleontology, I'd be pissed off" (ibid., pp. 55–56).

4. Robert Frost's poem "Fire and Ice" is especially eloquent on this issue:

> Some say the world will end in fire,
> Some say in ice.
> From what I've tasted of desire
> I hold with those who favor fire.
> But if it had to perish twice,
> I think I know enough of hate
> To say that for destruction ice
> Is also great
> And would suffice.

24
THE SCIENCE OF ETHICS

LAURA PURDY

Is there a legitimate source of ethical[1] guidance apart from the alleged will of God that the Religious Right (RR) is attempting to impose on everyone? In 2006, only the woefully ignorant could see this as a serious question. Yet it has become an urgent matter in a democracy where a majority of citizens have not acquired the critical thinking skills or intellectual background to reject such a move or recognize alternatives.

What has gone wrong? First, people are being sold a view of ethics as a set of rules demanded of them by authority. Second, there is no need for these rules to make sense in terms of human welfare or happiness. Third, facts are often regarded as irrelevant or as fair game for manipulation and misrepresentation. Fourth, consistency (and the rules of logic and critical thinking generally) are often ignored. These assumptions appear to relieve individuals of any personal responsibility for the moral consequences of their decisions: their sole duty is to follow the rules—and condemn those who fail to do so. Worse still, these rules are now alleged to be the only legitimate basis for government and law, as the United States is allegedly a "Christian Nation."

In short, the public is now being presented with a momentous choice. Are we (allegedly) God's creatures, brought to life to follow (one group's conception of) his divine plan? Or are we an intelligent form of life that has evolved with the capacity and right to make our own choices about the good life and good societies? If the first claim is true, then ethics is just the enterprise of trying to figure out what God wants and then doing it; this is not science. But if the second claim is true, then it is plausible to maintain that ethics is a form of science, albeit a unique one because it is an overtly normative project. That is, it requires well-supported and relevant facts, and clear and consistent principles; it tests the conjunction of the two against their outcomes, modifying the principles as needed to conform to the overriding goal of the project, the welfare of sentient creatures.[2] I will argue here that there are many objections to the model of ethics now being promulgated by the Religious Right, and that there is no reasoned alternative but the scientific model.

THE TROUBLE WITH GOD'S ETHICS

The most obvious problem with the RR's approach to ethics is that there are numerous alleged sources of moral authority. So how are people supposed to make sure they've chosen the right one? They obviously need some standard for judging moral authorities—and once one has that there is no further need for such an authority at all.

Moreover, having acknowledged an authority does not relieve one of vigilance, for any authority could make a moral error, requiring of one seriously immoral actions. After all, even the military—arguably the most authoritarian body in any democracy—recognizes the doctrine of superior orders.[3] Equally important, even if there were one recognizable, true moral authority, encouraging individuals to accept claims on faith has far-reaching negative consequences, as W. K. Clifford pointed out long ago.[4]

This authority-based approach to ethics also maintains that no source of morality other than God's will is possible, so the failure to accept it leaves us adrift in a sea of moral relativism. Yet this ignores millennia of rich and varied philosophizing about ethics. These are just some of the most obvious problems with the moral epistemology now being urged on us by the Religious Right.

The content of the moral life now being pressed upon us by the Religious Right—the so-called culture of life (CL)—is equally problematic from the scientific point of view. The CL asserts that protecting and promoting life is the highest moral priority, trumping all other moral goals. At its core are two key propositions. One, articulated by Christian ethics professor Gilbert Meilaender, asserts that it is wrong deliberately to end human life, except perhaps in self-defense.[5] The other asserts that sex must always be open to reproduction. Yet these assertions together with the concrete rules alleged to follow from them violate all the assumptions inherent in a scientific approach to ethics.

First, the CL promotes the view that ethics is more about following rules than about using them to advance a desirable goal. Second, the precepts of the CL are often incompatible with the welfare of sentient creatures. Third, important elements of the CL are based on false claims about relevant states of affairs. Fourth, the CL cannot withstand critical scrutiny based on logic and reason.

THE GOAL OF ETHICS

Many people—and the RR encourages and promotes this view—seem to believe that ethics chiefly involves following rules. Acceptable rules allegedly aim at doing good and avoiding evil, but that is such a vague goal that following the rules is sufficient for demonstrating moral purity. Such individuals are ripe for the message of the RR purporting to supply the appropriate rules, obviating the need for critical examination by the moral "consumer."

This conception is analogous to the emphasis on the act of voting in elections, at the expense of thoroughgoing analysis of the competing platforms, or discussions of how one might choose among them. Instead, many children are taught to avoid discussions of politics and religion. Schools run mock elections, but often exclude the kind of systematic study of candidates' positions and critical thinking about them that would help children learn to make political decisions on a rational basis. As a result, voters seem to rely on family tradition, spousal pressure, or impulses based on emotionally appealing ads—with disastrous results for democracy and human welfare.

Wanting to do good and avoid evil is, of course, an essential part of ethics. But learning how to reason about what the good might look like, and how to achieve it is also crucial. A scientific approach to ethics would ask us to consider the various possible goals that might be appropriate for ethics, along the general lines Bentham follows in *Utilitarianism*. Aiming at the net welfare or happiness of sentient creatures is a plausible candidate. It both reflects most people's individual goals, yet requires significant sacrifices to ensure that the welfare of all affected parties is taken into account. Be that as it may, the general point here is not to argue specifically for utilitarianism, but rather to urge on society a process of rational analysis of possible moral goals based on people's most fundamental values, rather than choices based on authority or randomly chosen rules. This would include recognition that a satisfactory ethics must also make a place for significant and widely accepted values such as equality, justice, welfare, and liberty.

The CL violates this approach. First, its value system is not the result of a systematic consideration of alternatives, but is rather, as mentioned earlier, allegedly required of us by God, the ultimate moral authority. Second, the overriding emphasis on promoting life fails to acknowledge other values with which it might come into conflict. Because of that latter fact, one of its most common consequences is an increase in misery.

Why? The answers are familiar, even if ignored and the conflicting values discounted by the RR. Sometimes dying is terribly painful. Sometimes fetuses develop diseases or disabilities that will cause great suffering. Criminalizing the expression of sexual love between consenting adults who are not married (whether heterosexual or homosexual) frustrates basic needs. Pregnancy can threaten women's life or health. Preventing women from controlling their bodies and their reproductive lives can thwart their deepest desires. And so on.

Perhaps the most misery-inducing (and most irrational) expression of the CL is the current situation in El Salvador, where doctors cannot operate on women with ectopic pregnancies. Ectopic pregnancy is a condition where the embryo becomes lodged in a woman's fallopian tube. If it dies, doctors in El Salvador can remove it before it harms the woman. But if it does not die, they must wait until the woman's fallopian tube bursts, seriously endangering her life. The woman's life is subordinated to that of the embryo, even though it has no chance of becoming a child.[6]

A close competitor might be the war on condoms. Allegedly, they are less effective at preventing pregnancy and protecting against sexually transmitted diseases than people have been led to believe. Even if those claims were true—which they aren't—they would still be preventing some pregnancies and some disease. Discouraging people from using them therefore promotes unwanted pregnancy and often life-threatening disease. This is inconsistent with any culture of life and suggests quite another underlying agenda. Even stranger and more misery-inducing, however, is the position that it is immoral for gay men to use condoms. After all, in the context of heterosexual intercourse, the basic objection to the use of condoms is that preventing conception is immoral. Yet clearly the wickedness of preventing conception is now being attributed to the condom, so that using them is immoral even where conception is unimaginable. Moreover, their use is apparently so wicked that it is morally preferable to risk-transmitting, life-threatening diseases like AIDS.

THE ROLE OF FACTS

The most disturbing use of allegedly factual claims occurs in the promulgation of the second core assertion of the CL, that only sex acts open to the creation of life are moral. The argument is therefore that preventing conception or aborting fetuses is immoral. And if preventing sexually transmitted disease thwarts conception, such prevention, too, is immoral, and the immorality is inherent not just in the goal but in the instruments used, as the foregoing example shows.

Although these rules are allegedly entailed by the CL's two core assumptions, the RR also gives consequentialist arguments in support of them. This is where the RR most egregiously violates the truth. For instance, as we have just seen, the RR holds that condoms neither prevent conception nor disease reliably and is insisting that this information be included in abstinence-only sex education. But those claims are patently false.[7] It is also pushing the notion that abortion causes breast cancer or long-lasting psychological distress,[8] as well as inaccurate claims about fetal development.[9] It is now also being claimed (without a shred of evidence) that if girls are inoculated with the HPV vaccine that prevents cervical cancer, they might be more likely to become sexually promiscuous and that that worry outweighs the benefit of ending cervical cancer.[10] Other false claims are routinely made.[11]

Interestingly, the alleged connection between the principle that direct killing is always wrong and the principle that every sex act must be open to conception is hardly clear, let alone justifiable on its own merits. Eggs and sperm are not humans, so killing them (by preventing them from developing) cannot be entailed by the principle that direct killing is always wrong. Could they—or at least sperm—have a right to life anyway? Perhaps so, if one harks back to ancient theories that attributed the formation of new individuals solely to sperm, either because of their special powers or because they already contained the new persons as homunculi.[12] But discredited biological speculation is not a proper ground for contemporary moral precepts.

In any case, preventing conception does not involve killing, although it does involve letting one egg and one sperm die that might (but might not) have gone on to fertilization; all the other millions of sperm would die anyway, even if conception did take place. Of course, it is now well known that a huge percentage (some 80 percent) of conceptuses fail to develop anyway. Yet as we see below, the activities of the RR show that its focus is on the alleged evil of killing, not letting die.

LOGIC AND CRITICAL THINKING

The CL also fails in various ways to survive logical scrutiny. If a core principle is that killing is always wrong, except perhaps in self-defense, then it involves serious contradictions. Most obviously, RR proponents of the CL should be fighting to prohibit capital punishment, war, and the failure to take public health measures known to save lives. Yet their policies are just the opposite.

How do they justify these apparently contradictory positions? They implicitly appeal to universalizability, the principle that two cases can be treated differently if there is a morally relevant difference between them. So, for example, capital punishment is justifiable because there is a morally relevant difference between those who may or may not be killed—the former are guilty, whereas the latter are innocent. But with this distinction, the apparently simple and clear prohibition on killing becomes significantly less clear. What constitutes guilt? What degree of guilt justifies death? And who makes these decisions? In short, killing is now permissible for good reasons or in the right circumstances. Yet this way of thinking about the principle is simply ignored or rejected without argument in other contexts where it seems no less relevant (sex and reproduction, terminal illness). This is inconsistent and cannot be justified. Indeed, it is much more plausible to argue that physician-assisted suicide or active voluntary euthanasia are justifiable than capital punishment. In the first case, but not the second, killing prevents suffering and is desired; in the second, neither of these things is true. The same is true with respect to issues connected with sex and reproduction: the goals attained by killing are desired by all parties, prevent suffering, and advance the welfare of women, children, men, and society as a whole.

The antikilling principle becomes still less clear as proponents of the culture of life attempt to show why war, say the current war on Iraq, is justifiable. For even if one posits the requisite guilt for Saddam Hussein, it is difficult to show why the deaths of innocent Iraqis—innocent by any criterion at all, such as children—is therefore justified. Can one person's guilt be so enormous as to justify myriad innocent deaths?[13]

Last and not least, justifying the failure to take public health measures that are known to save lives requires still further questionable moves. For example, if experience shows that extensive safety measures, carefully enforced, saves miners' lives then how can one justify weakening those measures or failing to enforce them? The only available moral move is to posit a critical moral distinction between killing and letting die, acts and omissions, or the lack of responsibility for mere "statistically expected" deaths.[14] But why is ending life by indirectly rather than directly morally relevant?

CONCLUSION

It is a sad commentary on the state of US culture and politics that the concept of scientific ethics is now so controversial. Despite its promise of a way of life that attempts to satisfy our most fundamental needs and desires, it confronts a society that condones and encourages decision making based on emotion and wishful thinking. No wonder that "junk" ethics—provided by organizations intent on their own aggrandizement by manipulating our need for community—is becoming ever more prevalent. It is no coincidence that this state of affairs appeals to those who want to protect the political and moral status quo from the critical scrutiny it deserves. Moreover, scientific ethics provides the only hope for dealing with the increasingly numerous and complex problems posed by developments in basic science and technology.

As always, education is key: public schools are one of the main battlegrounds where the fight for a scientific approach will be won or lost, as the RR is well aware. But proponents of scientific ethics also need to clearly and accessibly lay out the case wherever they can—in the media, in the courts, and wherever else opportunity arises. In short, philosophers must increasingly become public intellectuals since we cannot be philosopher-kings.

NOTES

1. I am using "ethical" and "moral" interchangeably.

2. It is possible, of course, to develop ethics that do not have that goal, but I would argue that they are to be regarded as offshoots of the authority-driven view of ethics. It is hard to see why any such approach should be preferred to one that advances human welfare.

3. The doctrine of superior orders requires that military personnel disobey obviously immoral orders. Even the Nazi military code included this doctrine.

4. See W. K. Clifford, "The Ethics of Belief," in *Lectures and Essays* (London: Macmillan, 1879).

5. Gilbert Meilaender, "Living Life's End," *First Things* 153 (May 2005): 17–21, http://www.firstthings.com/ftissues/ft0505/articles/meilaender.html (accessed September 11, 2006). Meilaender holds the Duesenberg Chair of Christian Ethics at Valparaiso University. Meilaender never mentions God in this article, which is clearly intended to address the Schiavo case.

6. Jack Hitt, "Pro-Life Nation," *New York Times Magazine*, April 9, 2006; on the Web at http://www.nytimes.com/2006/04/09/magazine/09abortion.html?ex=11581 20000&en=f5b4f81aac0dc38e&ei=5070 (accessed September 11, 2006).

7. See the Waxman Report, *The Content of Federally Funded Abstinence-Only*

Education Programs, http://72.14.205.104/search?q=cache:OSSa1KNLuvEJ:www
.democrats.reform.house.gov/Documents/20041201102153-50247.pdf+Waxman
+Report&hl=en&gl=us&ct=clnk&cd=1&client=firefox-a (accessed September 11,
2006).

8. Ibid.

9. The most egregious misrepresentation about the development of fetuses was
presented in the antiabortion film *The Silent Scream.*

10. See, for example, the much-quoted comment by Bridget Maher of the Family
Research Council: "Giving the HPV vaccine to young women could be potentially
harmful because they may see it as license to engage in premarital sex." Cited in Katha
Pollitt, "Virginity or Death!" *Nation*, May 30, 2005, http://www.thenation.com/doc/
20050530/pollitt (accessed September 11, 2006).

11. For more, see the Waxman Report, note 8 above. For other alleged harms
caused by contraception, see *Humanae Vitae* (Pope Paul VI). For an excellent critique,
see Carl Cohen, "Sex, Birth Control, and Human Life," *Philosophy & Sex*, ed. Robert
Baker and Frederick Ellison (Amherst, NY: Prometheus Books, 1975).

12. Nancy Tuana, *The Less Noble Sex: Scientific, Religious, and Philosophical
Conceptions of Woman's Nature* (Bloomington: Indiana University Press, 1993), chaps.
6–7.

13. None of this answers the question why war is still justified once the "guilty"
party (such as Saddam Hussein) has been captured.

14. See my "The Politics of Preventing Premature Death," in *Public Health Policy
and Ethics*, ed. Michael Boylan (Kluwer, 2004).

25
POLICY, ETHICS, BELIEF, AND MORALITY

TOM FLYNN

C ontroversies regarding policy and ethical judgments often founder on issues of faith and belief. The positions defended by some participants in moral debate may be strongly influenced, sometimes even determined, by their religious beliefs. Zealots may answer every ethical question—and many questions of policy—with reference to their faith.

Which complicates discussion, since some religious people claim to obtain guidance from their beliefs that no amount of real-world evidence can overcome. Consider a superficial example. As a secular humanist, I hold that birth control and abortion are morally licit, in part because of the this-worldly consequences of continued unchecked growth in human numbers and in part because a scientific view gives us no reason to suppose that a human fetus possesses a status that would make its destruction morally unacceptable. In contrast, many Christians hold that abortion is forbidden—some would go so far as to forbid even birth control, because of their belief that God imbues each fertilized ovum with a supernatural essence, the soul, that renders its destruction unacceptable.

If a devout believer thinks abortion should be forbidden because fetuses, perhaps even blastocysts, have souls, he or she has every right to think that—

Portions of this essay were prefigured in Tom Flynn, "The Morality of Unbelief," *Free Inquiry* (Spring 1989): 6–8.

and every right to say so. Still, when real-world policy questions need to be solved, progress is difficult when humanists and other naturalists argue from the likely consequences of a given course of action in this world, while religious believers argue from what they believe God said on the subject.

When we are among our own, we humanists like to think that our single-minded focus on a consequential ethics firmly rooted in the world of ordinary experience gives us an advantage. We imagine that because our solutions are firmly rooted in an intersubjectively checkable reality, they are thereby made more persuasive. Yet believers view that as a disadvantage. To them humanists' refusal to consider causes beyond the natural world is a limitation—in effect a kind of blindness. Believers consider themselves advantaged because they can speak of this world and the next while we confine ourselves to speaking solely of this one. To them, thinking only in terms of this world is like philosophizing with one hand tied behind our backs.

The situation is further complicated by the deference Western societies generally demand toward religious beliefs and those who express them. It is sometimes good and proper that cultural mores encourage us to grant one another substantial leeway in matters of belief. If Muslims consider themselves forbidden to eat pork or if pacifist Quakers refuse to serve in the armed forces, every effort is properly made to accommodate them. But when some Muslim parents agitate for sexual segregation in schools or campaign against coeducational swimming, things get edgier. Western societies privilege religion, but there will inevitably be circumstances in which believers belonging to one religious community will want something altogether different—and fundamentally incompatible—with what believers belonging to another community insist upon. Of course, both of their proposed solutions might be quite different than the solution a naturalistic humanist might hit upon after contemplating the worldly situation unassisted by metaphysical pre-assumptions.

Strong religious belief can also impose artificial limits on debate. Believers may be unwilling to argue the issues past a certain point. From the believer's viewpoint, this can seem eminently reasonable. If they trace their answer to a certain policy or ethical question to a revelation from a deity, and if that deity in his, her, or its eternal wisdom chose to share the revelation with them but not with us, then we humanists are out of luck. From the believer's viewpoint we can be *disqualified* to continue discussion after the believer has intoned, "God said it, I believe it, that settles it."

Are naturalists trapped when debating opponents who claim the right to maneuver in one more realm of being than we can? Are we helpless before the ability of determined believers to short-circuit our rational examination of consequences at any time by invoking the supposed sanctity of their own religious beliefs? Have we no way to slash through this Gordian knot so that important policy and ethical debates move forward? Fortunately, we can break impasses of this sort. We need not—indeed, we must not—allow believers to do the equivalent of tying our shoelaces together whenever they make reference to their own beliefs. If their beliefs lead them toward specific ethical positions, we can probe the morality of their beliefs. We can argue—successfully, I think— that some beliefs have so little supporting evidence that it is *immoral* to hold them in a way that shapes one's position on ethical and policy issues.

If believers can appeal to their faith to judge what is moral, we can appeal to morality to separate legitimate from illegitimate applications of faith. Best of all, the philosophical argument in defense of this position is compact, extremely powerful, and surprisingly fun to read. I speak, of course, of "The Ethics of Belief," an essay published in 1876 by the short-lived English mathematician and philosopher William Kingdon Clifford.[1] Humanists and other naturalists engaging in ethical and policy debates would do well to take the lessons of Clifford's essay to heart before they contend in the marketplace of ideas.

For those unfamiliar with the work, Clifford's "The Ethics of Belief" presents an outspoken defense of evidentialism, the view that it is morally binding to assent only to propositions for which we have satisfactory evidence. "It is wrong always, everywhere, and for anyone, to believe anything upon insufficient evidence," Clifford famously declared.

In this paper I will summarize Clifford's contentions, place his arguments in historical context, and offer a taxonomy of beliefs by which we can probe whether those making ethical or policy claims on religious grounds are morally entitled to rely on their faith in the way that they do.

Is it meaningful to talk about an ethics for belief—and if so, *what* can we say about it? Let us examine Clifford's argument. (I apologize in advance for the sexism that pervades these quotes; Clifford was a man of his time and the time was 1876.)

"The Ethics of Belief" opens with one of the most powerful word-pictures in philosophy. A shipowner has reason to suspect that an older ship in his fleet may not be seaworthy; he considers spending heavily to have the craft refitted. At length he succeeds in overcoming his doubts, and orders the vessel to sail to the New World as is. The ship goes down in mid-ocean. There are no survivors. "What shall we say of him?" Clifford asked of the shipowner. "Surely this, that he was verily guilty of the death of those men." (And of the women and children, too, might I add.) "It is admitted that he did sincerely believe in the soundness of his ship; but the sincerity of his conviction can in no wise help him, because *he had no right to believe on such evidence as was before him.*"[2]

Next Clifford asked: What if, despite its frailties, the ship had safely completed its Atlantic crossing? The owner would be no less guilty, Clifford charged, because based on the evidence before him he had no right to *expect* that outcome. Clifford urged peerless vigilance so that no one's belief should ever be misplaced. "[Belief]," he wrote, ". . . is desecrated when given to unproved and unquestioned statements, for the solace and private pleasure of the believer; to add a tinsel splendour to the plain straight road of our life and display a bright mirage beyond it."[3] He continued, "Every time we decide to let ourselves believe for unworthy reasons, we weaken our powers of self-control, of doubting, of judicially and fairly weighing evidence. . . . If I let myself believe on insufficient evidence, there may be no great harm done by that belief; it may be true after all, or I may never have occasion to exhibit it in outward acts. But I cannot help doing this great wrong toward Man, that I make myself credulous."[4]

Does Clifford set forth an impossible ideal? Does he demand too much of his hearers? Anticipating that objection, Clifford responds by quoting an imaginary opponent: "'But,' says one, 'I am a busy man; I have no time for the long course of study which would be necessary to make me in any degree a competent judge of certain questions. . . .'" "Then," Clifford thunders, that person "should have no time to believe."[5]

Who was William Kingdon Clifford? He was a prodigy—a professor of applied mathematics at University College London, a student of Darwin, an outspoken atheist, and, at age twenty-nine, the youngest man ever to join the Metaphysical Society, an exclusive London debating club whose members included William Gladstone, Thomas Henry Huxley, and Alfred Lord Tennyson.[6] Clifford delivered "The Ethics of Belief" as a lecture to that group on April 11, 1876. It was immediately published in the influential journal *Contemporary Review*. Two years later, William Kingdon Clifford lay dead of tuberculosis at age thirty-three.

Though Clifford was gone, his essay continued to exert influence. Ironically, it inspired what may be, from the naturalist's point of view, the most damaging single discourse on belief ever published.

In 1896 William James composed a muscular rebuttal to "The Ethics of Belief," a far better-known essay called "The Will to Believe." Perhaps modern philosophy's most respectable celebration of impulsive assent, "The Will to Believe" lay the groundwork for the explosion in credulity that rocked twentieth- and twenty-first-century thought. What did "The Will to Believe" consist of? Primarily, in James's words, a "defence of our right to adopt a believing attitude in religious matters, in spite of the fact that our merely logical intellect may not have been coerced."

In plain terms, James strove to establish, more or less by sheer bluster, a human right to believe without evidence. Millions took him up on it, neo-Romantics and anti-intellectuals perhaps most of all. "The Will to Believe" has had an impact that is immense and to my mind largely insidious. Sadly, it has been far more influential than "The Ethics of Belief." The West's dalliance with Eastern religion, the New Age movement, postmodernism, the contemporary fascination with alternative and complementary medicine—the naturalist cannot help wondering how differently our society might have turned out if "The Will to Believe" had never been written.

For my part, I side with Clifford. Despite its occasional flamboyances, "The Ethics of Belief" sets out an impressive intellectual and, yes, a *moral* case for evidentialism—a case for applying scientific methodology to the moral question of when it is, or is not, acceptable to believe.

For what follows, let us establish a new term: we shall describe a person who willfully believes in the absence of evidence as a *credulist*.

Following Clifford, I contend that belief without empirical justification can be inherently immoral. The moral wrong lies in the adverse effects that the credulist may have upon the world and upon other persons when he or she acts on an unjustified belief. In other words, it is not in the *act of believing* without evidence, but rather in the *willingness to act upon* unjustified belief, that moral hazard lies.

This seems a simple enough principle, until we remember the importance generally attached to freedom of thought and expression. Isn't it contrary to intellectual pluralism to argue, as Clifford did, that the real world has characteristics that can make one choice *morally better* than another, and that this moral superiority can be discerned in ways about which independent observers can agree? As critical thinkers who wish to prevent persons of faith from hijacking policy discussions, we wish to uphold reasonable, objective moral standards for belief—yet we also wish to respect freedom of expression and belief. Can we do both? I would say yes.

In part, we can overcome the conflict between free expression and objective accuracy by recognizing that they hail from separate streams of discourse. Our commitment to free expression is primarily *political*; our commitment to objective accuracy is primarily *methodological*. We can uphold both freedom of inquiry and an objective ethical evidentialism by recognizing varying categories of belief, to which we can assign varying epistemic and moral weights.

Here I will offer a taxonomy of beliefs, categorizing them according to their evidential support and their moral implications.

TABLE I. TAXONOMY OF BELIEF TYPES, EVIDENTIARY CHARACTERISTICS, AND PUTATIVE MORAL STATUS.

Belief Type	Characteristics	Moral Status
Assertional	Belief held without sufficient evidence that creates no predisposition toward action	Inconsequential
Motivating	Belief held without sufficient evidence that creates a predisposition toward action	Immoral; "Rogue Belief"
Evidencing	Belief held on the basis of sufficient evidence; may or may not predispose toward action	Morally Licit

At the lowest level, a belief may be nothing more than an innocuous proposition about reality. If it may be unsupported by evidence, it is also unlikely to predispose its holder toward behavior that can have significant moral consequences. For example, a belief that the moon is made of green cheese is not supported by evidence. But holding that belief puts one no closer to nor further from pursuing any morally significant course of action. It makes me no more likely to benefit or to harm other persons or society. I propose to call the belief in propositions of this sort *assertional*. Assertional beliefs are harmless so long as they remain assertional. This is fortunate, as assertional beliefs are also extremely common.

I should admit that in claiming the moral innocence of assertional beliefs, I am departing from Clifford. Clifford denied that there could exist any belief that held *no* implications for future behavior. With due respect I disagree, for two reasons. First, as in the case of "green-cheese-ism," we can easily imagine earnestly held beliefs that would predispose their holders toward no specific actions. Second, it is at this very point that we confront one of those previously mentioned collisions between political and methodological domains of discourse. Our commitment to freedom of inquiry embodies a political recognition that in a society of human beings, room must be allowed for people to follow their thoughts where they lead. Within limits, room must be allowed for people to be hideously wrong. This is a human necessity which Clifford's method alone cannot encompass.

Having defined assertional belief, let's move on to a form of belief that once held is likely to alter our likelihood to perform or refrain from morally significant actions. Consider the proposition that abortion is murder. Randall Terry, founder of the radical pro-life group Operation Rescue, used to tell his followers, "If you believe that abortion is murder, act like it." Some did—notably James Kopp, who in 1998 assassinated abortion provider Barnett Slepian in his Amherst, New York, home. Antony Flew has written of *motivating belief*, and that is the term I will apply here.[7] A motivating belief constitutes assent to a proposition whose content alters our probable behavior in morally significant ways. Note carefully, however, that its power to motivate has nothing to do with whether it is true. A motivating belief can be true or false, or its truth may be unknown.

It is time, then, to take the next and final step. How can we know a belief is true? We can have substantial confidence if we have assented to a proposition that enjoys powerful evidential support of the kind that lends itself to intersubjective validation, that is, verification upon scientific principles. Flew calls belief on such grounds *evidencing belief*, and I will accept that nomenclature here.[8]

If someone holds a well-supported evidencing belief, does that tell us anything about his or her likely behavior? I don't think so. One can imagine an evidencing belief that does not predispose its holder toward or away from any morally significant action. For example, there is copious evidence that noble gases like neon do not participate in chemical reactions. But it's hard to imagine a moral act that I might be more or less likely to perform because I understand this behavior of noble gases.

Equally, one can hold a well-supported belief that *does* incline one toward or away from a particular moral course. For example, if I hold a small number of well-grounded beliefs regarding architecture, human psychology, and the behavior of flames, I can easily deduce that shouting "Fire!" in a crowded theater is an immoral act.

We can now return to our consideration of debating ethical or policy issues with an interlocutor who is religious. Which category of beliefs comes into play when believers use their faith to obstruct ethical and policy debates? In the terminology established above is the set of beliefs that are *motivating* but not *evidencing*. Such beliefs are very likely to engender action but may have little or no factual support. I call them "rogue" beliefs.

With this vocabulary and these concepts before us, can we formulate a general principle for assessing the morality of belief? I believe so.

Begin by considering an assertional belief—in essence, a mere opinion. It may be foolish, but my decision to embrace it has no moral consequences. Now consider a motivating belief—a proposition whose content, if accepted, will likely predispose me toward a course of action with moral consequences. Unfortunately, some propositions that have no more weight than an assertional belief nonetheless, almost necessarily, lead the people who accept them into action because of the nature of their content. To accept such beliefs at all is all but inevitably to accept them *as motivating beliefs*. Religion, paranormal belief systems, utopian sociopolitical systems such as Communism, and similar belief complexes almost always act as motivating beliefs. To hold them *is*, all but unavoidably, to act on them. So we ought to be very careful about which such beliefs we come to hold. For any person to accept a body of propositions of this type without first subjecting it to detailed scrutiny is—let's not mince words— an immoral act. The credulist is immoral in his or her practice of epistemology.

The moment when beliefs "go rogue" is the moment when an unsubstantiated assertional belief morphs into an unsubstantiated motivating belief— when beliefs that others are entitled to hold only as assertions become potential platforms for morally significant actions.

Knowing this, we can better appreciate the value of Clifford. Whatever his excesses, Clifford firmly demonstrates *why* the believer who has chosen to accept not merely an assertional belief, but a motivating belief, without compelling evidence courts grave moral risk. Clifford gives us a stance from which to push back when believers obstruct policy debate, then claim that their faith is not subject to our review.

This brings us, finally, to the stance which critical thinkers should adopt when we debate credulists on issues of policy or ethics. Every contender has the right to state his or her opinion or preference so long as it is presented as such, without making any claim that it is an objectively truthful description of reality and without making any claim that it justifies any morally significant course of action. But we know that often, our opponents will reinterpret their assertional belief as a motivating belief, as a justification for some morally significant course of action, even if there is no good warrant for accepting the belief at all.

To accept beliefs that necessarily imply actions with moral consequences—to embrace an unsupported motivating belief while anticipating that one might act according to its precepts—is on my view and in Clifford's memorable phrase "always and everywhere" immoral.

This does not mean that critical inquirers should demand that credulists not be heard. Far from it. But we must reserve the right—and we should never avoid the obligation—to step in when an unsupported motivating belief is expressed, and to urge listeners to assign to that statement no greater weight than one would grant to a mere personal assertion. *Because that is all it is.*

A conservative Christian may declare that cloning is impermissible because only God can create a human life. We can acknowledge that person's right to hold that opinion, but note that expressing it does not put forward any genuine argument because its epistemic weight depends on an unsupported belief that other participants in the debate are not obliged to share. We can respond, "Thank you for stating your preference, but why should someone who does not believe in God exactly as you do be swayed by it? Further, on what grounds should your unsubstantiated personal preference justify limiting the freedom of others to explore cloning technology?"

When critical thinkers contend with credulists in debates concerning policy and ethics, we need never feel that our commitment to freedom of thought and expression compels us to accept moral relativism. We can object in the strongest terms—Cliffordian terms—to unsubstantiated beliefs that predispose toward morally negative outcomes. We can do this consistently, and scientifically. Following the example of Clifford, not that of William James, critical thinkers can fairly apply high standards of scrutiny to extraordinary claims. To my mind, this justifies us in maintaining—if, one hopes, sparingly— the position that the critical inquirer's reluctance to believe is morally superior to the credulist's unquestioned belief.

NOTES

1. Timothy J. Madigan, ed., *The Ethics of Belief and Other Essays* (Amherst, NY: Prometheus Books, 1999).

2. Ibid.

3. Ibid., p. 74.

4. Ibid., p. 76.

5. Ibid., p. 78.

6. Timothy J. Madigan, "Ethics and Evidentialism: W. K. Clifford and 'The Ethics of Belief,'" *Journal for the Critical Study of Religion, Ethics, and Society* 2, no. 1 (Spring/Summer 1997): 9–18.

7. Antony Flew, "W. K. Clifford and the Presumption of Atheism," *Journal for the Critical Study of Religion, Ethics, and Society* 2, no. 1 (Spring/Summer 1997): 5–7.

8. Ibid.

NATURALISTIC ETHICS

PART VIII

26

SCIENTIFIC NATURALISTIC ETHICS
Weird Science and Pseudo-Ethics?

WILLIAM A. ROTTSCHAEFER

Ascientific naturalistic ethics proposes among other things that there are moral facts that partially explain what makes action morally right. Separatists claim that the sciences and ethics are fundamentally distinct. They argue that (1) the sciences explain factual phenomena of the natural world by means of theories about natural kinds and (2) ethics establishes moral values that guide us in fashioning norms for determining what is the right thing to do. Separatist, therefore, find a scientific naturalistic ethics to be weird science and pseudo-ethics. More specifically, moral facts are explanatorily irrelevant or epiphenomenal. They refer to weird properties that never enter into scientific explanations. Nor could these facts ever be the source of genuine moral motivation. In this paper, I argue that a scientific naturalistic ethics neither uses weird science nor manufactures a pseudo-ethics. In particular, I use empirical findings and theories about moral internalization to show that moral facts are causally relevant to moral actions. I illustrate how moral explanations have an explanatory structure similar to the selection theories in biology and psychology. Finally, I use an empirically based theory of agency and empirically based theories of representational moral motivation to understand how moral facts are relevant to genuine moral motivation. I conclude that attempts to provide naturalistic ethics with scientific support are encouragingly successful and ought to be vigorously pursued. A scientific naturalistic ethics can be both scientifically based and about ethics.

INTRODUCTION

What are the relationships between ethics, the philosophical discipline concerned with the study of morality, and the sciences? A common opinion is that since their subject matters and methodologies are entirely distinct, they are essentially distinct disciplines. Substantively, ethics is concerned with moral values and the sciences with natural facts. The methodology of ethics is nonempirical and that of the sciences empirical.[1]

This Separatist view implies that any relationships between the sciences and morality are external. Scientists, just as all members of society, are bound by moral values built into ethical norms. Thus they are obliged to follow accepted ethical norms for scientific investigation and to consider the moral consequences of their scientific work. But given the ethical legitimacy of a scientific investigation, the standards for pursuit of scientific truth ought not to be compromised for the sake of achieving moral values, no matter how noble. Science is concerned with cognitive values and ethics with moral values. Both values bring norms to bear on practice, but the values and norms are distinct, even though in the pursuit of the scientific the scientist must respect the ethical, giving it primacy.

Integrationists challenge the Separatist view by denying either the methodological or substantive distinction between cognitive and moral values. Some feminist epistemologists and not a few sociologists of science have denied the methodological distinction. They have done so by either denying the existence of cognitive values or maintaining that even within the internal practice of science, any methodologically salient cognitive values are themselves ultimately subordinated to noncognitive values, whether moral or not. On the substantive side, some scientific naturalistic moralists have argued that natural features of the world constitute moral values and, thus, are open to scientific investigation. Such methods of investigations would themselves be guided by the cognitive values pursued in the other sciences. These scientific naturalists also deny the methodological distinction, but unlike the above-mentioned feminists or sociologists of science, maintain that the study of moral values should itself be guided by the cognitive values exemplified in the sciences.

Thus it is clear that the denial of Separatism leads to two very distinct outcomes. One outcome produces the subjectivization of science, according to which, though the substantive distinction between the sciences and morality remains, the methodological distinction disappears, leaving in its place pursuits guided ultimately, and, perhaps, only by noncognitive values. The second outcome results in the objectivization of ethics, according to which the substantive and methodological distinctions disappear, but the methodology now asserted to be common to both ethics and the sciences is itself guided by cognitive values. *Prima facie*, the subjectivization seems to threaten the sciences' autonomy and epistemic authority. Objectivization seems to imperil the autonomy of ethics; the subjectivist view seems to eliminate the sciences, and the objectivist view postulates a science (or sciences) of morality, a scientifically based naturalized ethics.

In this essay I explore some advantages of an Integrationist approach that maintains the objectivity of both the sciences and ethics.[2] I do so by outlining a scientifically based naturalized ethics, one using the scientific disciplines of biology and psychology.[3] I argue that one way to understand such a scientific naturalization of ethics is to consider it as a theory of moral agency. This enables me to outline some of the requirements for a successful scientific naturalization of ethics in terms of a series of increasingly controversial hypotheses. Focusing on what I call the ontological connection hypothesis, I proceed to examine the role of moral values in the origin of moral agency using findings and plausible theories from evolutionary and developmental biology and operant and social cognitive psychology. In doing so, I attempt to meet three recent objections that ethics cannot meet the standards of theoretical scientific explanation. On this basis I maintain that a scientific naturalized ethics shares an explanatory pattern common to explanations in these scientific disciplines. Insofar as it does, it is a moral science, a science of morality. It is neither weird science nor pseudo-ethics. I conclude that although the project of the scientific naturalization of ethics is only in its beginning stages, it merits pursuit.

A SCIENTIFIC NATURALISTIC ACCOUNT OF MORAL AGENCY

Following this naturalizing hypothesis, I suggest that human moral agency is a central phenomenon of morality.[4] On this understanding ethics concerns itself in the first instance with human moral agency. Consequently, it is helpful to understand the questions of metaethics as questions about moral agency. For instance, (1) what counts as moral capacities and actions, both substantively and functionally? (2) How does one acquire moral capacities? (3) How does one put these moral capacities to work? (4) How does one assess the adequacy of the operation of these moral capacities and actions? And (5) what is the function or purpose of moral agency? To count as being scientifically based, a scientifically naturalized ethics will make significant use of the relevant sciences to answer the questions of moral agency.[5] Although I believe that the social sciences may come to play an even more important role in a science of moral agency than the natural sciences, at this point in time the potential contributions of biology and psychology seem clearer.[6]

The scientific naturalistic account of moral agency that I am proposing is constituted by seven increasingly controversial substantive hypotheses concerning the connections between the ethics and biology and psychology.[7,8]

1. *Informational Connection Hypothesis*: Because of the relevant information about the circumstances and conditions of moral action that they have, the biological and psychological sciences can provide a moral agent with factual information important in ethical decision making and significant for ethical understanding.

2. *Explanatory Connection Hypothesis*: Moral capacities have genetic, developmental, behavioral, affective, and cognitive components. Biology and psychology provide descriptive, explanatory, and predictive knowledge concerning the origin, development, maintenance, use, change, or extinction of the cognitive, affective, and behavioral capacities that are employed in ethical action.

3. *Critical Connection Hypothesis*: An account of the biological and psychological bases of moral agency can effectively critique the claims of common sense and nonscientifically based philosophical or religious theories concerning human moral capacities and the nature and function of morality.

4. *Normative Connection Hypothesis*: We can use knowledge of our moral capacities, as well as knowledge from other sources, for instance, perceptual and social sources, to formulate some general prima facie normative principles about what it is good for us to do morally, what is morally permissible and impermissible, and what is morally obligatory.

5. *Epistemological Connection Hypothesis*: If the explanatory hypothesis is substantiated, we can conclude that the capacities of moral agency provide us with relatively reliable mechanisms for achieving moral goals. So we can appeal to their use in attempting to justify moral beliefs, motivations, and actions and in trying to understand the nature and function of morality.

6. *Ontological Connection Hypothesis*: If the explanatory hypothesis is substantiated, we can give a naturalistic ontological account of the nature and role of moral values in human agency.

7. *Meaningfulness Hypothesis*: An account of the biological and psychological bases of moral agency can make an important contribution to the vision of a meaningful human life, one connected in fulfilling ways to other humans, nonhumans, and the environment.

Separatists accept the Informational Connection Hypothesis and often a minimalist version of the Explanatory Connection Hypothesis. However, they find the other hypotheses to be woefully misguided. I shall focus on their critique of the Ontological Connection Hypothesis, the claim that adequate explanations of moral agency enable a naturalistic account of the nature moral values. Separatists maintain that this hypothesis represents either weird science or pseudo-ethics. I address this general complaint by examining three prominent problems facing the Ontological Connection Hypothesis. First, they argue that the appeal to moral facts in explaining moral agency is an appeal to explanatorily inert factors. In response I show how appeals to empirical psychological findings in moral developmental psychology about the phenomenon of moral internalization can help make the case for moral realism against the charge of explanatory inertness. Second, even if such facts have explanatory power, they are scientifically weird facts unacceptable in any reputable science. I use some generalizations about selection theories in evolutionary biology and cognitive social learning theory in psychology to support moral realism in the face of the problem of the weirdness of moral properties. Finally, even if these moral facts are not so scientifically weird after all, they are irrelevant to any explanation of moral motivation.[9] I shall employ results concerning cognitive social learning theories in psychology and ecological theories of emotion to support moral realism's ability to explain moral motivation. By addressing these three problems, I show how moral values, by playing a significant explanatory role, help confirm what I have called the Ontological Connection Hypothesis.[10] In this way I lend support to the Integrationist approach to the relationships between the sciences and the philosophical discipline of ethics, one that argues that ethics is a moral science.[11]

MORAL REALISM, EXPLANATORY INERTNESS, AND MORAL INTERNALIZATION

In addressing the first objection, I address a dispute between two naturalists' positions, the moral realist view—maintained with variations by such philosophers as Nicholas Sturgeon, Richard Boyd, Richard Miller, and Peter Railton—and an antirealist naturalist position supported prominently by Gilbert Harman.[12] I focus on the exchanges between Sturgeon and Harman.[13] Roughly, moral realists hold that there are moral facts constituted by both subject-side and object-side factors. Besides the moral beliefs, attitudes, and actions of the subject there are moral facts about practices, institutions, situations, and objects. Some of the latter object-side factors are morally valuable;

others are not. Moral antirealists hold that the only moral facts are subject-side, including intersubjective-side facts, such as pro and con attitudes or collective pro or con tendencies.

Gilbert Harman has argued in a number of places that object-side facts are explanatorily inert.[14] They explain nothing about an agent's moral perceptions, beliefs, and actions. Indeed, they are irrelevant to such explanations. On Harman's view such facts, if they exist, are epiphenomenal. On the other side, Sturgeon contends that adequate explanations of moral phenomena require the invocation of object-side moral facts. Each party supports his position by considerations of linguistic practice and appeals to imaginary and hypothetical cases. I contend that this discussion has ended in a stalemate and suggest that findings about moral internalization coming from moral developmental psychology break this stalemate and lend tentative support to moral realism.[15]

Moral internalization is a way that developmental psychologists often describe what moralists have discussed as the development of conscience. It designates a psychological state, and its development, in which one feels or believes that he or she has an obligation to act in accord with moral norms. Developmental psychologists mean various things by moral norms, but one acceptable and non-biasing version is that a moral norm is a norm that enjoins one in a specific situation to act for the welfare of another. An agent manifests moral internalization when, in situations where a conflict of interests exists between the welfare of another and her own interests, she consistently acts to promote the welfare of another person rather than to attain social approval or egoistic aims.

Parental discipline situations are particularly apt occasions for promoting moral internalization. Psychologists have identified three importantly different methods by means of which parents/caregivers facilitate moral internalization.[16] First, caregivers use assertions of power, which involve such measures as the use of force, deprivation of privileges, threats, and commands. Second, parents use withdrawal of love, which includes expressions of disapproval and anger. Finally, in inductive techniques, caregivers point out to the child, either directly or indirectly, the effects of the child's behavior on others, provide information about moral norms, and communicate their values regarding the consideration of others.

The current consensus concerning the results of both naturalistic and experimental studies is that the most effective means of moral internalization are inductive techniques.[17] It is hypothesized that this technique is effective because it associates moral norms with empathic feelings, in particular empathic distress and guilt feelings, producing what psychologists call a "hot cognition," one that has motivational power. A hot cognition can enter into future considerations independently of any considerations about approval or disapproval or fear of punishment.

Consider, then, a hypothetical moral learning situation. Michelle is a moral neophyte, though not necessarily of the blank slate type, since she possesses some empathic capacities. Suppose she is hitting her baby brother, Mickey, for no reason whatsoever. No matter what internalization technique she might employ, her caregiver considers Michelle's current activity to be morally wrong. So her caregiver tells Michelle that what she is doing is wrong and that she should stop hitting little Mickey. Idealize the situation and suppose that there are three versions of our drama differentiated by the three different discipline methods employed, power assertion, love withdrawal, and inductive techniques. The findings tell us that inductive techniques will be the most effective in enabling Michelle to internalize moral norms. What this indicates is that when object-side facts play a role in discipline techniques, those techniques are more effective in producing moral internalization than when they do not, as is the case in the techniques of power assertion that invoke fear of punishment and love withdrawal that invoke anxiety.

Returning now to the dispute between moral realists and antirealists, these findings support, at least *prima facie*, the moral realist position. Moral internalization is best accomplished and explained by postulating a complex type of property with related subject-side and object-side components than by attributing it merely to subject-side factors.

MORAL REALISM, EXPLANATORY WEIRDNESS, AND SELECTION THEORIES

Assume that it is this complex property that appears to have more explanatory power than the simpler subject-side ones. That's still a very weird property, not likely to be one that any reputable scientific theory invokes. On a standard view of scientific explanation the properties that play an explanatory role constitute natural kinds, for instance, the phenomenal properties of uranium are caused by a particular element of the periodic table. Uranium possesses a set of identifiable properties that have nothing to do with the subject doing the identifying nor are they constituted by complex relationships with other elements. Moral properties are not at all like these properties.[18]

In reply the moral realist argues that there are a whole group of perfectly respectable scientific theories that invoke the same general type of weird property. These are selection theories.[19]

Selection theories have the following form:[20]

(1) Capacity C (e.g., empathy) in organism O (e.g., a human) tends to bring about effect E (e.g., helping) in situation S (e.g., when someone is hurt). (**Causal clause**)

(2) C is there in O because in the past C has often been successful in bringing about E in S. (**Goal Clause**)

(3) Having C and bringing about E in S allowed O-1s to do better than O-2s that had trait C* (e.g., a tendency to act fearfully) rather than C, or better than O-1s themselves would have done, if they had had C** (a tendency to feel personal distress) rather than C. (**Benefit Clause**)

(4) When Es are in the moral realm, O-1's doing better than O-2 means doing better morally. (**Moral Benefit Clause**) In the case of humans, some of these goods are moral goods. That is, they are (1) the goods of human flourishing, for instance, food, shelter, clothing, safety, companionship, the development of intellectual, creative, practical, and social capacities and (2) goods of the human community, for instance, social and distributive justice and moral rights. The schema leaves open whether these goods are to be understood to be reduced to, supervene on, or emerge from their nonmoral bases. In any case, these goods, including moral goods, are understood in an entirely naturalistic fashion, that is, as instantiated in physical, chemical, and biological properties, so that they can play an explanatory role in the acquisition, activation, and operation of the moral capacities constitutive of moral agency.

To see how selection theories work, we can consider how they help explain the acquisition of moral agency. Psychologist Albert Bandura has developed a highly confirmed model of general human agency.[21] I extend that model and use it to understand moral agency.[22] In addition, I supplement my model with what I call a base level, making use of evolutionary psychology, operant theory, and Martin Hoffman's theory of empathic distress.[23] The model of moral agency consists of four functionally described levels of agency:[24]

1. A *base level* consists of evolutionarily acquired and behaviorally learned capacities and tendencies that incline the agent to act morally in given situations;
2. A *behavioral level* is made up of a set of moral beliefs and desires that are the immediate sources of moral actions and that are influenced by both base-level and higher-level components;
3. A *reflective level* is comprised of higher-level beliefs and desires, including moral norms or their equivalents, that influence the behavioral-level beliefs and desires; and

4. A *self-referential level* is constituted by conceptions of the self, including the self as moral agent, that motivate the use of moral norms and, indirectly, moral action.[25]

Consider the question of acquisition and how selection theories play a role in explaining the acquisition of the component capacities of moral agency.[26] These capacities enable intentional activity at the higher levels of agency and goal-directed activities at the lowest level. We can sketch the origin of the component capacities of moral agency by appealing to a selecting environment in which capacities for the instantiations of moral goods are selected for. Explanations of the acquisition of the subcapacities of moral agency all display a common teleological structure, where the consequences serving to explain the acquisition and use of the moral capacities in question are moral values.

We can conceive of the base-level capacities to consist of those that are evolutionarily based adaptations or are the result of operant conditioning. The other component capacities of moral agency derive from various forms of individual and social cultural learning. In each type of selection process, the presence of the disposition or capacity is due in part, at least, to *successful* past performances. Since a selection process is involved there is selection among variant capacities. In the case of organisms with relevant, heritable genetic differences the selection is evolutionary. With respect to organisms that differ because of nongenetically based noncognitive or cognitive capacities the selection is social/cultural and/or intentional. What is selected for is differentially good or bad for the organism and others.

In these environments those agents that seek to satisfy moral ends will tend to do better than those that do not or who do not do so to the same extent. Because of this relative difference in success the capacities that produce the more successful actions will be relatively more plentiful in the next generation. Of course, this is not to say that there are no other opposing selective forces and human tendencies, or that morality is the ultimate, let alone the only, end of human activity.

The goal is to find adequate selection-based accounts of the origin of each of the component capacities of moral agency. Such selection-based accounts require the weird sorts of properties that the Separatist finds so objectionable. They appeal to both object- and subject-side properties and the relationships between them. To the extent that selection explanations are scientifically respectable, to that extent explanations of the origin of each of the components of moral agency that are based on selection theories are scientifically respectable. I conclude that either some acceptable scientific theories concern themselves with weird properties or these properties aren't so weird after all.

MORAL REALISM, MOTIVATIONAL VACUITY, AND APPRAISAL THEORIES

Let us grant that these weird moral facts exist. Let us also concede that such facts play an explanatory role with respect to what we do. The Separatist argues that that makes no difference for moral agency. To be moral, moral acts demand proper motivation. Such proper motivation necessarily involves moral requiredness. But if moral goodness and rightness are based ultimately on objective facts, no matter how ordinary or weird, they are in the end incapable of being a source of moral requiredness. Such facts can never be motivating, let alone morally motivating.[27]

But the objection fails. Clauses (3) and (4) show us that normative requiredness is a feature of selection explanations. Clause (3) makes clear that what is selected for is beneficial for the organism because it is required for the organism's success in that environment. This benefit is relative to benefits accruing from other alternatives within a pool of candidate capacities and with respect to a given external or internal environment. And when, as Clause (4) suggests, the goods in question are moral goods, the benefit and success in question is moral.[28] Thus, selection theories have a value and normative component built into them. Explanations in terms of moral properties having normative requiredness are just a subtype of explanation as it occurs in selection theories. The Integrationist suggests that such theories provide an account of the sought-for morally motivational capacities.[29]

Appraisal theories of emotion illustrate how to forge this connection between, on the one hand, the object- and subject-side properties appealed to in selection explanations and on the other hand, motivational capacities. Appraisal theories of emotion take them to be ecological theories, that is, theories about the significance of the environment for an organism.[30] They differ from other accounts of emotions that focus on the motivational content of emotional states, for instance, cognitive accounts that understand emotions to be fully formulated judgments or phenomenological accounts that focus on the noncognitive feelings associated with emotions. Rather, they emphasize the relevance of the environmental situation for the organism. This significance can concern various sorts of substantive ends, evolutionary and nonevolutionary, including moral significance. Certain features of the environment, its relevant dimensions, elicit various levels of emotional responses in an organism. These responses are the organism's appraisals of the environment in the light of the stimulus's relevant dimensions.

Thus, we can hypothesize that these levels of emotional response differ in terms of their conceptual content.[31] Some of these appraising responses are automatic and lead immediately to certain bodily changes, bodily expressions, and dispositions to act. Others involve conscious, fully conceptually formulated assessments. At the highest level of conceptual elaboration, there are distinct types of propositional attitudes, beliefs with factual content, and desires with desiderative content. At the lowest level we have what Paul Griffiths has characterized as attitude collapse.[32] States concerning what is the case merge with those about what ought to be the case. Lower-level responses ensure that basic adaptive actions are performed early in such a way that costly and fatal mistakes are minimized. On the other hand, higher-level responses enable one to use her cognitive capacities to appraise a situation accurately and thus act appropriately in cases where appearances may be deceiving and long-term consequences are more significant than short-term ones.[33]

Griffiths has suggested that the ecologically significant features of the environment be understood as action affordances. That is to say the environment furnishes an opportunity for action. Affordances, he argues, are organism-relevant dispositional properties of the environment.[34] In particular, we can add, they are relevant to an organism's action in the environment. I propose that object-side features of the weird properties that I have earlier argued for as the ontological instantiations of moral values have this character of being action affordances. These dispositions are actualized by moral action. We have here, I claim, a link between moral fact and moral motivation, though in a multilevel fashion corresponding to the various levels of emotional response and also to the various levels of moral agency that I have described above.

CONCLUSION

In this essay, I have sketched how the use of both biological and psychological empirical findings and theories allow the scientific naturalistic moral realist to begin to solve three central problems for her position, those of explanatory inertness, weird explanatory properties, and motivationally vacuous explanations. The solution of these problems goes a long way in supporting the Ontological Connection Hypothesis urged by Integrationists, that is, the claim that if the explanatory hypothesis is substantiated, we can give a naturalistic ontological account of the nature and role of moral values in explaining human moral agency. This result bolsters an approach to the relationships of the sciences and the philosophical discipline of ethics that seeks to integrate these disciplines rather than keeping them separate. A science of morality is neither weird science nor pseudo-ethics.

NOTES

1. For instance, Kantians and rationalist moral philosophers argue for a transcendental distinction between the two. Science studies the causal relations of the phenomenal world; ethics concerns the rational reasons for the actions of noumenal agents. Anglo-American linguistic philosophers argue for a necessary conceptual distinction. The concept of a moral agent is necessarily distinct from that of a physical cause. The elimination of this distinction is a category mistake. Even some naturalistic and empiricist moral philosophers, while placing morality within the natural world, keep morality separate from that part of the natural world with which the sciences are concerned. For instance, though moral agency requires a physical substrate, morality itself concerns subjective or idealized preferences that are neither true nor false. On the other hand, science concerns itself with objective phenomena and makes claims about such phenomena that can be either true or false.

Other reasons for this common opinion stem from methodological and epistemological concerns. Natural facts are discoverable by objective methods; moral values seem to be matters of rationality, preference, or consensus. Consequently, on some understandings, scientific claims are cognitively meaningful and capable of truth and falsity. On the other hand, ethical expressions, such as ethical norms, are neither cognitively meaningful nor capable of being true or false. Rather, they are expressions of emotion or imperatives. The methods of the sciences are methodologically objective and empirical, those of the discipline of ethics reflective, a priori and conceptual.

2. The two parts that I have in mind are a scientifically based naturalized epistemology, including a scientifically naturalized epistemology of science, and a scientifically based naturalistic ethics. Though I shall not argue for it here, there is good reason to think that the former enterprise is even more advanced than the latter.

3. In Rottschaefer 1998, I have laid out this project in some detail. Here I focus on one aspect of that project.

4. Traditionally conceived, ethics is a philosophical discipline concerned with morality, that is, with the nature of the human good and how it might be attained. Modern characterizations of ethics in the Anglo-American tradition have often divided it into three distinct parts, metaethics, normative ethics, and applied ethics. Metaethics deals with the nature and function of morality. Normative ethics is concerned with ethical principles and norms. Finally, applied ethics has to do with the application of ethical principles and norms to particular areas of moral concern. Although the traditional Anglo-American conception of ethics need not be taken as normative, I will use it to illustrate how the scientific naturalization of ethics might go. In this paper I focus on the crucial part of metaethics.

5. To understand scientific naturalization we need, of course, to have some account of science. Unfortunately, even if there were such an account, I would not have time to go into it here. I shall assume, for purposes of this discussion, that if ethics in each of its parts is related in a proper way to one or another of the recognized scientific disciplines such as biology or psychology, then ethics has been scientifically natural-

ized. Thus, as I see it, the proponent of a scientific naturalized ethics must establish that ethics in each of its parts can be related in a proper way to one or another of the recognized scientific disciplines. I shall attempt to sketch how ethics can be related in the proper fashion to biology and psychology. As will become apparent below, this criterion of scientific naturalization has both a substantive and methodological component. My focus will be on the methodological component with important substantive implications, specifically, shared explanatory pattern.

6. Postulating an important role for biology and psychology in accounting for moral agency does not exclude in principle the contributions of common sense since there is, I maintain, a continuity between scientific and commonsense methods. However, I set aside in this essay the issue of the extent to which a scientifically naturalized ethics will fit with or replace what we might call a commonsense or folk ethics.

7. What are the relationships, if any, between ethical and scientific knowing? Scientific knowing is typically described in terms of observation, experimentation, the formulation and testing of hypotheses and theories, prediction, and explanation. The issue of methodological connections concerns the question of whether there are similar sorts of cognitive processes involved in ethical knowledge. Although I believe that there are significant methodological connections between a scientific naturalistic account of ethical methodology and the methodologies of the sciences, I cannot pursue that issue here. I have argued for that position elsewhere (Rottschaefer 1997, 1998).

8. What is the status of these hypotheses? The Informational Connection Hypothesis is uncontroversial. Both biology and psychology can tell us things about ourselves and the circumstances in which we make decisions that are relevant to good moral decisions. This sort of factual input into ethical decision making leaves unaffected any claims about norms and moral values. Indeed, many antinaturalist Separatists also grant the Explanatory Connection Hypothesis. They concede, on the basis of the principle that "ought implies can" that the sciences have a role in the determination of moral values insofar as these are bound up in moral obligations, and the latter are tied to a moral agent's capacities. Thus, insofar as biology and psychology can tell us something about a moral agent's abilities and limitations, they set the parameters for any action, including moral action.

However, the remaining five hypotheses are controversial. In particular, what antinaturalists are not willing to concede is that the sciences are capable of bridging the is-ought and fact-value gaps that scientific naturalists assert can be bridged in these five hypotheses. The critical connection hypothesis is not specific about whether the proposed critiques are factual or evaluative or both. Insofar as it involves evaluative criticism, it, of course, relies on confirmation of at least the epistemological and normative hypotheses. From an epistemological perspective antinaturalists deny the possibility of justifying any claim about positive moral values, norms, or obligations, whether universal, general, particular, or individual, using only naturalistic means. Thus, they reject the scientific naturalistic hypotheses (3), (4), and (5). From an ontological point of view, antinaturalists deny the possibility of accounting for the nature and role of moral values using only naturalistic means. As a result, they reject hypothesis (6). Their reason in both instances is straightforward: the sciences deal with facts, and ethics deals with values and normative issues. To confuse these different tasks is to commit some form of the naturalistic fallacy. The classical formulations are Hume's deductive fallacy and Moore's open question argument. Finally, the failure of both the epistemological hypotheses (3, 4, and 5) and the ontological hypothesis (6) dooms the meaningfulness hypothesis (7).

9. The alleged widespread disagreement about moral matters and widespread agreement about scientific issues is also thought to pose a major problem for a scientifically based ethics. I shall not address this problem.

10. I do not have the time to do full justice to any of these examples. In each case, I merely present a sketch to illustrate the significant role of scientific results in the solution of major issues in moral philosophy.

11. More precisely, I view ethics as a philosophical discipline that has been scientifically naturalized, that is, it makes use of the best current findings and theories in relevant sciences.

12. Sturgeon (1985, 1986a, 1986b, 1995, 2000). See also Richard Boyd (1988), Richard Miller (1984), and Peter Railton (1986, 1995).

13. I have examined this exchange in detail in my (1999) paper.

14. Harman (1977, 1988).

15. Rottschaefer (1999).

16. See Eisenberg (1992); Eisenberg and Mussen (1989); Hoffman (1970, 1977, 1988); Macoby (1982); Macoby and Martin (1983); Moore and Eisenberg (1984); Radke-Yarrow et al. (1983); Zahn-Waxler et al. (1979); Zahn-Waxler and Radke-Yarrow (1990).

17. See, for instance, Eisenberg (1992). More recent studies have shown that assertive inductive techniques, those that use induction along with the arousal of an appropriate amount of fear and anxiety, are most effective in enabling internalization for children who exhibit a passive inhibitory temperament. Such a technique is not as effective with those who exhibit an active inhibitory system. For them, parental style, in particular, the style of engaging in mutual responsive interactions, is more important in facilitating internalization. On the other hand, power-assertive techniques are ineffective for internalization with either temperament, though they may produce immediate compliance. Researchers conjecture that semantic processing is facilitated in the first two cases by assertive induction and mutual responsiveness, respectively. However, power assertion makes for resentment, external attribution, and shallow processing in episodic memory.

18. Suppose that scientific natural kinds may not be constituted by a set of necessary and sufficient conditions, but, rather, are homeostatic property clusters (Boyd 1998). Moral kinds are not like homeostatic property clusters either. For the latter are objective, that is, they are properties of the object, not also of the subject or relations between two objects. So the objection to a scientifically based moral realism stands. Respectable scientific theories don't deal with the weird sort of kind that is a moral kind.

19. There are various ways to understand explanation in the sciences (Kitcher and Salmon 1989). The deductive nomological, the causal, the unificatory, and the pragmatic are prominent among these. I shall make use of the causal understanding. I take causal explanations to include explanations in terms of constitutive factors or in terms of either efficient or final causes. Constituent factors identify what a thing is, and they can be characterized either functionally or substantively. Below, I suggest a functional model of moral agency leaving open the substantive issue of how the functional elements are instantiated. We can distinguish efficient and final causes as mechanical and teleological respectively. Typically, mechanical causes are forces and teleological causes goals. More generally, mechanical and teleological explanations refer respectively to explanations in terms of a phenomenon's antecedents and consequences respectively. I use a selectionist model of explanation to show how teleological explanations play a part in some scientific causal explanations. With respect to an explanation of moral agency, I argue that moral values play an explanatory role as teleological causal factors in the acquisition of the moral capacities constitutive of the four levels of moral agency. If I am correct, then the account of the origin of moral agency that I am suggesting has the same sort of explanatory pattern as accounts of other nonmoral phenomena that have resulted from selectional factors, namely, a selectionist pattern of explanation. The account of moral agency differs from these other explanatory patterns only insofar as the consequences of the capacities in question are moral, and the selecting environment is one constituted in part by a set of moral values.

20. Larry Wright (1973, 1976) is the source of modern discussions of the structure of teleological explanation. I follow roughly the modified versions of Millikan (1989), Kitcher (1993), and Godfrey-Smith (1994) as they apply to biological adaptations and functions, without taking sides on their differences. Ringen (1976) has worked out the case for operant conditioning.

21. Albert Bandura (1986).

22. Rottschaefer (1998).

23. Martin Hoffman (1984, 2000).

24. As a functional description, the model addresses the processes involved in moral agency. An adequate description of moral agency, something that answers completely what I call the constitutive question, what makes a moral agent a moral agent, must also address the substantive question concerning the subject matter of morality. Sociobiologists, evolutionary psychologists, and moral developmental psychologists have not been of one mind on this issue (Rottschaefer 1998). But there is enough agreement about prototypical cases of morality for us to proceed in terms of this agreement with respect to the substantive question. Such prototypical cases are those of helping others in need, telling the truth, and being fair.

25. In the complete model that I am proposing, then, I conceive of moral agency in its fullest extent as cognitively and morally motivated agency that is both reflective and self-referential. However, I do not contend that for an action to be moral it requires the engagement of all four levels of moral agency. Arguably, operation at the behavioral level is required; but I shall leave the matter open. I do suggest, however, that Bandura's model

as applied to moral agency captures the phenomenon sufficiently well to take it as a working description of the phenomenon to be explained. Though cast in folk-psychological terms, I am not committed to a folk-psychological account of moral agency.

26. A complete theory of moral agency includes proposed answers to questions about the nature, origin, maintenance, well functioning, and improvement of moral agency.

27. Critics of a scientifically based moral realism might initially object by arguing that scientific theories do not deal with motivational content at all. Scientific theories are about physical things, living and nonliving, not humans. This reason is clearly inadequate since under any nonbiasing account, many scientific disciplines deal with humans and human motivation, indeed human moral motivation. These are behaviorist, social learning, cognitive moral developmental, and social cognitive theories of moral motivation. Critics may grant that there are scientific theories of motivation, but argue that they do not deal with motivation in the right way. At best, they provide explanations of human moral behavior in which motivational factors play an explanatory role. Such accounts of moral actions show how a set of causal factors brings about a behavior or how and why they regularly do so. We get a set of facts, what is, has been, will be, or might be the case. We get nothing about how and why what ought to be the case moves an agent to bring that ought to being. Such accounts are externalist in character and what is required is an internalist account concerned with properly moral motivation. This objection fails because there are several scientific theories available, in particular, the appraisal theory of emotions, Hoffman's theory of empathic development, and social cognitive theories of agency that provide accounts of moral motivation.

28. It can be objected that Clause (4) commits the "Euthyphro Mistake," that is, it maintains both that traits are selected for because they are moral and that traits are moral because they are selected for. I note, however, that clause (4), the moral realm clause, does not serve to justify claims about what is valuable. That is, I am not here claiming or denying that the effects and the capacities that they select for are morally valuable because they have been selected for. I am interested here only in pointing out that if the effects in the selecting process are moral values, then they help explain the presence of the selected for capacities. The schema I have presented is explanatory. As such it presupposes that an adequate justification of the hypotheses it contains has been provided. Specifically, it assumes that there are justified ways of establishing that there are some moral effects that play a role in selection processes. It does not specify how hypotheses about such moral values are established. Typically, researchers in the relevant sciences, such as moral development, make claims about paradigm cases of morality and immorality whose epistemic status depends upon commonly held beliefs about moral values. Scientific naturalistic philosophers cannot be satisfied with that level of justification. Though explanatory power is at times legitimately invoked as a source of justification, questions about the explanatory power of moral values are distinct from questions about the justification of moral values. I thank my colleague Nick Smith for posing this objection in a very forceful and fruitful fashion.

29. Of course, theists and Kantians rule out a priori the possibility that any empir-

ical theory can provide an adequate account of moral motivation. I assume that scientific naturalists have adequately countered these moves.

30. Griffiths (2004) and Scherer (1999). Griffiths argues that the ordinary conception of emotion does not refer to a natural kind, and contends that appraisal theories provide a way to understand differences between emotion systems, in particular, affect systems and higher-level cognitive emotional responses.

31. Hoffman (2000) and Charland (1997).

32. See also Charland (1997).

33. Griffiths (2004). According to the model of moral agency that I have proposed, the base level is the locus for the lower-level responses while the behavioral, reflective, and self-reflective levels of agency are the locus for distinct propositional attitudes. As far as I know, we have no adequate general theory of the relationships between factual and desiderative contents.

34. Griffiths, using the work of Scarantino (2003), distinguishes between deterministic and probabilistic affordances and between goal-affordances and happening-affordances. The import of the former set of distinctions is relatively clear. Organisms actualize goal-affordances through the successful performance of goal-directed behavior. Happening-affordances are manifested when the environment acts on the organism in such a way that the disposition of the environment is actualized. A prey provides a goal-affordance for a predator—the actualization of nourishment—if and when the predator captures it. The air as a happening-affordance for an organism is actualized by its automatic receipt into the mouth and lungs of an organism.

REFERENCES

Alexander, J. "Group Dynamics in the State of Nature." *Erkenntnis* 48 (2000): 1–14.

Bandura, A. *Social Foundation of Thought and Action: A Social Cognitive Theory*. Englewood Cliffs, NJ: Prentice Hall, 1986.

Bradie, M. *The Secret Chain: Evolution and Ethics*. Albany: State University of New York Press, 1994.

Brandon, R. *Adaptation and Environment*. Princeton, NJ: Princeton University Press, 1990.

Boyd, R. "How to Be a Moral Realist." In Sayre-McCord, *Essays on Moral Realism*, 181–228.

Brink, D. *Moral Realism and the Foundations of Ethics*. New York: Cambridge University Press, 1989.

Campbell, R., and B. Hunter, eds. "Moral Epistemology Naturalized." *Canadian Journal of Philosophy*, Suppl vol. 26 (2000).

Casebeer, W. "Natural Ethical Facts: Evolution, Connectionism, and Moral Cognition." PhD dissertation, University of California at San Diego, 2000.

Charland, L. "Reconciling Cognitive and Perceptual Theories of Emotion: A Representational Proposal." *Philosophy of Science* 64 (1997): 555–79.

Churchland, P. "Neural Representation in the Social World." In May, Friedman, and Clark, *Minds and Morals*, 91–108.

————. "Rules, Know How and the Future of Moral Cognition." In Campbell and Hunter, "Moral Epistemology Naturalized," 291–307.

Clark, A. "Connectionism, Moral Cognition, and Collaborative Problem Solving." In May, Friedman, and Clark, *Minds and Morals*, 109–28.

————. "Making Moral Space: A Rely to Churchland." In Campbell and Hunter, "Moral Epistemology Naturalized," 307–12.

————. "Word and Action: Reconciling Rules and Know-How in Moral Cognition." In Campbell and Hunter, "Moral Epistemology Naturalized," 267–90.

Collier, J, and M. Stingl. "Evolutionary Naturalism and the Objectivity of Morality." *Biology and Philosophy* 8 (1993): 47–60.

Copp, D., and D. Zimmerman. *Morality, Reason and Truth*. Totowa, NJ: Rowan and Allanheld, 1985.

Dagleish, T., and M. Power, eds. *Handbook of Cognition and Emotion*. Chichester: John Wiley and Sons, 1999.

Darwall, S., A. Gibbard, and P. Railton. " Toward Fin de siècle Ethics: Some Trends." *Philosophical Review* 101 (1992): 115–89.

Dunn, J. "The Beginnings of Moral Understanding: Development in the Second Year." In *The Emergence of Morality in Young Children*, edited by J. Kagan and S. Lamb, 91–111. Chicago: University of Chicago, 1987.

Eisenberg, N. *The Caring Child*. Cambridge, MA: Harvard University Press, 1992.

Eisenberg, N., and P. Mussen. *The Roots of Prosocial Behavior in Children*. Cambridge: Cambridge University Press, 1989.

Flanagan, O. "Ethics Naturalized: Ethics as Human Ecology." In May, Friedman, Clark, *Minds and Morals*, 19–43.

————. *Self Expressions: Mind, Morals, and the Meaning of Life*. New York: Oxford University Press, 1996.

Gillespie, N., ed. "Spindel Conference, 1986: Moral Realism." *Southern Journal of Philosophy*, Suppl vol. 24 (1986).

Godfrey-Smith, P. "A Modern History Theory of Functions." *Nous* 28 (1994): 344–62.

Goldman, A. I. *Liaisons: Philosophy Meets the Cognitive and Social Sciences*. Cambridge, MA: MIT Press, 1992.

Griffiths, P. "Towards a 'Machiavellian' Theory of Emotional Appraisal." In *Emotion, Evolution and Rationality*, edited by P. Cruse and D. Evans, 89–105. Oxford: Oxford University Press, 2004.

Harman, G. "Ethics and Observation." In *Essays on Moral Realism*, edited by G. Sayre-McCord, 119–24. Ithaca, NY: Cornell University Press, 1977.

————. "Is There a Single True Morality?" In Copp and Zimmerman, *Morality, Reason and Truth*, 27–48.

————. "Moral Explanations of Natural Facts—Can Moral Claims Be Tested?" In Gillespie, "Spindel Conference, 1986, 57–68.

Hoffman, M. "Moral Development." In P. Mussen, (Ed), *Carmichael's Manual of Child Psychology*, 3rd ed., edited by P. Mussen, 261–359. New York: Wiley, 1970.

———. "Moral Internalization, Parental Power, and the Nature of the Parent-Child Interaction.", *Developmental Psychology* 11 (1975): 228–39.

———. "Moral internalization: Current Theory and Research." In *Advances in Experimental Social Psychology*, edited by L. Berkowitz, 86–135. New York: Academic Press,1977.

———. "Is Altruism Part of Human Nature?" *Journal of Personality and Social Psychology* 40 (1981): 121–37.

———. "Affective and Cognitive Processes in Moral Internalization." In *Social Cognition and Social Development: A Sociocultural Perspective*, edited by E. Higgins, D. N. Ruble, and S. W. Hartup, 236–74. Cambridge: Cambridge University Press, 1983.

———. "Empathy, Its Limitations, and Its Role in a Comprehensive Moral Theory." In *Morality, Moral Behavior, and Moral Development*, edited by W. Kurtines and J. Gewirtz, 283–302. New York: Wiley, 1984.

———. "Moral Development." In *Developmental Psychology: An Advanced Textbook*, edited by M. Bornstein and M. Lamb, 497–548. Hillsdale, NJ: Lawrence Erlbaum Associates, 1988.

———. *Empathy and Moral Development: Implications for Caring and Justice.* New York: Cambridge University Press, 2000.

Kitcher, P. "Function and Design." In *Midwest Studies in Philosophy*, vol. 18: *Philosophy of Science*, edited by P. French, T. Uehberg Jr., and H. Wettstein, 379–97. Notre Dame, IN: University of Notre Dame Press, 1993.

———. "The Naturalist Returns." *Philosophical Review* 101 (1992): 53–114.

Kitcher, P., and W. Salmon, eds. *Scientific Explanation.* Minneapolis: University of Minnesota Press, 1989.

Kochanska, G., and R. Thompson. "The Emergence and Development of Conscience in Toddlerhood and Early Childhood." In *Parenting and Children's Internalization of Values: A Handbook of Contemporary Theory*, edited by Joan E. Grusec and Leon Kuczynski, 53–77. New York: John Wiley and Sons, 1997.

Kornblith, H. "Introduction: What Is Naturalistic Epistemology." In *Naturalizing Epistemology*, 2nd ed., edited by H. Kornblith, 1–14. Cambridge, MA: MIT Press, 1994.

Kurtines, W., and E. Grief. "The Development of Moral Thought: Review and Evaluation of Kohlberg's Approach." *Psychological Bulletin* 81 (1974): 453–70.

Macoby, E. "Trends in the Study of Socialization: Is There a Lewinian Heritage?" *Journal of Social Issue* 48 (1982): 171–85.

Macoby, E., and J. Martin. "Socialization in the Context of the Family: Parent-Child Interaction." In Mussen and Hetherington, *Handbook of Child Psychology*, 1–101.

May, L., M. Friedman,and A. Clark, eds. *Minds and Morals: Essays on Ethics and Cognitive Science.* Cambridge, MA: MIT Press, 1996.

Miller, R. "Ways of Moral Learning." *Philosophical Review* 94 (October 1985): 507–56.

Millikan, R. "An Ambiguity in the Notion of 'Function.'" *Biology and Philosophy* 4 (1989): 172–76.

Millikan, R. G. "Pushmi-Pullyu Representations." In May, Friedman, and Clark, *Mind and Morals*, 145–61.

Moore, B. S., and N. Eisenberg. "The Development of Altruism." In *Annals of Child Development*, vol. 1, edited by G. Whitehurst, 107–74. Greenwich, CT: JAI Press, 1984.

Mussen, P. H., and E. M. Hetherington. *Handbook of Child Psychology*, vol. 4: *Socialization, Personality, and Social Development*. New York: Wiley and Sons, 1983.

Nichols, S. "Mindreading and the Cognitive Architecture Underlying Altruistic Motivation." *Mind and Language* 16 (2001): 425–55.

———. "How Psychopaths Threaten Moral Rationalism: Is It Irrational to Be Amoral?" *Monist* 85 (2002): 285–303.

———. "Norms with Feeling: Toward a Psychological Account of Moral Judgment." *Cognition* (forthcoming).

———. "Sentimentalism Naturalized: The Role of Affect in Moral Judgment." In *The Psychology and Biology of Morality*, ed. W. Sinnott-Armstrong. Forthcoming.

Radke-Yarrow, M., C. Zahn-Waxler, and M. Chapman. "Children's Prosocial Dispositions and Behaviors." In Mussen and Hetherington, *Handbook of Child Psychology*, 469–545.

Railton, P. "Moral Realism." *Philosophical Review* 95 (1986): 163–207.

Richards, R. *Darwin and the Emergence of Evolutionary Theories of Mind and Behavior*. Chicago: University of Chicago Press, 1987.

Ringen, J. "Explanation, Teleology and Operant Behaviourism: A Study of the Experimental Analysis of Purposive Behavior." *Philosophy of Science* 43 (1976): 223–54.

Rottschaefer, W. "Skinner's Science of Values." *Behaviorism* 8 (1980): 99–112.

———. "Social Learning Theories of Moral Agency." *Behavior and Philosophy* 19 (1991): 61–76.

———. "Evolutionary Ethics: An Irresistible Temptation: Some Reflections on Paul Farber's *The Temptation of Evolutionary Ethics*." *Biology and Philosophy* 12 (1997): 369–84.

———. *The Biology and Psychology of Moral Agency*. Cambridge: Cambridge University Press, 1998.

———. "Moral Realism and Moral Internalization." *Behavior and Philosophy* 27 (1999): 19–50.

———. "Naturalizing Ethics: The Death of Ethics and the Resurrection of Moral Science." *Zygon* 35 (2000): 253–86.

Rottschaefer, W., and D. Martinsen. "Really Taking Darwin Seriously: An Alternative to Michael Ruse's Darwinian Metaethics." *Biology and Philosophy* 5 (1990): 149–74.

Sayre-McCord, G., ed. *Essays on Moral Realism*. Ithaca, NY: Cornell University Press, 1988.

———. "The Many Moral Realism." In Sayre-McCord, *Essays on Moral Realism*, 1–23.

Scarantino, A. "Affordances Explained." *Philosophy of Science* 70 (2003): 949–61.

Scherer, K. "Appraisal Theory." In Dagleish and Power, *Handbook of Cognition and Emotion*, 637–64.

Skyrms, B. *Evolution of the Social Contract*. New York: Cambridge University Press, 1996.

Stingl, M. "All the Monkeys Aren't in the Zoo." In Campbell andHunter, "Moral Epistemology Naturalized," 245–66.

Sturgeon, N. "Moral Explanations." In Copp and Zimmerman, *Morality Reason and Truth*, 49–78.

———. "Harman on Moral Explanations of Natural Facts." In Gillespie, "Spindel Conference, 1986," 69–78.

———. "What Difference Does It Make if Moral Realism Is True?" In Gillespie, "Spindel Conference, 1986," 115–41.

Teasdale, J. "Multi-Level Theories of Cognitive-Emotion Relations." In Dalgleish and Power, *Handbook of Cognition and Emotion*, 665–82.

Wright, L. "Functions." *Philosophical Review* 82 (1973): 139–68.

———. *Teleological Explanation*. Berkeley: University of California Press, 1976.

Zahn-Waxler, C., and M. Radke-Yarrow. "The Development of Altruism: Alternative Research Strategies." In Eisenberg and Mussen, *Development of Prosocial Behavior*, 109–37.

———. "The Origins of Empathic Concern." *Motivation and Emotion* 14 (1990): 107–30.

Zahn-Waxler, C., M. Radke-Yarrow, and R. A. King. "Child-rearing and Children's Prosocial Initiations toward Victims of Distress." *Child Development* 50 (1979): 319–30.

27

ON THE NATURALISTIC FALLACY
A Conceptual Basis for Evolutionary Ethics

CHRISTOPHER DiCARLO AND JOHN TEEHAN

In debates concerning evolutionary approaches to ethics, the Naturalistic Fallacy (i.e., deriving values from facts or "ought" from "is") is often invoked as a constraining principle. For example, Stephen Jay Gould asserts the most that evolutionary studies can hope to do is set out the conditions under which certain morals or values might have arisen, but it can say nothing about the validity of such values, on pain of committing the Naturalistic Fallacy. Such questions of moral validity, he continues, are best left in the domain of religion. This is a common critique of evolutionary ethics but it is based on an insufficient appreciation of the full implications of the Naturalistic Fallacy. Broadly conceived, the Naturalistic Fallacy rules out any attempt to treat morality as defined according to some preexistent reality, whether that reality is expressed in natural or nonnatural terms. Consequent to this is that morality must be treated as a product of natural human interactions. As such, any discipline which sheds light on the conditions under which values originate, and on the workings of moral psychology, may play a crucial role in questions of moral validity. The authors contend that rather than being a constraint on evolutionary approaches to ethics, the Naturalistic Fallacy, so understood, clears the way, conceptually, for just such an approach.

Originally published in *Evolutionary Psychology* 2 (March 2004): 32–46.

I. INTRODUCTION

The title of this essay is intended to be a bit provocative insofar as the Naturalistic Fallacy (NF) is most often seen as an obstacle to evolutionary ethics rather than a basis for it. The NF prohibits deriving value statements from purely factual statements about the way the world is. Since evolutionary studies seek to provide strictly factual statements about the world it seems, to many, to follow that such studies cannot provide the basis for an ethical system. There are many variations of this claim and a great debate on the topic. In order to focus on the salient aspects of this issue we will focus on one particular version of this objection, that presented by noted evolutionary thinker, the late Stephen Jay Gould.

Gould addresses the issue of evolution and ethics in his work entitled *Rocks of Ages: Science and Religion in the Fullness of Life* (1999). In that work he sets out a principle that sets the boundaries between science and religion, which he terms NOMA, i.e., Non-Overlapping Magisteria. A magisterium, Gould tells us, "is a domain where one form of teaching holds the appropriate tools for meaningful discourse and resolution" (5). Science and religion, according to Gould, each have their respective magisterium where their teaching is authoritative, and it follows, given the logic of magisteria, that neither has any authority to teach in the other's domain. The domain of science is the empirical world. As Gould says, "Science tries to document the factual character of the natural world, and to develop theories that coordinate and explain these facts" (4). The domain of religion is "the realm of human purposes, meanings, and values—subjects," he continues, "that the factual domain of science might illuminate, but can never resolve" (4). The consequences of this setting of boundaries is that "religion can no longer dictate the nature of factual conclusions residing properly within the magisterium of science" and that scientists cannot claim higher insight into moral truth from any superior knowledge of the world's empirical constitution" (9–10).

It is this latter claim that directly concerns us here: that the superior knowledge of the empirical nature of the world does not provide a higher insight into ethics than that provided by nonempirical methods, such as religion. It is clear that the Naturalistic Fallacy lurks beneath this claim. Gould writes of ethics, that "fruitful discussion must proceed under a different magisterium, far older than science," a discussion "about ethical 'ought,' rather than a search for any factual 'is' about the material construction of the factual world" (55).

Gould is really not adding anything new to this debate. (Nor, in all fairness, does he claim to be. In fact, Gould includes a lengthy footnote admitting that he oversimplifies the topic, but justifies his use of the is/ought distinction as "broad-scale treatment" of a "central principle," notes 55–57). Still, he does set out a useful schema for understanding the issue. There are empirical facts about the world and there are value judgments about those facts. Facts are ascertained via the scientific method; religion is barred from speaking about the empirical constitution of the world because it does not employ the scientific method. So far, so good. Then we see that science is barred from speaking about values; but religion is not similarly barred—and why? Because the line between facts and values is guarded by the NF and it is presumed that the NF prohibits any scientific approach to ethics but passes through any religious or philosophical approach (at least, any nonempirical philosophical approach) (59–60).

It is here that we see a confusion which needs to be addressed to fully appreciate the role of the NF in ethical theory. While it is true that the NF does prohibit a certain scientific approach to ethics, it does not follow that it prohibits any scientific approach. Furthermore, a deeper reading of the NF shows that it does not allow *all* religious or philosophical approaches to ethics, but places a constraint on this magisterium, as well. The thesis here is that once this confusion is cleared away, we will see that not only is an evolutionary approach to ethics permissible, but it may in fact be indispensable. In order to justify this final claim, we must first delve into the NF.

II. UNDERSTANDING THE NATURALISTIC FALLACY

We find the first historical reference to the Naturalistic Fallacy in David Hume's *Treatise of Human Nature*, in which he states:

> In every system of morality, which I have hitherto met with, I have always remark'd, that the author proceeds for some time in the ordinary way of reasoning, and establishes the being of a God, or makes observations concerning human affairs: when of a sudden I am supriz'd to find, that instead of the usual copulations of propositions, *is*, and *is not*, I meet with no propositions that is not connected with an *ought*, or an *ought not*. This change is imperceptible; but is, however, of the last consequence. For as this *ought*, or *ought not*, expresses some new relation or affirmation, 'tis necessary that it shou'd be observ'd and explain'd; and at the same time that a reason should be given, for what seems altogether inconceivable, how this new relation can be a deduction from others, which are entirely different from it. (469)

Scholars have generally taken this to mean that one cannot make logical inferences of value from observations of natural facts—at least, not without the inclusion of an additional (suppressed or hidden) premise. "Is" does not imply "ought," as they say. It has also been referred to as the Fact/Value Gap, but it reached its greatest popularity as the Naturalistic Fallacy in the *Principia Ethica* of G. E. Moore. Moore maintained that any attempt to define "good" in naturalistic terms was fallacious. But as with many scholars, the intended meaning of an idea can become lost, misrepresented, caricatured, etc., if we ignore the primary sources.

Few realize that there is a feature in Moore's ethical system which is often overlooked and that is his claim that metaphysicians also commit the naturalistic fallacy. Understandably so, Moore dubbed his famous fallacy in order to reveal the problems associated with defining Good in naturalistic terms. However, Moore stretches the boundaries of this fallacy by claiming that it applies to those who define Good in metaphysical terms, as well.

In the first chapter of his *Principia*, Moore states that any attempt to define Good in terms of natural properties commits the naturalistic fallacy. This, he believed, was due to the unique nature of Good, which is, he claimed, indefinable. "'Good' . . . is incapable of any definition . . . 'good' has no definition because it is simple and has no parts. It is one of those innumerable objects of thought which are themselves incapable of definition, because they are the ultimate terms by reference to which whatever *is* capable of definition must be defined" (9–10).

Now, although Moore realizes that Good is not actually indefinable, i.e., that no definition of it is possible, he is trying to point out that its elusive nature is the substantive to which any adjective of "good" must apply. In other words, although we may experience many good things, that which is Good about these things is not found in their properties. To offer any definition of Good we may ask, says Moore, whether that definition is good. This, of course, is Moore's open question argument. "If 'good' was definable it was a complex, and so it could be asked of any definiens if it was good. After all, a definition should not be merely "analytic," it should give information about the definiendum; therefore whatever definition is offered, it may always be asked, with significance, of the complex so defined, whether it is itself good" (Hill, 99). Good is what it is and not another thing; anyone attempting to define it through the use of any natural properties commits the naturalistic fallacy.

In the fourth chapter of the *Principia*, Moore goes on to state that any metaphysical definition of Good commits the naturalistic fallacy as well. Unlike naturalists, metaphysicians did not believe that ethics could be explained in terms of natural properties but instead believed, like Moore, that Good was a super-sensible property. Unlike Moore, however, the metaphysicians came under attack because they tried to define Good as actually existing supersensible objects (Warnock, 28). This is somewhat confusing due to the fact that Moore earlier defined Good as supersensible and known only through intuition yet he also maintains that goodness does not exist. The main difficulty with Moore's definition of Good seems to lie in its precarious mode of existence. There is a similarity here between Moore's theory of Good and Plato's theory of Forms.

Moore believed the central problem with the metaphysicians involved their attempt to equate Good with some supersensible property such as the true self or the real will (Warnock, 32). In this respect they seem, prima facie, to have committed the naturalistic fallacy (though not because they have equated Good with a natural property). As Frankena points out, Moore tends to confuse matters by lumping natural and metaphysical properties into one class. Perhaps Frankena is correct in claiming that Moore should have called it the "definist fallacy," i.e., the fallacy is committed when the attempt is made to define Good as a natural or a metaphysical property (cited in Warnock, 13). Mary Warnock points out that Moore didn't care much for the name: "It does not matter what we call it provided we recognize it when we meet it; the true fallacy is the attempt to define the indefinable" (Warnock, 13). Nevertheless, an important distinction can be made between committing the naturalistic fallacy by equating Good with a natural property and committing the naturalistic fallacy by equating Good with a metaphysical property. What Moore is asserting is that any argument of the form:

(1) "Reality is of this nature" à "This is good in itself"
     (where à designates "implies")

commits the naturalistic fallacy (NF). Since this differs in type from the attempt to define Good in terms of natural properties, we shall distinguish it by calling it the metaphysical fallacy (MF). Though it differs in type (or species) from that of defining Good in terms of natural properties, we may consider it, as does Moore, to belong to the overall genus of the naturalistic fallacy.

It has been suggested that Moore treats Good and the naturalistic fallacy in this manner because if naturalistic or metaphysical definitions were synony-mously identified with Good, the autonomy of ethics would be destroyed: "If Good is identified with some empirically verifiable biological tendency (say, what is more evolved) Ethics becomes a branch of biology. If Good is defined in psychological terms (say, whatever anyone prefers) Ethics becomes a branch of psychology. And so on" (Regan, 201–202). If naturalistic or metaphysical definitions were synonymous with Good, Regan states, Moore believed our freedom to judge intrinsic value would be lost. For example, if Good means "more evolved" then there could be no room for individual judgment about what sort of things ought to exist for their own sakes. In this way, those that are most knowledgeable about what things are more evolved (i.e., biologists) would become our authorities. The same holds true if Good is defined in psychological or metaphysical terms. If Good is not defined in either naturalistic or metaphysical terms, the autonomy of the individual is assured:

> At the deepest level it is the autonomy of the individual judgment about what has intrinsic value, not the autonomy of the Science of Morals. . . . *Individuals* must judge for themselves what things ought to exist, what things are worth having for their own sakes. No natural science can do this. No metaphysical system can do this. (Regan, 204)

Moore here articulates a more general concern over evolutionary ethics—that such an ethics will somehow dictate to the individual what and how he or she ought to value. However, we will later argue that an evolutionary ethics based on a deeper understanding of the NF rules out any such concern. For now we can see that extending the NF to metaphysical definitions of the good poses a problem for Gould's insistence on the exclusivity of the Religious Magisteria concerning ethics, and, we believe, creates an opening for evolutionary ethics.

III. IMPLICATIONS OF THE NATURALISTIC/METAPHYSICAL FALLACY

Given this understanding of the Naturalistic Fallacy we can see that certain moves from facts to values are ruled out. For example, any attempt to read a value statement directly from a simple statement of fact would be to commit the NF. An instance of such a fallacious move can be found in a 1984 article by philosopher Michael Levin entitled "Why Homosexuality Is Abnormal." In support of the notion that there is something "unnatural" about homosexuality Levin writes,

> The erect penis fits the vagina, and fits it better than any other natural orifice; penis and vagina seem made for each other. This intuition ultimately derives from, or is another way of capturing, the idea that the penis is not *for* inserting into the anus of another man–that so using the penis is not the way it is *supposed*, even *intended*, to be used. [Italics in the original] (251)

Here the NF comes into play and asks the key question: Even though x (the penis) evolved to do y (be inserted into the vagina) why ought we to do y, instead of z? To reply that y is the evolved function of x, and z is not, is merely to restate the original premise. It is a circular argument, and is without merit.

Now Levin, being a professional philosopher, does not present such a simplistic argument as this, but it is not merely professional philosophers who moralize and the NF can be a useful tool in assessing popular moral arguments, which are often more socially influential than philosophical arguments. Of course, we are here most interested in the role of the NF in moral philosophy and it does play a role in assessing Levin's larger position.

While he does not mention the NF, Levin goes to great lengths throughout the article to avoid suspicion of this charge. He begins by stating that homosexuality is abnormal "not because it is immoral or sinful . . . but for a purely mechanical reason. It is a misuse of bodily parts" (251). Still, for Levin, the evolution-determined function of the penis clearly sets the boundaries for the normative use of the penis (256–58). Levin does not argue, overtly at least, that since evolution shaped the penis to do x that to do ~x is immoral. His argument is that the use of the penis in accord with its evolutionary purpose is conducive to happiness, and to act counter to what is conducive to our happiness is abnormal. He attempts to present this conclusion as a prudential assessment, rather than a moral one but he undermines such an interpretation. He writes:

> Homosexual acts involve the use of the genitals for what they aren't for, and it is a *bad* or at least *unwise* thing to use a part of the body for what it isn't for. Calling homosexual acts "unnatural" is indeed to sum up this entire line of reasoning. "Unnatural" carries disapprobative connotations, and any explication of it should capture this. [Italics in the original] (253)

His argument comes down to: homosexuality is bad because it makes us unhappy, and it makes us unhappy because it is unnatural–i.e., contrary to the design of nature. With this formulation Levin may be able to avoid the more egregious violation of the NF previously discussed, but he falls into a variation of the fallacy, nonetheless, i.e., he uses a natural description to make a moral prescription.

It may be legitimate to argue that one ought not to act in a way incompatible with one's happiness and so one ought not to do x because x is incompatible with happiness. But then one must support the premise that "x is incompatible with happiness." Levin's primary support for this premise is that "Nature is interested in making its creatures like what is (inclusively) good for them" (259). Therefore using our bodily parts (not merely the penis) for the purpose for which they were intended/evolved will lead to a life that is, on whole, more enjoyable, and a life so lived will be a happier life (260). Levin's explication of this position is marred by an equivocation between "enjoyment" and "happiness" but more importantly he seems to rule out, by definition, any sense of happiness generated by using body parts in an "unnatural" manner. "Homosexuality," he asserts, "is likely to cause unhappiness because it leaves unfulfilled an innate and innately rewarding desire" (261). This "innate desire" is not simply to experience sexual release, or to ejaculate, but to "introduce semen into the vagina" (261). Any other means of release will fail to truly satisfy this desire.

Levin is here treading on treacherous grounds, not only logically, but empirically. There are more serious problems with this line of reasoning than violating the NF, but that this is an example of the NF we can see by posing the question: What if an individual does not find vaginal sex innately rewarding, but instead finds anal sex or even no sex more rewarding? In such instances it follows that fulfilling the natural function of the penis will not be enjoyable, and will not conduce to happiness. Therefore, one ought not to act in the way nature intended for to do so would violate the principle that one ought not to do what is incompatible with happiness. (It is, perhaps, telling that Levin allows that volitionally celibate individuals, such as Catholic priests, do not face the same problem in being happy as homosexuals do—despite their similar violation of the natural impulse [271].)

It is, we believe, arguments like Levin's which cause the most anxiety over evolutionary ethics. The concern seems to be that if we allow evolutionary thinking into our ethics we are going to end up with a reactionary moral system which supports an oppressive patriarchal value system in which women are consigned to the kitchen, homosexuals to the closets, the poor and disadvantaged to the fringes of society, all in the name of the natural moral order. The Naturalistic Fallacy cuts off any such strategy by pointing out that simply because something has played a certain role in the evolution of the species it does not follow that it ought to continue to play that role, or that it can play no other role. How we ought to behave is a moral question which cannot simply be read out of the world of facts.

Curiously, this is just the point that opponents of evolutionary ethics, such as Gould, want to make, and it is a valid point. However, it does not do all the work Gould and others attribute to it. For one, it does not hand ethics over to religion and metaphysics —as we can see from an examination of the MF.

The Metaphysical Fallacy holds that value statements cannot be derived from a simple statement of religious or metaphysical "fact." As an example let's explore an aspect of Immanuel Kant's ethics. Kant developed a dualistic view of humans as phenomenal beings, with passions, needs, and desires, and noumenal beings, capable of grasping the laws of pure reason (1788). Morality, for Kant, is derived from these intellectually grasped laws of pure reason. This is, of course, the Categorical Imperative (in its various manifestations).

The question to consider here is, what grounds the Categorical Imperative, not as a rule of reason (we can grant Kant that) but as a moral law? Why ought one to follow the Categorical Imperative? Or in Moore's terms, why is it good to follow the Categorical Imperative? Kant addressed this question and deemed it unanswerable: "It is wholly impossible to explain how and why the *universality of a maxim as a law* [italics in original]—and therefore morality—should interest us." However he then asserts that this interest is connected to the fact that the law has "sprung from our will as intelligence and so from *our proper self*" (emphasis added) (1785,128–29). Our essential nature as rational beings is the foundation for the moral force of the rule of reason. In effect, Kant is arguing:

p1 Humans are Essentially Rational Beings
p2 Pure Practical Reason dictates certain rules for behavior
C—We ought to follow these rules.

The argument is, of course, much more complicated but this will serve, I believe, without too much harm being done to Kant.

Now we ask the Open Question. When we ask Kant why we ought to follow the dictates of rationality, his answer, ultimately, is because it is an expression of our rational nature. Even if we were to grant the notion of an essential nature, it seems we can still ask why we ought to fulfill that nature. If it is supposedly good to do so, a justification seems called for. Kant, however, absolutely rejects any consequential justification of ethics. We cannot claim, for example, that we will be happier if we follow the dictates of reason. We are simply obliged by virtue of our rational natures to act rationally.

We can now notice a circularity lurking in the argument: We ought to do x because it is rational, and we ought to be rational because we are, *essentially*, rational beings—in effect this is to derive an "ought" (act according to rationality) from an "is" (we are rational). Whether the "is" is an empirical statement or a metaphysical statement, it is an invalid move. This is not to deny that we must be rational in order to engage in moral discourse. Kant is correct in emphasizing the necessity of rationality as a precondition of any moral deliberation. He goes astray, however, in deriving the principles of morality strictly from the notion of rationality, per se.[1] He in effect identifies the "good" with the "rational," which not only begs the question of reason's moral authority, but rules out of consideration, a priori, emotional and consequential concerns.

The Metaphysical Fallacy prohibits certain religious/philosophical attempts at developing an ethics, just as the Naturalistic Fallacy prohibits certain scientific attempts at developing an ethics. This is, in fact, what we believe the Naturalistic Fallacy does: it does not demarcate the boundaries between science and ethics, or between science and religion—it invalidates certain attempts at developing an ethics. Specifically, it invalidates ethical arguments of the form

X is the natural function of Y; therefore one ought to do X

It also rules out:

X is an expression of Ultimate Reality: therefore X is morally correct

We can see, then, that Gould's NOMA is mistaken in placing ethics under the magisterium of religion. Religious and metaphysical systems can be just as misguided in their approach to ethics as scientific approaches can be. However, our goal was not to critique religion, but to argue for a positive role for evolution in ethical theorizing, and to that we must now turn.

IV. THE NATURALISTIC FALLACY AND EVOLUTIONARY ETHICS

The message to be taken from this understanding of the NF is that no factual statement about the world—be it empirical or metaphysical—entails a value statement. The deeper message is that values are not to be *found*, at all, whether in the natural universe, or in some transcendent realm. Now, this may seem an unpalatable conclusion that does not bode well for any ethical system, much less an evolutionary one, but we do not believe this is to be the case. Moral dilemmas exist; values conflict; "What ought we to do?" is still a meaningful question. There needs to be some way of dealing with these ethical concerns, even after the NF/MF has done its work.

To see how to proceed we need to adjust our traditional notions of the subject of moral philosophy. The notion that ethical truths are "out there" waiting to be discovered is itself the remnant of a prescientific mode of thought. It stems back to a time when not only ethics, but science itself was under the magisterium of religion. The progress of modern science can be viewed as a process of freeing the study of nature from religious/ metaphysical constraints and establishing its own magisterium. For example, our understanding of species increased dramatically once we surrendered the notion that there are fixed essences embodied by species, and saw instead that species are what they are because of a complex, dynamic process of interaction between individuals and their environments.

This provides an important lesson for understanding ethics. While the universe is value-neutral in the sense of not entailing any moral imperatives, it does contain the conditions that give rise to valuing and to creatures who make value judgments. These value judgments are not the expression of some pre-existing moral essence but rather arise from the complex interactions between individuals and the environment. In effect, morality is not "out there" waiting to be found, it is constructed by individuals—who value, who live in an environment which provides the conditions for both satisfying and frustrating our desires, and who must live with others who may or may not value the same things, in the same way. Morality is both the result of and a contributor to complex social interactions.

This approach should not be construed as an endorsement of a noncognitivist or antirealist approach to ethics. In one sense this critique of the NF/MF is neutral on these metaethical issues. However, the goal of this critique is to clear the conceptual ground for an evolutionary ethics and such an ethics is aligned more consistently with cognitivist /realist approaches. Although in making this claim we would do well to keep in mind Simon Blackburn's warning that "realism" and "cognitivism" are "terms of art that philosophers can define pretty much at will" (120). In saying that values are not "out there" we do not mean to imply that values are therefore simply expressions of subjective attitudes or emotions.[2] What is being denied is any strict identification of a factual description of some property of the world with a normative evaluation of that property.

A complete inventory of the universe would not yield any property which in and of itself could be labeled "good" or "bad." But that inventory would contain creatures (e.g., humans) that have needs, desires, interests, etc., which in relationship to other things on the list yield satisfactions/dissatisfactions, which constitute "values." A "value" is not an object in the world, but is shorthand for an objective relationship between creatures with interests and other components of the universe.[3]

To view ethics in this way is to see it as an attempt to evaluate and critique certain responses to complex social situations, not as an attempt to divine some preexisting moral order. It is to view ethics as a practical discipline. This is not a radically new view of ethics. It was first suggested by Aristotle, and it has been more recently advocated by Michael Ruse and E. O. Wilson, who have urged us to see morality as an "applied science" (1986). It is also the approach to ethics developed by John Dewey (1898, 1902, 1925, 1929)—who, though woefully underappreciated, has much to offer evolutionary ethics and who is, in fact, the guiding light behind much of this article.[4]

Given this view of ethics, it becomes essential to gain greater insight into the conditions that underlie value judgment, their development and their consequences. These are empirical questions and so fall under the magisterium of science. Any science which helps us to understand and assess morally problematic situations has something to contribute to moral philosophy. Evolution, as a scientific study of human cognition, emotions, and predispositions—core elements of moral situations—rather than being barred becomes a most valuable tool in the study of ethics.[5]

V. CONCLUSION

Before concluding, we need to deal with the most common objection to this position, and again we can allow Gould to speak for the opposition. It is quite reasonable, Gould says, to accept that science can highlight the conditions of moral experience or the history of moral systems, what he calls the "anthropology of morals," but it can go no further. Factual information can contribute nothing to normative ethics; or as Gould puts it, "Science can say nothing about the morality of morals" (65–66). John Dewey responded to just this type of criticism, one hundred years ago. Here is his formulation of the criticism of what he calls the "historical method," i.e., an evolutionary approach to ethics in which the cultural as well as natural development of morality is assessed:[6]

> The opponent argues thus: It is of course true that morality has a history; that is, we can trace different moral practices, beliefs, customs, demands, opinions, various forms of outward manifestation. We can say that here such and such moral practices obtained, and then gave way in this point or that. This indeed is a branch of history, and an interesting one. . . . But when this is said and done the result remains history, not ethics. What ethics deals with is the moral worth of these various practices, beliefs, etc. . . . The historian of ethics can at most supply only data; the distinctive work of the ethical writer is still all to be done. (1902, 22)

The problem with this objection is that it misconstrues the purpose of the historical/ evolutionary approach to ethics, and the nature of ethical deliberation. Dewey's imaginary critic, and Gould, are correct that this process will not reveal the "Good," or the "Right" (as those terms are understood in traditional philosophical jargon). But this is not the purpose of such an approach. For Dewey, we engage in moral inquiry *because* there is no clear, objective moral truth at hand. We investigate in order to better understand the conditions of human valuations and so be better equipped to understand and resolve those dilemmas which we must face. He writes, "It might be true that objective history does not create moral values as such, and yet be true that there is no way of settling questions of valid ethical significance in detail apart from historical consideration" (23).

Dewey believes moral dilemmas are problematic situations in which there is a question about what to do. They arise when there is a disjunct between the desires/ interests of an agent and the environing conditions in which one finds oneself. Such situations call for deliberation in order to reach a judgment that "x" is the right/good thing to do. For Dewey, to claim "x" is "good" is not to commit the naturalistic fallacy of identifying a natural property with a moral evaluation. It is to judge that "x" will resolve the problematic situation (1925a, 1925b, 1929, 1939b). From Dewey's perspective the entire situation is composed of natural elements, and so the moral conclusion must follow from naturalistic premises. But, as should be clear at this point, such conclusions are not violations of Moore's injunction; nor is Dewey's approach subject to the Open Question criticism. To say "x resolves the dilemma, but is x good?" is confused. Once we have established that "x" resolves the dilemma to then ask if it is good is either redundant, or it is to ask for further evaluation of the proposed resolution—i.e., it is to ask "Does x truly resolve the dilemma?" "Does it resolve the dilemma in the short run but create greater long-term problems?" "Does it resolve the problem by frustrating other significant interests?" etc. These are all fair questions, indeed important questions. They do not imply, however, that there is some fallacy lurking beneath the moral judgment, they merely seek to continue the process of moral inquiry in a metaethically and epistemically responsible way.

In order to resolve a problematic situation, to make a moral judgment, we need to have a clear grasp of the situation at hand and the possible consequences of various options. Whatever contributes to our understanding of the situation, contributes to our judgment of what we may construe as the good in that situation. As Dewey says, "Whatever modifies the judgment . . . modifies conduct. To control our judgments of conduct . . . is insofar forth to direct conduct itself" (38). In other words, whatever contributes to that moral judgment has normative and not merely descriptive significance. Evolutionary studies clearly can make such a contribution.

This is not to imply that evolution will have something to offer each dilemma; our moral experience is too complicated to make any such generalized claim. The point is that evolutionary studies, by helping to uncover the workings of human emotions and cognition provide a wealth of resources that can inform, in a practical way, our moral deliberations. Philosophers/ethicists can no longer turn a blind eye to the evolutionary sciences and related disciplines uncovering relevant information regarding human nature. We believe that the attribution of such information to the field of ethics is a clearly defined epistemically responsible method for framing ethical concepts.

So, in conclusion, rather than excluding evolutionary considerations from ethics the Naturalistic Fallacy actually opens up space for evolution to contribute to moral philosophy. The deeper lesson of the Naturalistic Fallacy is that ethics is not about identifying preexisting moral definitions. It is, instead, an ongoing process of deliberation concerning what is right/good to do. Given this, any discipline which contributes to an understanding of the human condition, contributes to this process. Evolutionary studies aspire to offer insights into the physical, psychological, and social aspects of human existence and, to the degree that these insights are valid, may prove invaluable to our moral thinking.[7]

NOTES

1. For a more detailed discussion of Kant's ethics from an evolutionary perspective see Teehan (2003).

2. Simon Blackburn has developed a naturalistic approach to ethics which also seeks to overcome the constraints of the naturalistic fallacy. His theory, which cannot be given its due here, bears apparent kinship with the approach developed in this paper, but differs in relation to the cognitivist/realist issue. While appropriately wary of such labels, Blackburn accepts that his theory falls near the nonognitivist/antirealist end of the spectrum (although he prefers the term "quasi-realism"). Ethical propositions are properly seen as projections of our concerns and attitudes, rather than as references to some property of the world. As such there are no truth conditions applicable to ethical proposition. (1998) As it stands this is in agreement with the Deweyan position underlying this paper, but it does not go far enough in assessing ethical propositions. Dewey would agree that ethical propositions are rooted in human concerns but he would insist they are more than projections. They are themselves practical judgments which address those concerns (1925, 1945). To use an example from Blackburn, to say "fat is bad" is

not to identify "fat" with some objective moral quality "badness" but neither is it simply an expression of a subjective attitude. If it were, then for Dewey it would not be an ethical proposition (1945, 684). As an ethical proposition "fat is bad" works against, is inconsistent with, somehow conflicts with some desired state of affairs (which is also a real property of the world). Such a proposition is open to a cognitive assessment, despite the fact that noncognitive factors play an essential role in moral judgments (here Dewey and Blackburn are in agreement). Much more can and should be said on this issue than can fit within the scope of this paper.

3. DiCarlo has mentioned elsewhere ("Problem Solving and Religion in the EEA: An Endorphin Rush?" presented at the New England Institute Cognitive Science and Evolutionary Psychology Conference, August 2003, Portland, Maine) that an evolutionary concept of human value begins with the drive to maintain biomemetic equilibria in order to achieve survival-reproductive value. As a starting point for acknowledged value, that which would have best favored survival and reproduction would have garnered the most value. The eventual emergence of nonconscious humans to conscious, socially active language users, created the environment in which humans were capable of measuring ideas with actions in terms of their own survival strategies. Hence, the emergence of consciously recognized "value" in terms of survival and reproduction. See also diCarlo 2002/2003, 2000a, 2000b.

4. It is worth noting some recent works on evolution and ethics consistent with a Deweyan approach. Larry Arnhart (1998) makes a compelling case for an Aristotelian evolutionary ethics which shares much with Dewey's approach—not surprising, given Dewey's affinity with Aristotle. Also, Robert Hinde (2002) has quite effectively set out the role biology may play in moral philosophy, given that moral philosophy is concerned with ethical deliberations, rather than with a search for absolutes. Most significantly, William Casebeer (2003) sets out, in effective detail, the case for an Aristotelian/Deweyan ethics grounded in evolutionary biology and cognitive science consonant with the ethical approach being developed in this paper. His work also contains a critique of the NF, but from a different, though complementary, angle.

5. One way in which we can see this in application is to briefly consider diCarlo's "Relations of Natural Systems" project. This is essentially a multidisciplinary Web-based approach to understanding human behavior by examining our species and its environmental interactions as a complex synthesis of relational systems. It is anticipated that though the understanding of such interactive systems may not provide us with "oughts" it will certainly clarify matters in terms of the "is's," i.e., the physical substrates. And we believe this to be epistemically responsible. For we are now taking the initiative to ask the other humanities, social and natural sciences what makes humans "tick" at various levels. Such a synthetic view—in conjunction with a clear understanding of the NF/MF—will shed light on the origin and development of human values.

6. Dewey's conception of an evolutionary account of ethics is not a strictly biological approach. His concern is to study the developmental history of moral judgments, which on a certain level may not include biological considerations. But Dewey's naturalism sees "culture" as an outgrowth of the needs, desires, and predispositions of

humans who are the product of natural evolution. Therefore "natural" evolution and "cultural" evolution are points on a continuum and are both part of a full appreciation of human experience. The contemporary evolutionary study of ethics seems a continuation of the project Dewey is defending in his 1902 essay. For a further discussion of Dewey's views on evolution see Teehan 2002.

7. Perhaps, the role to be played is even more urgent. Dewey warns, "A culture which permits science to destroy traditional values but which distrusts its power to create new ones is a culture which is destroying itself" (1939, 172).

BIBLIOGRAPHY

Arnhart, Larry. *Darwinian Natural Right: The Biological Ethics of Human Nature.* Albany: State University of New York Press, 1998.

Blackburn, Simon. *Ruling Passions.* Oxford: Clarendon Press, Oxford University Press, 1998.

Casebeer, William D. *Natural Ethical Facts: Evolution, Connectionism, and Moral Cognition.* Cambridge, MA: MIT Press, 2003.

Dewey, John. *Evolution and Ethics.* 1898. In *John Dewey: The Early Works*, vol. 5: *1895–1898.* Edited by Jo Ann Boydston. Carbondale and Edwardsville: Southern Illinois University Press, 1972.

———. *The Evolutionary Method as Applied to Morality.* 1902. In *John Dewey: The Middle Works*, vol. 2: *1899–1924.* Edited by Jo Ann Boydston. Carbondale and Edwardsville: Southern Illinois University Press, 1976.

———. *Experience and Nature.* 1925a. *John Dewey: The Later Works*, vol. 1: *1925.* Carbondale and Edwardsville: Southern Illinois University Press. 1988.

———. *The Meaning of Value.* 1925b. *John Dewey: The Later Works*, vol. 2: *1925–1927.* Carbondale and Edwardsville: Southern Illinois University Press, 1988.

———. *The Quest for Certainty.* 1929. *John Dewey: The Later Works*, vol. 4: *1925–1953.* Carbondale and Edwardsville: Southern Illinois University Press, 1988.

———. *Freedom and Culture.* 1939a. *John Dewey: The Later Works*, vol. 13: *1938–1939.* Carbondale and Edwardsville: Southern Illinois University Press, 1988.

———. *Theory of Valuation.* 1939b. *John Dewey: The Later Works*, vol. 13: *1938–1939.* Carbondale and Edwardsville: Southern Illinois University Press, 1988.

———. "Ethical Subject-Matter and Language." *Dewey and His Critics*, edited by S. Morgenbesser, 676–87. New York: Journal of Philosophy, 1977.

diCarlo, Christopher. "The Evolution of Morality." *Humanist in Canada*, no. 143 (Winter 2002/2003): 12–19.

———. "Critical Notice of Anthony O'Hear's *Beyond Evolution: Human Nature and the Limits of Evolutionary Explanation.*" Biology and Philosophy 16, no. 1 (2000a): 117–30.

————. Abstract: "The Influence of Selection Pressures and Secondary Epigenetic Rules on the Cognitive Development of Specific Forms of Reasoning." *Journal of Consciousness Studies: Consciousness Research Abstracts* (2000b): 137.

Gould, Stephen Jay. *Rocks of Ages: Science and Religion in the Fullness of Life*. The Library of Contemporary Thought. New York: Ballantine, 1999.

Hill, John. *The Ethics of G. E. Moore: A New Interpretation*. Amherst, NY: Prometheus Books, 1976.

Hinde, Robert A. *Why Good Is Good: The Sources of Morality*. London: Routledge, 2002.

Hume, David. (1740) *A Treatise of Human Nature*. 1740. Edited by P. H. Nidditch. 2nd ed. Oxford: Oxford University Press, 1978.

Kant, Immanuel. *Groundwork of the Metaphysics of Morals*. 1785. Translated by H. J. Paton. New York: Harper and Row.

————.*Critique of Practical Reason*. 1788. Translated by Lewis Beck White. The Library of the Liberal Arts. New York: Macmillan, 1993.

Levin, Michael. "Why Homosexuality Is Abnormal." *Monist* 67 (1984):251–83.

Moore, G. E. *Principia Ethica*. Cambridge: Cambridge University Press, 1903.

Regan, Tom. *Bloomsbury's Prophet*. Philadelphia: Temple University Press, 1986.

Ruse, Michael, and E. O. Wilson. "Moral Philosophy as Applied Science." *Philosophy* 61 (April 1986): 173–92.

Teehan, John. "Evolution and Ethics: The Huxley/Dewey Exchange." *Journal of Speculative Philosophy* 16, no. 3 (2002): 225–38.

————. "Kantian Ethics: After Darwin." *Zygon* 38, no. 1 (March 2003): 49–60.

Warnock, Mary. *Ethics Since 1900*. Oxford: Oxford University Press, 1978.

BIOLOGY, SOCIAL SCIENCE, COMMON SENSE

28
THE COMMON GROUND BETWEEN SCIENCE AND MORALITY
A Biological Perspective

DONALD B. CALNE

THE NATURE OF SCIENCE

Most scientists would agree with Thomas Huxley's metaphor that science is "nothing but trained and organized common sense, differing from the latter only as a veteran may differ from a raw recruit; and its methods differ from those of common sense only in so far as the guardsman's cut and thrust differ from the manner in which a savage wields his club" (Huxley 1895).[1] So if common sense is at the root of science, what is at the root of common sense? The answer must surely be "reason." But the term "reason" is used in different ways by different people, so it is necessary to formulate a working definition. *Reason is built upon logical deduction and induction. It assigns priority to observations over theories, and simplicity over complexity. It demands consistency, coherence, and efficiency* (Calne 1999).

So science derives from reason, and may be regarded as its most highly developed expression. If reason is the tool that enabled our ancient ancestors to select rich soil along the banks of rivers for their crops, science is the tool that enabled our more recent ancestors to produce the chemical agents necessary to keep the soil fertile, and the irrigation plants necessary to sustain the harvest. Reason and science are tools that assist us in reaching our goals, but they cannot set those goals. For motivation, we need to satisfy physiological, instinctive, emotional, or cultural drives. Morality is the hub of our cultural drives.

THE NATURE OF MORALITY

From a biological viewpoint, individuals of the species *Homo sapiens* are not physically powerful. There are many animals with greater stature, more muscular jaws, sharper teeth, and longer claws. To survive, *Homo sapiens* evolved in groups. Individuals fared much better living together, rather than living alone. The formation of social groups facilitated reproduction, care of the young, acquisition of food, and defense from predators (including other assemblies of *Homo sapiens*). Language, first spoken and then written, increased the efficiency of the groups, and as they grew in size, subgroups developed specialized skills that allowed societies to improve the length and quality of their lives—of course they could also use their power to kill and destroy.

For a social group to operate efficiently, a compromise must be established between the competition that motivates individuals, and the cooperation essential for the organization and operation of a group. This compromise is achieved though the development of guide lines for behavior. For each individual, a blueprint of these guidelines is integrated psychologically into a conscience that encapsulates the morality of the group. The conscience is formed by personal acceptance of impersonal rules that are shaped by secular institutions as laws, and by religious institutions as commandments. What determines the content of the laws and commandments? The most important elements select themselves by promoting survival. If the rules and commandments work—as tools for survival—they are grafted into the "operating system" of the culture. If they do not work, they are, sooner or later, rejected or relegated to a low priority. Laws and commandments buttress the strength and unity of the group, thereby increasing the society's ability to withstand internal disruption, external attack, and the hazards of an unstable physical environment. Without laws that work there will, sooner or later, be anarchy, and anarchy does not lead to survival.

EVOLUTION OF THE INTELLECT

The biological success of *Homo sapiens* has been achieved though interrelated developments—anatomical organization of the larynx, and the neuronal systems that control language; anatomical organization of the hand, and the neuronal systems that control fine finger and thumb movements. But perhaps the most important evolutionary advance has been the development of the human intellect, and the new (in evolutionary terms) portions of the brain that have made this possible.

We can study chimpanzees to find clues about the evolution of the primate brain. In doing so, we find a curious mismatch between how chimpanzees behave normally in the wild, and how they behave artificially in the laboratory. Their behavior appears much more "clever" in experimental settings, compared with their behavior in their normal environment. Laboratory tests reveal "intellectual" abilities in excess of those they display—or seem to need—in their natural habitat.

How can this paradox be explained? In the words of Nicholas Humphrey: "Social primates are required, by the very nature of the system they create and maintain, to be calculating beings; they must be able to calculate the consequences of their own behavior, to calculate the likely behavior of others . . . 'social skill' goes hand in hand with intellect" (Humphrey 1992). Emil Menzel gives a good example of how intelligence is used in the social interaction of primates—here, chimpanzees. The major characters are Rock, a dominant male, and Belle, a clever female. In an experiment where food was hidden in a field, Belle was proficient at finding it, and once found, she shared it with most of the other chimpanzees—providing Rock was not present. When Rock appeared, Belle became

> increasingly slower in her approach to the food. The reason was not hard to detect. As soon as Belle uncovered the food, Rock raced over, kicked or bit her, and took it all. Belle accordingly stopped uncovering the food if Rock was close. She sat on it till Rock left. Rock, however, soon learned of this, and when she sat on one place for more than a few seconds, he came over, shoved her aside, searched her sitting place, and got the food. Belle next stopped going all the way. Rock, however, countered by expanding the area of his search through the grass near where Belle had sat. Eventually, Belle sat farther and farther away, waiting until Rock looked in the opposite direction before she moved toward the food at all—and Rock, in turn, seemed to look away until Belle started to move somewhere. On some occasions, Rock started to wander off, only to wheel around suddenly precisely as Belle was about to uncover the food. (Menzel 1988)

In any culture that has survived for more than a few generations there is a core of rational morality that embraces certain universal guidelines—not to kill, steal, lie, or violate sexual customs. These guidelines are universal because they "work"—they contribute to the survival of the group. Cultures generally have other guidelines that are idiosyncratic, and differ from one culture to another. These are woven into religious teachings—for example, to cover the head—or not to cover the head when praying, to avoid eating pork or to avoid eating beef. These idiosyncratic commandments are distinguishable from universals because they lack stability when followed over thousands of years. Nevertheless idiosyncratic guidelines reinforce social structure through their ability to promote powerful bonding between members of the group.

HOW DOES MORALITY WORK?

Morality is achieved by the creation of a conscience that motivates us to accept certain acts, and to reject others. In other words, our consciences determine what we want (beyond biological cravings)—reason is the "hired gun" that helps us get it. The limitations of reason—and its derivative, science, come from their having no capacity to make us "feel" anything. We are motivated by seeking mental rewards, and avoiding mental punishments. Most obviously, we are motivated to seek satisfaction of physiological, instinctive, and emotional drives, such as hunger, thirst, and sex. In addition, we are motivated by our society through an ethical system that can assign powerful mental rewards and punishments. We seek to obtain the approval of our culture—family and friends—and to avoid being criticized or cast out. Religious and political institutions utilize morality to generate feelings such as awe, ecstasy, obligation, guilt, and fear. The power of such mental rewards and punishments is illustrated by their ability to overcome instincts as basic as self-preservation; for example, in soldiers who risk their lives for their country, and suicide bombers who go beyond the risk of death for their religion.

Morality is learned within the family. Developmental psychologists use the term "internalization"(Rottschaefer 1998) for the process by which conscience is established—conscience being a set of values such that acts in compliance with the set leads to mental rewards, fulfilling an obligation that is like satisfying an emotion. Correspondingly, failure to meet an obligation results in anguish just as failure to satisfy an emotion leads to frustration. Acceptance of obligations leads to social cohesion that facilitates survival of the group. In general, cohesion is achieved when individuals act to help others rather than themselves, so the central theme of morality is unselfishness.

We have little understanding of the process of internalization of morality to create a conscience, but it is likely to involve parental discipline, parental approval/disapproval, and, when the child is old enough, explanation. Internalization is a special form of learning, and the capacity for moral internalization is greatest in the young, just as the capacity for learning language is greatest in the young. But moral internalization is not confined to infants and children.

The conscience can be changed in adults; for example, propaganda can remodel the conscience without any awareness of what is happening.

SCIENCE AND MORALITY IN THE BRAIN

We have already argued that reason (at the root of science), and social behavior (at the root of morality) evolved together as the primate brain enlarged. The region of the brain that underwent the greatest increase in size and complexity was the frontal lobes. Damage to the frontal lobes can lead to selective loss of the ability to reason—leaving memory, language, sight, and hearing intact. This "dysexecutive syndrome" is characterized by inability to assemble a rational series of thoughts. For example, we can take a case report of a patient who said that "money is green (in the United States) and so are trees, so money must grow on trees." She was equally unable to put together a rationally organized series of actions—she would do the laundry by placing a box of detergent in the washing machine with her clothes (Campbell 1994).

Damage to the frontal lobes can also lead to selective impairment of morality. A classical case from the neurological literature illustrates the point. In 1848, Phineas Gage was laying track in Vermont when an accidental explosion blew an iron bar through the front of his head. Before the explosion, Gage was reported by the railroad company as having been "the most efficient and capable" man in their employ. The circumstances following the accident are graphically recorded; the explosion threw Gage onto his back and he had a "few convulsive movements of the extremities." Then he spoke a few words and was carried to an oxcart; he was taken, sitting, to the nearest town where he received prompt medical attention. He made an excellent recovery, but he displayed a remarkable change in behavior. His physician, Dr. Harlow, described him as "fitful, irreverent, indulging at times in the grossest profanity which was not previously his custom, manifesting but little deference to his fellows, impatient of restraint or advice when it conflicts with his desires." Antonia Damasio comments that "the foul language was so debased that women were advised not to stay long in his presence, lest their sensibilities be offended. The strongest admonitions from Harlow himself failed to return our survivor to good behaviour" (Damasio 1994) In essence, the iron bar had altered Gage's morality.

CONCLUSIONS

Traditionally there has been a tendency to regard science and morality as totally separate and independent from each other. I have argued that the evolution of the human brain was driven by the need for higher primates to form social groups in order to succeed in a competitive environment, where supplies of food, water, and space were limited. Social groups, by themselves, were necessary but not sufficient for survival. The social groups had to develop a morality, with rational laws derived from this morality, to deal with problems that go beyond the need to share natural resources. Geoffrey Warnock gives an eloquent summary: (8).

> Knowledge, skills, information, and intelligence are limited; people are often not rational, either in the management of their own affairs or in the adjustment of their own affairs in relation to others. Then, finally, they are vulnerable to others, and dependent on others, and yet inevitably often in competition with others; and, human sympathies being limited, they may often neither get nor give help that is needed, may not manage to co-operate for common ends, and may be constantly liable to frustration or positive injury from directly hostile interference by other persons. (Warnock 1971)

Large frontal lobes—capable of new social skills—also brought the capacity to improve the faculty of reason, and reason was the platform upon which science was built. The same large frontal lobes enabled larger groups of *Homo sapiens* to live together, and this in turn generated a need for the creation of a code of rules—morality—to reconcile individual self-interest with the cooperation needed for the efficient operation of a tribe, city-state, or nation. So science and morality have similar origins.

Can science be employed to help morality, and vice versa? The answer must be yes to both questions. As an example of science helping morality, we can consider the death penalty. Science can design and perform a double blind, controlled prospective study—with strictly defined inclusion and exclusion criteria for randomly allocated subjects—to see whether the death penalty has a deterrent effect. Such studies are demanded to determine whether a new medication has a therapeutic effect. Surely our standards should be no less rigorous if we have to decide whether the death penalty is desirable. Loose retrospective comparisons are unacceptable.

Can morality be employed to help science? For many years it has been recognized that ethicists help in the evaluation of research that involves human subjects or animals. It is now customary to have ethical screening of scientific projects. This extends beyond biomedical research to include, for example, assessment of the risks of unwanted environmental consequences resulting from industrial contamination by toxic chemicals or radiation.

In summary, the evidence indicates that science and morality have similar evolutionary origins. They can no longer be regarded as totally separate and independent, and they are certainly not in conflict.

NOTE

1. The traditional view of science stressed the principle of verifying a hypothesis as its essence, but in more recent years Karl Popper has emphasized the importance of failure to falsify a hypothesis. Experiments can never establish total verification but they can readily and totally refute a hypothesis. This emphasis does not, in any way, detract from Huxley's claim that science is refined common sense.

REFERENCES

Calne, D. B. *Within Reason: Rationality and Human Behavior*. New York: Pantheon, 1999.

Campbell, J. J. "The Regional Prefrontal Syndromes: A Theoretical and Clinical Overview." *Journal of Neuropsychiatry and Clinical Neuroscience* 6 (1994).

Damasio, A. R. *Descartes' Error: Emotion, Reason, and the Human Brain*. New York: Putnam, 1994.

Humphrey, N. "The Social Function of Intellect." In *Growing Points in Ethology*. Edited by B. P. G. Bateson and R. A. Hinde. Cambridge: Cambridge University Press, 1992.

Huxley, T. H. *The Method of Zadig*. In *Collected Essays (1893–94)*. London: Macmillan, 1895.

Menzel E. W. "A Group of Young Chimpanzees in a One-acre Field: Leadership and Communication." In *Machiavellian Intelligence*. Edited by R. W. Byrne and A. W. Whiten. Oxford: Clarendon Press, 1988.

Rottschaefer, W. A. *The Biology and Psychology of Moral Agency*. Cambridge: Cambridge University Press, 1998.

Warnock, G. J. *The Object of Morality*. London: Methuen, 1971.

29

CARL MENGER AND EXACT THEORY IN THE SOCIAL SCIENCES

DAVID R. KOEPSELL

The social sciences, no less than any other scientific realm, have suffered for the effects of multiculturalism, relativism, and postmodernism, all of which suggest that there are no objective truths when it comes to human, social phenomena. But this assumption is unfounded, and potentially dangerous. Accepting this assumption requires setting humans somehow above the realm of the natural world, where science and its methods have given us so much prediction, understanding, and control. This assumption is also challenged by the work of a few Austrian philosophers whose work was influential to what would later come to be known as the Vienna Circle, and whose work should be looked at again with some scrutiny for its potential impact on modern social science. I will look primarily at the innovations of Carl Menger, and his influence on the Austrian school of philosophy and its potential for revitalizing the social sciences, looking particularly at its potential for ethical studies.

CARL MENGER

Carl Menger, in his seminal works, begins with the premise that methods of investigation of laws of economics have hitherto proceeded in error. Smith, Marx, and others have depended in their research of economics on examining historical trends, which only give us imprecise, inexact "laws" of economics. This is an a posteriori method that will never give us a scientific law of the sort we ought to strive for. Menger employs a "phenomenological" approach typical of the Austrian movement, described by Franz Brentano in *Psychology from an Empirical Standpoint* (1874). Brentano's form of phenomenological empiricism is based upon the view that we can discover general laws of human and social behavior, which laws are the objects of science, by uncovering necessary relations in ordinary experience. This method has been called both methodological essentialism (Popper, *The Poverty of Historicism*) and methodological individualism.

In *Investigations into the Method of the Social Sciences with Special Reference to Economics*, Carl Menger discusses the method and means of arriving at "exact" laws of economics while assailing what he calls the "realistic-empirical" method of classical economics, which, he says:

> Offers us in all realms of the world of phenomena results which are formally imperfect, however important and valuable they may be for human knowledge and practical life. They are theories which give us only a deficient understanding of the phenomena, only an uncertain prediction of them, and by no means an assured control of them. (p. 59)

According to Menger, there are two types of knowledge: (a) individual, and (b) general. Only general knowledge affords one a true understanding of phenomena. He states:

> Either there are concrete phenomena in their position in space and time and their concrete relationships to one another, or else there are the empirical forms recurring in the variation of these, the knowledge of which forms the object of our scientific interest. The one orientation of research is aimed at cognition of the concrete, or more correctly, of the individual aspect of phenomena; the other is aimed at cognition of their general aspect. (p. 35)

Menger criticizes the realistic-empirical method of the social science as poorly suited to determining exact laws of human phenomena:

> Real human phenomena are not strictly typical [and] just for this reason, and also as a result of the freedom of the human will ... empirical laws of absolute strictness are out of the question in the realm of human activity. (*Problems of Economics and Sociology*, p. 214)

According to Menger, exact laws of human phenomena cannot be derived from standard empirical social research. But it is those exact laws that must be the object of the study of human phenomena:

> [Exact theory is] an aim which research pursues in the same way in all realms of the world of phenomena, [it] is the determination of the strict laws of phenomena which do now present themselves as absolute, but which in respect to the approaches to cognition by which we attain to them simply bear within themselves the guarantee of absoluteness. (p. 59)

How, then, can exact laws of human phenomena be investigated if standard empirical study must fail? The key to the correct methodology lies in recognizing the correct "object-world" of one's study. In the case of human phenomena, human consciousness is the correct object world. Exact laws of social phenomena can be formulated or discovered only by discovering the laws of thought which comprise those phenomena. Menger concludes that

> The error of the social philosophers consists in the fact that they try to arrive at exact social laws by means of empirical research, and thus in a way in which exact laws of phenomena cannot be established at all, neither exact social laws nor exact natural laws. (*Problems*, p. 214)

Methodological individualism, which seeks through introspection to uncover the precise and general mental phenomena underlying social acts is, according to Menger, the only allowable method for uncovering the exact laws he seeks in economics. Adolf Reinach utilizes this method in his *Aporiori Foundations of the Civil Law* in examining the exact laws of claims. The result of such research is to give us synthetic, a priori truths about ranges of phenomena hitherto believed by Kant to not be amenable to such inspection.

Husserl explains the structure of social reality offered by such a method of inquiry thusly:

> There obtain firmly determined relations of necessity, laws determinate in their content which vary with the species of dependent contents and accordingly prescribe one sort of completion to one of them and another sort of completion to another. (1900/1901, vol. II, A244f, translation 454)

This Husserlian view of synthetic *a priori*, and its phenomenological method offer us breakthroughs in an understanding of social phenomena such as economics and law, but can they offer us insight into ethical inquiry?

METHODOLOGICAL INDIVIDUALISM IN ECONOMICS

Menger's criticism casts doubt upon the work in economics that still predominates. Most economists study trends in economies by looking at microeconomic transactions. The purposes to which these economists put their study are generally prospective. That is, with economic data and a general view of economic trends, both at a macro- and a microlevel, economists make predictions that help guide governmental fiscal policies, and investments. As we can see by the relative lack of success in these areas, with large-scale market unpredictability, and investment failures, economic theory that utilizes the realistic-empirical method is imperfect at best.

Menger's insight is twofold: despite the unpredictability of economies, there are still (a) laws that regulate economic *behavior* and (b) we can *know* those laws. The overall implication for economics as a science is profound in that it leaves open an avenue for fruitful study of the mechanisms of valuation, desire, need, profits, and other related economic entities, while suggesting that this understanding leaves little room for prediction and control of economies.

For value theory, the upshot of Menger's theory is apparent in the work of the exact theory of value developed by Ehrenfels, who rejects supply-and-demand definitions of value, holds that value is an objective property of a valued object, and agrees with Menger in holding that the value of an object is in every case a product of individual valuing acts by the marketplace of valuers.

Assume for a moment that ethics is such a field of study. It is both a social phenomenon and a human phenomenon. The study of ethics, for the most part, has been a little more fruitful than that of economics, but the lack of consensus as to the worth of any one ethical theory may well speak to a failure of methodology. Can we strive toward general laws of ethics as Menger urges in the study of economics?

EXACT LAWS OF ETHICS

Let us assume that there is such a thing as the good, for without this assumption, the argument cannot be made. Now, without deciding upon the mode of existence of the good, how does Menger's method inform a study of ethics? First, we agree that the good is prone to phenomenological investigation in the same manner as are economic phenomena. There is little reason to question this so long as we posit some human interaction in the good. Even given some theological basis for morality, the participation of the human will in willing the good gives us a basis to inquire, for instance, what the general and necessary conditions are behind any particular human ethical choice. The problem in ethics is, however, in many ways like that of economics. We have many conceptions of the good, and historicism will fail to allow us to derive exact ethical laws for precisely the same reasons. Are there common enough concepts, however, to serve as a starting point for study using methodological individualism?

Utilitarians of both the classical and average utility school start with the supposition that the good is akin to that which increases pleasure. Assuming this to be so, Utilitarianism seems a good candidate for study using methodological individualism. The experience of pleasure is akin to individual acts of valuing. Examination of the exact laws of pleasure seems fruitful, and would provide a missing chunk to Utilitarian theory given that this is one of the great criticisms of the theory.

Deontological theories of the good certainly already presuppose accommodating methodologically individualist study. If the good exist in something like "nature" as with natural law theories, then the natural laws of the good are as amenable to scientific examination as other laws. Just as the exact laws of economics are uncovered by discovering the laws behind acts of individual valuation, so, too, should the exact law behind the good be discoverable by individual acts of participation in natural moral laws. Exact laws of duties and obligations, such as those touched upon by Reinach's discussion of the a priori nature of claims, can ground secular deontological notions of ethics.

WHAT METHODOLOGICAL INDIVIDUALISM IMPLIES FOR ETHICS

In economics, the Austrian school of economics grew out of Menger's methodological individualism and remains on the outskirts of practical economics. There are not many working Austrian economists outside of academia. One reason for this is that the implications of this school of thought, as discussed above, are that generalizations made from individual acts of valuation will necessarily be vague. Economies cannot be guided, predictions can only be imprecisely made, and governments can only maintain a very small degree of control over economies in the long run due to the unpredictability of individuals and their acts of will.

The breakthrough of Austrian economics gives us a greater scientific understanding of the phenomena underlying economic activity, even while uncovering the flaws in generalizing from that understanding. I suspect that Menger's methods prove somewhat more useful when applied to ethics, however.

Assuming that ethics is a field of study amenable to methodological individualism, then at least we can conclude that ethics can be studied scientifically and that exact and general laws can be discovered, even if, as in economics, the degree of prediction and control we will have over human ethical behavior is just as uncertain as is economic behavior.

Menger's method strengthens the bases of current ethical theories by providing the phenomenological bases for our decisions as to the *importance* of certain things taken for granted, such as *pleasure*, *duty*, or *obligation*. Even contractarian models, such as Rawls's theory of "justice as fairness," base parts of their theories on assumptions that ought to be supported by something. Menger's phenomenology provides a means of bridging such gaps and curing those assumptions.

Finally, if the result of methodological individualism leads us finally to conclude that, like economics, no degree of prediction or control is ultimately possible, and that individual acts of will toward pursuing differing ends are all we can know, then the fruits of that determination, from a purely scientific standpoint, are themselves worth knowing.

THE PROBLEM WITH REALISTIC-EMPIRICAL ETHICS

Much current work in applied ethics ignores the important questions of ethical theory: specifically, is there a "ground" for ethical judgment? By focusing on ethical behaviors, instead of the ontological grounding of the "good," normative ethics makes the same fatal error as classical economics. It can never derive "exact" laws of ethics from such a normative approach. At best, as in economics, it can reach statistical answers, but can never give us the sort of scientific certainty we should seek to attain if ethics is ever to be a proscriptive science.

Discovering the "exact" laws of ethics starts not with observation of external behaviors of individuals or cultures, but rather with the nature of human intentionality as an aspect of consciousness. Reinach did a kernel of this in his *Apriori Foundations of the Civil Law*. He saw that certain legal entities such as contracts are grounded in certain facts of human intentionality and speech. They are bound together as social objects. He examined the ontology of claims, stating that "a claim arises in the one party and an obligation in the other. What are these curious entities (*Gebilde*)? They are surely not *nothing*." Elucidated now by speech act theory, we can see that the complex phenomenon involving explicit acts of promising and the concurrent intentional states of acceptance and perceived freedom give rise to a real set of entities: claims and obligations, wholly apart from the social norms, institutions, or conventions that provide for remedies for breaches of contract. Reinach argues that this state of affairs is a simple law of being, preceding any legal or social norm of contracts.

What Reinach describes is an *a priori* theory of right. Claims, duties, and obligations arise in certain circumstances not by the creation of institutions, laws, or norms of behavior, but rather prior to them, based upon necessary and sufficient conditions rooted in human intentionality and speech acts. Some "enactments" (laws, norms, or institutions) are "grounded" in simple laws of being, according to Reinach. He argues that enactments such as contract law, which recognize the a priori nature of obligations and duties arising from agreements, are grounded, whereas positive laws that would contravene such laws of being are not. Here is an objective basis for judgment of the relative justice of enactments and norms, rooted not in divine law, nor in changing, relativistic cultural phenomena, but in universal facts about human intentionality and speech.[1]

Personal bodily autonomy, property rights, freedom of speech, and other liberties may also be similarly argued to be grounded naturalistically in "simple laws of being." If so, then there is a solid basis for judgment about moral and ethical norms, and normative prescriptions can be rooted in something objective and real, rather than surmise.

IMPLICATIONS FOR THE SOCIAL SCIENCES IN GENERAL

The same implications hold for the social sciences in general. What postmodernism and multiculturalism have done to the social sciences is to further "soften" them, making them of little use in understanding or describing human behavior generally. We instead assume without question that the social sciences will never yield scientific knowledge of the sort we find in the "hard" sciences. It is a shame to give up so easily and quickly on a field whose investigations may be necessary to avert calamities such as starvation, war, genocide, and other human-made horrors. Perhaps by returning to the innovations of Menger and his ilk, we can revive the scientific bases for investigations in all the social sciences. It is at least worth a second look.

NOTE

1. For a discussion of applications of moral apriorism to property rights see David Koepsell, "Ethics and Ontology: A New Synthesis," *Metaphysica* 8, no. 2: 20–27. Forthcoming.

30

DEFENDING SCIENCE— WITHIN REASON
The Critical Common-Sensist Manifesto

SUSAN HAACK

> That men should rush with violence from one extreme, without going more or less into the contrary extreme, is not to be expected from the weakness of human nature.
> —Thomas Reid, *Essays on the Intellectual Powers* (1875)

Attitudes to science range all the way from uncritical admiration at one extreme, through distrust, resentment, and envy, to denigration and outright hostility at the other. We are confused about what science can and what it can't do, and about how it does what it does; about how science differs from literature or art; about whether science is really a threat to religion; about the role of science in society and the role of society in science. And we are ambivalent about the value of science. We admire its theoretical achievements, and welcome technological developments that improve our lives; but we are disappointed when hoped-for results are not speedily forthcoming, dismayed when scientific discoveries threaten cherished beliefs about ourselves and our place in the universe, distrustful of what we perceive as scientists' arrogance or elitism, disturbed by the enormous cost of scientific research, and disillusioned when we read of scientific fraud, misconduct, or incompetence.

From *Skeptical Inquirer* 28, no. 4 (2004): 28–34

Complicated as they are, the confusions can be classified into two broad kinds, the scientistic and the antiscientific. Scientism is an exaggerated kind of deference toward science, an excessive readiness to accept as authoritative any claim made by the sciences, and to dismiss every kind of criticism of science or its practitioners as antiscientific prejudice. Antiscience is an exaggerated kind of suspicion of science, an excessive readiness to see the interests of the powerful at work in every scientific claim, and to accept every kind of criticism of science or its practitioners as undermining its pretensions to tell us how the world is. The problem, of course, is to say when the deference, or the suspicion, is "excessive."

Disentangling the confusions is made harder by an awkward duality of usage. Sometimes the word "science" is used simply as a way of referring to certain disciplines: physics, chemistry, biology, and so forth, usually also anthropology and psychology, sometimes also sociology, economics, and so on. But often—perhaps more often than not—"science" and its cognates are used honorifically: advertisers urge us to get our clothes cleaner with new, scientific, Wizzo; teachers of critical thinking urge us to reason scientifically, to use the scientific method; juries are more willing to believe a witness when told that what he offers is scientific evidence; astrology, water-divining, homeopathy, or chiropractic or acupuncture are dismissed as pseudosciences; skeptical of this or that claim, people complain that it lacks a scientific explanation, or demand scientific proof. And so on. "Scientific" has become an all-purpose term of epistemic praise, meaning "strong, reliable, *good.*" No wonder, then, that psychologists and sociologists and economists are sometimes so zealous in insisting on their right to the title. No wonder, either, that practitioners in other areas—"Management Science," "Library Science," "Military Science," even "Mortuary Science"—are so keen to claim it.

In view of the impressive successes of the natural sciences, this honorific usage is understandable enough. But it is thoroughly unfortunate. It obscures the otherwise obvious fact that not all or only practitioners of disciplines classified as sciences are honest, thorough, successful inquirers; when plenty of scientists are lazy, incompetent, unimaginative, unlucky, or dishonest, while plenty of historians, journalists, detectives, etc., are good inquirers. It tempts us into a fruitless preoccupation with the problem of demarcating *real* science from pretenders. It encourages too thoughtlessly uncritical an attitude to the disciplines classified as sciences, which in turn provokes envy of those disciplines, and encourages a kind of scientism—inappropriate mimicry, by practitioners of other disciplines, of the manner, the technical terminology, the mathematics, etc., of the natural sciences. And it provokes resentment of the disciplines so classified, which encourages antiscientific attitudes. Sometimes you can even see the envy and the resentment working together: for example, with those self-styled ethnomethodologists who undertake "laboratory studies" of science, observing, as they would say, part of the industrial complex in the business of the production of inscriptions; or—however grudgingly, you have to admit the rhetorical brilliance of this self-description—with "creation science." *And*, most to the present purpose, this honorific usage stands in the way of a straightforward acknowledgment that science—science, that is, in the descriptive sense—is neither sacred nor a confidence trick.

Science is not sacred: like all human enterprises, it is thoroughly fallible, imperfect, uneven in its achievements, often fumbling, sometimes corrupt, and of course incomplete. Neither, however, is it a confidence trick: the natural sciences, at any rate, have surely been among the most successful of human enterprises. The core of what needs to be sorted out concerns the nature and conditions of scientific knowledge, evidence, and inquiry; it is epistemological. (No, I haven't forgotten Jonathan Rauch's wry observation: "If you want to empty the room at a cocktail party, say 'epistemology'";[1] but the word is pretty well indispensable for my purposes because, unlike "theory of knowledge," it has adjectival and adverbial forms.) What we need is an understanding of inquiry in the sciences, which is, in the ordinary, nontechnical sense of the word, realistic, neither overestimating nor underestimating what the sciences can do.

What we have, however, is a confusing Babel of competing, unsatisfactory accounts of the epistemology of science. How did we come to such a pass?

FROM THE OLD DEFERENTIALISM TO THE NEW CYNICISM

Once upon a time—the phrase is a warning that what follows will be cartoon history—the epistemological bona fides of good empirical science needed to be defended against the rival claims of sacred scripture or a priori metaphysics. In due course it came to be thought that science enjoys a peculiar epistemological authority because of its uniquely objective and rational method of inquiry. In the wake of the extraordinary successes of the new, modern logic, successive efforts to articulate the "logic of science" gave rise to umpteen competing versions of what I call the "Old Deferentialism": science progresses inductively, by accumulating true or probably true theories confirmed by empirical evidence, by observed facts; or deductively, by testing theories against basic statements and, as falsified conjectures are replaced by corroborated ones, improving the verisimilitude of its theories; or instrumentally, by developing theories which, though not themselves capable of truth, are efficient instruments of prediction; or, etc., etc. There were numerous obstacles: Humean skepticism about induction; the paradoxes of confirmation; the "new riddle of induction" posed by Nelson Goodman's "grue"; Russell Hanson's and others' thesis of the theory-dependence of observation; W. V. O. Quine's thesis of the underdetermination of theories even by all possible observational evidence. But these, though acknowledged as tough, were assumed to be superable, or avoidable.

It is tempting to describe these problems in Kuhnian terms, as anomalies facing the Old Deferentialist paradigm just as a rival was beginning to stir. Thomas Kuhn himself, it soon became apparent, hadn't intended radically to undermine the pretensions of science to be a rational enterprise. But most readers of *The Structure of Scientific Revolutions*, missing many subtleties and many ambiguities, heard only: science progresses, or "progresses," not by the accumulation of well-confirmed truths, or even by the elimination of conjectures shown to be false, but by revolutionary upheavals in a cataclysmic process the history of which is afterward written by the winning side; there are no neutral standards of evidence, only the incommensurable standards of different paradigms; the success of a scientific revolution, like the success of a political revolution, depends on propaganda and control of resources; a scientist's shift of allegiance to a new paradigm is less like a rational change of mind than a religious conversion—a conversion after which things look so different to him that we might almost say he lives "in a different world."

Even so, a quarter of a century ago now, when Paul Feyerabend proclaimed that there is no scientific method, that appeals to "rationality" and "evidence" are no more than rhetorical bullying, that science is not superior to, only better entrenched than, astrology or voodoo, he was widely regarded—he described himself—as the "court jester" of the philosophy of science. Post-Kuhnian Deferentialists, adding "incommensurability" and "meaning-variance" to their list of obstacles to be overcome, modified and adapted older approaches; but remained convinced not only of the rationality of the scientific enterprise, but also of the power of formal, logical methods to account for it.

But then radical sociologists, feminists and multiculturalists, radical literary theorists, rhetoricians, semiologists, and philosophers outside strictly philosophy-of-science circles began to turn their attention to science. Proponents of this new almost-orthodoxy, though they disagreed among themselves on the finer points, were unanimous in insisting that the supposed ideal of honest inquiry, respect for evidence, concern for truth, is a kind of illusion, a smokescreen disguising the operations of power, politics, and rhetoric. Insofar as they were concerned at all with the problems that preoccupied mainstream philosophy of science—theory-dependence, underdetermination, incommensurability, and the rest—they proclaimed them insuperable, further confirmation that the epistemological pretensions of the sciences are indefensible. Appeal to "facts" or "evidence" or "rationality," they maintained, is nothing but ideological humbug disguising the exclusion of this or that oppressed group. Science is largely or wholly a matter of interests, social negotiation, or of mythmaking, the production of inscriptions or narratives; not only does it have no peculiar epistemic authority and no uniquely rational method, but it is really, like all purported "inquiry," just politics. We arrived, in short, at the New Cynicism.

Feyerabend, who seems in retrospect the paradigm Old Cynic, promised to free us of "the tyranny of . . . such abstract concepts as 'truth,' 'reality,' or 'objectivity'." Now New Cynics like Harry Collins assure us that "the natural world has a small or non-existent role in the construction of scientific knowledge"; and Kenneth Gergen that the validity of theoretical propositions in the sciences "is in no way affected by factual evidence." Ruth Hubbard urges that "[f]eminist science must insist on the political nature and content of scientific work"; and Sandra Harding asks why it isn't "as illuminating and honest to refer to Newton's laws as 'Newton's rape manual' as it is to call them 'Newton's mechanics.'" Ethnomethodologist of science Bruno Latour announces that "[a]ll this business about rationality and irrationality is the result of an attack by someone on associations that stand in the way"; and rhetorician of science Steve Fuller proposes "a 'shallow' conception . . . that locates the authoritative character of science, not in an esoteric set of skills or a special understanding of reality, but in the appeals to its form of knowledge that *others* feel they must make to legitimate their own activities." Richard Rorty informs readers that "[t]he only sense in which science is exemplary is that it is a model of human solidarity," and Stanley Fish that "the distinction between baseball and science is not finally so firm."[2] Reacting against the scientism toward which the Old Deferentialism sometimes veered uncomfortably close, rushing with violence into the opposite extreme, the New Cynics take an unmistakably antiscientific tone.

Perhaps it is no wonder that many scientists came to regard philosophy of science as at best irrelevant—"about as useful to scientists as ornithology is to birds." With the exception of a few enthusiastic Popperians, working scientists seem to have been mostly unaware of or indifferent to Old Deferentialist aspirations to offer them advice on how to proceed. But in 1987—provoked by Alan Chalmers's observation, at the beginning of his popular introduction to philosophy of science, that "[w]e start off confused and end up confused on a higher level"[3]—physicists Theocharis and Psimopoulos published an impassioned critique of "betrayers of the truth": Popper, Kuhn, Lakatos, and Feyerabend, "the worst enemy of science." And as the influence of New Cynicism grew, more scientists were moved to defend the honor of their enterprise: Paul Gross and Norman Levitt in *Higher Superstition*; Max Perutz denouncing rhetoric of science as "a piece of humbug masquerading as an academic discipline"; Sheldon Glashow deconstructing his letter of invitation to a conference on The End of Science; Alan Sokal parodying postmodernist "cultural critique" of science; and Steven Weinberg replying to the "cultural adversaries" of science.[4] Sometimes they made a good showing; but, not surprisingly, they didn't aspire to supply the realistic account of the epistemology of science required for an adequate defense against the extravagances of the New Cynicism.

Mainstream philosophy of science, meanwhile, had become increasingly specialized and splintered. Though many philosophers of science ignored the New Cynicism, a few tackled it head-on: John Fox criticizing self-styled "ethnomethodologists of science"; Larry Laudan in running battles with proponents of the "Strong Programme" in sociology of science; Mario Bunge protesting the influence of Romanticism and subjectivism; Noretta Koertge wrestling with the social constructivists.[5] Sometimes they made a good showing, too. And with an increased readiness to accommodate social aspects of science, a turn toward one or another form of naturalism, and, since Bas Van Fraassen's influential defense of constructive empiricism, something of a retreat from strong forms of scientific realism, there were efforts to acknowledge the elements of truth to which the New Cynicism gestures, without succumbing to its extravagances. But some mainstream philosophers of science—especially, perhaps, those most anxious not to offend the feminists—seem to have gone too far in the direction of the New Cynicism: as when Ronald Giere suggested that there might be something in the Nazi concept of "Jewish physics," as in feminist complaints of the masculinity of science;[6] and many others, still clinging to the Old Deferentialist reliance on formal, logical methods as sufficient to articulate the epistemology of science, seem not to have gone far enough. In my opinion, anyway, the realistic understanding we need still eludes us.

Still, as I articulate my Critical Common-sensist account—which I believe can correct the overoptimism of the Old Deferentialism without succumbing to the factitious despair of the New Cynicism—I won't forget the cautionary story of the student who is said to have observed in his Introduction to Philosophy examination that while some philosophers believe that God exists, and some philosophers believe that God does not exist, "the truth, as so often, lies somewhere in between." Though there are elements of truth in both the Old Deferentialism and the New Cynicism, a crude split-the-difference approach won't do; for as Algernon observes in Oscar Wilde's *The Importance of Being Earnest*, the truth "is seldom pure and never simple."

CRITICAL COMMON-SENSISM

Critical Common-sensism acknowledges, like the Old Deferentialism, that there are objective standards of better and worse evidence and of better and worse conducted inquiry; but proposes a more flexible and less formal understanding of what those standards are. Critical Common-sensism acknowledges, like the New Cynicism, that observation and theory are interdependent, that scientific vocabulary shifts and changes meaning, and that science is a deeply social enterprise; but sees these, not as obstacles to an understanding of how the sciences have achieved their remarkable successes, but as part of such an understanding.

The core standards of good evidence and well-conducted inquiry are not internal to the sciences, but common to empirical inquiry of every kind. In judging where science has succeeded and where it has failed, in what areas and at what times it has done better and in what worse, we are appealing to the standards by which we judge the solidity of empirical beliefs, or the rigor and thoroughness of empirical inquiry, generally. Often, to be sure, only a specialist can judge the weight of evidence or the thoroughness of precautions against experimental error, etc.; for such judgments require a broad and detailed knowledge of background theory, and a familiarity with technical vocabulary, not easily available to the layperson. Nevertheless, respect for evidence, care in weighing it, and persistence in seeking it out, so far from being exclusively scientific desiderata, are the standards by which we judge *all* inquirers, detectives, historians, investigative journalists, etc., as well as scientists. In short, the sciences are not epistemologically privileged.

They are, however, epistemologically distinguished; the natural sciences at least, fallible and imperfect as they are, have succeeded remarkably well by the core epistemological standards of all serious inquiry. But distinction, unlike privilege, has to be earned; and the natural sciences have earned, not our uncritical deference, but our tempered respect.

The evidence for scientific claims and theories—consisting, not simply of the "data" or "observation statements" of the Old Deferentialism, but of experiential evidence and reasons working together—is like empirical evidence generally, but even more complex and ramifying. Think of the controversy over that four-billion-year-old meteorite discovered in Antarctica, thought to have come from Mars about 11,000 years ago, and found to contain what might possibly be fossilized bacteria droppings. Some space scientists think this is evidence of early Martian life; others think the bacterial traces might have been picked up while the meteorite was in Antarctica; others again believe that what look like fossilized bacteria droppings might be merely artifacts of the instrumentation. How do they know that the meteorite's giving off these gases when heated indicates that it comes from Mars? that it is about 4 billion years old? that this is what fossilized bacteria droppings look like?—like crossword entries, reasons ramify in all directions.

How reasonable a crossword entry is depends on how well it is supported by its clue and any already completed intersecting entries; on how reasonable those other entries are, independent of the entry in question; and on how much of the crossword has been completed. Similarly, what makes evidence stronger or weaker, a claim more or less warranted, depends on how supportive the evidence is; on how secure it is, independent of the claim in question; and on how much of the relevant evidence it includes.

While judgments of evidential quality are perspectival, dependent on background beliefs about, for instance, what evidence is relevant to what, evidential quality itself is objective; the determinants of evidential quality are not subjective or context-dependent, as New Cynics suppose. Neither, however, are they purely logical, as Old Deferentialists thought; they are *worldly*, depending both on scientists' interactions with particular things and events in the world, and on the relation of scientific language to kinds and categories of things. Observation interacts with background beliefs, as clues interact with already completed crossword entries: what observations are taken to be relevant, and what is noticed when observations are made, depends on background assumptions; and the workings of instruments of observation, such as the mass spectrometer and ultra-high resolution transmission microscope on which those space scientists relied, depend on other scientific theories.

Scientific inquiry is continuous with the most ordinary of everyday empirical inquiry. There is no mode of inference, no "scientific method," exclusive to the sciences and guaranteed to produce true, probably true, more nearly true, or more empirically adequate, results. As Percy Bridgman put it, "[T]he scientific method, as far as it is a method, is nothing more than doing one's damnedest with one's mind, no holds barred."[7] And, as far as it is a method, it is what historians or detectives or investigative journalists or the rest of us do when we really want to find something out: make an informed conjecture about the possible explanation of a puzzling phenomenon, check how it stands up to the best evidence we can get, and then use our judgment whether to accept it, more or less tentatively, or modify, refine, or replace it.

Inquiry is difficult and demanding, and we very often go wrong. Sometimes the problem is a failure of will; we don't really want to know badly enough to go to all the trouble of finding out, or we really *don't* want to know, and go to a lot of trouble *not* to find out. And even with the best will in the world, we often fail. Our senses, our imaginations, and our intellects are limited; we can't always see, or guess, or reason, well enough. The remarkable successes of the natural sciences are due, not to a uniquely rational scientific method, but to the vast range of "helps" to inquiry devised by generations of scientists to overcome natural human limitations. Instruments of observation extend sensory reach; models and metaphors stretch imaginative powers; linguistic and conceptual innovations enable a vocabulary that better represents real kinds of thing and event; techniques of mathematical and statistical modeling enable complex reasoning; the cooperative and competitive engagement of many people in a great mesh of subcommunities within and across generations permits division of labor and pooling of evidence, and—though very fallibly and imperfectly, to be sure—has helped keep most scientists, most of the time, reasonably honest.

As you and I can complete the crossword faster and more accurately if your knowledge of Shakespeare and quick ear for puns complements my knowledge of popular music and quick eye for anagrams, so scientific inquiry is advanced by complementary talents. And interactions among scientists, both within and across generations, are essential not only to the division of scientific labor, but also to the sharing of scientific evidence, to a delicate mesh of reasonable confidence in others' competence and honesty. Moreover, scientific claims are better and worse warranted, and there is a large grey area where opinions may reasonably differ about whether a claim is yet sufficiently warranted to put in the textbooks, or should be subjected to further tests, assessed more carefully relative to an alternative, or what. There can no more be rules for when a theory should be accepted and when rejected than there could be rules for when to ink in a crossword entry and when to rub it out; "the" best procedure is for different scientists, some bolder, some more cautious, to proceed differently.

Scientific theories are (normally) either true or else false. A scientific claim or theory is true just in case things are as it says; e.g., if it says that DNA is a double-helical, backbone-out macromolecule with like-with-unlike base pairs, it is true just in case DNA *is* a double-helical, backbone-out macromolecule with like-with-unlike base pairs. Truth, like evidential quality, is objective; i.e., a claim is true or false, as evidence is better or worse, independent of whether anybody, or everybody, believes it to be so. But there is no guarantee that every scientist is entirely objective, i.e., is a completely unbiased and disinterested truth-seeker, immune to prejudice and partisanship; far from it. Nevertheless, the natural sciences have managed, by and large and in the long run, to overcome individual biases by means of an institutionalized commitment to mutual disclosure and scrutiny, and by competition between partisans of rival approaches.

A popular stereotype sees "the scientist" as objective in the sense, not merely of being free of bias or prejudice, but as unemotional, unimaginative, stolid, a paradigmatically convergent thinker. Perhaps some scientists are like this; but not, thank goodness, of all them. "Thank goodness," because imagination is essential to successful scientific inquiry, and a passionate obsession with this or that problem, even a passionate commitment to the truth of this or that elegant but as yet unsupported conjecture, or a passionate desire to best a rival, can contribute to the progress of science. Another stereotype, this time perhaps more philosophical than popular, sees "the scientist" as an essentially critical thinker, refusing to take anything on authority. A systematic commitment to testing, checking, and mutual disclosure and scrutiny *is* one of the things that has contributed to the success of natural-scientific inquiry; but this is, and must be, combined with the institutionalized authority of well-warranted results. Not that crossword entries once inked-in never have to be revised; but only by taking some for granted is it possible to isolate one variable at a time, or to tackle a new problem with the help of others' solutions to older problems.

Not all scientific theories are well supported by good evidence. Most get discarded as the evidence turns out against them; nearly all, at some stage of their career, are only tenuously supported speculations; and doubtless some get accepted, even entrenched, on flimsy evidence. Nevertheless, the natural sciences have come up with deep, broad, and explanatory theories which are well anchored in experience and interlock surprisingly with each other; and, as plausibly filling in long, much-intersected crossword entries greatly improves the prospects of completing more of the puzzle, these successes have enabled further successes. Progress in the sciences is ragged and uneven, and each step, like each crossword entry, is fallible and revisable. But each genuine advance potentially enables others, as a robust crossword entry does—"nothing succeeds like success" is the phrase that comes to mind.

*   *   *

Earlier, I stressed the complicated interactions among individuals that enable division of scientific labor and pooling of scientific evidence. But of course science is a social enterprise in another sense as well: it is a social institution embedded in the larger society, both affecting and affected by other social institutions; subject to political and cultural forces, it both influences and is influenced by the beliefs and values of that larger society. Earlier, I stressed the ways in which the social character of natural-scientific inquiry has contributed to its success. But of course both the internal organization and the external environment of science may hinder, as well as enable, good, fruitful, inquiry.

The disasters of Soviet and Nazi science remind us how grossly inquiry can be distorted and hindered when scientists seek to make a case for politically desired conclusions rather than to find out how things really are. Less melodramatic, but still disturbing, among the other potential hindrances that come immediately to mind are the necessity to spend large amounts of time and energy on obtaining funds, and to impress whoever supplies them, in due course, with your success; dependence for resources on bodies with an interest in the results coming out this way rather than that, or in rivals being denied access to them; pressure to solve problems perceived as socially urgent rather than those most susceptible of solution in the present state of the field; a volume of publications so large as to impede rather than enable communication. It would be less than candid not to admit that this list does not encourage complacency about the present condition of science. Once, important scientific advances could be made with the help of a candle and a piece of string; but it seems scientists have made most of those advances. As science proceeds, more and more expensive equipment is needed to obtain more and more recherché observations; and the more science depends for resources on governments and large industrial concerns, the worse the danger of some of the hindrances listed. While scientific techniques and instruments grow ever more sophisticated, the mechanisms needed to sustain intellectual integrity are strained.

*   *   *

Where the social sciences are concerned, it isn't so easy to think of examples of discoveries analogous to plausibly filled-in, long, much-intersected, crossword entries, nor to be so sure that real progress has been made—it's no wonder that some people deny that the social "sciences" are really sciences at all. Social scientists' enthusiasm for the mathematical techniques and the cooperative and competitive inquiry that have helped the natural sciences to build on earlier successes has sometimes encouraged a kind of affected, mathematized, obscurity, and prematurely gregarious (or dogmatically factional) thinking. More immediately to the present point, where the social sciences are concerned some of the prejudices apt to get in the way of honest inquiry are political as well as professional. Where the physical sciences are concerned, given the manifest irrelevance of sex, race, class, to the content of physical theory, the New Cynics' complaints of pervasive sexism, racism, classism, etc., seem far-fetched. But where the human and social sciences are concerned, given the manifest relevance of sex, race, or class to the content of some theories, political and professional preconceptions can come together, and the complaints seem only exaggerated.

Perhaps it is because the social sciences are especially susceptible to the influence of political prejudice and bias that sociologists of science seem especially susceptible to a dreadful argument ubiquitous among New Cynics—the "Passes-for Fallacy": what has passed for, i.e., what has been accepted by scientists as, known fact or objective evidence or honest inquiry, etc., has sometimes turned out to be no such thing; *therefore* the notions of known fact, objective evidence, honest inquiry, etc., are ideological humbug. The premise is true; but the conclusion obviously doesn't follow. Indeed, this dreadful argument is not only fallacious, but also self-undermining: for if the conclusion were true, the premise could not be a known fact for which objective evidence had been discovered by honest inquiry. Dreadful as this argument is, however, it has played a significant role in encouraging the recent alliance of radical sociology of science with the New Cynicism.

As a result, many sociologists of science have been cool or even hostile not only towards mainstream philosophy of science, but also to science itself; and this has reinforced the disinclination already felt by some mainstream philosophers of science, and by scientists themselves, to take sociology of science seriously as a potential ally in the task of understanding the scientific enterprise. This unfortunate quarrel between epistemology and sociology has obscured the potential for a sensible sociology of science to contribute to our understanding of what arrangements encourage, and what discourage, good, thorough, honest inquiry, efficient communication of results, effective testing, and criticism.

*   *   *

Since both scientism and antiscientific attitudes have their roots in misunderstandings of the character and limits of scientific inquiry and scientific knowledge, up till now I have focused on epistemological issues. But I don't at all mean to deny the legitimacy or denigrate the importance of those difficult ethical, social, and political questions about the role of science in society: who should decide, and how, what research a government should fund? who should control, and how, the power for good and evil unleashed by scientific discoveries?

As this suggests, the vexed question of science and values *is* vexed, in part, because of its many ambiguities. Scientific inquiry is a kind of inquiry; so epistemological values, chief among them creativity and respect for evidence, are necessarily relevant—which is not to say that scientific inquiry always or inevitably exemplifies such values. But moral and political values are relevant, too; it is legitimate to ask, for instance, whether some ways of obtaining evidence are morally unacceptable, or whether, and if so how, and by whom, access to and applications of potentially explosive scientific results should be controlled.

Some New Cynics suggest that the fact that scientific discoveries can be put to bad uses is a reason for doubting the bona fides of those discoveries; and some hint that those of us who believe that science has made many true discoveries, or even that there is such a thing as objective truth, reveal themselves to be morally deficient in some way. But it isn't enough to point out the obvious confusion, nor to protest the blatant moral one-up-personship. It is essential, also, to articulate sober answers to those difficult questions about the role of science in society: to point out, inter alia, that only by honest, thorough inquiry can we find out what means of achieving desired social changes would be effective. And, as always, it is essential to avoid the exaggerations of the scientistic party as well as the extravagances of the antiscience crowd: to point out, inter alia, that decisions about what ways of handling the power that scientific knowledge of the world gives us are wise or just, are not themselves technical questions that may responsibly be left to scientists alone to answer.

NOTES

1. Jonathan Rauch, *Kindly Inquisitors* (Chicago: University of Chicago Press, 1993), p. 35.

2. Harry Collins, "Stages in the Empirical Programme of Relativism," *Social Studies of Science* 11 (1981): 3-10; Kenneth Gergen, "Feminist Critique of Science and the Challenge of Social Epistemology," in *Feminist Thought and the Structure of Knowledge*, ed. Mary Gergen (New York: New York University Press, 1988), 27–48; Ruth Hubbard, "Some Thoughts about the Masculinity of the Natural Sciences," in Gergen, *Feminist Thought and the Structure of Knowledge*, 1–15; Sandra Harding, *The Science Question in Feminism* (Ithaca, NY: Cornell University Press, 1986); Bruno Latour, *Science in Action: How to Follow Scientists and Engineers Through Society*

(Cambridge, MA: Harvard University Press, 1987); Steve Fuller, *Philosophy, Rhetoric, and the End of Knowledge* (Madison: University of Wisconsin Press, 1993); Richard Rorty, "Science as Solidarity," in *The Rhetoric of the Human Sciences*, ed. John S. Nelson, Allan Megill, and Deidre McCloskey (Madison: University of Wisconsin Press, 1987), pp. 38–52; Stanley Fish, "Professor Sokal's Bad Joke," *New York Times*, May 22, 1996, p. A23.

3. Alan Chalmers, *What Is This Thing Called Science? An Assessment of the Nature and Status of Science and Its Methods* (Atlantic Highlands, NJ: Humanities Press, 1976; Milton Keynes, UK: Open University Press, 1978). (I can't find this sentence in the third [1999] edition of the book.)

4. Theo Theocharis and M. Psimopoulos, "Where Science Has Gone Wrong," *Nature* 329 (October 1987): 595–98; Paul Gross and Norman Levitt, *Higher Superstition: The Academic Left and Its Quarrels with Science* (Baltimore: Johns Hopkins University Press, 1994); Max Perutz, "A Pioneer Defended," review of Gerald Geison, *The Private Science of Louis Pasteur*, *New York Review of Books* (December 21, 1995): 54–58; Sheldon Glashow, "The Death of Science!?" in *The End of Science? Attack and Defense*, ed. Richard Elvee (Lanham, MD: University Press of America, 1992), pp. 23–32; Alan Sokal, "Transgressing the Boundaries: Towards a Transformative Hermeneutics of Quantum Gravity," *Social Text* 46–47 (Spring–Summer 1996): 217–52; Steven Weinberg, *Facing Up: Science and Its Cultural Adversaries* (Cambridge, MA: Harvard University Press, 2001).

5. John Fox, "The Ethnomethodology of Science," in *Realism and Relativism in Science*, ed. Robert Nola (Dordrecht, The Netherlands: Kluwer, 1988), pp. 59–80; Larry Laudan, "The Pseudo-Science of Science?" (1981), in Laudan, *Beyond Positivism and Relativism: Theory, Method, and Evidence*, (Boulder, CO: Westview, 1996), pp. 183–209; Noretta Koertge, "Wrestling with the Social Constructor," in *The Flight from Science and Reason*, ed. Paul Gross, Norman Levitt, and Martin W. Lewis, Annals of the New York Academy of Sciences, vol. 775 (1996) (Baltimore: Johns Hopkins University Press, 1997), pp. 266–73.

6. Ronald Giere, "The Feminism Question in the Philosophy of Science," in *Feminism, Science, and the Philosophy of Science*, ed. Jack Nelson and Lynn Hankinson Nelson (Dordrecht, The Netherlands: Kluwer, 1996), pp. 3–15.

7. Percy W. Bridgman, *Reflections of a Physicist* (1950) (New York: Philosophical Library, 1955).

CONTRIBUTORS

BARRY BEYERSTEIN is professor of psychology and a member of the Brain Behaviour Laboratory at Simon Fraser University. His research has involved many areas related to his primary scholarly interests: brain mechanisms of perception and consciousness and the effects of drugs on the brain and mind. Dr. Beyerstein is a Fellow and a member of the Executive Council of CSICOP and serves on the editorial board of CSICOP's journal, *Skeptical Inquirer*. He is a founding member of Canadians for Rational Health Policy and a contributing editor of the journal *Scientific Review of Alternative Medicine*. He has published in these areas himself and is a frequent commentator on such topics on TV and radio and in the print media.

DEREK BOLTON is professor of philosophy and psychopathology at Kings College in London and hon. consultant clinical psychologist, and associate director, Clinical Governance, South London & Maudsley NHS Trust. He has authored, among others: "Meaning and Causal Explanations in the Behavioural Sciences," in *Nature and Narrative: International Series in Philosophy and Psychiatry*, vol. 1, and (with J. Hill, W. Yule, O. Udwin, S. Boyle, and D. O'Ryan) "Long-term Effects of Psychological Trauma on Psychosocial Functioning," *Journal of Child Psychology and Psychiatry* 45 (2004).

BERIT BROGAARD is assistant professor of philosophy at University of Missouri, St. Louis. Her primary research interests are in the philosophy of language, metaphysics, and epistemology. Recent publications include "Number Words and Ontological Commitment," *Philosophical Quarterly* (2007); "Descriptions: Quantifiers or Predicates?" *Australasian Journal of Philosophy* (forthcoming); "Span Operators' *Analysis*" (forthcoming); "Tensed Relations," *Analysis* (2006); "The 'Gray's Elegy' Argument, and the Prospects for the Theory of Denoting Concepts," *Synthese* (2006); and (with Joe Salerno) "Anti-Realism, Theism, and the Conditional Fallacy," *Nous* (2005).

VERN L. BULLOUGH (deceased) was a SUNY Distinguished Professor Emeritus, and also founded the Center for Sex Research at California State University, Northridge. He was the author, coauthor, or editor of more than fifty books, about half of which deal with sex and gender issues. A past president of the Society for the Scientific Study of Sexuality, he earned numerous awards for his writing and research, including the Kinsey award. He wrote more than 150 refereed articles, and hundreds of others. During his career, he lectured in most of the fifty states and in more than twenty-five foreign countries.

MARIO BUNGE is the Frothingham Professor of Logic and Metaphysics at McGill University. He has taught theoretical physics and philosophy in his native Argentina, the United States, Germany, Switzerland, and Mexico. He is the author of fifty books and five hundred articles, including *Causality, Foundations of Physics, Scientific Research, Treatise of Basic Philosophy, Social Science under Debate*, and *Emergence and Convergence*.

DONALD CALNE received his BA, BSc, and DM at Oxford. From 1974–1981 he was clinical director at the National Institute of Neurological Diseases, Bethesda, Maryland. From 1981–2001 he was director of the Neurodegenerative Disorders Centre at the University of British Columbia. In October 1998 he received the Order of Canada. In 2001 he was elected to the Royal Society of Canada, and in 2002 he received the degree DSc *honoris causa*.

ARTHUR CAPLAN is one of the most preeminent bioethicists in the United States. He is currently the Emmanuel and Robert Hart Professor of Bioethics and director of the Center for Bioethics at the University of Pennsylvania in Philadelphia. Caplan is the author or editor of twenty-five books and more than five hundred papers in refereed journals of medicine, science, philosophy, bioethics, and health policy. His latest book is *Smart Mice, Not-So-Smart People: An Interesting and Amusing Guide to Bioethics*.

CHRISTOPHER W. DiCARLO is an assistant professor of philosophy cross-appointed in the Faculties of Health and Social Sciences at the University of Ontario Institute of Technology in Oshawa, Ontario. He is a past visiting research scholar at Harvard University in the Faculty of Arts and Sciences: Department of Anthropology and the Peabody Museum of Archaeology and Ethnology. Here, he conducted research for two books he is currently writing: *The Comparative Brain: The Evolution of Human Reasoning* and *The Evolution of Religion: Why Many Need to Believe in Deities, Demons, and the Unseen.*

TOM FLYNN, a longtime secular humanist activist, was a founding coeditor of the newsletter *Secular Humanist Bulletin*. He is editor of *Free Inquiry* magazine, director of the Robert Green Ingersoll Birthplace Museum, and director of Inquiry Media Productions, the electronic media arm of the Center for Inquiry. He has authored *The Trouble with Christmas* as well as two irreverent science-fiction novels, and is editor of the forthcoming *New Encyclopedia of Unbelief.*

MARIN GILLIS is the director of Medical Humanities and Ethics at the University of Nevada School of Medicine. She holds two graduate degrees in philosophy: an LPh from the Higher Institute of Philosophy, KU Leuven, in Belgium, and a PhD from the University of Calgary in Canada. Her areas of research include the normative aspects of science and technology, especially stem cell research and reproductive technologies, and the scholarship of teaching and learning. She is an executive member of the Association of Feminist Ethics and Social Theory and sits on the board of the International Ethical Humanist Union in New York City.

TED GOERTZEL is a professor of sociology at Rutgers University. He is the author of numerous books and articles, including *Linus Pauling: A Life in Science and Politics* (with Ben Goertzel, Mildred Goertzel, and Victor Goertzel).

SUSAN HAACK (Cooper Senior Scholar in Arts and Sciences, professor of philosophy, and professor of law, University of Miami) has published highly regarded books on logic, espistemology, philosophy of science, social and cultural issues, etc. Her *Putting Philosophy to Work: Inquiry and Its Place in Culture* will be published by Prometheus Books in 2007.

JAMES HUGHES, PhD, teaches Health Policy at Trinity College in Hartford, Connecticut, and serves as the executive director of the World Transhumanist Association and its affiliated Institute for Ethics and Emerging Technologies. Dr. Hughes produces the weekly syndicated public affairs talk show

Changesurfer Radio, and is the author of *Citizen Cyborg: Why Democratic Societies Must Respond to the Redesigned Human of the Future*.

ELAINE M. HULL is professor of psychology and neuroscience, Florida State University, Tallahassee, and the author of scores of scientific articles, including most recently: (with J. M. Dominguez and M. Gil) "Preoptic Glutamate Facilitates Male Sexual Behavior," in the *Journal of Neuroscience* (in press); (with S. Sato) "The Nitric Oxide-cGMP Pathway Regulates Dopamine Efflux in the Medial Preoptic Area and Copulation in Male Rats," *Neuroscience*; (with R. I. Wood and K. E. McKenna) "The Neurobiology of Male Sexual Behavior," in *The Physiology of Reproduction*, 3rd ed.

RICHARD T. HULL is professor emeritus of philosophy at the University at Buffalo, and currently serves as executive director of the Text and Academic Authors Association of St. Petersburg, Florida. He has authored numerous articles and edited several books on bioethics, including *Ethical Issues in the New Reproductive Technologies*, 2nd ed., and *A Quarter Century of Value Inquiry: Presidential Addresses of the American Society for Value Inquiry*.

DAVID KOEPSELL has a PhD in philosophy and a JD from the University at Buffalo. He is executive director of the Council for Secular Humanism. He has authored numerous articles on law, ethics, philosophy, science, and technology, as well as the books *The Ontology of Cyberspace: Law, Philosophy, and the Future of Intellectual Property* and (coedited with Laurence Moss) *John Searle's Ideas about Social Reality: Extensions, Criticisms, and Reconstructions*. He is currently the Donaghue Initiative Visiting Scholar in Research Ethics at Yale for the 2006–2007 academic term.

PAUL KURTZ is professor emeritus of philosophy at the University at Buffalo. He has taught at Vassar, Trinity, and Union colleges. His specialty is the philosophy of religion, ethics, value theory, and the paranormal. He is founder and chairman of the Committee for the Scientific Investigation of Claims of the Paranormal (CSICOP), the Council for Secular Humanism, Center for Inquiry, and Prometheus Books. He is editor in chief of *Free Inquiry* magazine, a publication of the Council for Secular Humanism. He was copresident of the International Humanist and Ethical Union (IHEU). He is a Fellow of the American Association for the Advancement of Science, and Humanist Laureate and president of the International Academy of Humanism. He is author or editor of forty-five books, including *The Transcendental Temptation, Skepticism and Humanism: The New Paradigm, Embracing the Power of Humanism, The*

Courage to Become, and *Promethean Love*, and has edited *Science and Religion: Are They Compatible?* He drafted *Humanist Manifesto II* and *Humanist Manifesto 2000*.

SCOTT O. LILIENFELD, PhD, is associate professor in the Department of Psychology at Emory University. Lilienfeld is president of the Society for a Science of Clinical Psychology (SSCP), and the 1998 recipient of the David Shako Award for Early Distinguished Contributions to Clinical Psychology, presented by the American Psychological Association Division 12. He is founder and editor in chief of the *Scientific Review of Mental Health Practice*, and sits on the editorial boards of nine other publications, including *Clinical Psychology*, the *Journal of Clinical Psychology*, the *Journal of Abnormal Psychology*, and the *Journal of Social and Clinical Psychology*.

RONALD A. LINDSAY is by training both a philosopher and a lawyer. He has published articles on bioethics, the philosophy of religion, and constitutional law in various publications, including the *Kennedy Institute of Ethics Journal*; the *Journal of Law, Medicine & Ethics*; and *Free Inquiry*. He is currently legal director for the Center for Inquiry–Transnational, headquartered in Washington, DC.

DON MARQUIS is professor of philosophy at the University of Kansas, Lawrence. He has authored a widely reprinted secular argument that abortion is immoral. He is the author of "Leaving Therapy to Chance: An Impasse in the Ethics of Randomized Clinical Trials," *Hastings Center Report* (1983); "Why Abortion Is Immoral," *Journal of Philosophy* (1989); and "An Ethical Problem Concerning Recent Therapeutic Research on Breast Cancer," *Hypatia: A Journal of Feminist Philosophy* (1989).

LAURA M. PURDY is professor of philosophy and the Ruth and Albert Koch Professor of Humanities at Wells College, New York. She completed her PhD in philosophy at Stanford University in 1974. From 1997–2000 she held the position of bioethicist at the University Health Network, the University of Toronto Joint Centre for Bioethics, where she also acted as cochair of the Women's Health Research Network. At Wells College, she has been associate dean for academic affairs and coordinates the minor in Science, Health, and Values. She has taught, presented, and published extensively in the field of ethics. Her books include *Reproducing Persons*, and she is coeditor of *Feminist Perspectives in Medical Ethics*, *Embodying Bioethics* and, most recently, *Bioethics, Justice and Health Care*.

WILLIAM ROTTSCHAEFER is professor emeritus of philosophy at Lewis and Clark College, Portland, Oregon. His research and publication have focused on the relationships between science and religion and science and values, in particular the biological and psychological bases of moral agency. He has published in many journals, including *Philo*, *Zygon: The Journal of Science and Religion*, *Behavior and Philosophy*, *Biology and Philosophy*, and *Philosophy of Science*. Cambridge University Press published his book *The Biology and Psychology of Moral Agency* (1998).

JOHN SHOOK is provost and research fellow at the Center for Inquiry–Transnational in Amherst, New York. He received his PhD in philosophy at the University at Buffalo and was a professor of philosophy at Oklahoma State University for six years. Shook's research and writing focuses on American philosophy, philosophy of science, epistemology, and political theory. His most recent book is the *Blackwell Companion to Pragmatism*, edited with Joseph Margolis. He authored *Dewey's Empirical Theory of Knowledge and Reality*, and edited *Pragmatic Naturalism and Realism* and *Dictionary of Modern American Philosophers*. He is also coeditor of the journals *Contemporary Pragmatism* and the *Pluralist*.

THOMAS SZASZ, AB, MD, DSc (Hon.), LHD (Hon.), is professor of psychiatry emeritus at the State University of New York Upstate Medical University, in Syracuse, New York. He is the author of thirty-one books, among them the classic *The Myth of Mental Illness*. His forthcoming book, *Coercion as Cure: A Critical History of Psychiatry*, is scheduled for publication in the spring of 2007. Dr. Szasz is widely recognized as the world's foremost critic of psychiatric coercions and excuses.

JAMES STACEY TAYLOR is an assistant professor of philosophy at The College of New Jersey. He is the editor of *Personal Autonomy: New Essays*, and the author of *Stakes and Kidneys: Why Markets in Human Body Parts Are Morally Imperative*. He has published numerous papers in applied ethics (especially medical ethics), theoretical ethics, and autonomy theory.

RICHARD TAYLOR (deceased) was professor emeritus of philosophy at the University of Rochester. His best-known book is *Metaphysics* (1963). Other works include: *Action and Purpose* (1966), *Good and Evil* (1970), and *Virtue Ethics* (1991).

JOHN TEEHAN is associate professor of philosophy in the Department of Religious Studies, Hofstra University, Hempstead, New York. He is the author of numerous articles exploring the impact of evolutionary theory on ethical and religious traditions, and is currently working on an analysis of religious ethics and violence from the perspective of evolutionary psychology.

DAVID J. TRIGGLE, PhD, is a university professor and a distinguished professor in the School of Pharmacy and Pharmaceutical Sciences at the University at Buffalo. He serves on the editorial boards of a number of publications, was the editor and founder of *Pharmaceutical News* and the perspectives editor of the *Journal of Medicinal Chemistry*, and is currently the Chemical Diversity editor of *Drug Development Research* and coeditor of *CNS Drug Reviews*.

FRED WILSON, PhD, FRSC, is professor emeritus of philosophy, University of Toronto. Wilson received his PhD at the University of Iowa. He has published extensively in the history of philosophy and the philosophy of science, with books on Hume, John Stuart Mill, Darwin, and Carnap; in the philosophy of science; and on the philosophical problems of death. His most recent books are *The Logic and Methodology of Science and Pseudoscience* and *Logic and the Methodology of Science in Early Modern Thought*. Wilson has also served as president of the Canadian Association of University Teachers.